D1324425

WITHDRAWN

INTELLECT AND HOPE

Other titles in this series:

John Wild, *Human Freedom and Social Order:
An essay in Christian philosophy*

Kenneth W. Thompson, *Christian Ethics and
the Dilemmas of Foreign Policy*

Francis P. Canavan, s.j., *The Political Reason
of Edmund Burke*

Paul Ramsey, *War and the Christian Conscience:
How shall modern war be conducted justly?*

Edgar H. Brookes, *Power, Law, Right, and Love:
A study in political values*

Carl J. Friedrich, *Transcendent Justice:
The religious dimension of constitutionalism*

John H. Hallowell, *ed., Development: For What?*

INTELLECT AND HOPE

Essays in the thought of Michael Polanyi

Edited, with an Introduction, by

Thomas A. Langford *and* William H. Poteat

PUBLISHED FOR THE LILLY ENDOWMENT RESEARCH
PROGRAM IN CHRISTIANITY AND POLITICS BY THE
DUKE UNIVERSITY PRESS, DURHAM, N.C.   1968

*Printed in the United States of America
by Kingsport Press, Inc., Kingsport, Tenn.*

Acknowledgments

The editors wish to thank all those whose moral support, counsel and material aid made this venture possible.

Provost R. Taylor Cole was the first to underwrite us in the name of Duke University, with encouragement and with travel monies; the Committee for the Lilly Endowment Research Program in Christianity and Politics at Duke granted us money to publish this volume as a part of its work. It was these who provided the occasion, if not indeed the *conditio sine qua non,* for our coming into the debt of so many others.

We received invaluable counsel from Professors Marjorie Grene, Richard Gelwick, and Ruel Tyson—all in privileged situations *vis à vis* Polanyiana. Without our conversations with Professor Tyson, our Introduction would have been very different—an acknowledgment which will no doubt evoke a most equivocal response in him.

Thanks are due also Messrs. Routledge and Kegan Paul for permission to use "Michael Polanyi and Max Weber" from their *The Logic of Personal Knowledge* (1961), and to that essay's author, M. Raymond Aron; and also to the Royal Institute of Philosophy and to Professor H. B. Acton, editor of its journal, *Philosophy,* for permission to use Polanyi's "Sense-Giving and Sense-Reading" which first appeared in the pages of this journal.

Finally, we thank and remember with pleasure those whose personal pride in the task and whose professionalism made the day-to-day unfolding of our enterprise intrinsically interesting: Mrs. Mary Chestnut and Mrs. Bettie Bedell, who typed; and Miss Harriet Leonard of the Duke Library staff, an indefatigable sleuth, who always found the fugitive citation, and who never failed to make us feel that even the most tedious work she did for us was fun.

T.A.L.
W.H.P.

May, 1967
Durham, N.C.

Table of Contents

Abbreviations   ix

UPON FIRST SITTING DOWN TO READ *PERSONAL
KNOWLEDGE*   An Introduction   3

TACIT KNOWING AND THE PRE-REFLECTIVE CO-
GITO   *Marjorie Grene*   19

POLANYI AND THE PROBLEM OF METAPHYSICAL
KNOWLEDGE   *Edward Pols*   58

MAN THE MEASURE: PERSONAL KNOWLEDGE
AND THE QUEST FOR NATURAL LAW
                                    Carl J. Friedrich 91

PERSONAL KNOWLEDGE AND THE CRISIS OF THE
PHILOSOPHICAL TRADITION   *Helmut Kuhn*   111

POLANYI AND WITTGENSTEIN   *C. B. Daly*   136

POLANYI AND J. L. AUSTIN   *Ian Ramsey*   169

MYTHS, STORIES, HISTORY, ESCHATOLOGY AND
ACTION: SOME POLANYIAN MEDITATIONS
                                    William H. Poteat 198

POLANYI'S INTERPRETATION OF SCIENTIFIC IN-
QUIRY   *Chaim Perelman*   232

THE GENTLE RAIN: A SEARCH FOR UNDER-
STANDING   *William T. Scott* 242

PERSONAL KNOWLEDGE AND CONCEPTS IN THE
BIOLOGICAL SCIENCES   *Sir Francis Walshe* 275

PERSONAL KNOWING AND MAKING
                         Harold G. McCurdy   315

MAX WEBER AND MICHAEL POLANYI
                           Raymond Aron   341

"MORAL INVERSION" OR MORAL REVALUATION?
                          Zdzislaw Najder   364

IN PURSUIT OF DISCOVERY   *Donald Weismann*   386

SENSE-GIVING AND SENSE-READING
                         Michael Polanyi   402

A BIBLIOGRAPHY OF MICHAEL POLANYI'S SOCIAL
AND PHILOSOPHICAL WRITINGS
                        Richard L. Gelwick   432

            Appendix   447

            Index   456

            Notes on Authors   461

Abbreviations

References in the text to the published books of Michael Polanyi will be made by means of the following symbols:

S.F.S. for *Science, Faith and Society* (Chicago: University of Chicago Press, 1946; Phoenix edition, 1964).

L.L. for *The Logic of Liberty* (Chicago: University of Chicago Press, 1951).

P.K. for *Personal Knowledge: Toward a Post-Critical Philosophy* (Chicago: University of Chicago Press, 1958; London: Routledge and Kegan Paul, 1958; New York: Harper Torchbooks, 1964).

S.M. for *The Study of Man* (Chicago: University of Chicago Press, 1959; London: Routledge and Kegan Paul, 1959; Phoenix edition, 1964).

T.D. for *The Tacit Dimension* (Garden City, New York: Doubleday and Company, Inc., 1966; Anchor Books, 1966).

The unpublished Duke Lectures entitled *Man in Thought* and consisting of five lectures: "The Metaphysical Reach of Science," "The Structure of Tacit Knowing," "Commitment to Science," "The Emergence of Man," and "Thought and Society" will be cited as *Duke*. These were delivered in February–March, 1964 and have been microfilmed and copyrighted at The Pacific School of Religion, Berkeley, California by Dr. Richard Gelwick.

INTELLECT AND HOPE

L'esprit croit naturellement, et la volonté aime naturellement; de sorte que, faute de vrais objets, il faut qu'ils s'attachent aux faux.

PASCAL

UPON FIRST SITTING DOWN TO READ
PERSONAL KNOWLEDGE . . . .

AN INTRODUCTION

Personal Knowledge is an exasperating book. It is the very antithesis of prepossessing. To some readers, it is a book against the over-all thrust and vision of which it requires no great acuity to defend oneself. To others, it seems too good to be true, too obvious to be important, or too simplistic to square with what even the simple-minded know to be the case. To still others, it presents a comprehensive view of things toward which even the most patient and sympathetic reader must struggle as toward some fugitive coherence. Even when one's initial hesitations are overcome and one seeks more fully to articulate for oneself its central theses, the whole enterprise, which seems to betray a fundamental instability, falls apart. At the same time, one is being subtly changed in unspecified ways, and against one's will all before one has decided the proper way to take up a critical attitude toward what sometimes appears to be an argument, or, alternatively, the fruitful way to meet more than halfway what at others seems not an argument but a personal invitation. Worst of all, one is alternately and sometimes simultaneously all the above readers.

Yet it is just when we have persuaded ourselves that we can place these epithets between ourselves and Michael Polanyi that the sense of being trapped in a maze overtakes us. On one level the undertaking of the book seems senseless, but at another, perhaps inarticulable, level, the text keeps intimating a new kind of sense. It is a sense which we distrust, which perhaps we even fear insofar as we rely on our inherited models of intellectual probity or existential stability, yet a sense which, insofar as we have already begun, however tentatively, to slip our moorings to these inherited models, resonates with moral and intellectual passions. Such passions too are inherited, yet by now so weakened by neglect, so much the subject of our profoundest ambivalence, as to cause a deep discord. Thus we find ourselves unable or unwilling to go forward, incapable quite of going back; our exasperation is complete.

Quite accountably, the sane man tries to give some name to his torment, some explanation for his discomfiture. And if, as we would suggest, the confusion is not a superficial one, not merely an intellectual non-confrontation, not a loss of direction upon paths, which however new, have familiar signposts, but rather that kind of deep disorientation that cuts to the very heart of one's personal existence—so that one feels a counterattack is at once a highly personal act of self-defense and a kind of *ad hominem* directed at oneself—then the explanation will necessarily show that kind of highly personal impatience which one does not associate with the rhetoric of scholarly debate.

Of course, it is not inevitable that one should read *Personal Knowledge* in this way, for we all come to such a rendezvous along very different roads. But an examination of the reviews of this set of Gifford Lectures, to say nothing of one's own experience with the book and with one's students, who struggle with it, suggests not only that this is a common occurrence, but even more, that if one does not find it exasperating one has not *really* read it! One must suspect a student who moves gracefully into *Personal Knowledge*.

One reviewer, in the peroration of the review, writes:

I have not been gentle with Polanyi who is, I am sure, a fine and noble gentleman as well as a distinguished chemist. But apart from the abundant evidence provided by his comments on the history of science, logic, mathematics, and philosophy for the old truth that cobblers should stick to their lasts, something else should also be said. It is late in the day for these tender-minded assaults on the life of reason. They have had and still have far too much company. They are in fact quite the fashion. It is not necessary to be a scientific materialist, as I am not, to recognize that it is time once again to stand up and be counted against the forces of irrationalism wherever they appear, in no matter how benign a guise.[1]

We cite this eloquent judgment not to hold it up to ridicule. On the contrary. It is different from many others only in the uninhibited indignation which it expresses. Indeed, this is precisely the kind of honest exasperation which one ought to expect. And one can well appreciate how purged its author must have felt, how, once she had written those words, everything gradually settled back into a more familiar shape.

Even so urbane, sophisticated, comprehending and sympathetic a reviewer as Michael Oakeshott—himself an elegant stylist and the author of a work on epistemology which makes no concession to the irresolute reader—even he seems inclined to attribute in part his own exasperation with *Personal Knowledge* to its putative stylistic and editorial lapses. Of Polanyi's book he says, *inter alia*: "It is disordered, repetitive, digressive and often obscure; as a work of art it leaves much to be desired."[2]

Perhaps the most cryptically revealing expression of the malaise which overtakes one in reading *Personal Knowledge* is the briefest and most unself-conscious: C. P. Snow's aside directed toward Polanyi in a long reply to critics of his "Two Cultures" thesis.[3] He says: "[Polanyi] is arguing, as it were, at right angles to my original line. I have had a great, though somewhat mystified, regard for him, as he knows, for years. . . ."

At this point the reader of this Introduction may well wonder about the good faith of its authors. Are these observations, apparently directed at *explaining* why it is that *Personal Knowledge* evokes reactions of this sort, anything more than a vicious form of *ad hominem* argument, as if the criticisms leveled at it were unjust (though no attempt to show why this is the case is made)? The answer must be that we wish to sidestep the question of the merit of these charges in order to suggest that even if they were fully supported by the book, they might still (indeed, we

1. May Brodbeck in *American Sociological Review*, XXV (Aug., 1960), 583.

2. *Encounter*, No. 3 (Sept., 1958), 77-80.

3. *Encounter*, No. 2 (Feb., 1960), 64-68.

believe they do) disguise the nature of Polanyi's enterprise and therefore the real reasons for our initial exasperation with it.

The book may well be a failure as a work of art, as Oakeshott suggests. But suppose Polanyi's objectives move, as Snow intuits they do, at right angles to our expectations; would we not properly invoke a different set of critical canons from the conventional, would not our evaluation of the rhetoric of *Personal Knowledge* be different? And if this were so, would not persistent appeal to standard canons, continual use of these evaluations of its rhetoric, defer indefinitely the realization of the manner of "argument" we have before us?

I

There can be no doubt that *Personal Knowledge* comes at us with its rhetoric all out of focus. It is a mixed-bag.

It is quite beyond the scope of these remarks to give an exhaustive form-criticism of the text. But it may be of some help to the reader of the essays which follow—and let us hope of *Personal Knowledge* itself—to examine some of its isolable rhetorical strategies.

The book's subtitle, "An Essay in Post-Critical Philosophy," suggests that it is a work on philosophy and, in the use of "post-critical," links it to a specific period in the philosophical tradition —the period, let us say, begun in Descartes and culminating but not ended in Kant. Yet, philosophers by and large, at least English-speaking philosophers on both sides of the Atlantic, find *Personal Knowledge* annoying because it is dangerously loose, innocuous because what it says has been said elsewhere and better, or irrelevant because its preoccupations are no legitimate concern of philosophy or of philosophers.

Now, clearly there are many passages throughout the book which are elegant illustrations of philosophical argument—even construing that in the most rigorous and currently fashionable sense. For example, discussing randomness and order:

> Now why this sudden change in our methods of inference?
> Actually, there is no change: we have merely stumbled on a
> tacit assumption of our argument which we ought to make

explicit now. We have assumed from the start that the arrangement of the pebbles [at a border railway station, saying: 'Welcome to Wales'] which formed an intelligible set of words appropriate to the occasion represented a distinctive pattern. It was only in view of this orderliness that the question could be asked at all whether the orderliness was accidental or not. When the pebbles are scattered irregularly over the whole available area they possess no pattern and therefore the question whether the orderly pattern is accidental or not cannot arise.[4]

This would appear to be a solid piece of dialectic both in its form and content. Yet, lost in a bewildering landscape of what appear incongruent rhetorical devices, it seems to promise something only to snatch it away. Thus one never "gets going."

Secondly, there is much concern with psychological theories and experiments regarding learning and perception: detailed reports on learning in planaria, upon the work of Tolman, Köhler, Piaget, and others. This is first a mere canvass, then a comparison, and finally an argument to Polanyi's own view of perception as a model of knowing-doing derived at once from a variant interpretation of the findings of these experimentalists and an unpacking of their hidden assumptions, which lead to their qualification, if not indeed to their refutation. Yet, although no independent experimental evidence is given, and although the criticism of the material cited is dialectical, i.e., "philosophical," the further, larger coherence toward which we are being directed by these unaccustomed materials is not easily specifiable. On their face, these passages appear to be no more than a part of the literature of psychology *simpliciter*, albeit one offered by an unconventional if not irreverent practitioner.

Further, there are also "digressions" into what may perhaps be described as sociology of knowledge.

[The] assimilation of great systems of articulate lore by novices of various grades is made possible only by a *previous act of affiliation*, by which the novice accepts apprenticeship to a community which cultivates this lore, appreciates its values and strives to act by its standards. This

4. *P.K.,* p. 34.

affiliation begins with the fact that a child submits to education within a community, and it is confirmed throughout
life to the extent to which the adult continues to place
exceptional confidence in the intellectual leaders of the
same community.[5]

This seems to bear indirectly upon some of the interests of
epistemology—in a way more explicit, say, than Mannheim or
even Scheler—so that it must seem out of place to a more
straightforward, neo-Marxian analysis of the social foundations
of knowledge; yet it derives its material from very ordinary social
"facts." Nevertheless, it is neither a transcendental, a linguistic,
nor a phenomenological analysis of such facts. Well then what
is it?

In the same vein:

> The sentiments of trust and the persuasive passions by
> which the transmission of our articulate heritage is kept
> flowing, bring us back once more to the primitive senti-
> ments of fellowship that exist previous to articulation
> among all groups of men and even among animals.[6]

Yet here, too, there is startling heterodoxy. In the midst of this
discourse on pure conviviality, the distinction between men and
animals seems totally ignored. The sociologist or the epistemologist must be startled to read: "A newly hatched chicken soon
learns to join the flock around its mother and to seek protection
under her wings."[7] This is not the sort of disclosure that either of
them is accustomed to regard as germane to their inquiries.
Is Polanyi a cobbler who would more profitably have stuck to his
lasts, or is he an innovator who would have us see all familiar
things in a new but only subtly refocused way?

Sometimes, again, Polanyi writes in a form suggestive of a
kind of political philosophy now out of fashion:

> . . . no order of society is thoughtless: it embodies the civic
> sense and moral convictions of those who believe in it and
> live by it. To a happy people its civic culture is its civic

5. *Ibid.*, p. 207.
6. *Ibid.*, p. 209.
7. *Ibid.*

home; and to this extent the intellectual passions sustaining this culture are in fact esoteric.[8]

Yet, again, and most importantly, there is also conceptual innovation, innovation of such sweeping import, undertaken with such ingenuousness as to outrage those who grasp this import and to confuse those who do not—notwithstanding the warnings which have been issued. "I am attempting to resolve by conceptual reforms the apparent self-contradiction entailed in believing what I might conceivably doubt."[9] This clear-eyed but muted promise can hardly prepare one for what in fact is happening.

Consider, for example, the use of the concept of "commitment" to range over cases as diverse as an exploratory movement of one's hand, a confident probing of a somatic cavity with a probe, the speaking of one's first word in one's native language, the making of a contract, the giving and receiving of promises.

Like the tool, the sign or the symbol can be conceived as such only in the eyes of a person who *relies on them* to achieve or to signify something. *This reliance is a personal commitment which is involved in all acts of intelligence by which we integrate some things subsidiarily to the centre of our focal attention.* Every act of personal assimilation by which we make a thing form an extension of ourselves through our subsidiary awareness of it, is a commitment of ourselves, a manner of disposing of ourselves.[10]

If this assertion has completely sprung our usual ways of using "commitment," then "personal" itself has been commandeered for new, perhaps exotic, but certainly conceptually innovative, force. "The tracing of personal knowledge to its roots in the subsidiary awareness of our body as merged in our focal awareness of external objects, reveals not only the logical structure of personal knowledge but also its dynamic sources."[11] If one makes this move, then the ordinary bonds among "commitment," "per-

8. *Ibid.*, p. 215.
9. *Ibid.*, p. 109.
10. *Ibid.*, p. 61.
11. *Ibid.*, p. 60.

sonal," "conscious," "intentional," are decisively loosened, if not in fact broken.

We can talk about "personal" and "commitment" as Polanyi does only when we realize at the very least that he has abandoned the classic dichotomies: thought-action, practical-theoretical, mind-body, subject-object—all with an innocence that alternately exasperates or bewilders. And in their places have been put alternative logical structures such as subsidiary-focal, attending-*from*—attending-*to,* tacit-explicit, particular-comprehensive entity, and in later writings,[12] proximal-distal.

> We have met here some primitive forms of commitment, and biology has been revealed as an appreciation of commitment. To swallow something in the hope that it may be wholesome is clearly a commitment, and *so is every act of seeing things in one particular way.* I have suggested before that in a generalized sense commitment may be acknowledged even at the vegetative level, since it is of the essence of a living organism that each part relies for its function, and for its very meaning as part of the organism, on the presence and proper functioning of a number of other parts.[13]

All the rhetorical devices so far enumerated, from straightforward argument to the sweep of innovative dialectic, irritate and strain the reader. But there is also alleviation of the strain. Amidst the bewildering profusion of rhetorical forms, the reader finds his mental cramp relieved again and again by elegant or trenchant apothegms, aphorisms, and maxims:

On speakers, sentences and assertion:

> An unasserted sentence is no better than an unsigned cheque; just paper and ink without power or meaning.[14]

On scientific investigation:

12. See *T.D., passim.*
13. *P.K.,* p. 363. (Italics added.) Readers with a more technical philosophical interest in the import of Polanyi's conceptual innovations should refer to the Appendix, p. 447.
14. *Ibid.,* p. 28.

To select good questions for investigation is the mark of scientific talent, and any theory of inductive inference in which this talent plays no part is a *Hamlet* without the prince.[15]

On personal knowledge:

All personal knowing appraises what it knows by a standard set to itself.[16]

On our belief in the existence of facts:

We do not believe in the existence of facts because of our anterior and securer belief in any explicit logical presuppositions of such a belief; but on the contrary, we believe in certain explicit presuppositions of factuality only because we have discovered that they are implied in our belief in the existence of facts.[17]

On the magic of Marxism and the "moral inversion" in which it issues:

Why should so contradictory a doctrine carry such supreme convincing power? The answer is, I believe, that it enables the modern mind, tortured by moral self-doubt, to indulge its moral passions in terms which also satisfy its passion for ruthless objectivity.[18]

On the personal:

The freedom of the subjective person to do as he pleases is overruled by the freedom of the responsible person to act as he must.[19]

Finally, we meet in *Personal Knowledge* a rhetorical device which is perhaps best called the homily. This is the form through which shines forth Polanyi's very personal appreciation of the import for the human spirit, distraught now by three centuries of self-denial, of his attempt to rediscover and reaffirm those fundamental beliefs to which he and *we* have all along

15. *Ibid.,* p. 30.
16. *Ibid.,* p. 63.
17. *Ibid.,* p. 162.
18. *Ibid.,* p. 228.
19. *Ibid.,* p. 309. (Italics original.)

clandestinely subscribed. Their eloquence and the grace of their style makes them "personal," in the ordinary, pre-Polanyian sense of that word, as is nothing else in *Personal Knowledge*.

Thus, at the confluence of biology and philosophical self-accrediting, man stands rooted in his calling under a firmament of truth and greatness. Its teachings are the idiom of his thought: the voice by which he commands himself to satisfy his intellectual standards. Its commands harness his powers to the exercise of his responsibilities. It binds him to abiding purposes, and grants him power and freedom to defend them.

And we can establish it now as a matter of logic that man has no other power than this.

He is strong, noble and wonderful so long as he fears the voices of this firmament; but he dissolves their power over himself and his own powers gained through obeying them, if he turns back and examines what he rejects in a detached manner. Then law is no more than what the courts will decide, art but an emollient of nerves, morality but a convention, tradition but an inertia, God but a psychological necessity. Then man dominates a world in which he himself does not exist. For with his obligations he has lost his voice and his hope, and been left behind meaningless to himself.[20]

Modern sensibility has brought us to suspect this kind of rhetoric as hollow, as false because too good to be true, has brought us, indeed, to believe that nobility is false *because* noble. If the author of *Personal Knowledge* has retraced in thought the path which has led to this issue, if, by so doing and by revisiting his own life, he has recovered in his book beliefs which he can sincerely hold, so as to *write* these words without self-consciousness—then, even if *Personal Knowledge* is not the whole story, would not one still wish to comprehend it in order to be able once more to *read* and even subscribe to these words without embarrassment?

II

Now, even if one had assurances in advance that it is toward some such consummation as this that these divergent strategies

20. *Ibid.*, p. 380.

I have enumerated are directed, and also that such a denouement would work in one's being an irreversible change of perspective, it might still be wondered how these several heterogeneous devices jointly contribute to a single end. By what magic do dialectic, empirical psychology, political philosophy, sociology of knowledge, conceptual innovation, maxims, aphorisms, and homilies become elements of an integral rhetoric?

Here it is that we must enter a Polanyian *caveat*. We must not overtrust our powers to explicate the way in which the particular rhetorical strategies are disposed towards one another in order to focus on the coherent view which they jointly mean. We must also note well that *Personal Knowledge* would not have proved a more congenial book had Polanyi tried to tell us in advance *how* he proposed to do *what* he has done; or, if it did prove more congenial, then it would surely have been a different, in fact, a trivial book. For it is of the very nature of a work of innovation that its author begins without knowing what he is doing; or whether indeed he has not embarked upon a disastrous course. If one does not know where one is going, it cannot be said how one might get there.[21]

Having said so much, however, it is possible to single out several passages in *Personal Knowledge* in which yet another rhetorical device is intimated, a device through which, while performing the task itself in which he is engaged, its author makes a reflexive commentary upon that very performance, thereby giving us and perhaps himself a clue to the rhetorical and personal center of the enterprise, in the light of which the particular strategies may achieve an integration. This we shall call the confessional mode, having in mind, as Polanyi himself does, the *Confessions* of St. Augustine. To this form of confession one might contrast, as we shall do later, the *Confessions* of Rousseau. The contrast is mentioned here only to indicate that the rhetorical device used by Augustine, and by Polanyi, has a very different intellectual setting from any which falls in the post-Cartesian (and pre-Polanyian) period, and for this reason has a wholly different impact.

Polanyi writes:

21. See Donald Weismann's "In Pursuit of Discovery," in this volume.

> The principal purpose of this book is to achieve a frame of mind in which I may hold firmly to what I believe to be true, even though I know that it might conceivably be false.[22]

What is most noteworthy in these words is, first, the unusual appearance of the first person singular pronoun, with its self-referential character. But, secondly, the reflexive force of the statement is a complex one. Polanyi tells us that the purpose of the book is "to achieve a frame of mind" in which he himself may dwell as in his own abode. At the same time he tells us that, while he is committed to such indwelling, he can conceive of inspecting this very frame of mind from outside the commit-ment situation. In the light of this compact sentence, then, the whole of *Personal Knowledge* is seen throughout the range of its many rhetorical strategies as a reflexive exercise in discovering one's beliefs, giving them articulation (and hence distance from oneself) in order that one may more fully dwell in them; but nevertheless (*since they have been articulated*) dwelling in them in such a way as to retain the sense of the fiduciary grounding of the beliefs *in his own subscription to them* by admitting to their *conceivable* falseness.

And again:

> . . . having recognized that an "impersonal allegation" is a contradiction in terms—just as an "anonymous cheque" would be—we shall no longer try to arrive at any justifica-tion of our allegations which would not in its turn be composed of personal allegations of our own. It should not be too difficult to justify my scientific beliefs, in particular, in terms of some logically antecedent beliefs of my own, this justification itself being acknowledged once more to involve a fiduciary act of my own. The trouble is in fact that this may appear so easy as to be quite pointless. For it will be objected that 'You can believe what you like'; which brings us back once more to the paradox of self-set stand-ards; if the criteria of reasonableness, to which I subject my own beliefs, are ultimately upheld by my confidence in

22. *P.K.*, p. 214.

them, the whole process of justifying such beliefs may appear but a futile authorization of my own authority.

Yet so be it. Only this manner of adopting the fiduciary mode is consonant with itself: the decision to do so must be admitted to be itself in the nature of a fiduciary act.[23]

Here one must notice that in the first paragraph there is an easy movement back and forth between the first-person singular pronoun and its plural. In this, too, is shown the confessional strategy—one which, unlike the *mere* confession, finds the singular and plural form almost equally congenial, for it is a confession having a universal intent—a rhetorical modality to use which, as we shall suggest, must seem an act of bad faith in the post-Cartesian ethos.

It is of interest also that after the unself-conscious use of the first-person pronominal style, Polonyi moves in the following sentence into a *third-person* form, which serves still further to reinforce the universal intent of *this* confessional form.

Once again, the confession, here employing the first-person plural:

This then is our liberation from objectivism: to realize that we can voice our ultimate convictions only from within our convictions—from within the whole system of acceptances that are logically prior to any particular assertion of our own, prior to the holding of any particular piece of knowledge.

. . . .

I believe that the function of philosophic reflection consists in bringing to light, and affirming as my own, the beliefs implied in such of my thoughts and practices as I believe to be valid; that I must aim at discovering what I truly believe in and at formulating the convictions which I find myself holding; that I must conquer my self-doubt, *so as to retain a firm hold on this programme of self-identification.*[24]

All this leads directly both to a first-person (plural) formulation such as:

23. *Ibid.,* p. 256.
24. *Ibid.,* p. 267. (Italics added.)

Thus to speak a language is to commit ourselves to the double indeterminacy due to our reliance both on its formalism and on our own continued reconsideration of this formalism in its bearing on experience. For just as, owing to the ultimately tacit character of all our knowledge, we remain ever unable to say all that we know, so also, in view of the tacit character of meaning, we can never quite know what is implied in what we say;[25]

and to a third-person summary, such as:

> For it is self-contradictory to secede from the commitment situation as regards the beliefs held within it, but to remain committed to the same beliefs in acknowledging their factual content as true.[26]

Polanyi explicitly recognizes St. Augustine's significance as a paradigmatic user of what we are here calling a confessional rhetoric, and refers specifically to his *Confessions*.[27] And having done so, he interprets the bearing of this model upon the rhetoric of his own enterprise. He says:

> . . . the process of examining any topic is both an exploration of the topic, and an exegesis of our fundamental beliefs in the light of which we approach it; a dialectical combination of exploration and exegesis.[28]

Finally, the self-reflexive character of Polanyi's enterprise and the need for a confessional rhetoric—a confession having a universal intent—is compactly given in the following statement:

> The passionate urge to fulfill self-set standards will appear *completely determinate* if we too accept the same standards as real and valid; but it is also seen to be *quite indeterminate,* for it is achieved by a supreme intensification of uniquely personal intimations.[29]

It is only in the light of these confessional passages that the other diverse rhetorical forms which comprise *Personal Knowl-*

25. *Ibid.,* p. 95.
26. *Ibid.,* p. 304. (Italics in the original.)
27. *Ibid.,* p. 267.
28. *Ibid.*
29. *Ibid.,* p. 396. (Italics in the original.)

edge can be rightly evaluated and interpreted, for it is only in their light that the meaning of these forms can be properly appreciated. It is, in short, these passages which reveal the otherwise never fully disclosed rhetorical and personal center of the book: a center which is both personal, and universal, in its intent.

If all this be so, then Polanyi's words in the preface, ". . . it is my own allegiance that upholds these convictions, and it is on such warrant alone that they can lay claim to the reader's attention," have invited some monstrous misreadings of his book. For on the contrary, its claim to a reader's attention lies, not in the individual root of the confession, but in its universal intent.

III

It only remains for us to ask why it is that a confessional form should be used with such diffidence by its author and greeted by such indifference or suspicion by the unsympathetic reader; and why it results in so much confusion even for the sympathetic reader.

As I have already suggested, an answer may well lie in the difference between the confessions of Augustine and Rousseau.

Let us go back for a moment to Descartes, on whose head so many errors have been laid. His program of methodological doubt developed an ethos in which mathematical rigor became paradigmatic for all thought. Thus our intellect was uprooted from its grounding in the past of our bodies. (An exception may be the *cogito* itself, but from the significance of this self-directed moment our sensibility has on the whole turned away.) The consequence of Cartesian method, therefore, was the notorious "bifurcation of nature," a dichotomy which carried with it the insistence on the utterly detached character of rational thinking. Such an insistence, however, entailed a rhetoric that eschewed the first-person in favor of a third-person form for transacting our serious business with one another about what is the case. This has meant, therefore, that the first-person form has become either a mere means to reveal the idiosyncratic uniqueness of the "interesting" individual (singular) or alternatively the form in which a historically conditioned (pejorative sense) community, somewhat nervously, declared its corporate faith (plural) .

But if one returns to or recovers an ancient, pre-Cartesian model—Augustine's *Confessions*—then one begins to realize that as a rhetorical device the confession—whether in the first person singular or plural—has a very different force. For it then ceases to be a soliloquy by an individual through which is revealed his merely personal and idiosyncratic uniqueness. Instead, it can be seen as a disclosure to oneself of one's basic beliefs, grounded, first, in one's own personal history, with its roots in a pre-personal somatic appearance in the world, bearing its genetic inheritance; and secondly, in a native language upon the insinuations of a larger coherence of which one has trustingly and acritically relied as the *conditio sine qua non* of one's coming ever more fully to possess one's human being.

Now, far from being a mere disclosure of one's unique idiosyncrasy, *this* form of confession is precisely the medium for seeking to appreciate how and who one is in order that one may more fully be so. Therefore it is a confession having a fully convivial setting in the double sense that, on one hand, one, in subscribing to one's own ever more fully self-disclosed and disclosing reality, is *discovering* and *affirming* that convivial setting as one's own; and on the other, one is ratifying this setting as something at once both *given* and *shared*. This recovery of the prepersonal and personal historical roots of one's own knowledge leads, not, as for the Cartesian, to subjectivism or relativism, but to the recognition of the inescapable, because necessary, universal intent of all our affirmation.

.   .   .   .

Upon first sitting down to read *Personal Knowledge,* then, one must begin by attending *from* the many independent "arguments," relying *upon* the various rhetorical strategies, in order to attend *to* the large coherence they jointly mean: a comprehensive view of things at once more plainly at right angles to what we *do* expect, yet more consonant with what we *should* expect than anyone would realize who only dwells successively in its rhetorical particulars.

TACIT KNOWING AND THE PRE-REFLECTIVE COGITO

Marjorie Grene

I

"Le coeur a ses raisons, que la raison ne connait point." Ever since Descartes announced the first modern program of unified science, there have been those who have protested: who have seen in his substitution of a principle of poverty for the traditional (though posthumously christened) principle of plenitude the death of the human spirit. Intellectually as well as terrestrially, however, we stand where our generativity has cast us. And so for the most part those protesters themselves, from Pascal's day to ours, have stood—could not help standing—on Cartesian ground. They have partly resisted, or have supplemented, but not in its essence rejected, the central Cartesian thesis of the wholly luminous, the clear and distinct idea as the single unit of all knowledge. They have set, as Pascal did, some other insight, some more quintessential inner "truth," over against the explicitly articulated, impersonal world of knowledge, but have not sternly faced the post-Cartesian dilemma: nature *or* spirit, body *or* mind, and pass between its horns to a new and firmer starting point than the vaunted *firmum et mansurum* of 1641.

As well as protesters, there have, admittedly, been synthesizers. Kant thought himself such. Yet his synthesis depends, in the last analysis, on the pietist faith which held, for him, nature and freedom unquestioningly together. That faith gone, we are left with the "as-if" of positivist science on the one hand and on the other the subjective gesturings of the alienated self, whether in arrogance or despair. One can find such alternatives in any generation from Kant's to our own. You may, if you like, pit Fichte, say, against Feuerbach, Mill against Kierkegaard, or Russell against Bergson. But in our time one book, *Being and Nothingness,* exemplifies *par excellence* this tragic to-and-fro of the modern mind. Nor, in my opinion, does Sartre's Marxist-existentialist dialectic, for all its ingenuity (and all its bulk) by one jot alter the impasse which in his classic work he has once for all embodied.[1]

What I want to do in this essay is to show, on the one hand, how the impasse of modern philosophy is displayed in *Being and Nothingness,* and, on the other, to demonstrate how the whole no-exit panorama of the Sartrean world is transformed by the substitution of tacit for explicit knowing, and of bodily indwelling for the *pour-soi/en-soi* dichotomy of Sartrean thought.

II

The *cogito* is for Sartre the only proper starting point of philosophy, but a *cogito* revised in the light of his study of Husserl. The Cartesian *cogito* is an *act* of thinking, identifiable with its content. But if all consciousness is *of* something, then the *something* seems to take over the whole, and to leave the act itself empty. That is, crudely, the argument of the *Transcendence of the Ego,* and its outcome is assimilated in *Being and Nothingness;* but with a difference. The *cogito* Sartre is working with in the central argument of *Being and Nothingness* is a prereflective *cogito,* which, he argues, is presupposed by the Cartesian.[2] If I am counting my cigarettes, he points out, I am conscious, not, in the first instance, of my existence, but of the cigarettes: "elles sont douze." But if you ask me what I'm doing, I answer quite spontaneously: "I'm counting."[3] So I *am* somehow conscious of

1. See Wilfred Desan, *The Marxism of Jean-Paul Sartre* (New York: Doubleday, 1965).
2. *L'Etre et le Néant* (Paris: Gallimard, 1943), p. 220; *Being and Nothingness,* trans. Hazel Barnes (New York: Philosophical Library, 1956), p. 172. In what follows, I have quoted, with a very few emendations, from the translation (and where I have altered the translation, I have added the original in parentheses). "Conscience (de) soi" I have simply referred to as such, since "self-consciousness" is seriously misleading.
3. *Being and Nothingness* (referred to henceforth as *B. & N.*), p. liii; *L'E. et Le N.,* p. 19.

myself, yet it is not of myself that, until questioned my (thetic) consciousness was conscious. Thus, Sartre argues, "every positional consciousness of an object is at the same time a non-positional consciousness of itself."[4] This non-thetic consciousness (of) myself saves me from the infinite regress: to know that I know that I know . . . and stops it short in a *non-substantial absolute*.

What, at first sight, could be less Cartesian than a non-thetic consciousness? Yet Sartre's prereflective *cogito* is still the bond slave of its Cartesian master in at least four ways.

First, it is *instantaneous*. Sartre comes back, over and over, to this point: the temporality of the for-itself breaks out of—flees—the instantaneity of the prereflective *cogito,* but only to be drawn back to it again.[5] Ultimately, it is true, there *is* in a sense no instant, yet "in the very development of our temporalization, we can produce instants if certain processes arise on the collapse of prior processses."[6] The instant *will* exist if—though only if—"we are a beginning and an end to ourselves within the unity of a single act."[7] But this is precisely the Sartrean free act, the for-itself projecting itself as having to be what it is not, and as not being what it was. There *are* no instants, but the instant as a "double nothingness" is nevertheless the pure, free decision, the original choice of myself, which I *am.* As Iris Murdoch puts it, ". . . the agent, thin as a needle, appears in the quick flash of the choosing will."[8]

Secondly, the prereflective *cogito* is self-directed. The transfer of attention, of thetic consciousness, to the object leaves a truncated, an unnoticed, yet still self-contained "conscience (de) soi" behind. Without the other-directedness of thetic consciousness, admittedly, the non-thetic consciousness (of) self would itself be nothing. Indeed, as it turns out, it is precisely nothingness, the nihilation of the in-itself, that, as for-itself, it *is.* But as (in

4. *Loc. cit.* Cf. *B. & N.,* p. 192; *L'E. et le N.,* p. 242. (I hope that these few parallel references will help readers using the original text to orient themselves in my references to the translation.)
5. *Ibid.,* e.g., pp. 84, 104, 149, 192, 239, 244, 268, 282, etc.
6. *Ibid.,* Pt. IV, pp. 466-467.
7. *Ibid.,* p. 466.
8. Iris Murdoch, "On 'God' and 'Good,'" paper written for the Study Group on Foundations of Cultural Unity, 1966.

Sartre's interpretation) the example shows (*I* am counting), it is
the hidden for-itself, which posits, gives meaning to, elects the
in-itself, that is here revealed. And an *I*, for Sartre, as for Descartes, as for all Cartesian thinkers, must be radically *other* than,
over against, the real, the given, the "out-there." It may be a
diminished ghost, a mere fellow in the cellarage, but ghost it is;
and a machine, "pure exteriority," is, but for its nihilating upsurge, the being to which, in its being, it stands opposed. Whether
like Kierkegaard you despise the machine, or like contemporary
"central-state materialists" you exorcise the ghost, the opposition,
the antagonism amounting to an agony, remains. True, the for-
itself's negation of the object, the negation by which alone it
makes the object be, is said by Sartre to be "internal." But it is a
pure internal, wholly cut off from the pure *exteriority* of mere
space, of the abstract out-there of common sense and its systematic elaboration in science. And in this sense the internality of the
for-itself's negation of being is *extrinsic* to, wholly other than,
the being-in-itself which it negates. This is Cartesian dualism,
minus Cartesian substance: Thus:

> . . . the revelation of the spatiality of being is one with the
> non-positional apprehension by the for-itself of itself as
> *unextended*. And the unextended character of the for-itself
> is not a positive, mysterious property (*vertu*) of spiritual-
> ity, which is hiding under a negative denomination; it is a
> natural ecstatic relation, for it is by and in the extension of
> the transcendent in-itself that the for-itself makes itself
> known to itself and realizes its own non-extension.[9]

Thirdly, as the in-itself is pure exteriority, relativity, and pas-
sivity, so the for-itself which is the elaboration of the prereflective *cogito*, is, along with its interiority and absoluteness,
purely active. This is again, as Sartre himself has stressed, pure
Cartesian freedom. It is my making of myself, my choice of
myself, in total, unalloyed liberty. Even God could not diminish
or divide the will.

Fourthly, and most important for my present purpose, the
prereflective *cogito*, because it is non-thetic, is *precognitive*.[10]

9. *B. & N.*, p. 179.
10. See, e.g., *ibid.*, pp. 69, 95, 150, 155, 172, 199.

Knowledge, Sartre argues in the Introduction, can be saved from the infinite regress of the *idea ideae* only by something less than knowledge. It is by "abandoning the primacy of knowledge" that "we have discovered the being of the knower and encountered the absolute."[11] This follows, indeed, from the fact that the prereflective *cogito* is wholly self-directed. Only thetic consciousness is *of* . . . an object. Thus knowing, as distinct from the being of the knower, appears throughout as "the act of a pure and attentive mind." True, this "mind" is no longer substantial. It is not even the pinpoint "that" of Kantian apperception; it is pure nihilation. It is the transference "out there" of the negation that I am. To see the inkwell on the table is to negate the inkwell's being the table, and so to read off from the surface of the world the not being either, not being the in-itself in general, that is the for-itself.

This is, again, only the logical outcome of the Cartesian starting point deprived of its props in God and substance. "There is only intuitive knowledge," Sartre writes.[12] "Discursive" knowing is only the transition from intuition to intuition. But intuition, the direct vision of consciousness, must be either reflection: consciousness turned thetically upon itself; or the positing of the in-itself which I have to *not* be: that is, once more, negation. Again, we are caught in the eternal antinomy, the hopeless to-and-fro of mind-against-nature: the antinomy that characterizes not only Sartrean thought, but its apparent contrary, empirical or analytical philosophy as well. For we have on the side of consciousness in the first instance the "phenomenon," which taken in itself breaks down into Humean psychological atoms or into some sort of sense-data. For Sartre, just as for Hume and his descendants, there is, there can be, no *person* here. The "circuit of selfness" which Sartre describes is, ontologically, illusory. The "ego" I construct as being myself is a tissue of pretenses, produced by a kind of bastard ("impure") reflection. In truth "my" aspirations, "my" feelings are a magical device for failing to face, in honesty and dread, my otherness than being (the emotive theory of ethics!) ; and the "meanings" of events, things, institu-

11. *Ibid.*, p. lvi.
12. *Ibid.*, p. 172.

tions are either my techniques for choosing to subdue, though unsuccessfully, the alien in-itself and the alien Other, or, if I take them seriously, the expression of my collapse into bad faith. What, in contrast, "pure" reflection might produce Sartre fails to say, although he hints in a footnote[13] that a radical "conversion" would be needed to achieve it: a conversion, one would imagine, to a Kierkegaardian inwardness, a still more radical negation of the in-itself. On the side of the in-itself, alternatively, we have a theory of pure exteriority, that is, positivism or behaviorism: self-contradictory, as Sartre can easily show,[14] but in this null-point situation a reasonable temptation for reasonable minds. No wonder that the third alternative, the most popular seeming evasion of this dilemma, is, once more, the Humean "escape," "to live at ease ever after," to abandon philosophical reflection altogether for the happy and ingenious chitchat of ordinary language "philosophy."

III

So much for the Cartesian character of Sartre's starting point. Let us look in very rough outline at the argument that follows from it. And—be it noted—it does follow. Students trained in the academic table tennis of the analytical tradition often object to *Being and Nothingness* that they can find no argument. It is of course a dialectical argument, and it is admittedly a repetitious one. The infant romancer of *Les Mots* has continued to spin words without a thought of pruning or condensation. But it is nevertheless an argument, moving relentlessly from the "phenomenon" of the Introduction to the closing question of a possible (or impossible?) alternative to bad faith.

In Part One the study of the "question" opens up the perspective of nihilation, finds dread as the instrument of self-recognition, and bad faith as its, apparently inevitable, alternative. Out of the initial positional consciousness of . . . an object, supported by a non-positional consciousness (of) myself, the

13. *Ibid.,* p. 412. Cf. pp. 155, 159f., 163.
14. *Ibid.,* p. 307: "Thus the concept of objectivity, which aimed at replacing the in-itself of dogmatic truth by a pure relation of real agreements between representations, is self-destructive if pushed to the limit."

contrast of the in-itself as plenum and the for-itself as opposing that plenum—as a "hole in being"—has opened up. Part Two examines the structures of the (in the first instance non-thetic and non-reflective) for-itself. First (Chapter I) its immediate structures. We discover the "presence to itself" which "supposes that an impalpable fissure has slipped into being. If being is present to itself, it is because it is not wholly itself. Presence is an immediate *deterioration* of coincidence, for it supposes separation."[15] What brings about this separation, however, is precisely *nothing:* this *is* the "fissure," the "hole in being," the "fall of the in-itself to the self," "by which the for-itself is constituted."

How can such nothingness come to be? Only by what Sartre calls an *ontological act,* the "perpetual act by which the in-itself degenerates into presence to itself."

> Nothingness is the putting into question of being by being—that is, precisely, consciousness or for-itself. It is an absolute event which comes to being by means of being and which, without having being, is perpetually sustained by being. Since being-in-itself is isolated in its being by its total positivity, no being can produce being and nothing can happen to being except for nothingness. Nothingness is the peculiar possibility of being and its unique possibility. Yet this original possibility appears only in the absolute act which realizes it. Since nothingness is nothingness of being, it can come to being only through being itself. Of course it comes to being through a particular being, which is human reality. But this being is constituted as human reality inasmuch as this being is nothing but the original project of its own nothingness. Human reality is being in so far as within its being and for its being it is the unique foundation of nothingness at the heart of being.[16]

Out of this original foundation of nothingness, then, Sartre elicits the further structures of the for-itself. First, its facticity, its character as *an unjustifiable act.* Secondly, its character as *lack*: human reality is the being which has to not-be what it is and to be what it is not. It is the over-against-being through which

15. *Ibid.,* p. 79. (My italics.)
16. *Loc. cit.*

negation, through which lack appears in the world. To assert this lack, it must itself *be* a lack. A lack of what? Of "the impossible synthesis of the for-itself and the in-itself."[17] Making itself as a *lack* of being, human reality is *on principle* both the aspiration to *be* (what it is not) and incapacity of such being, since it is precisely as *not* being that it *is*. To anticipate a later formulation, "we are condemned to be free."[18] We choose ourselves, we make ourselves be, as the unrealized and, by the very logic of our being, unrealizable completion of ourselves.

In this nihilating act, therefore, thirdly, consciousness not only posits value, it is *as* value. Value is the lacked which the for-itself lacks. It is the empty "for" of the for-itself: "The being of value qua value is the being of what does not have being. . . . Value is beyond being. . . . Value taken in its origin, or as the supreme value, is the beyond and the *for* of transcendence . . . the meaning and the beyond of all surpassing."[19]

Notice, we are still with the prereflective *cogito*. Value at this stage is not *known:*

> Value is not known at this stage since knowledge posits the object in the face of consciousness. Value is merely given with the non-thetic translucency of the for-itself, which makes itself be as the consciousness of being. Value is everywhere and nowhere; at the heart of the nihilating relation 'reflection-reflecting,' it is present and out of reach, and it is simply lived as the concrete meaning of that lack which makes my present being. In order for value to become the object of a thesis, the for-itself which it haunts must also come to the notice of reflection [*il faut que le pour-soi qu'elle hante comparaisse devant le regard de la réflexion*]. Reflective consciousness in fact accomplishes two things by the same stroke; the *Erlebnis* reflected-on is posited in its nature as lack and value is disengaged as the out-of-reach meaning of what is lacked. Thus reflective consciousness can be properly called a moral consciousness since it can not arise without at the same moment disclosing values. It is obvious that I remain free in my reflective consciousness to

17. *Ibid.*, p. 90.
18. *Ibid.*, p. 129.
19. *Ibid.*, p. 93.

direct my attention on these values or to neglect them—exactly as it depends on me to look more closely at this table, my pen, or my package of tobacco. But whether they are the object of a detailed attention or not, in any case they are.[20]

Note also that by implication the to-and-fro of honest and unhappy dread or of the relaxation into bad faith are already given here as our only alternatives. Either on the level of reflection I shall rise to face myself as pure lack—in freedom, anguish, total responsibility—or sink into a complacent taking of my values (which are *really* lacks) as substantive realities.

Short of the ultimate statement of this duality, Sartre adds here to facticity and value the concept of *possibility* as "*the something which the for-itself lacks in order to be itself,*"[21] a something already shown to be unattainable in terms of its starting point. Finally, the dialectic of the for-itself and the possible (*its* possible) is shown to produce the "circuit of selfness" in which the self seeks itself by its own surpassing, and in which the *world* appears as the fugitive structure, "haunted by possibles," which I *live*.[22]

The argument has been confined, so far, to the limits of the prereflective *cogito;* yet it has transcended these limits in the direction towards its possibles which constitutes the for-itself's nihilating upsurge. It becomes necessary, therefore, (Part II, Chapter II), to elicit the temporal structure of the for-itself. Given the instantaneity of the *cogito* from which it started, however, Sartre can find in temporality only *flight,*" the refusal of the instant."[23] Consciousness temporalizes itself as what it *was,* in sheer contingency, and *is not,* and as the future which is its lack, and which again it is not. Yet even so, as the very being which has to not-be what it is (was) and to be what it is not (yet), the for-itself, even as denial, is nevertheless primarily present:

20. *Ibid.*, pp. 94-95.
21. *Ibid.*, p. 102.
22. *Ibid.*, p. 104. Sartre has here been following closely Heidegger's analysis of *Dasein*, although, as we shall see presently, the position of temporality in his argument is, in the light of the *cogito*, very different from its place in *Sein und Zeit*.
23. *Ibid.*, p. 149. Cf. p. 610: "temporalization *is* flight"! (My italics.)

Finally, in the third dimension, the for-itself, dispersed in the perpetual game of reflection-reflecting, escapes itself in the unity of one and the same flight. Here being is everywhere and nowhere: wherever one tries to seize it, it is there before one, it has escaped. It is this game of musical chairs (chasse-croise) at the heart of the for-itself which is *Presence* to being.

As Present, Past, Future—all at the same time—the for-itself dispersing its being in three dimensions is temporal due to the very fact that it nihilates itself. No one of these dimensions has any ontological priority over the other; none of them can exist without the other two. Yet in spite of all this, it is best to put the accent on the present ekstasis and not on the future ekstasis as Heidegger does: for it is as a revelation to itself that the for-itself *is* its Past, as that which it has-to-be-for-itself in a nihilating surpassing; and it is as a revelation to itself that it is a lack and that it is haunted by its future—that is, by that which it is for itself down there at a distance. The Present is not ontologically "prior" to the Past and to the Future; it is conditioned by them as much as it conditions them, but it is the mould of indispensable non-being for the total synthetic form of Temporality.[24]

All this, in the life of consciousness, is still primarily nonthetic. I may try, in pure reflection (this is presumably what Sartre is attempting here), to seize on the character of original temporality itself: on the nihilating, empty eruption of the for-itself as *historicity*.[25] More frequently, however, consciousness falls prey to *impure* reflection, where, with their shadowy being, the structures of duration, of psychic life, of the "person" are spun out.

In Chapter III of Part II, "Transcendence," Sartre returns, in the light of the exposition of the for-itself, to the question he had posed, in the Introduction, of the phenomenon and its knowledge. ("Transcendence" here, it should be noted, is not the transcendence to the future, Heidegger's "existentiality," referred to in the "Temporality" chapter, but the transcendent relation

24. *Ibid.*, p. 142. Cf. also p. 194, on value as transcendence, for a succinct statement of the Cartesian ideal which dominates the argument.
25. *Ibid.*, p. 158.

between the for-itself and the in-itself.) We are now moving from the for-itself as the non-thetic *conscience (de) soi* to the thetic consciousness of . . . an object. What does the being of the for-itself have to be in order to be knowledge of the in-itself?

There is, Sartre announces (and as I have already mentioned) only intuitive knowledge, and intuition is the presence of consciousness to the thing. But presence—to . . . is, we have found, essentially negation. The for-itself puts itself in question as *not* being the being of the object. Knowing is a form of being; it is the for-itself as realizing its own being, and its otherness than being, in its internal negation of itself.[26] We meet, in other words, in the clear light of positional consciousness, the exacerbation of the *pour-soi/en-soi* conflict:

> The world is human. We can see the very particular position of consciousness: being is everywhere, opposite me, around me; it weighs down on me, it besieges me, and I am perpetually referred from being to being; that table which is there is being and *nothing* more; that rock, that tree, that landscape—being and *nothing* else. I want to grasp this being and I no longer find anything but *myself*. This is because knowledge, intermediate between being and non-being, refers me to absolute being if I want to make knowledge subjective and refers me to myself when I think to grasp the absolute. The very meaning of knowledge is what it is not and is not what it is; for in order to know being such as it is, it would be necessary to be that being. But there is this "such as it is" only because I am not the being which I know; and if I should become it, then the "such as it is" would vanish and could no longer even be thought. We are not dealing here either with scepticism—which supposes precisely that the *such as it is* belongs to being—nor with relativism. Knowledge puts us in the presence of the absolute, and there is a truth of knowledge. But this truth, although releasing to us nothing more and nothing less than the absolute, remains strictly human.[27]

Within this to-and-fro, all or none context, Sartre has handled, in this chapter, a surprising number of traditional (and some

26. *Ibid.,* pp. 179-180.
27. *Ibid.,* p. 218.

untraditional) epistemological categories and problems: quality, quantity, abstraction ("the revelation in profile of my future"), space, time, perception ("a conductor in the circuit of selfness"). He has elaborated, with a slight twist, Heidegger's theory of the instrumentality of things. And he has returned to value, the in-itself-for-itself, as the "perpetually indicated but impossible fusion of essence and existence," as "beauty," a beauty glimpsed implicitly as the imperfection of the world.

This is a *Symposium* emptied of content. It is true for Sartre, as for Plato, that only he who has seen beauty itself will breed true virtue, because he alone is in contact not with illusion but with truth; and, indeed, that all others are imitators of imitations. But the Sartrean ideal is vacuous, even self-contradictory. The for-itself is in its very being the nihilation of being, and its ideal reunion with being—the for-itself-in-itself—is thus by its very nature the self-canceling denial of itself. Could it come to an issue—which it cannot—it would be the pinpoint-being, the *un-*being of A~A which it had achieved. Wittgenstein at the close of the *Tractatus* threw away his ladder: exact speech issues in total silence. Sartrean existence *is* the ladder, forever aimed at its own extinction, or, in the downward direction, forever fleeing it. Indeed, on the ground of the *cogito,* of the claim to wholly self-contained and wholly explicit knowledge, that is the only existence we can have, or can be. Human reality, temporalization, is, and can only be, flight, deterioration, from the eternal perfection of an unattainable ideal:

> This perpetually indicated but impossible fusion of essence and existence does not belong either to the present or the future, it indicates rather the fusion of past, present, and future, and it presents itself as a synthesis *to be effected* of temporal totality. It is value as transcendence; it is what we call *beauty*. Beauty therefore represents an ideal state of the world, correlative with ideal realization of the for-itself; in this realization the essence and existence of things are revealed as identity to a being who, in this very revelation, would be merged with himself in the absolute unity of the in-itself. This is precisely because the beautiful is not only a transcendent synthesis to be effected but because it can be

realized only in and through a totalization of ourselves. This is precisely why we desire the beautiful and why we apprehend the universe as *lacking* the beautiful to the extent that we ourselves apprehend ourselves as a lack. But the beautiful is no more a potentiality of things than the in-itself-for-itself is a peculiar possibility of the for-itself. It haunts the world as an unrealizable. To the extent that man *realizes* the beautiful in the world, he realizes it in the imaginary mode. This means that in aesthetic intuition, I apprehend an imaginary object across an imaginary realization of myself as a totality in-itself and for-itself. Ordinarily the beautiful, like value, is not thematically made explicit as a value-out-of-reach-of-the-world. It is implicitly apprehended on things as an absence; it is revealed implicitly across the *imperfection* of the world.[28]

This is historicity confined within the iron grip of the *cogito;* but the *cogito,* deprived of supernatural or rational support, has itself collapsed into nothingness.

From this ground, further, in Part III, the compulsive dialectic of the body and of the Other necessarily follows. True, Sartre sometimes mentions a non-thetic awareness of body, which would, if he had started with it, have led him, as it did Merleau-Ponty and Marcel (and as, we shall see, it does Polanyi) to a different and more hopeful issue.[29] But he begins, fatally, with the body as the known;[30] and on his premises, and on the premises equally of traditional rationalism or empiricism, on the premises also of phenomenology, that is where he must begin. The prereflective *cogito,* being purely self-directed, is impotent to reach the body; it is only through thetic consciousness, through "knowledge," that the body comes into view. It appears as the alienated aspect of myself, the congelation into a thing of my facticity. But as object, secondly, it comes into view essentially as what the Other knows. Indeed, even taking my body as myself, my brain as my mind, as a materialist like Smart would do, I therewith take

28. *Ibid.,* pp. 194-195. Sartrean imagination, of course, like the Sartrean ego, is empty. See *The Psychology of the Imagination* (New York: Citadel Press, 3rd paperback edition, 1965).

29. See, e.g., *ibid.,* p. 454.

30. *Ibid.,* p. 218. Cf. p. 354, where the body is said to be *first* known, and second (and alternatively) *lived* and *not* known.

myself in effect as known by another. And as the Other's object, finally, my body becomes the opener for me of the dizzying spectacle of another's subjectivity: of another for-itself which degrades me into mere being, unless in my turn I succeed in so degrading it. The mechanics of sadomasochism, language as a form of seduction, "love" as purely the desire to be loved, the indirect reality of the us-object and the total unreality of the we-subject, the whole of Sartre's social philosophy, a philosophy of pure denial alternating with an unreal and abstract totalization—in short, his Marxist existentialism or his existentialist Marxism—all this follows inevitably from the confinement of the *cogito* with which he starts, and from which, wherever we turn, we have all started. What Sartre has done is to face with appalling honesty the consequences of our common crisis.

Finally, Part IV is a deepening and elaboration of the ontological foundations laid down in the argument so far. The for-itself, totally free, responsible even for its own being, and indeed for the meaning of being itself, in the teeth of its ineluctable contingency, of the fact that it is not its own foundation—the for-itself is essentially agent, actor, and maker. Yet for Sartre action in the last analysis is possession. Being sheer activity, as sheer nihilation of the alien object and the alien Other, it seeks to absorb the in-itself into itself, and so to escape its own non-entity. Even knowing, the act by which the for-itself posits its negation in the object, becomes a kind of having, a digestive process by which I seek to devour the alien world. Yet the for-itself, being in its nature nihilation, cannot possess its object; whether in practice or theory, the in-itself forever escapes it. So I either strive vainly and absurdly for an empty authenticity or relapse into bad faith and *l'esprit de sérieux*. Either way my action is suffering, my aspiration failure: man is a useless passion.

IV

The upshot, in summary, is this: we are a negation, a hole in being; our manner of existing is a disintegration of a unity, a flight from ourselves, and, inexorably, failure. And in this condition the only honest attitude is dread: a mood which swings, it seems, between blind arrogance—*I* am responsible, *I* give meaning, *I* make the world—and blind despair—I am nothing, an unjustifiable fact, a contradiction, prey to the Other's look, a mere means to the Other's end. Wherever we turn, an impasse.

V

Yet the way out is so simple. Non-thetic consciousness is essential, not only to the being of the for-itself, but to knowledge, that is, to the relation of the for-itself and the in-itself. It is not prereflectively reflexive, but outward directed; it directs the for-itself toward the in-itself. But I shall leave Sartre's language now and move to Polanyi's theory of tacit knowing, turning back then to see how easily, with his help, we can step over the Cartesian barriers of Sartre's thought.

Sartre's prereflective *cogito*, I pointed out, is still Cartesian in at least four ways. Take the last one first: the prereflective *cogito* is precognitive, since, it seems evident, all knowledge must be thetic. Polanyi's discovery is the contrary of this thesis. All knowing entails both subsidiary and focal awareness, both knowledge by relying on and knowledge by attending to. Nor is this a mere addition; it is *by means of* the clues we rely on (but do not, and cannot, insofar as we rely on them, attend to) that we attend to our focal object. A paradigm case is the practice of a skill, where if I attend to my particular movements, I destroy the pattern of the performance. The same relation holds, however, not only of "practice" but of the most theoretical performances as well: as, for example, in a mathematical proof, or in the appraisal of a work of art.

It is strange how close Sartre comes to this insight, only to be pulled back again by the power of his Cartesian ideal, the ideal of total clarity. The text fairly bristles with examples; I shall mention here just two. In his initial example of counting, Sartre refers to Piaget's demonstration that children who can perform an addition spontaneously cannot *explain* afterward how they set about it.[31] This, Sartre says, is a refutation of Alain's "to know is to know that one knows." It is also a refutation of Sartre's

31. *Ibid.*, p. liii.

equation of knowledge with pure intuition (in the Sartrean, not the Polanyian sense of that term). Or take the statement:

> Consciousness (of) reading is not consciousness (of) reading this letter or this word, or even this paragraph; it is consciousness (of) reading *this book,* which refers me to all the pages still unread, to all the pages already read, which by definition detaches consciousness from itself.[32]

At first sight this passage is strikingly reminiscent of Polanyi's discussion (*P.K.,* Part I, Chap. IV) of denotative meaning and the transparency of language. We have here a cluster of subsidiaries bearing on a performance: reading this book. Moreover, Sartre does here seem to be turning *conscience (de)* . . . (= subsidiary awareness) away from self to the clues bearing on the performance. But the parallel does not quite hold. For one thing, even the over-all performance (reading this book) is referred to entirely as subsidiary [consciousness (of)], not focal; that is, no relation has been established of the subsidiary to the focal aspects of the same performance. Or, a better statement in Polanyian terms: If I say that I rely on my awareness of words, paragraph *and* book, to attend to their *meaning*—that is, to pay attention to what the book is saying—then Sartre has simply omitted the focal aspect altogether.

The trouble, I believe, lies in the second of the four "Cartesian" principles I mentioned earlier. *Conscience (de)* . . . is too strongly inclined to swing back into *conscience (de)* . . . *SOI.* And then the stretch of attention becomes, as the passage just quoted suggests, a pure *de*tachment. My thetic consciousness of the letters, words or paragraph *might* be rolled up into a self-contained intuitive act, supported by an instantaneous prereflective *cogito.* But if I am reading this *book,* then the non-thetic consciousness which accompanies my activity is already a consciousness (of) myself as engaged with past and future, as "refusing the instant," and so once more detached from the plenitude of being. There is then, after all, only the to-and-fro of the

---

32. *Ibid.,* p. 100. Cf. also, e.g., p. 125 (playing tennis), p. 156 (the temporal structure of doubt), p. 258 (my awareness of my eyes in seeing), pp. 453 ff. (fatigue).

pour-soi and *en-soi,* the negation of being and the being negated. The alternatives, flashing back and forth in an everlasting aye and nay, are total. Thus "As soon as we wish to define a consciousness as doubt, perception, thirst, etc. we are referred to the *nothingness* of what is not yet."[33] As Sartre, in the same paragraph, says of Husserl's "protensions," so of his own dialectic of consciousness: we move, in following him, "like flies bumping their noses on the window without being able to clear the glass."[34] For-itself, its negation in the in-itself; for-itself as negation, against the plenum of the in-itself; future as negation of the present; the evanescent present against the congealing past; and so on, to and fro, forever—till death.

What Polanyi has done, in contrast, is to replace this hectic *to-and-fro* by the more viable structure of a *from-to* relation. But this means that *conscience (de) soi* is *not* in fact primarily self-directed. It is primarily other-directed. Of course subsidiary knowledge is *mine:* it is what, relevantly to the present focal point of my attention, I have assimilated to my very self; it is what, out of my being-in-the-world, I have interiorized to the point where I can rely on it to guide me toward a distally located goal. All knowing, whether tacit, as in perception or in skills, or explicit (though never totally so), as in the mastery of an intellectual discipline, displays this dual structure. I attend *from* a proximal pole, which is an aspect of my being, *to* a distal pole, which, by attending *to* it, I place at a distance from myself. All knowing, we could say, in other words, is orientation. The organism's placing of itself in its environment, the dinoflagellate in the plankton, the salmon in its stream, or the fox in its lair, prefigures the process by which we both shape and are shaped by our world, reaching out from what we have assimilated to what we seek.

From this follows, moreover, the contrary, also, of the two remaining "Cartesian" maxims: instantaneity and pure activity.

From-to knowledge cannot be instantaneous; it is a stretch, not only of attention, but of effort; effort must be lived, and living takes time. There is indeed no instant except as the concretion

33. *Loc. cit.*
34. *Loc cit.* Sartre's metaphor describes equally well the darting movements of ordinary language philosophy, and for the same historical reasons.

of history; its spectre need no longer haunt us. It is wrong to see temporality, as Sartre does, as the decompression of the instant; on the contrary, the instant is the compression of original time, of the span of living, the from-to dynamic of being-in-the-world from which we, like all living things, must take our start. Again, Sartre nearly comes to this recognition in a number of passages, only to fall back again into the voracious maw of the *cogito*.

Nor, finally, given the from-to structure of tacit knowing, need I now seek in some isolated, empty center the utter self-sufficiency of my original choice of myself. It is, indeed, quite true, as both Sartre and Polanyi convincingly argue, that pure potency, pure exteriority, is impotent to account for the existence of conscious life, or, indeed, Polanyi would add, of any life at all. Laplacean science contains no concepts which could by the wildest stretch of the imagination make intelligible the existence of an *I*. The atomic topography of my central nervous system *is* not myself; it is a set of objectified conditions of my existence; and only the grossest pseudo-substitution can equate my existence with its conditions, however complex and however necessary. But that is another story. The point here is that pure activity, like pure potency, is equally an illusion.

Sartre finds in *Avoir, Faire* and *Etre* the basic ontological categories of our being; but he assimilates *Faire* to *Avoir:* to make, or to do, is on principle to possess, or at least to aim at possessing. That *is* my being: I nihilate the in-itself, whose negation I am, and which is in its being my annihilation, by trying to *have* it. But my foundation in the in-itself forever escapes me: my pure action-as-having becomes pure suffering as failing to have. The same to-and-fro recurs here in agonizing, ultimately tragic form. For Polanyi, on the other hand, there is no pure action and therefore no pure possession, even as the goal we miss. Indeed, were it our goal we should have to miss it. The assimilation of the world into total inwardness would be as self-contradictory, as nihilating, as the collapse of the active center into the pure exteriority of atomism. But that is not our situation. In the from-to stretch by which we grope our way forward out of and into and within a world, we both make and are made, possess and are possessed, in tension, indeed, and even paradox, but not in contradiction. For what we have here is not an all-or-none affirmation or denial, but a *polarity*. We may even call it, following the lead of that Goethean concept, a tension between Faustean energy and *Hingabe*, *"das ewig Weibliche."* The action through which we appropriate is also the passion through which we give ourselves to being. Our self-integration is also self-surrender, our self-surrender is also the process through which we find ourselves. For Polanyi, indeed, as for Sartre, we are centers of responsibility, even of total responsibility. For Sartre, however, responsibility is wholly turned inward; it is pure self-assertion, as, for him, all assertion is. Except as *my* object, or as threat to my all-devouring subjectivity, there is no place for the other, for community and tradition, the ordinary sources and objectives of responsibility.

In *Personal Knowledge,* on the other hand, responsibility appears as the human way of being an active center: total, indeed, in that only *I* can surrender myself to being, to the sheer factual contingencies, the social lore, the practical and intellectual disciplines, to which, however, I must pledge myself in order both to affirm my being and at the same time to submit, through these manifold nexuses, to the goals of my further search. True, *I* make my values values, but by acknowledging them, responsibly, as standards, as principles which I assert, and accept, with universal intent. For Sartre, since such an acceptance takes me beyond myself, it is inevitably in bad faith. For Polanyi, it may be so, as it is, for instance, in the epistemological example of pseudo-substitution. But it need not be so. The risk of forfeiture, like the risk of error, is always with us; living is the hope of achievement and the risk of failure. But this risk, this tension, need not be, except for the mistaken dream of utter self-containment and pellucidity, a stretching on the rack. It evokes, rather, in the perspective of tacit knowing, a sense of calling. Within the limitations of my facticity, and relying on the limited powers it gives me, I ought to strive for an integration, a comprehension, which I could not, indeed, acquire by my own unaided efforts, but which I may, with grace, in part achieve.

In *The Tacit Dimension*[35] Polanyi has worked out more sys-

35. *T.D.*, chap. i.

tematically than in *Personal Knowledge* the fundamental aspects
of tacit knowing, and it may solidify my contrast with Sartre if I
look briefly at this recent account and compare it at some points
of contact with the topography of *Being and Nothingness*.
Polanyi starts with the fact that we know more than we can
tell (there *is* non-thetic knowledge) ; witness the import of experiments in subception. He could also take, as he has done
elsewhere, the case of seeing with inverting spectacles, the recognition of a physiognomy, the feat of medical diagnosis; the instances are endless. Take the second case: the achievement of
normal vision with inverting lenses. After a period of disorientation I come to rely on the clues available within my body in
order to attend to, to see, effectively the things out there. The
function of my subsidiary knowledge is to direct me to the
coherent sight of my surroundings. This is the *functional* import
of tacit knowing: it guides me from proximal, interiorized particulars to the integration of a coherent, distal whole.

This is the familiar lesson of Gestalt psychology. The bearing
of particulars on a total pattern produces the phenomenon of
pattern. And this is, secondly, the *phenomenal* aspect of tacit
knowing. The particulars, therefore, thirdly, bear on what they
mean. Reading, indeed, is, once more, a paradigm case of tacit
knowing. All *explicit* knowledge, however crystallized in the
formalisms of words, pictures, formulae, or other articulate devices, relies on the grasp of meaning *through* its articulate forms:
the comprehension that is its tacit root. And wholly tacit knowing, as in skills, is still a grasp of significance, though without the
mediation of articulate utterance. Thus tacit knowing directs us
from particulars to the whole which they signify: that is its
semantic aspect. But in so guiding us, finally, subsidiaries, which
are aspects of our being, draw us beyond ourselves to their distal
referent. They guide us toward the comprehension of something
real, in many cases, at least, to the comprehension of a reality
bearing the same structure as our knowing of it: that is, to a
whole of parts, whose significance ranges in ways perhaps un-
guessed by us beyond its specifiable particulars or even beyond
the presently visible outline of the whole. This is the *ontological*
import of tacit knowing.

I cannot of course begin to trace here the philosophical consequences of this doctrine; but let me just look back at cognate
points in *Being and Nothingness*. First, Sartre begins with the
phenomenal, and even recognizes the non-thetic aspect inherent
in our awareness of phenomena. But again, the grasp of the
phenomenon, seen *via* Descartes and Husserl, is instantaneous.
Thus when he touches on the *functional* study of consciousness it
is to reproach Husserl for confining himself to the merely functional as the merely *descriptive*, and so missing the underlying
existential, or ontological, dimension. In other words, for Sartre
even the functional is what is merely present. Polanyi, on the
other hand, starts with the function of tacit knowing, the non-
thetic as the indispensable servant of the thetic; and the very
appearance, for example, of organized perception, let alone of
articulate knowledge, already contains, accordingly, the dimension of achievement, that is, a temporal as well as a normative
aspect. The *semantic* theme, thirdly, is a recurrent one in *Being
and Nothingness*, and some of Sartre's formulations in this connection come close to the theory of tacit knowing (as: "The sign
is that which is surpassed toward meaning") .[36] Again, however,
these are almost-insights which cannot be sustained, since in the
last analysis meaning swings between the subjectivity of myself
who arbitrarily confer it ("The for-itself is compelled to decide
the meaning of being"), and the facticity, the objectivity which
absurdly cancels this meaning out. In the situation of tacit knowing, however, with its distally directed particulars tending to the
constitution of meaningful wholes, we are squarely within a
world of emergent significance, where we contemplate meanings
as truly, as honestly, as we confer them.[37] And in Sartre, finally,
the *ontological act* to which, from Husserl's pure phenomena, he
moves, proves, in the last analysis, to be the self-assertion of the
for-itself alone. True, the *ontological proof* of the Introduction
displays the necessary existence of the in-itself, but only as the
bare other-than-itself which the for-itself nihilates. And the devel-

36. *B. & N.*, p. 330; cf. also, e.g., pp. 193, 194, 373, 477, 556.
37. "Objective meanings" already there for me constitute of course a special
problem for Sartre; see *ibid.*, pp. 510 f. They have to be transformed into
techniques for me; the alternative would be *"l'esprit de sérieux."* See section 6
below.

oped ontology of Part IV concerns my being only. Polanyi, on the other hand, finds in the object, and in the analogue, of tacit knowing, a cosmic ontology, within which man, uniquely, but also biologically and historically, takes his proper place.

VI

To expand the last point will permit me also to parallel my account of *Being and Nothingness* by looking, in summarizing outline, at the way in which the cosmic panorama of *Personal Knowledge* is approached. I shall be, as I have been so far, dealing primarily with the foundation of Polanyi's argument in the theory of tacit knowing: a theory which he has made more explicit since, both in itself and in its ontological implications. *Personal Knowledge* is directed not so much to tacit knowing—as such a pervasive substructure of all intelligent behavior—as to the problem of intellectual commitment, the question how I can justify the holding of dubitable beliefs. Nevertheless, the theory of tacit knowing is the foundation of the doctrine of commitment; the former is more far-ranging, the latter probes deeper into the foundation of human personality.[38]

Applying, then, the vocabulary of tacit knowing to the argument of *Personal Knowledge,* we see—as I have already pointed out—that Polanyi begins with the *functional* aspect. It is from the conceptual nexus of problem-solving, heuristics, and originality that he sets out. What is a scientist doing when he devotes a lifetime to following a hunch; what is a theory, by what means is it pursued and discovered, by what means does it exercise its compulsion over our minds? In puzzling over these questions Polanyi comes to the analogy of knowing with skilful performance, and of problem-solving and discovery with the learning of skills. Here (I, Chapter IV, Skills) he lays bare his fundamental discovery: the two ubiquitous, integrally related, but mutually exclusive, kinds of awareness, subsidiary and focal, through which we strive, in every endeavor, whether "practical" or "theo-

38. For the relation between "personal knowledge" and "tacit knowing," see the introduction to the Torchbook edition of *Personal Knowledge* (New York: Harper and Row, 1964) , p. xi.

retical," to master or to contemplate our environment. All four aspects of tacit knowing are already prefigured here;[39] the dialectic of Parts II to IV serves to draw them out and in particular to focus on the problem of personal commitment to dubitable beliefs.

Before I go on, however, to trace in its major features the course of this development, I must emphasize two points briefly made in the Skills chapter, which Polanyi has developed at greater length in his later work, and which take us, with one stroke, beyond the underlying premise of the Cartesian—and the Sartrean—dilemma.

The use of a tool, a hammer or a probe, as a paradigm case of tacit knowing, displays for us the way in which we rely on our body to live in the world, both extending our body outward and interiorizing our tools—both visible and intellectual—to form part of our selves:

> Our appreciation of the externality of objects lying outside our body, in contrast to parts of our own body, relies on our subsidiary awareness of processes within our body. Externality is completely defined only if we can examine an external object deliberately, localizing it clearly in space outside. But when I look at something, I rely for my localization of it in space on a slight difference between the two images thrown on my retina, on the accommodation of the eyes, on the convergence of their axis and the effort of muscular contraction controlling the eye motion, supplemented by impulses received from the labyrinth, which vary according to the position of my head in space. Of all these I become aware only in terms of my localization of the object I am gazing at; and in this sense I may be said to be subsidiarily aware of them.
>
> Our subsidiary awareness of tools and probes can be regarded now as the act of making them form a part of our own body. The way we use a hammer or a blind man uses his stick, shows in fact that in both cases we shift outwards

39. The phenomenal by implication in connoisseurship (which is a subtler development of ordinary perception) : chap. iv, sec. 4; the functional (tools) : 4-7; the semantic (meanings) : 5-6; the ontological (commitment and self-set standards) : 9-10.

the points at which we make contact with the things that we observe as objects outside ourselves. While we rely on a tool or a probe, these are not handled as external objects. We may test the tool for its effectiveness or the probe for its suitability, e.g. in discovering the hidden details of a cavity, but the tool and the probe can never lie in the field of these operations; they remain necessarily on our side of it, forming part of ourselves, the operating persons. We pour ourselves into them and assimilate them as parts of our own existence. We accept them existentially by dwelling in them.[40]

We have here, first, in the from-to dynamic of tacit knowing, the resolution, indeed, the dissolution, of the mind-body problem. To Sartre, the body appears first as "known," that is, for him, as the explicit, positional object of my reflective intuition. Although, in some of his defining phrases, as, for example, "my body is the instrument which I am,"[41] or in some of his phenomenological descriptions, as, for example, in the beautiful account of fatigue in Part IV, he seems almost to have broken through to the acceptance of the whole personal, psycho-physically ambiguous "lived body" as a new starting point, he is too deeply imbued with the doctrine of pure, unextended consciousness to retain this new foundation.[42]

With the Polanyian starting point, however, the situation is fundamentally, even paradoxically, altered. For in from-to knowledge it is in the first instance[43] the *bodily* awareness that is *my own* and the *intellectual*—focal—pole of my attention that is *outside*. Indeed, this should be implicit in Husserl's revision of the *cogito,* were not he, and Sartre after him, still caught in the pursuit of an illusory self-referring instant, the dream of a "pure and attentive mind" which is sought in the *epoche,* in the resig-

40. *P.K.,* p. 59.
41. *B. & N.,* p. 359.
42. It was, of course, this alternative of the *lived body* which in their different ways both Merleau-Ponty and Marcel adopted, and their thought does indeed at points substantially coalesce with Polanyi's. That, however, is not my theme here. Suffice it to remark in passing that Polanyi's way out, though, in my view, in essential agreement with theirs, is more precisely articulated in epistemological terms and therefore also in its ontological consequences.
43. Though not always (see the closing paragraph of this section).

nation of the real world's claim to reality. No; to comprehend—all the way from the everyday perception we share with
other animals to the grandest visions of an Einstein or a Michel-
angelo—to comprehend is to rely on myself as *bodily* in order to
envisage a coherent, intelligible spectacle *beyond* myself. The
philosopher who has ascended out of the cave is still—no matter
how devotedly he may "practise" dying—an embodied person;
the objects in the cave, even their shadows, have, in such fragmentary coherence as they possess, already some intelligibility.
The dichotomy, or, more truly, the complementarity of self and
world, inner and outer, is not that between a secret, inner,
significance-conferring consciousness and a public, outer, meaningless "reality." It is the polarity of a bodily self and an intelligible world.

Starting, then, with ourselves as "embodied," with the subsidiary awareness of our bodies as the bridge to our functional
awareness of a real world, we have at our disposal, secondly, as
the paragraphs already quoted indicate, the dialectic of *interiorization* and *indwelling* which has proved a major instrument both
in *Personal Knowledge* and in the later development of Polanyi's
thought. Of all "tools," conceptual or technical, aesthetic or
ritualistic, we may say that "we pour ourselves out into them *and*
assimilate them as parts of our own existence. We accept them
existentially *by* dwelling in them."[44] This is, if you like, a paradox. I both assimilate the world to myself, *appropriate* it, and
give myself to it, *dwell in* it. But it is the paradox of a polarity, of
the organic unity-in-difference of the focal and subsidiary poles of
our awareness, rather than the flat contradiction which the Sartrean situation displays. Even the literal, everday meaning of
"dwelling-in" shows us what is involved. I build a house and in
so doing assert myself in the world: these bricks and boards
become part of myself, just as the home of my childhood, the
poems learned, the cakes baked, the earthworms dissected, the
persons loved and hated in my youth have done. And of course
by such appropriation I have in my small measure changed the
world; but by the very same movement, by the same temporal

44. *P.K., loc. cit.* (My italics.)

dialectic, I have been metamorphosed too. I have become what I am, and am yet to be, not only by seeking to *have*, to assimilate, being, but by the character of the entities—landscapes, customs, institutions, persons—by which in my time I have been possessed, to which I have surrendered. In the penultimate section of the "Skills" chapter Polanyi writes:

> I have described the effort which we put into acquiring the art of knowing as the attempt to assimilate certain particulars as extensions of our body, so that by becoming imbued with our subsidiary awareness they may form a coherent focal entity. This is an action, but one that has always an element of *passivity* in it. We can assimilate an object as a tool if we believe it to be actually useful to our purposes and the same holds for the relation of meaning to what is meant and the relation of the parts to a whole. The act of personal knowing can sustain these relations only because the acting person believes that they are apposite: that he has not *made them* but *discovered them*. The effort of knowing is thus guided by a sense of obligation towards the truth: by an effort to submit to reality.[45]

Thus, as I have already pointed out *contra* Sartre, the organic unity-in-difference of internal and external, bodily and mental, self and other, which the theory of tacit knowing allows us to envisage becomes at the same time the duality of *action* and *passion*, appropriation and surrender. This provides us, in fact, a broader polarity than the from-to structure of tacit knowing seemed in the first instance to warrant. There are always two poles, proximal and distal, of tacit knowing, and in the most obvious cases, of perception, for example, or of scientific knowledge, the proximal pole, the subsidiaries, are mine, while the distal pole, the focus of my effort, is that aspect of the world toward which I am straining, to which I am *giving* my attention. This is the most evident direction of our everyday indwelling, of being-in-the-world.[46] But this direction may be reversed. Then my

45. *Ibid.*, p. 63.
46. Polanyi holds that his concept of indwelling is identical with Heidegger's being-in-the-world; see Torchbook edition of *P.K.*, p. viii. I am not sure about this, since in *Sein und Zeit* there is no conception of authentic community and no ground on which to establish a relation of *Dasein* to nature; but there is certainly a kinship.

actions *in* the world become the subsidiary particulars which bear on the integration of myself as focal point of my activity. This process of integration is, in general, I believe, more easily seen in our acquaintance with others than in ourselves, since usually throughout our daily lives the proximal-distal vector as an inner-outer direction is compelling. That is why, though indeed we seldom know others, it is so appallingly difficult to know ourselves. That is why, in Heideggerian language, we lose ourselves, for the most part, in the everyday mode of forfeiture. But on the one hand, this is not, in Polanyi's terms, a "bad" loss: it is the essential process by which we make sense of things, the process that carries the achievements of science, art, institutional lore, even of religion. And on the other hand, the direction can be and sometimes is reversed: my practice of a discipline—which must be at many points partially focused on in its particulars in order, ultimately, to strengthen the integral performance—serves, *from* out-there, to deepen the coherence of my own existence. The performance of religious rituals involves a repetition of external actions which serve to strengthen my inner giving of myself to a higher power. Finally, moreover, the direction may be mutual: in attending through bodily clues to a loved person or a loved work of art or science, I interiorize, at the same time, the beloved object as I interiorize the subsidiaries which bear on the enrichment of myself. In following Diotima, one should not forget Aristophanes' comic insight: love as the begetting on the beautiful is both the discovery of beauty through the beloved and the completion of oneself.[47]

VII

To return to the argument of *Personal Knowledge:* Part II paints on a broader canvas the tacit component in language and in the whole range of mental development which the existence of language has supported (Chapter V: Articulation: the exposition of the semantic aspect of tacit knowing) ; in heuristics, from science, through art, to religion (Chapter VI: Intellectual Pas-

47. The amplification of "indwelling" to include self-integration is suggested in Polanyi's essay in this volume.

sions); and in the interiorization of our society's standards by which we accept social lore (Chapter VII: Conviviality). To compare in detail Polanyi's study of meaning with Sartre's would need a separate essay; I shall concentrate here on the metamorphosis, through the from-to relation of tacit knowing, of the concepts of emotion, of value and of community.

Sartre retains in *Being and Nothingness* his hysteria theory of emotion. He sees feeling as magic, as an incantation by which I refuse an active attack upon the in-itself and pretend to deny it by screaming.[48] As so often in his writings, what looks like a bizarre distortion of the facts is but a rigorous exploitation of a premise to which we all subscribe without admitting it. In this case he has simply stated in extreme form the logical consequence of the separation of thought and feeling which has haunted Western thought since Plato. The white horse of the *Phaedrus,* the Θυμοειδες of the *Republic* are no solution; nor is the Sartrean theory. The separation has been mistaken all along. What characterizes human life is not the opposition of passion to some separate principle of Reason or Will, or even to their pinpoint descendant, the nihilating for-itself. What characterizes human, as distinct from animal, life is the transcendence, and the transmutation, of the biological principles of appetite and aversion into *intellectual passion,* the responsible submission of ourselves to an aim which we not only desire as an individual satisfaction, but aspire to out of an obligation because we believe it to be true and right. Since he is basing his argument primarily on the study of scientific knowledge and its roots in scientific discovery, Polanyi stresses here the intellectual passions which support such knowledge, but he also generalizes this conception, in the final sections of the chapter, to include the aspirations by which art and religion are brought into, and sustained, in being. Indeed, the concept of intellectual passion is equivalent in scope and meaning to Spinoza's "intellectual love," which transforms human bondage into human freedom.[49]

48. Cf. *Sketch of a Theory of the Emotions,* trans. P. Mairet (London: Methuen, 1962).

49. Cf. also F. J. J. Buytendijk's concept of "desire-free love" in "Zur Phänomenologie der Begegnung," *Das Menschliche* (Stuttgart: Koehler, 1958), pp. 60-100.

In all knowing, in all our manipulation of and giving of ourselves to, our environment, our passions are assertive, in that (as, indeed, Sartre's "ontological proof" also demonstrates) they entail the putative existence of an appropriate object. As animals, we share such passions with all animals. Yet although the passions which move the scientist, or the artist, or the judge to seek the truth, are still passions, affirming—in hazard—the existence of their object, their object is different, and so is the passion that seeks it:

> The parallel with intellectual passions is clear, and so is the contrast to them. As the pursuit of our drives implies the supposition that there exist objects which we have reason to desire or to fear, so similarly, all passions animating and shaping discovery imply a belief in the possibility of a knowledge of which these passions declare the value; and again, in accrediting these passions with the power to recognize the truth, we do not assume their infallibility—since no rule of scientific procedure is certain of finding the truth and avoiding error—but we accept their competence. Our intellectual passions, however, differ essentially from the craving and emotions which we share with the animals. The satisfaction of these terminates the situation which evoked them. Discovery likewise terminates the problem from which it started, but it leaves behind knowledge, which gratifies a passion similar to that which sustained the craving for discovery. Thus intellectual passions perpetuate themselves by their fulfilment.[50]

It is through the power of symbolic systems that we have achieved this self-perpetuating mode of desire:

> This distinctive quality of intellectual passions is largely due to the fact that they are attached to an articulate framework. A scientist seeks to discover a satisfying theory, and when he has found it, he can enjoy its excellence permanently. The intellectual passion which animates the student to grapple with the difficulties of mathematical physics is gratified when he feels at last that he understands it, but it is the resulting sense of mastery that gives him

50. *P.K.*, p. 173.

permanent intellectual satisfaction. While the purely intellectual joy of the animal who has contrived a trick already
shows the same enduring quality, the articulate powers of
man can extend the range of such joys to whole systems of
cultural gratification.[51]

This difference brings us to the *social* ground of tacit knowing,
which is expanded in the following chapter, and indeed throughout Part III ("The Justification of Personal Knowledge"). Since
we have here the nub of the argument which overcomes the
emptiness of Sartrean value, as well as the hysterical character of
Sartrean emotion, I shall quote it in full. Polanyi continues:

> This wider perspective brings us back to the fact that
> scientific value must be justified as part of a human culture
> extending over the arts, laws and religions of man, all
> contrived likewise by the use of language. For this great
> articulate edifice of passionate thought has been reared by
> the force of the passions to which its erection offered crea-
> tive scope, and its lasting fabric continues to foster and
> gratify these same passions. Young men and women brought
> up in this culture accept it by pouring their minds into its
> fabric, and so live the emotions which it teaches them to
> feel. They transmit these emotions in their turn to succeed-
> ing generations, on whose responding fervour the edifice
> relies for its continued existence.[52]

We can see plainly, moreover, the criterion by which such
interiorized indwelling is differentiated from appetite:

> By contrast to the satisfaction of appetites, the enjoyment
> of culture creates no scarcity in the objects offering gratifi-
> cation, but secures and ever widens their availability to
> others. Those who obtain such goods increase their univer-
> sal supply and teach others to enjoy them by practising
> what they were taught. The pupil submits to what he
> acquires and improves himself by its standards.[53]

This permanence and universality of cultural frameworks
makes possible the rootedness of individual choice, as responsible

51. *Loc. cit.*
52. *Ibid.*, p. 173-174.
53. *Ibid.*, p. 174.

choice, in allegiance to communal standards: whether of a family, a profession, a nation, or even of humanity itself:

> Accordingly, the social lore which satisfies our intellectual passions is not merely desired as a source of gratification; it is listened to as a voice which commands respect. Yielding to our intellectual passions, we desire to become more satisfying to ourselves, and accept an obligation to educate ourselves by the standards which our passions have set to ourselves. In this sense these passions are public, not private: they delight in cherishing something external to us, for its own sake. Here is indeed the fundamental difference between appetites and mental interests. We must admit that both are sustained by passions and must ultimately rely on standards which we set to ourselves. For even though intellectual standards are acquired by education, while our appetitive tastes are predominantly innate, both may deviate from current custom; and even when they conform to it, they must both ultimately be accredited by ourselves. But while appetites are guided by standards of private satisfaction, a passion for mental excellence believes itself to be fulfilling universal obligations.[54]

The distinction between appetites and passions, Polanyi concludes, "is vital to the existence of culture. If it is repudiated, all cultural life becomes subordinated in principle to the demand of our appetites and of the public authorities responsible for the advancement of material welfare."[55] In other words, all cultural life is reduced once more to a Sartrean to-and-fro: the empty ego magically remaking an eternally resistant other, thus generating a Hobbesian war of all against all as the only possible manner of existence; or an abstract totalization which can recognize only a "scientific" rationalization of techniques (since there are no meaningful ends except the empty ego's unrealizable freedom). And indeed, for an instantaneous, reflexive, purely appropriative, non-cognitive *cogito,* no other issue is possible. Sartre himself remarks: we can draw from the *cogito* only what we put into it.[56] Hence, inevitably, the Sartrean analysis whereby the "already

54. *Loc. cit.*
55. *Loc cit.*
56. *B. & N.,* p. 73.

meaningful" world into which the for-itself springs—the world of
the Luxembourg, the Metro, the Deux Magots, of waiters and
books and cigarettes and wars and revolutions—must be, on pain
of the for-itself's extinction, an aggregate of *techniques* for self-
assertion.

If, however, our starting point is an endeavor (in the Spinozis-
tic, not the merely Hobbesian sense), a from-to process by which
we both grasp and give meaning, then the dialectic of interiorization and indwelling inherent in such a structure can give us,
though not the certainty, nevertheless the hope of a more fruitful
issue, an issue in which we can recognize that although community and tradition make us, although our being has been shaped
parochially and contingently, and hence in the last analysis "absurdly," we can assimilate these factual foundations of ourselves,
often in criticism of, but also in respect and gratitude for, the
values to which, in becoming human, we responsibly submit.
Thus my original choice of myself is also a choice of standards to
which I freely submit myself. They are neither written on the
heavens with no reference to my choice of them, nor made by fiat,
as expressions of, and identical with, my own nihilating eruption
out of an indifferent being. They are the expressions of my
calling, which I accept as laws, as universally compelling, yet in
the knowledge of my contingency, in the awareness that try as I
may, I may be wrong. We are not so much *condemned* to be free,
as we are given, as right and duty, the responsibility of freedom,
the responsibility of service to what, to the best of our limited
abilities, we judge to be the truth.

Since I have elicited here the essential theme of the Conviviality chapter from its anticipation in Chapter VI, I shall not stop
to elaborate it further—although, again, a detailed comparison of
Polanyi's critique of Marxism with Sartre's Marxist program
would be a fruitful theme for further study.

So far Polanyi has been tracing, descriptively, the range of tacit
knowing. Part III moves to a new, reflective level, and asks how I
can justify to myself my hazardous reaching out to the world in
passionate assertion and responsible self-surrender. This part of
the argument parallels, therefore, the movement in *Being and
Nothingness,* in the Transcendence chapter, from the prereflec-

tive *cogito* to the level of reflection. Sartre, we have seen, distinguishes between pure and impure reflection: pure reflection he returns to only in the mysterious footnote I have already mentioned, and in the conclusion, where he points to some (not yet written) further work which will investigate this theme. This pure reflection looms as either the result of a conversion (and a conversion proved impossible by the argument of *Being and Nothingness*—for it would, in its own realization in the world, inevitably collapse into bad faith) or as a reinstatement, in all its isolation and impotence, of the original Cartesian *cogito*. *Impure* reflection, on the other hand, produces the illusory proliferation of a psychological object world, a pretended ego, which honesty can only demolish. Now what tacit knowing does here, it seems to me, is to allow us, not, indeed, complacency, but at least a hopeful dwelling in impure reflection. Given tacit knowing, no reflection, *qua* reflection, can be "pure"; yet it need not therefore be alternately despairing or dishonest; as Sartrean reflection is compelled to be. For Sartre, belief, when I examine it, is necessarily "troubled"; and if, naïvely, I fail to examine it, of course I am living in the "spirit of seriousness," in the illusory acceptance of illusions as real. For Polanyi, belief when I examine it is admittedly hazardous; all belief, from belief in kinds of things—ordinary "universals"—to belief in God, "carries its own dubiety," but also its own well-founded sense of competence:

> I shall go on, therefore, to repeat my fundamental belief that, in spite of the hazards involved, I am called upon to search for the truth and state my findings. To accept commitment as the framework within which we may believe something to be true, is to circumscribe the hazards of belief. It is to establish the conception of competence which authorizes a fiduciary choice made and timed, to the best of the acting person's ability, as a deliberate and yet necessary choice. The paradox of self-set standards is eliminated, for in a competent mental act the agent does not do as he pleases, but compels himself forcibly to act as he believes he must. He can do no more, and he would evade his calling by doing less. The possibility of error is a necessary element of any belief bearing on reality, and to withhold belief on the

grounds of such a hazard is to break off all contact with reality. The outcome of a competent fiduciary act may, admittedly, vary from one person to another, but since the differences are not due to any arbitrariness on the part of the individuals, each retains justifiably his universal intent. As each hopes to capture an aspect of reality, they may all hope that their findings will eventually coincide or supplement each other.[57]

Thus both the hoped-for reality and the hoped-for mutuality of my objectives may be reasonably confirmed by my reflection on them and on the contours of the situation in which and through which I accept them. Impure reflection, that is, reflection falling short of a Cartesian transpicuity, proves an appropriate, and by no means a tragic, destiny for the philosophic mind.

Nor do we, in Polanyian terms, simply abandon pure reflection as an ideal. As the culmination of the *via negativa,* it, or its equivalent, appears as the total transcendence, in mystic experience, of my ordinary being-in-the-world. Not that, as with Sartre, I "try to become God and fail," but that in the development of the passive, the *devotional* aspect of tacit knowing, I may come to the act of worship as the positive expression of my negativity, the embodiment of reverence for what is totally greater than myself. Indeed, this sacramental dimension underlies Polanyi's account of knowledge throughout, as its radical denial does that of Sartre:

> The stage on which we thus resume our full intellectual powers is borrowed from the Christian scheme of Fall and Redemption. Fallen Man is equated to the historically given and subjective condition of our mind, from which we may be saved by the grace of the spirit. The technique of our redemption is to lose ourselves in the performance of an obligation which we accept, in spite of its appearing on reflection impossible of achievement. We undertake the task of attaining the universal in spite of our admitted infirmity, which should render the task hopeless, because we hope to be visited by powers for which we cannot account in terms of our specifiable capabilities. This hope is a clue to God. . . .[58]

57. *P.K.,* p. 315.
58. *Ibid.,* p. 324.

It remains, in Part IV, to found the epistemology so far developed in an appropriate ontology, and in this again *Personal Knowledge* parallels *Being and Nothingness,* where Part IV delves into the ontology demanded by the description of, and reflection on, the being of consciousness. But while for Sartre the ontological proof of the in-itself has been left far behind, as a necessary and limiting *un*intelligible, and only the agonizing doom of the for-itself remains, Polanyi seeks to ground commitment, and its root structure, tacit knowing, in the full hierarchical order of an emergent universe:

> Having decided that I must understand the world from my point of view, as a person claiming originality and exercising his personal judgment responsibly with universal intent, I must now develop a conceptual framework which both recognizes the existence of other such persons and envisages the fact that they have come into existence from primordial inanimate beginnings.[59]

Polanyi has since developed and elaborated this ontological foundation of tacit knowing, and I have myself attempted elsewhere to trace some of its essential constituents. Instead of repeating here either Polanyi's arguments or my own exposition of them, I shall return briefly to the metaphor of *orientation* which I mentioned earlier. All living things not only have an ecological niche, but take their place in it, and by so doing help to make it the niche it is. It develops through them, as they through it. The from-to structure of tacit knowing, and its development into responsible commitment in all its forms, not only intellectual, but aesthetic, moral, religious, this structure as we know it and live it, is the human emergent from the universal self-orienting processes of life. Knowing, our way of being open to the world, is one highly developed, and hence both grandiose and greatly imperiled, form of living. Knowing about knowing, therefore, entails knowing about life, life at all levels, since no higher level can exist except in intrinsic dependence upon its lower-level conditions.[60] Thus the whole panorama of biological knowledge,

59. *Ibid.,* p. 327.
60. The foundations for this have been laid earlier; I have not space to point them out here. Cf. *B. & N.,* p. 155: "What we ordinarily call knowing presupposes depths (reliefs), levels, an order, a hierarchy." But no use is made of this clue except to deny its applicability to the case of reflection.

biochemistry, physiology, morphology, embryology, evolution, forms the necessary underpinning for the epistemology of tacit knowing and of personal commitment. Since, moreover, to carry on the implications of the orientation metaphor, all organisms must right themselves not only in relation to the physical and chemical features of their environment, but in relation to a complex biotic community, this whole panorama exhibits from the start not only a hierarchy of individual development, but of social structures and generic norms. Not only goals, but *meanings,* which are prior to goals, acquire an ontological reality in reference to which life is not only, by us, interpreted, but *is.* Yet all such meanings, in the perspective of organic life, are also goals or aspirations: not only meaningful *sub specie aeternitatis,* but intrinsically time-borne, giving sense—that is, significance and direction—to process. Granted, this is a difficult ontology to articulate correctly and to assimilate effectively; it is in his theory of emergence, in my view, that Polanyi's philosophy still lacks a conclusive, and a wholly convincing, statement. But, in contrast to Sartre, it is the locus of Polanyi's argument here that matters. For Sartre, like all Cartesians, lacks the category of the organic (and in this almost all contemporary philosophers, especially philosophers of science, are still Cartesian). Although he can say on occasion, "I live my body," he is only expressing here (as Descartes had already done in *The Passions of the Soul*) the self-contradictory togetherness of a body which is felt as mind and a mind which, looked at "objectively," is all body. The vast range of living functions, the countless modes of emergent individuality, the countless styles of living together which both make possible and enrich such individual existence, the unquestionably and intricately hierarchical organization of living matter and living function, the recurrent mystery of individual development, the cosmic originality of evolution: all this is forgotten, indeed was never known by the consciousness for which the chestnut root is but the source of nausea, and nausea the honest expression of its contact with reality.[61] Polanyi's ontology, in contrast, is the philosophical expression of a different vision, more hopefully questioning:

61. Cf. *B. & N.*, p. 338.

O chestnut tree, great-rooted blossomer,
Are you the leaf, the blossom or the bole?
O body swayed to music, O brightening glance,
How can we know the dancer from the dance?

VIII

The outcome of *Personal Knowledge,* as compared with *Being and Nothingness* (Section 4 above), can be briefly put. We are not a pure negation of being, since as living things we also *are;* but it is nevertheless a tension between the from- and to-poles of tacit knowing that defines our way of being. Merleau-Ponty's metaphor a "fold in being," therefore, is more apposite than Sartre's "hole." We exist, not as disintegration, but as a search for coherence, as the striving for, and, in many directions and on many levels, the achievement of, integration. We may indeed flee ourselves, but the primary direction of our "flight"—our direction outwards—is at the same time the movement by which we *discover* the inexhaustibly promising features of a real world. This search, though dangerous, is by no means foredoomed to failure. Indeed, the very emergence of life, of sentient life, and of responsible life on this planet is, against the meaninglessness of mere matter, already the expression of a cosmic achievement which we acknowledge as the ground, as well as the limitation, of all we strive to achieve. In this situation, finally, the appropriate mood is neither arrogance nor despair, but hope.

IX

I have tried to indicate the premises of Sartre's argument in *Being and Nothingness,* its main outline, and its outcome, and to parallel this with a similar statement for *Personal Knowledge*: the transformation of the Cartesian *cogito,* whether prereflective or reflective, into the dynamic of tacit knowing, the argument which follows from this altered starting point, and its outcome in contrast to the "tragic finale" of the Sartrean dialectic. It remains to mention very superficially, what other contributors to this volume will have treated in depth, the prognosis for philosophy in so far as we in fact succeed in taking up the concept of tacit knowing as an instrument of philosophical discovery. I need hardly mention again the dead end to which Sartre in so many directions brings us, and shows us that we have brought ourselves: in epistemology, a choice between some form of phenomenalism, a Kierkegaardian subjectivity, or a naïve renunciation of philosophy for the merely practical; in ontology, the agony of the I-other as the alternative to a meaningless materialism; in aesthetics, the assertion of a beauty which is the hypostatization in emptiness of the ugliness of the real, an aesthetic of which Genet is the Saint; in ethics, the illusory pursuit of a null-point total freedom haunted by its ubiquitous collapse into *mauvaise foi;* in theology, God as the self-contradictory goal of man's fruitless self-assertion. By the simple expedient of accepting the from-to vector of tacit knowing, and turning the prereflective *cogito* away from its empty inwardness, we can open with one gesture all these closed doors. From perception through the natural sciences to mathematics, knowing turns out to be the way in which as responsible persons we grope our way forward, relying on clues within ourselves to comprehend the complex patterns of the real world:[62] a real world which, moreover, in Polanyi's ontology, includes not only the extended out-there and the non-extended within, but a host of inter-organized, stratified entities, both embodied and intellectual: living beings, works of art, institutions, theories, all the "worlds" of nature and culture through participation in which our lives are shaped.[63] Moreover, in acknowledging the reality of comprehensive entities such as problems, laws, works of art, and so on, and the obligation we owe to the standards we set ourselves, *Personal Knowledge* opens the way to what contemporary philosophy desperately needs: a viable theory of value. As intellectual beauty serves the scientist as a clue to discovery, so in art: beauty is the lure which guides the

62. For specific applications to epistemological problems, see "Tacit Knowing: Its Bearing on Some Problems of Philosophy," *Rev. Mod. Phys.*, XXXIV (1962), 601-616.
63. See, e.g., *The Tacit Dimension;* "The Structure of Consciousness," *Brain*, LXXXVIII (Sept. 1965), 799-810; "Science and Man's Place in the Universe" in *Science as a Cultural Force* (Baltimore: Johns Hopkins, 1964), pp. 54-76.

artist or the spectator, not as the empty negation of the imperfections of the world, but as the focal gathering point of the manifold subsidiaries through which we attend to it. Tacit knowing in its semantic aspect can be elaborated as well into an aesthetics as into a general theory of meaning.[64] The accrediting of standards as making a valid claim to our assent, moreover, the central role allotted the person even in theoretical activity, and the rooting of responsible personhood in the many-leveled foundation of the organic world—all this calls for a development in ethical terms. In particular, as Polanyi's recent article on the Hungarian Revolution points out, it demands a rethinking of the methodology of the behavioral sciences, where the false ideal of an essentially positivist objectivity has done, and continues to do, most harm.[65] For with the instrument of tacit knowing we can rectify the mistaken view of science which has led to these absurdities and proceed toward the understanding of persons and their practical activities on a foundation continuous with the methods of the natural sciences yet congruent with the substantive insights of our ordinary lives.[66] Finally, for theology, Polanyi exhibits belief and hope as the means whereby we make contact with the reality around us, and interprets that reality, in its broadest sweep, as a "cosmic field,"[67] to which our proper approach is devotion, and whose gifts to us are those of grace.[68]

64. There are some suggestions for this in *P.K.* Cf. Donald Weismann, "The Collage as Model," in *Towards a Unity of Knowledge: Psychological Issues* (New York: International Universities Press, 1968).
65. "The Message of the Hungarian Revolution," *The American Scholar,* XXXV (Sept., 1966), 661-676.
66. There are also obviously leads in the stress on learning, on tradition, and so on, for a philosophy of education.
67. *P.K.,* p. 405.
68. See Richard Gelwick, "Michael Polanyi: *Credere Aude,* His Theory of Knowledge and Its Implications for Christian Theology" (Th.D. Dissertation, Pacific School of Religion).

POLANYI AND THE PROBLEM OF
METAPHYSICAL KNOWLEDGE

Edward Pols

I

Polanyi addresses himself in *Personal Knowledge* and in his later work to certain problems philosophy has been left with as a result of the epistemological development from Descartes through Hume. There seem to be five chief problems, the first four of which all bear on the question whether metaphysical knowledge is possible; the fifth problem is one version of that very question. The chief concern of this essay is with the fifth problem and with the adequacy of Polanyi's approach to it. I shall first state these problems, but without attempting to give a detailed account of how they arose.

The *first* is the separation between knowing and valuing. It is not a separation that has always troubled philosophy: the whole of Plato's work and the Platonic tradition is evidence for that. For that tradition the knower directed himself towards what was most real because also most valuable, and it required consequently the complete integration of his passional nature into the order of the virtues for his cognitive nature to function as it should and to permit him to know what Plato called the really real. The epistemological and metaphysical sections of *The Republic* offer us probably the most coherent version of such an outlook. In this limited sense of an interdependence of our valuing and cognitive "faculties," knowledge of the real is for Plato a personal matter. For Descartes it is patently less so. The thinking substance in its ideal state—a state in which it sees itself as it is, its utter separability from matter, the dependence of itself and matter upon a Perfect Being, and the paradoxical union of thinking and material substance in human nature—has at the most a negative relation with the passions: it must be free of them to see things clearly. That theme may of course also be found in Plato, in much of the *Phaedo,* for instance. That, however, tells us only that Plato was aware of, and struggled continuously with, the paradox of a soul bent upon the generality and (in one sense) impersonality of truth and yet dependent upon the complex forces and drives of some particular person. Descartes surely builds his whole case upon the generality of the consciousness that is joined with some particular body. So thoroughgoing is his concentration upon generality and impersonality that he does not in the end seem to be talking about the consciousnesses of a plurality of thinking substances, but about the consciousness of *one* thinking substance that manifests itself in a variety of instances. The separation of knowing and valuing thus begun in Descartes finds its culmination, in different ways, in Hume and in Kant. For the Hume of the ethical writings, reason and sentiment are quite separate things, the one concerned with consequences of the actions to which we are moved, the other issuing in the "valuations" that move us to action. That Hume in his epistemological writing puts sentiment (habit, custom, gentle force) at the root of much of our "reasoning" argues against his consistency, but it does not alter his explicit view of the separation of fact and value. Kant is concerned in the first critique to analyze the necessary structure of our knowing, but turns in the second and third critiques to consider the springs of right action and of aesthetic judgment. The two realms are separate, and their findings are at odds about the most important matters. It is the whole point of the later critiques that they are not concerned with what we can know, but with what we can judge to be right or beautiful.

The *second* problem is the one to which Whitehead has perhaps given the definitive name: the bifurcation of nature. It is, of course, intimately related to the previous problem, and has roughly the same historical roots. As Whitehead saw it, the prevailing scientific attitude, based upon the success of Cartesianism and Newtonian science, divides nature into the two realms of body and mind, and then attempts to derive mind, and indeed the whole world of subjectivity, from the laws of matter. It is the passionate insistence of the knower that he is not a by-product, but an authentic reality issuing in an authentic view of the world; yet he appears an unaccountable and tragic intrusion in a world whose constitution is of a different sort.

The *third* is an epistemological problem that takes various forms, but that appears perhaps most vividly in Hume's question: By what right do we move, from a host of disconnected, often interrupted, and partial data to the conviction that we are dealing with a world of substantial entities in causal interaction? How do we, in short, transcend the immediacy of empirical data to establish truths that exceed any assemblage of empirical data? Kant has furnished us with a kind of answer, but it is one that Polanyi will not accept, since to do so would leave the first two problems I have sketched unresolved. Kant's affirmation of transcendental principles of the mind—principles which do indeed enable us to account for our capacity to transcend the fragmentary and manifold character of experience—is possible only at the expense of a separation of knowing and valuing, and a distinction between the laws of causally connected nature and the freedom of our will.

The *fourth* problem is the lack of reflexivity in at least some post-Cartesian theories of knowledge. It would seem to be an indispensable feature of an adequate theory of knowledge that it should be capable of accounting for its own origins and its own adequacy. If the epistemologist professes to tell us something about the structure of knowing that would be inaccessible to a mind so constituted, we have reason to distrust his doctrine. It has, for instance, long been apparent to critics that if one holds the representative theory of ideas, and supposes that the mind of the epistemologist who propounds it is also subject to the restrictions that theory proposes, then it is difficult to see how the epistemologist could ever determine the truth of the doctrine without introducing premises that the theory does not tolerate. By what right, for instance, can Locke claim that our ideas do not represent substance as it really is when none of his (representative) ideas can tell him *what* substance is or indeed *that there is* any substance? The general point is not of course restricted to doctrines in which the representative theory plays a significant role. We may put it in the form of some questions that are evidently considered to be too unsporting to put to an epistemologist. Could, for instance, a mind constituted as Hume claims it to be, have produced the *Treatise*? Could it indeed have enunciated and defended the premise that all our knowledge is founded upon atomic impressions? Although much of the force of Hume's criticism of our knowledge of causation rests upon his contention that all events are loose and disconnected, and although this in turn rests upon his premise about the atomic character of impressions, there are probably few philosophers who would accept that premise *au pied de la lettre*. Their willingness nevertheless to see Hume's conclusions as persuasive is a measure of their willingness to exempt the theoretician from the consequences of his theory. The other side of this willingness is the fear—often well grounded —that a properly reflexive theory will also be viciously self-confirmatory.

The *fifth* problem can be seen as a natural outcome of the others: at least the solution to it will seriously affect the adequacy of the solutions we can give to the other problems. It is the question of the validity of metaphysical knowledge. If we should in some sort be equipped to go beyond the immediate data of experience, does our act of transcendence of the immediate ever afford us a knowledge of what is, in Plato's phrase, really real, or must we content ourselves in our science, our commonsense attitudes, and our valuations (since we may not share Kant's views on the separability of knowledge and valuation) with the phenomenal—content ourselves, that is, with forms of thought and attention that we ourselves have shaped, and that consequently while enabling us to cope with reality, also always hide it from us?

We need not take Kant as our final authority on the question whether we have a capacity for metaphysical knowledge, since he does less than justice to metaphysical claims that lie outside the rationalistic tradition against which his criticism is directed. Nevertheless, we can hardly avoid testing the pretensions of any supposed metaphysical knowledge against the findings of the first critique. No metaphysics has any chance of satisfying us if it does not offer us an authenticated knowledge of entities that are substantial in a sense more basic than the phenomenal "substances" Kant maintains we are limited to. The word "substantial" is a stumbling block. Most of us would be content if it meant, in this supposed new metaphysical context, something rather different from its various pre-Kantian senses. The insistence that it should mean something more than an appearance engendered by a categorial habit is, however, impossible to give up. For presumably an entity that was not *merely* a phenomenon, or appearance, would necessarily yield us *something* of a reality that transcended it and upon which it depended. Which is, of course, only to take the word "appearance" in a somewhat more positive sense than it has in Kant, where what is stressed is not what a phenomenon might yield us of what lies behind it, but rather what it hides or veils from us. Kant, in erecting the thing-in-itself as an impossible ideal towards which we might turn if we were provided with an intellectual intuition, almost persuades us that this is what metaphysicians have always been after. Yet few, if any, philosophers have ever claimed that it was within our capacity to know an absolute reality unqualified by a relation to realities of lesser degree. No doubt if someone should want to possess a transcendence so pure as to be isolated from all the manifestations that depend upon it, Kant gives him good reasons why he cannot have it. But we have a right to hope for a knowledge that should yield us *something* of the domain that he held to be inaccessible to reason. Certainly we shall not settle for less and still wish to call it metaphysical knowledge.[1] It should yield us something of the absolute *in* the relative; transcendence *in and through* the particulars it transcends; the really real *refracted in* various degrees of reality; Being *appearing* to us in appearances. If we look for pure Reality in the sense of a thing-

1. There are of course many Pickwickian senses of "metaphysics." Hume, for instance, calls his own epistemology, which purports to show metaphysics impossible, "true metaphysics." Kant gives us more than one such sense. Various contemporary analytic writers use the term to designate any analytic investigation dealing with expressions that have turned up in traditional metaphysics.

in-itself we shall certainly find pure Nothing: nothing happening; nothing at issue; no diversity, but instead a stolid and inane Unity. It clears our minds to be persuaded of the impossibility of this extreme case, even if there are some of us who can honestly say that we have never been tempted to look in that direction. And we are convincingly taught by Kant that, if there are more profitable directions to look in, there is profit there only if our glance is simultaneously upon the nature of our own cognitive powers.

It is important to remember that Polanyi did not enter the philosophical arena primarily as a metaphysician. It would appear, rather, that he was moved to take up these issues because he felt that philosophers, by dealing with them inadequately, or by ignoring them entirely, had permitted the development of a philosophy of science and an attitude towards science whose cultural consequences were disastrous. While science grew more and more imperialistic in its pretensions, the epistemology in the light of which it understood itself remained completely unsatisfactory. Scientism and the reductionism that is the consequence of it went hand in hand with an epistemology, founded upon Hume and roughly classifiable as positivism, that was in no position whatsoever to sustain such pretensions. Polanyi was concerned of course not just to curb the excesses of scientism, but to protect the integrity of science itself, which he felt to be threatened by its preoccupation with an inadequate image of itself. His first concern, then, was the establishment of an epistemology adequate to account for the real achievements of science, and it is, I take it, only because the first four problems lead naturally to the fifth that he must also be judged as a metaphysician. For it is hardly possible to cope adequately with any of the first four problems without taking up a position on the question whether our minds are fitted for metaphysical knowledge.

The way Polanyi deals with the first four problems in his epistemology is obviously congruent with various contemporary efforts to revive metaphysics. A philosophy that purports to be "postcritical" could hardly do otherwise. I shall try to answer the question whether his epistemology gives us any grounds for holding that metaphysical knowledge is possible. By "metaphysical knowledge" I shall mean something like what I set forth in dealing with the fifth problem.

In Section II I shall state the main lines of the argument Polanyi has evolved to deal with the first four problems. In the later sections I shall examine the bearing of various parts of his argument on the fifth problem. In pursuit of this metaphysical interest we shall have to neglect much of the very rich texture of *Personal Knowledge*.

II

Polanyi's argument falls naturally into three stages. The *first stage*, which is the most clearly epistemological one, is concerned chiefly with his distinction between explicit and tacit knowing. The distinction appears vividly in the contrast between our knowledge of a countryside by way of a map and our knowledge of it gained by the direct familiarity that comes of walking about in it. The former knowledge is critical, articulated, and often acquired by way of strict rules based upon specifiable premises, as a map, for instance, may be constructed by applying mathematical rules to our data. The latter is acritical, preverbal, and instinctive in somewhat the same way in which our reliance upon our senses is instinctive. We tend to value explicit knowledge more highly, and accept it as the standard both for finished knowledge and for the acquiring of knowledge.

And yet this exalted valuation of strictly formalized thought is self-contradictory. It is true that the traveller, equipped with a detailed map of a region across which he plans his itinerary, enjoys a striking intellectual superiority over the explorer who first enters a new region—yet the explorer's fumbling progress is a much finer achievement than the well-briefed traveller's journey. Even if we admitted that an exact knowledge of the universe is our supreme mental possession it would still follow that man's most distinguished act of thought consists in producing such knowledge; the human mind is at its greatest when it brings hitherto unchartered domains under its control. Such operations renew the existing articulate framework. Hence they cannot be performed within this framework but have to rely (to this extent) on the kind of plunging reorientation which we share with the animals. Fundamental novelty can be discovered only by the same tacit powers which rats use in learning a maze.[2]

We must be clear at once about one thing: what Polanyi calls the "personal component" in knowledge is identical with this tacit component.[3] Thus, the productive or creative component in human knowledge is identified with this tacit "plunging reorientation which we share with animals."

Except for this last point—and the exception is an important one—we should be fairly safe in seeing Polanyi's distinction as one more in a series of classical distinctions between a lower and a higher form of mind. Aristotle's distinction between demonstrative knowledge (epistēmē) and rational intuition (nous) comes first to mind, the former concerned with the logical articulation and development of principles (or premises), the latter with the creative acquisition of principles. The distinction derives from a similar one made by Plato in the image of the divided line and elsewhere, although Plato uses different terms on different occasions to designate the two levels. Descartes' distinction between the deductive and intuitive capacities of the mind also belongs to this tradition. The tradition does not, however, insist upon the body-rooted character of the higher, or intuitive, capacity, and thus does not hold that there is a continuity of this power with animal instincts. Indeed, its emphasis lies in the other direction: intuition is taken to be so elevated and detached from the particularity of the person and his body as to seem impersonal and even Godlike. Plato often maintains that it comes into its own only after death; and Aristotle often represents it as the intrusion of a higher and divine principle. Kant, while denying that an intellectual intuition is possible to us, makes the same kind of point by maintaining that it is the interpenetration of our sensory (body-rooted) and our rational capacities that *prevents* us from having an intellectual intuition.

2. *S.M.,* p. 18.
3. *Ibid.,* p. 17.

Polanyi, on the other hand, wishes to stress the important role played in our intuitive capacity[4] by its bodily roots. This positive interest in the role of the body in intuition is to be found elsewhere in twentieth-century philosophy. Perhaps the clearest parallel to Polanyi's point is Bergson's distinction between intellect and intuition, in which the creative, vital feature of intuition is seen as an expression of the *élan vital*—the highest point, as it were, of the "plunging" force that makes itself also felt in the growth and development of our bodies.

Polanyi's contention that knowledge is personal in the sense that its creative or intuitive side is animated by bodily and passional vitality avoids the image of a disembodied intelligence, which is so often encouraged by the older tradition. These older writers, however, were interested in the universality or generality of the knowledge that results from intuition or insight. In a perfectly usual sense of the word, such knowledge was "impersonal." Since many of them insisted that the highest reaches of intuition were open only to those in whom the passions were subdued into the order of the virtues, they had to contend with the paradox that such impersonality had personal roots of a kind.

Although Polanyi also recognizes passionate commitment as the most important personal element in the "plunging" component of tacit knowledge, he does not maintain that knowledge is open only to the virtuous. He thus gives "personal" a somewhat different emphasis from that I have given it in applying it to the Platonic tradition. But, beginning with what is in *some* sense personal, rather than with (impersonal) universality, he must cope with the other side of the Platonic paradox. He must, that is, account for the impersonal side of knowledge. This he does by way of what he calls the universal intent of personal knowledge—a sense of responsibility, or commitment beyond the personal.[5] The paradoxical mingling of personal and impersonal in knowledge creates problems in any philosophy that attempts to cope with it. Plato claims that we attain a direct rational satisfaction in our grasp of what is universal. Polanyi's claim that the

4. Polanyi occasionally calls the tacit component "intuitive." See *P.K.*, pp. 16, 91 n., 130-131.
5. *S.M.*, p. 27. See *P.K.* as indexed under "universal intent."

whole cognitive enterprise must rest on a tacit personal component which is a commitment to a quest rather than the realization of a quest, must therefore find some way other than Plato's
for coping with the problem of universality. We shall, however,
defer for a while consideration of this and other difficulties inherent in Polanyi's way of dealing with the personal element in
knowledge.

The distinction between tacit and explicit knowing is paralleled by another distinction, which is addressed to the way we
know parts and wholes. Polanyi intends the distinction to apply
to parts and wholes of all sorts, but it will be well to begin with
some natural entity, an animal or plant for instance. When we
are aware of some such whole *as* a whole, so that we are attending
to *it* rather than to its parts, our awareness of it is said to be *focal*.
We do not focus upon the components, say the mane or hooves of
the horse, the bark or leaves of the oak tree, but upon the horse
and the oak tree. It is not that we are unaware of the parts—
indeed our awareness of the parts contributes to our focal awareness of the whole—but our awareness of the parts is *subsidiary*
rather than focal. We have no need to catalogue the parts,
although in other circumstances we might want to do so. There is
in fact something creative in the way in which we bring together
our awareness of the parts into a joint awareness of the whole.

> We may say that when we comprehend a particular set of
> items as parts of a whole, the focus of our attention is
> shifted from the hitherto uncomprehended particulars to
> the understanding of their joint meaning. This shift of
> attention does not make us lose sight of the particulars,
> since one can see a whole only by seeing its parts, *but it
> changes altogether the manner in which we are aware of the
> particulars. We become aware of them now in terms of the
> whole on which we have fixed our attention.* I shall call this
> a *subsidiary awareness* of the particulars, by contrast to a
> *focal awareness* which would fix attention on the particu-
> lars in themselves, and not as parts of a whole. I shall also
> speak correspondingly of a *subsidiary* knowledge of such
> items, as distinct from a *focal* knowledge of the same items.[6]

6. *S.M.*, pp. 29-30.

Evidently, then, the distinction between focal and subsidiary knowledge is not a precise parallel with the distinction between tacit and explicit knowledge. It seems rather that the first distinction is clearest when we think of it as a further exploration of the structure of tacit knowing. Indeed shortly before the passage just quoted he has made this very point in the course of drawing a parallel between his doctrine and that of Gestalt psychology.

> The structure of tacit knowing is manifested most clearly in the act of understanding. It is a process of *comprehending:* a grasping of disjointed parts into a comprehensive whole. The characteristic features of this process have been carefully traced by the psychology of gestalt in the course of the last forty years. Yet that enquiry has missed an aspect of its subject which I believe to be decisive for our understanding of knowledge and for our corresponding appreciation of man's position in the universe. Psychologists have described our perception of gestalt as a passive experience, without envisaging that it represents a method—and indeed the most general method—for acquiring knowledge. They were probably unwilling to recognize that knowledge was shaped by the knower's personal action. But this does not hold for us. Having realized that personal participation predominates both in the area of tacit and explicit knowledge, we are ready to transpose the findings of Gestalt-psychology into a theory of knowledge: a theory based primarily on the analysis of comprehension.[7]

It would appear then that Polanyi holds that the plunging, direct, personal, or tacit aspect of reason is present whenever we are able to make our awareness of the parts contribute in a subsidiary way to our focal awareness of the whole. The awareness of the parts then stands in tacit support of our awareness of the whole. We can also call our awareness of the whole an example of tacit knowing for it is our "plunging," personal, and in that sense, tacit, faculty that has brought together our awareness of the parts into a joint awareness of the whole.

There are many difficulties about the term "explicit." Some of them can be avoided by noticing that Polanyi seems to feel that

7. *S.M.*, pp. 28-29.

absolute explicitness is an ideal—a false one, to be sure—and that any real explicitness is always relative to an ineradicable tacit component. Thus, although he gives "words, graphs, maps and symbols in general"[8] as examples of the explicit or articulate, he does not mean that any of these are wholly explicit. It is an important part of his doctrine that *no* knowledge, not even that embodied in a logistic system,[9] is explicit in the sense of being neutrally transferable from person to person without reference to its tacit base. When we *are* able to transfer, as it would seem impersonally, some body of knowledge "immediately present to the mind," we can do so only by virtue of operating within another, and for the moment unnoticed, framework that is tacit and personal. He puts this by observing that the distinction between subsidiary and focal transcends the distinction between tacit and explicit.[10] His point is that any symbol or symbol structure, which we might suppose to be explicit in the sense of being neutrally transferable, can only be apprehended *as* a symbol by making our awareness of it subsidiary "while fixing our focal attention on [its] meaning."[11] Explicitness in the absolute sense is, then, an illusion.

Besides the relative sense (*a*) in which symbol structures are explicit, there is another sense of the word that tends to confuse the issue. This sense turns up in two rather different contexts and we shall for convenience treat it as two different senses. (*b*) If my focal awareness of some whole, an awareness that is an achievement of tacit knowing, issues in an articulate judgment, say, "That is a house" or "That is an oak tree," then we must surely say that our awareness of the whole is explicit, in a perfectly usual sense of that word. Yet that achievement is, in Polanyi's sense, personal and not neutrally transferable.[12] (*c*) Subsidiary awareness is tacit in the sense, already noticed, of contributing to

8. *S.M.*, p. 30.
9. *P.K.*, pp. 117 ff., 190 ff., 255 ff.
10. *S.M.*, p. 30.
11. *Loc. cit.*
12. Marjorie Grene uses this expression to describe the ideal of explicitness. I am not sure whether the phrase is actually used by Polanyi, but it is admirably descriptive of what he is after. See Marjorie Grene, *The Knower and the Known* (London: Faber and Faber; New York; Basic Books, 1966), p. 25 *et passim*. Cited hereafter as *K.K.*

our tacit knowledge of wholes. When, however, we wish to justify our knowledge of a whole or to analyze it for some other purpose, we must make what was subsidiary focal, and thus explicit in at least sense (b). So, we might say "That is a white oak. Note the evenly lobed, hairless leaves; see the characteristic acorn: its cup is bowl-shaped and covers very little of it; and the bark is whitish and rather evenly scaled." The point of the example is, however, to enable someone else to recognize white oaks by a tacit achievement. And the items we make explicit as we focus upon them (leaves, bark, acorn) must themselves be grasped by an act of tacit knowing. According to Polanyi we are never able to stand quite outside our tacit achievements. Tacit knowing, when it functions properly, rests upon a certain relation between focal and subsidiary; when what was tacit becomes explicit we upset that relation at least temporarily. It is, however, a faulty emphasis to say that the focal is explicit (except in sense (b)).

Although the example was drawn from the class of natural entities, Polanyi wishes these distinctions to apply much more widely. The oak tree is a natural entity, its leaf a natural part, but we may think of the recognition of the tree as founded alternatively on a set of sense data (roundness, pointedness, whiteness, glossiness, greenness, etc.) that are subsidiarily known. The distinction, then, applies wherever we are concerned with the recognition of wholes on the basis of a subsidiary awareness of what are in *some* sense parts. He also uses the distinction to apply to organic integrations that may have little or no strict cognitive significance. Tacit knowing becomes, then, a subtype of tacit achievement in general. Polanyi has used examples drawn from at least the following fields: (1) the acquiring of a skill like riding a bicycle, playing tennis, or using some tool; (2) the discernment of a fruitful problem in science; (3) the discovery of a successful scientific theory; (4) the recognition of a physiognomy; (5) the act of perception; (6) the acquiring of speech; (7) the recognition of natural entities either in the sense of merely being aware of them or in the stricter sense of being able to name them as individuals or types; (8) the recognition of sensory patterns, forms, or *Gestalten* of a variety of fields; (9) the making of a work of art; (10) the enjoyment of a work of art.

Conversely, all the unifications are subject to the kind of explicit analysis I noticed under sense (c) above. Thus he gives the following examples of analyses of tacit knowing:

(1) the analysis of skills by motion studies, (2) the characterization of a physiognomy by listing the typical features, (3) the giving of detailed directions for carrying out a test or using a tool, (4) the analysis of speech by grammar, and (5) the physiological analysis of perception.[13]

The *second stage* of Polanyi's argument is of mixed epistemological and metaphysical import. He claims that our tacit knowledge is animated by the confidence that there is a hidden reality for us to discover. It is this confidence that makes our passionate and personal impulse also a responsible one having universal intent. We are therefore not enslaved by the participation of subjectivity in our knowledge. Sometimes our search is rewarded by a confrontation with the real that evokes a kind of intellectual joy in the beauty of what is discovered. For the moment I shall pass by the difficulties of the word "reality" except to notice that Polanyi seems to think of the solving of a problem, the creation of a work of art, the invention of a machine as all of them discoveries of what "was there before" and in that sense real.

The *third stage* is a more clearly metaphysical one. It amounts to a claim that we have in tacit knowing a model of the discernment of distinct levels of reality.

It seems plausible then to generalise to all other instances of tacit knowing that the structure of comprehension reappears in the structure of that which it comprehends and to go further and expect *to find the structure of tacit knowing duplicated in the principles which account for the stability and effectiveness of all real comprehensive entities.*[14]

Consider again what I called a natural entity, but which Polanyi often calls a comprehensive entity. When we know it tacitly we focus upon one level (its level) and we are subsidiarily aware of

13. Michael Polanyi, "Tacit Knowing: Its Bearing on Some Problems of Philosophy," *Review of Modern Physics*, XXXIV (October, 1962), 601-616.
14. *Duke*, IV, p. 5.

a lower level (that of its parts). When we turn our focal attention to the lower one the meaning of the higher is lost. Polanyi puts this by saying that the higher one "is logically unspecifiable in terms of its particulars."[15] The example is, however, not restricted to natural entities: the purpose of a machine, for instance, cannot be discerned from a focal awareness of the several parts. Reduction of any entity to its components by focusing upon *them* is to attend to a different and lower level from the one we began with. The logical unspecifiability of a higher in terms of a lower level is the heart of Polanyi's criticism of Laplacean reductionism. If there *should* be a level of ultimate particles, the laws reigning there cannot yield us the laws of higher levels.

Since such a shift of focus can be made indefinitely downwards, focusing upon the components of components, it would appear that the epistemology requires a doctrine of degrees or levels of reality. To attempt to revive this ancient doctrine is to step squarely into the metaphysical arena. We shall be concerned in later sections with the question whether Polanyi manages to defend his claim. Here what is important is that the distinction between focal and subsidiary is answered by a distinction between the comprehensive entity and its components. The first distinction is relative to our attention, and the validity of it depends upon our personal or tacit upholding of the reality of what we attend to. The second distinction is similarly relative and its authenticity similarly dependent upon the tacit component. The ontological claim is based upon an epistemological one. The point is made clearly enough by the following passage:

> We can anticipate then the ontological characteristics of a comprehensive entity on the following lines.
> 1) Tacit knowing relies on our awareness of the particulars of an entity for attending to it.
> 2) If we switch our attention to the particulars, this function of the particulars is cancelled and we lose sight of the entity to which we had attended.
>
> The ontological counterpart of this would be
> 1) The principles controlling a comprehensive entity

15. *S.M.*, p. 45. See *P.K.*, pp. 56, 63 *et passim.*

would be found to rely for their operations on laws governing their particulars in themselves.

2) At the same time the laws governing the particulars in themselves would never account for the organising principles of a higher entity which they form.[16]

It is not, however, a case of basing a metaphysics on an epistemological *theory,* for the theory is not only *about,* but *involves* a personal commitment.

The metaphysical claim is, however, also applied to the knower who makes the commitment: he too is a comprehensive entity and his cognitive act can therefore be understood as a level of reality making use of subordinate levels. Polanyi indeed holds that there are many comprehensive levels, or comprehensive functions, in man, no one of which is reducible to lower levels even though it makes use of them.

We thus come full circle: the entity upon whose personal, or tacit, knowledge the whole epistemological viewpoint is based is taken as an example of the ontology that epistemology opens up; and, being so considered, he is seen to be capable of that same tacit knowledge. There are many loose ends. Thus, although the indwelling of a mind in its physiological basis is rather different from the mind's indwelling in data of which it is subsidiarily aware (say the leaves and acorn of the oak), in order to achieve a focal awareness of a whole (say the oak tree), Polanyi occasionally confuses the two. Thus now and again[17] he seems to suppose that some physiological event basic to consciousness (say the movement of an action potential along an axon) is used as a subsidiary clue to what we are aware of in the same sense in which the rounded lobes of the leaf are clues to the white oak. But the essentials of the doctrine are clear enough: it would appear that the doctrine is reflexive in a way that might enable

16. *Duke,* IV, p. 6.
17. The point is not that he supposes subsidiary physiological "clues" to be conscious, but rather that the frequent use of the word "clue" and the expression "subsidiary awareness" assimilates all cases of a higher function's making use of a lower one to the particular case of cognition. An example of what I mean may be seen in Polanyi's otherwise admirable article "The Structure of Consciousness," *Brain,* LXXXVIII, Part IV (1965), 799-810. See especially p. 802.

the epistemologist to avoid at least the fourth problem mentioned in Section I.

III

We have so far been talking of metaphysics in a rather loose sense—have been, that is, assuming that where an interpretative scheme involves such terms as "entities" and "levels of reality" it is a metaphysical one. We now have to ask whether Polanyi's doctrine is sufficient to confirm our capacity for metaphysical knowledge, where "metaphysical knowledge" has somewhat the sense I gave it in Section I. In asking this we are not asking whether the doctrine purports to carry us beyond the merely phenomenal. We are asking whether it really does carry us there—that is, whether it confirms us in our right to "at least something of the domain that Kant held to be inaccessible to reason."

It should be noticed at once that Polanyi's doctrine *does* purport to give us something beyond the "merely phenomenal." Any doctrine must do so (at least by implication) that claims that there are degrees of reality (or being) and that we can know at least some of them. For the "degree of being" doctrine is logically incompatible with a distinction between the merely phenomenal on the one hand and absolute reality, Being, Transcendence, or the thing-in-itself on the other. If there should be degrees of being and *all* the degrees should be phenomenal, it must still be true that a higher degree yields us *more* of being than a lower, so that the pejorative sense of "phenomenal" is blurred sufficiently for us not to wish to speak of the *"merely* phenomenal." *Something* of being discloses itself in a phenomenon that has a higher degree of being than some other phenomenon.

The different sense given the doctrine of phenomena by Kant naturally has its historical antecedents in the same tradition from which we get the doctrine of the Great Chain of Being. Yet few of the philosophers in that tradition give the doctrine the extreme sense it has in Kant. Perhaps Spinoza does, although he, unlike Kant, agrees with that tradition's view that reason is capable of penetrating behind appearances. Plato, to whom we owe the most influential statements about the distinction between appearance and reality, qualifies their opposition in many ways. Many of the dialogues—notably *The Republic*—insist on a gradual movement in which our cognitive powers go from mere appearance of appearances to what is highest and most real, the Form of the Good; and the Forms themselves, while they are in some passages identified with Being itself, are in other and perhaps more decisive passages made a function of the Good, which is in that sense more real than they. Platonism can be read just as easily in terms of the graded disclosure of Being itself as in terms of its absolute sequestration behind appearances. What Platonism really tells us we cannot have, at least not as the embodied knowers we are, is Being alone, isolated from the multiplicity and process in which it is manifest. If that should be a deprivation, it is a lesser one than Kant announces to us in the first of the critiques, in which all the phenomena accessible to our understanding are of the *same* degree, equally distant from Being, which they do not so much disclose as make inaccessible to the knower.

If Polanyi, in maintaining a traditional doctrine of a Scale of Nature, degrees of being, or levels of reality, is also necessarily defending the possibility of metaphysical knowledge, that does not settle the question whether the defense implicit or explicit in his doctrine is a sound one. Before this question can be examined it will be necessary to examine some of the things Polanyi has to say about the topic of reality and its accessibility to us. Most important is the sense of "reality" proper to the doctrine of levels of reality (or degrees of being) we have already met, which is developed in terms of the doctrine of comprehensive entities. We shall call this sense *four*. There are, however, at least three other ways in which he deals with the topic of reality; as they would appear to be less satisfactory I shall deal with them first. They are, of course, related to the more important sense, but they are more clearly bound up with the purposes of the physical sciences than with those of metaphysics. It would also appear that they occasionally obscure some of the important features of the doctrine of comprehensive entities.

The *first* of these three senses of "reality" often appears in conjunction with the theme of the universal intent of personal knowledge:

> An empirical statement is true to the extent to which it reveals an aspect of reality, a reality largely hidden to us, and *existing therefore independently of our knowing it.* By trying to say something that is true about a reality believed to be existing independently of our knowing it, all assertions of fact necessarily carry *universal intent. Our claim to speak of reality serves thus as the external anchoring of our commitment in making a factual statement.*
>
> The framework of commitment is now established in outline for this particular case. The enquiring scientist's intimations of a hidden reality are personal. They are his own beliefs, which—owing to his originality—as yet he alone holds. Yet they are not a subjective state of mind, but convictions held with universal intent, and heavy with arduous projects. It was he who decided what to believe, yet there is no arbitrariness in his decision. For he arrived at his conclusions by the utmost exercise of responsibility. He has reached responsible beliefs, born of necessity, and not changeable at will. In a heuristic commitment, affirmation, surrender and legislation are fused into a single thought, bearing on a hidden reality.[18]

Whatever else this means, it also means that what we commit ourselves to by intent is that which is objectively true,[19] in a sense of "true" that must be compatible with the existence of other statements or theories that might be "more true." There is truth in Newtonian physics and presumably more truth in relativity physics. The term "real" then must mean "whatever it is that our (more or less) true scientific theories put us in touch with." If the real, understood in this sense, admits of degree, it is a degree defined in terms of the advance of science. If *all* mathematical physics deals, as Polanyi thinks it does, with the same level of reality, where "reality" is taken in the sense proper to the theory of comprehensive entities (sense *four*), then presumably the sense of "real" we are now dealing with (sense *one*) is less basic.

18. *P.K.*, p. 311.
19. *Ibid.*, p. 104.

Sense *two* is closely related to, and perhaps dependent upon, sense *one*. It turns up especially in his recent work, in which he now and again lays down a *criterion* for reality.

> The structural kinship between knowing a person and discovering a problem, and the alignment of both with our knowing of a cobblestone, call attention to the greater depth of a person and a problem, as compared with the lesser profundity of a cobblestone. Persons and problems are felt to be more profound, because we expect them to reveal themselves more richly and unexpectedly in the future. Since I have attributed the capacity of things to reveal themselves inexhaustibly in the future, to the fact that they are an aspect of reality, I shall say that minds and problems possess a deeper reality than cobblestones, even though cobblestones are more tangible. And since the significance of a thing is more important than its tangibility, I shall say that minds and problems are more real than cobblestones.[20]

A thing is therefore more real to the degree that it is more meaningful or significant, that is, to the degree that it reveals itself "more richly and unexpectedly in the future." As Polanyi uses it, the criterion gives us not only the superior reality of mind, for which the theory of comprehensive entities would already have provided a *rationale,* but also the superior reality of what are in some sort mind products—not just problems, but as Marjorie Grene has pointed out in defending the criterion,[21] theories, works of art, inventions, and laws as well. The sense of "reality" we are now concerned with (sense *two*) is the one generated in connection with the application of the criterion to these latter items.

There are obviously many difficulties here. The context as a whole requires us to talk of degrees of reality, or levels of reality, and, though one can see the importance of this and perhaps agree with the viewpoint when it is a question of molecules, cells, plants, animals, intelligence, and the like comprehensive entities (sense *four*) , this language does not illuminate in the same way such things as problems, theories, and machines. The idea of

20. *Duke,* IV, pp. 4-5.
21. *K.K.,* pp. 221-223.

stratification is not always present, and when it is, it is deceptive. It should be possible, for instance, to construct a machine having the same *number* of levels of function as a man, but Polanyi would not, I take it, wish to accord it the same degree of reality he accords its creator. If, puzzled by the ill-fit of the stratification principle, we say that such entities as theories and problems are not to be judged in that way, but merely in the light of the reality principle just enunciated, the picture does not become much clearer. For theories and the like do not just *have* a degree of reality, they also *put us in touch with* aspects of reality (sense *one*). Indeed the theory manifests its reality (sense *two*), that is, reveals itself "more *richly* and unexpectedly" precisely by putting us into touch with aspects of reality (sense *one*) in more and more ways. The criterion for the degree of reality (sense *two*) of the theory is thus the degree to which it puts us in touch with reality (sense *one*). And though this may be true, it also makes the criterion of little use: we still have to recognize that troublesome thing, reality, when we see it. It would also appear that the application of the criterion, at least to such things as theories, depends upon whatever criteria we employ to judge that an advance has been made in science, and our commitment in advance to a theory because of its beauty is a reality commitment in a way similarly tied to sense *one*.

Sense *two*, as we saw it at its first introduction, can also be taken to be equivalent to "meaningful" and "significant." Since the meaningfulness, or significance, of a comprehensive entity like a man is presumably rather different from that of a theory, the criterion will presumably have a different sense in the former case, presumably one consistent with sense *four*. Since Polanyi's whole doctrine about comprehensive entities that are real in sense *four* requires that we should uphold tacitly our knowledge of them, the point of an explicit criterion where that sense is at issue seems puzzling.

The *third* sense to be considered is a questionable one. At least, it is questionable whether we find it in Polanyi's work, although we *do* often find the expression that causes us to raise the question. Polanyi often uses the expression "aspect of reality." On the face of it this expression might seem to bear upon the degrees-

of-being doctrine of sense *four*. The notion of degree or level may
be illustrated, at least in some cases, by giving instances of the
entities that occupy it. A man occupies a higher level in Polanyi's
scheme than does an amoeba, and one of the reasons he does is
that he also "comprehends" (in the sense of subsidiarily employing in order to exist at *his* level) the cellular level. The notion of
"aspect" has certain parallels with this, although we probably
cannot precisely clarify an *aspect* of the real by pointing to some
entity that *illustrates* it. It would seem, nonetheless, that some
aspects of the real are less real than others. If, for instance, we
consider some real thing only under its measurable aspect, or
more precisely, only under such an aspect as is expressible in a
formal system, we presumably fail to capture *some* of its reality.
When Whitehead calls philosophy "the critic of abstractions" he
appears to have something like that in mind: it is the duty of the
philosopher to judge in terms of their relative abstractness aspects of the real that are expressed, it might be, in common sense
and in the sciences and arts. On its positive side philosophy
becomes therefore a search for the concrete (the more real, the
more important), in which a mode of seeing concretely is developed concurrently with a language in which the vision is expressible. Thus it would be Whitehead's point about ultimate "particles," which are at least one concern of mathematical physics, not
only that they occupy a lower level of reality than the amoeba, or
man, but also that *even that low level* is too abstractly seen by
mathematical physics. A more appropriate, or at least more concrete understanding, is given by philosophy, which, though it
may have in the long run to make do with aspects, is really
concerned to overcome the kind of externality suggested by the
word "aspect."[22] It would, of course, presumably be the case that
entities occupying higher levels afford both the philosopher and
the scientists deeper and more important aspects.

It does not appear that this sense of "aspect of the real" is
developed in Polanyi's doctrine. Indeed it will be noticed that, in
the quotation in which our *first* sense of "real" was introduced,

22. I have dealt with the topic "aspect of reality" elsewhere. See Edward
Pols, *The Recognition of Reason* (Carbondale, Ill.: Southern Illinois University Press, 1963), pp. 159-161.

the expression in fact used was "aspect of reality." There and wherever else the expression is used, the governing sense is our *first* sense of "real." The expression usually seems to mean that one physical theory reveals some true things about nature, another physical theory other things, without there necessarily being a distinction in the ontological import of what is revealed. Generally speaking, Polanyi, in wishing to defend the integrity of the physical sciences, claims their ontological adequacy to what they deal with—hence, presumably, his hostility to positivism and conventionalism of every kind. Of course positivisms and conventionalisms do not claim the ontological irrelevance of science, but rather the irrelevance of ontology. Polanyi's objection to a scientism based on mathematical physics is to the application of mathematical physics to levels of reality for which it is unfitted. He seems to take it for granted that it is ontologically adequate to its proper subject matter, and this is what a doctrine like Whitehead's would call in question.

For the purposes of metaphysics we are thrown back upon our *fourth* sense of "reality"—the traditional notion of which the doctrine of comprehensive entities is so very fresh and lively a version. I have already claimed that such a doctrine, if sustained and confirmed, can be thought of as providing metaphysical knowledge in the sense mentioned in Section I. The weight of the confirmation Polanyi gives rests squarely on the doctrine of personal, or tacit, knowing, of which a preliminary sketch has already been given in Section II.

IV

It is unfortunate that much of what he has to say about the personal element in our knowledge casts it in a negative role. We lack a mode of knowing that is self-justifying in its impersonal self-evidence and clarity; failing that, we must make do with a kind of *fides quaerens intellectum*—a faith in search of understanding—a plunging, groping movement that is justified in its issue, but has no justification in itself except in the sense that we cannot get along without it. The language of much older fideisms and voluntarisms is often used: faith, belief, will, desire move us

towards our desired object: we even hear of "fiduciary hazard."[23]
The newer language of existentialism—terms like "commitment," "passionate," and "affirmation"—is used concurrently,
reminding us that existentialism can be profitably seen as the
most recent of the voluntarisms. Polanyi is not really urging an
existentialism upon us: he sees his task as the overcoming of the
traditional and unprofitable disjunction between subjectivity
and objectivity,[24] and, though some existentialists might be
thought of as having a similar aim, they are never motivated by
an interest in defending scientific knowledge. Yet there is present
at least what existentialisms share with voluntarisms: an emphasis on the person as a dark dynamism. Polanyi sees the dark
dynamism as directed towards a light that is not yet, as bringing
about the "unification of the manifold" in which he thinks all
knowledge and indeed all achievement consists. The Kantian
expression is not out of order when we are dealing with a philosopher who has such an acknowledged debt to Gestalt psychology.

The negative justification that we cannot get along without
the dark, groping, dynamic, tacit, and in that sense personal side
of knowledge is not to be despised. If we can only "uphold"
knowledge by our passionate participation in it, and cannot give
our knowledge any foundation of a fully articulated, and in that
sense "self-evident," sort, it is well to say so and proceed as best
we can from there. If to know is to possess with a clarity, lucidity,
and articulation in which the mind finds rest, and if we cannot
know the foundations of knowledge in that way, then we must
"know" them as best we can, even if that "knowing" must be
described in the language of belief.

So far it might appear that Polanyi has one quite unexpected
bedfellow—Hume. Polanyi's account of belief is *toto caelo* different: the knower *as a person* asserts his commitment to his knowledge, and in doing so asserts himself to be a person. Hume
ascribes what we call knowledge to a belief that is a "gentle
force" and though it is a gentle force that leads us also to the
assertion of personal identity (if not precisely of personhood),
one is not really *asserting* personal identity but finding a reason

23. *P.K.*, p. 313.
24. *P.K.*, pp. 17, 48.

for that "assertion." Yet despite the difference there is a point of
agreement that is important: there is no authenticating satisfaction or self-evidence, rational or empirical, in our "knowledge"
of any entity. For Hume this "knowledge" therefore never becomes knowledge; for Polanyi our upholding makes it so, and if
it did not, we could not proceed at all—could not even assert, for
instance, the premises Hume needs to get his investigation under
way.

Polanyi's failure to admit what I have called an authenticating
satisfaction raises a major difficulty for his doctrine, considered as
a restoration of metaphysics. Why does he refuse to consider such
an authentication? I suspect that one reason is his rejection of the
explicit where "explicit" means "statable in propositions that are
transferable from one mind to another without a tacit 'upholding.' " If we follow him in his claims (a) that there are no such
propositions except within a framework whose soundness the
knower assumes, and (b) that no such framework can have its
justification in explicit propositions, then we are left with no
other justification but the tacit one. Yet it does not appear that
the alternative he urges upon us between explicit and tacit
(where those words have his special sense) exhausts the possible
foundations for knowledge. Indeed, to say that it does is to
misread much of the tradition that seeks a formulation for
knowledge in some sort of self-evidence. No doubt all the traditional answers of that sort are ultimately unsatisfactory in one
respect or another, but on the other hand there are few of them
indeed that can be taxed with making self-evidence identical with
the kind of explicit foundation Polanyi rightly takes to be impossible. Even Descartes, who might be supposed to be the arch-
advocate of what Polanyi calls the explicit, often speaks of the
effort needed to hold metaphysical truths in contemplation.[25]
There is no need, however, to contend with so extreme a case.
Plato will serve very well. There are important points of similarity with the doctrine of Polanyi, but also important points of
difference. At every stage of the progress of the knower there is an

25. For example in his reply to Objections II. See *The Philosophical Works
of Descartes*, trans. and ed. Elizabeth S. Haldane and G. R. T. Ross (Cambridge: Cambridge University Press, 1911), II, 49-50.

expenditure of effort not unlike the groping and plunging Polanyi speaks of. The knower, while drawn towards what is still obscure to him, is, however, rewarded at every stage of his effort to see by a corresponding satisfaction. Certain of the satisfactions have an explicit character: exploration of the pattern of the virtues, for instance, is supposed to lead to clear definitions. But all knowledge remains without a sure foundation until the Form of the Good itself is seen, and *that* foundation, while clear, satisfying, and present to rational intuition when at last it is reached, is not at all explicit in the sense Polanyi employs. It has been won by a kind of personal effort; it must be kept in view with a personal effort; and, while it satisfies the reason, it does not do so explicitly.

In order to call in question the need for a tacit foundation for knowledge that is without a self-evidential character we need not demonstrate that a successful "self-evidence" doctrine has ever been propounded. We need only show that a "self-evidence" doctrine need not depend upon the kind of explicitness that Polanyi deprecates. Failing some sort of self-evidence at the foundations, one is left only with the pragmatic consolation that our tacit knowing works—works indeed in the very fundamental sense that we cannot get along without it. The "unifying of the manifold" we perform with the help of our tacit dynamism supplies us with a world of comprehensive entities that can be seen in terms of levels of reality. It is a world in which common sense can live, more comfortably indeed than in many worlds. And as the same tacit dynamism can be conceived of as yielding us simultaneously the gradual advance of our scientific theories, it is a world hospitable to science as well. But such pragmatic considerations do not carry us beyond what we knew we already had: a viable common sense and a viable science. They do not persuade us that the levels of reality we think we see have any more than a common-sense significance. Our science too then becomes an extension of common sense. Indeed our whole approach to the first four epistemological problems discussed in Section I, which had so much to recommend it, now becomes infected by the suspicion that we are not dealing with comprehensive entities that are expressions of the Being metaphysicians have always sought, but with figments of an impassioned common sense. An epistemology adequate to enable us to speak of levels of reality must complete itself in a confirmation of our access to Being through the beings we claim to know. A concession that there is in the act of knowing a self-evidential factor that epistemology has not so far managed to elucidate might permit Polanyi to complete the metaphysical dimension of his philosophy. The image of sight has been so much used by rationalistic philosophers as to be in some discredit. Yet there may be a defensible sense in which the committed knower can be said both to *see* his object for what it is and to *see himself* in genuine engagement with the object. And it is also possible that the satisfaction thus gained may satisfy the demands of both reason and experience.

That he is perfectly aware that self-evidence of a kind is bound up with certain personal commitments, we know from what he says about our reasons for accepting a scientific theory in advance of its proved empirical fruitfulness. We commit ourselves to, and thus uphold the truth of, a certain theory because the very beauty of it persuades us. The intellectual beauty of a theory is a token of contact with reality,[26] so that we know that the beautiful theory will be fruitful as soon as we understand it. In this, at least, there is no undue voluntarism. The dark, groping, or plunging function of reason, guided presumably by some foretaste of what it is to enjoy,[27] finds a completion in the beauty it

26. *P.K.*, pp. 144-145.
27. This theme, which suggests that the tacit function is rather more than a blind will, becomes stronger in Polanyi's latter work. Consider, for instance, the following passage from "The Creative Imagination," *Chemical and Engineering News*, XLV (April, 1966). "I have spoken of our powers to perceive a coherence bearing on reality, with its yet hidden future manifestations. But there exists also a more intensely pointed knowledge of hidden coherence: the kind of foreknowledge we call a problem. And we know that the scientist produces problems, has hunches, and, elated by these anticipations, pursues that quest that should fulfill these anticipations. This quest is guided throughout by feelings of a deepening coherence and these feelings have a fair chance of proving right. We may recognise here the powers of a dynamic intuition.

"The mechanism of this power can be illuminated by an analogy. Physics speaks of potential energy that is released when a weight slides down a slope. Our search for deeper coherence is guided likewise by a potentiality. We feel the slope towards deeper insight as we feel the direction in which a heavy weight is pulled along a steep incline. It is this dynamic intuition that guides the pursuit of discovery." The theme, however, seems to be confined to our pursuit of scientific truths; it does not offer a self-evidential base for our knowledge of comprehensive entities in general.

has discovered. It is the familiar Platonic point about the affinity of beauty and truth, and here we can take it to mean that the commitment *has a reason* in the self-evident truth-in-beauty of the theory. To "uphold" a beautiful theory is to have some warrant in the very act of upholding. Had we so persuasive a warrant to back up our belief in comprehensive entities and the levels of reality they comprise, we should have less cause to stress the "voluntaristic" side of Polanyi's use of such terms as "commitment" and "belief."

A slight shift in emphasis in Polanyi's account of our knowledge of comprehensive entities might give us such a warrant and thus a way of confirming our assertion that there are indeed graded *beings,* some of which may disclose more of Being to us than others. The shift might come about by regarding our tacit upholding of the reality of a comprehensive entity as a *recognition.*[28] If our grasp of comprehensive entities is to be a grasp of them *as they are* then it is not so much a tacit *upholding* of their status that is at issue, but a *recognition* or *enjoyment* of them as having that status. Seen in this light, the plunging, groping character of tacit knowing is no more vital than the simultaneous discovery that is its issue. The unification or grasping together is, then, not so much creative as re-creative. Nor does this quite make the subtle point, for the re-creation at the same time satisfies itself that it is just that. It is important, then, both that we *recognize* an entity as such and that we *take it to be a recognition* that we are engaged in. We dwell in the entity (in somewhat Polanyi's sense) when we recognize it, but the recognition is not in the drawing together of elements, but in a (subsidiary) *taking of satisfaction* in the way in which the elements *are* the elements of the entity. The assurance or self-evidence is part of the act itself, and though no *explicit* assurance, it is no less important for that.

An entity *is* a unity in a manifold: to confirm our capacity to discern that kind of unity is to confirm our capacity to *recognize* beings as an expression of Being. For the unity we find in recognizing the unity of a comprehensive entity is not just *its* unity—not just the unity of a particular among many particu-

28. Polanyi does use this term, but not, I think, in the technical sense I have given it here and elsewhere.

lars—but a unity that is general or universal. Our recognition transcends the particularity of the entity we recognize: the presence of a particular entity among the Many is the partial presence of the (One) transcendence it exemplifies.

In this sense the quality of the satisfaction we achieve in recognition is "rational" as well as "empirical": the demand of the reason to rest in the general is satisfied simultaneously with the demand for experiential presence. Solving the problem of universality in this way avoids also the kind of difficulty Polanyi must confront in his idea of universal commitment, in which ". . . the universal is constituted by being accepted as the impersonal term of [the] personal commitment."[29] There the word "constituted" is an important one, for the general or universal theory we may one day have to give up in favor of a better one is certainly in some sense *constituted* by the mind. *That* kind of universal would become, on the basis of the suggestion I am now putting forward, a surrogate for the (universal) unity of Being, which is present in another and more concrete sense in our recognition of such entities as men and other comprehensive (natural) entities.[30]

It is idle to have it in mind to give metaphysics a foundation and yet be diffident about our claim to be in touch with Being. If we claim less our claim may be sufficient for some purposes but it will not confirm us in our right to ontology. I should therefore want to restate Polanyi's chief philosophical position in this way: as knowers we recognize (a) beings as unities in a manifold; (b) beings as expressions of Being (the recognition is at once particular and universal, is engaged both with the Many and the One) ; (c) the being of the knower, part of whose own unity-in-a-mani-

---

29. *P.K.*, p. 308.

30. Marjorie Grene expresses Polanyi's doctrine of universals in this way: ". . . general concepts are concretions out of a world of flux. They are movements in history, claiming universal validity, eternal rightness, yet always in danger of error, of the need of correction, because they are achievements of living individuals within a world which is radically engaged in change." *K.K.*, p. 61. The claim to universality is, however, more than a claim to constitute a concretion out of the flux: it is in fact a claim to transcendence—to what the concretions *represent*. It is well to recognize the tentativeness of one's universal formulations, but one's claim is presumably to be in touch with what those tentative formulations are designed to express, and *that* is universal in a different sense.

fold is precisely this capacity for recognition; (d) the reflexivity of this capacity for recognition—a reflexivity that gives us the contents of (a), (b), and (c); (d) that the capacity for recognition yields its own self-evidence in its exercise. Only an argument that permits this capacity its confident exercise has a hope of establishing metaphysics. It is much as though we managed to call into being the full exercise of the faculty we are trying to defend.

V

There is, however, another and more traditional sense in which knowledge may be personal, and in a way equally decisive for the question of metaphysical knowledge. Polanyi's doctrine is put forward as a kind of knowledge. Much of it purports to be knowledge about scientific knowledge; but some of it purports to be knowledge about man and his nature. It appears fair to call all of it the philosophical knowledge Polanyi is offering us. As an expression of what he terms the "calling" of the philosopher, it engages a richer complex of one's personal nature than does scientific knowledge. Plainly, although he does not put it this way, it is an effort to find our highest, most important, and, in Whitehead's sense, most concrete subject matter. More is at issue here than in scientific knowledge: we want and need this with all our heart. It may even be, as Plato thought, that its real and desired object is such that we cannot begin to move towards it, let alone reach it, unless the whole of our personal nature becomes ordered and integrated in the process. Its personal character lies not so much in the groping and plunging, but in the complexity and richness of the personal drives that are engaged in the groping and plunging, and in the potential unification of the person at a higher level that they foreshadow.

It is personal in the further sense that the structure of the person is part of the subject matter upon which it is directed. Much of the affective richness of the knower is engaged in the effort, but the *nature* of that affective complex and its interaction with the more narrowly "rational" part of our nature is part of its reflexive concern. We cannot successfully engage our affective nature in a transforming search for our highest subject matter unless our own nature becomes part of that subject matter.

Although one of the major themes of Polanyi's work is precisely the calling of the philosopher, and although his conception of man as a comprehensive entity is a rich and illuminating one, he does not really, it seems to me, complete the task of supplying a foundation for the philosophic knowledge from whose vantage point he contemplates the sciences. In Section II, I noticed that the three stages of his argument come full circle: he shows, that is, that man as a comprehensive entity exhibits a structure that enables him to know comprehensive entities tacitly. But the circle, for all its inclusion of the passions in its scope, does not allow for a sufficiently clear distinction of philosophic knowledge from other kinds.

Yet the first concern of the philosopher, even if it is his chief wish to understand and defend science, is to offer a justification for philosophic knowledge sufficient to show by what right he is able to pronounce upon the role of science. The content of *Personal Knowledge* is not in itself a scientific theory, and cannot be justified in the way in which scientific theories are justified. A justification like that suggested in the previous section might meet the case, but the complete expression of such a justification should include a distinction between what a scientific theory can give us of reality, and what that same philosophic knowledge can give us of reality. Such a distinction would presumably take account of the greater concreteness with which we cope, or attempt to cope, with the problem of being in a philosophic mode of attention. In this sense the justification of the philosophic mode of attention is also a justification of metaphysics—a deliberately concrete mode of attention that permits us to judge the relative concreteness of other modes of attention.

My point, for all that it is about concreteness, is made in too abstract a way. It may help to return again to our discussion of the expression "aspect of reality" in Section III. If we took that expression in the sense Whitehead might give it, we might conclude that even the most adequate mathematical physics is committed to an aspect of reality somewhat lacking in concreteness, and so committed that any advance in the science will exhibit the same lack. The nature of the lack may be expressed by pointing to one of science's virtues: that it is partly by means of an imaginative construction founded upon a quantitative aspect of things that it achieves its deepest understanding. It is an overstatement to say that the scientist understands what he has constructed, seeing that he is also *discovering as he constructs* formal possibilities inherent in the quantitative aspect of things. But surely there is an illuminating sense in which, say, quantum mechanics *is* a construct. The overstatement is a concession to the truth that there is in the conventionalist approach to philosophy of science, and presumably it is one that Polanyi would not wish to accept. Pursued far enough this suggestion might lead us to the conviction that even if mathematical physics were made considerably more adequate and then confined to its appropriate level, it would still not do justice to the concreteness of that level, but would require supplementation by a philosophic knowledge analogous in its intent, though not in its conclusions, to what Whitehead was after.

We saw that Polanyi does not criticize mathematical physics in this way, but only deplores its extension to levels of reality for which it is not appropriate. His own doctrine even seems to suggest that we may hope to have one day a number of sciences, none reducible to a science of a lower level; each adequate to its own level; each enunciating laws, ordering principles, or operating principles[31] that give us, without supplementation by an informing philosophical knowledge, the reality of each of these levels. An alternative view, and one that fits more happily with his own best insight, is that of the penetration of each science by the philosophic mode of attention in such a way that the scientist might see with a philosophic eye the concreteness of his subject matter, and see consequently in what respects techniques or modes of explanation he might employ might blur that full concreteness. Such a scientist would hardly be a reductionist of the kind Polanyi deprecates. He might, however, avoid another kind of reductionism that is inherent in the image of a group of graded scientific disciplines each co-ordinated with a level of reality. The notion that understanding completes itself in the

31. *P.K.*, pp. 35, 344-346, 381, 384-385, 397.

statement of laws, ordering principles, or operational principles
may also be a reductionism. Such laws or principles may be only
partially adequate to *any* level, and our reverence for them may
be a legacy of the success of physics. What consequences such a
philosophic penetration would have for the organization of the
sciences is hard to foresee. But, to take only biophysics as an
example, it is obvious that we shall have more of it before we
have less of it. Neither philosophy nor other kinds of biology
need have anything to fear from this. What is reductionist is not
the practice of biophysics but a kind of philosophy sometimes
held by biophysicists. And though a biophysicist who recognized
"organismic" laws would therefore not hold that biology is
reducible to physics, it is not clear that that in itself would lead
him to an adequate *philosophical* grasp of the organic. For this
last, one suspects, one must deal directly with the problem of
Being.

MAN, THE MEASURE: PERSONAL KNOWLEDGE AND THE QUEST FOR NATURAL LAW

Carl J. Friedrich

The achievement of Michael Polanyi makes possible a new discussion of natural law.

He argues[1] that the values of a society have a fiduciary grounding in the personal backing given to them by men who, moved as they are by moral and intellectual passions, perceive and uphold these values with universal intent within a convivial order. By insisting upon this fiduciary grounding, he suggests that there are roots for a natural-law theory in *human* nature; by holding that this commitment to values springs from moral and intellectual passions which have *universal intent,* he provides the basis for some appeal from laws to justice in human *nature;* and by showing that an appeal from the partial judgments of individual men to a "transcendent" norm has always a convivial setting, he clearly implies that the embodiment of justice in laws and in judicial decisions is both necessarily incomplete and yet

1. See especially *S.F.S.*, chap. ii *et passim; L.L., passim, P.K.*, pp. 203-245 *et passim;* "The Republic of Science, Its Political and Economic Theory," *Minerva*, I (Autumn, 1962), 54-73; "The Growth of Science in Society," *Minerva*, V (Summer, 1967), 533-545; *T.D.*, chap. iii.
For example: "Articulate systems which foster and satisfy an intellectual passion can survive only with the support of a society which respects the values affirmed by these passions, and a society has a cultural life only to the extent to which it acknowledges and fulfills the obligation to lend its support to the cultivation of these passions," *P.K.*, p. 203; "No order of society is thoughtless: it embodies the civic sense and moral convictions of those who believe in it and live by it. To a happy people its civic culture is its civic home; and to this extent the intellectual passions sustaining this culture are in fact esoteric" *P.K.*, p. 215.

also achieved in part by more or less skilful acts of legislative and judicial discrimination.

These skilful feats, supported by moral and intellectual passions with universal intent, are accredited by and subject to the superintendency of the convivial order within which they are achieved and whose very basis is in turn precisely these same passions.

For those to whom natural law is repugnant or meaningless either by reason of its presumed inhuman inflexibility and remoteness or the implausibility of a transcendent justice inscribed eternally upon the "nature of things," Polanyi shows that the values upon which natural law rests are on the contrary disclosures to our human powers of discernment; that natural law, in short, has in common with all structures of meaning that it is manifest to *men* in the convivial exercise of their unique human powers. Against those who fear that if justice have no more substantial ground than the judgments of men, then it will simply be identical with the law, his argument shows that these judgments have universal intent and therefore bear upon a reality which though never exhaustively disclosed is nevertheless truly manifest.

By this form of argument he overcomes the dogmatism of rationalists and the relativism of positivists. By showing that all human enterprises of knowing or doing are neither as subject to explicit articulation nor as merely relative to the subjective whims of individual men as the traditional views have held, Polanyi provides a postcritical basis for reinterpreting the nature of these enterprises. His thought therefore bears *a fortiori* upon the enterprise and its interpretation of attempting to embody justice in law—which has always been the concern of natural-law theory, whatever may have been its varying formulations.

. . . .

However, let us look more closely at natural law, which is equivocal both in conception and in interpretation.

It has rightly been observed by one of its most learned contemporary analysts that "its poetic and religious, its practical and theoretical formulation depend upon each particular mode of

thought and the Weltanschauung of each thinker."[2] This multiplicity of meanings has both its positive and its negative aspects.
It reveals the inherent dialectic of law and justice. Indeed the
unfolding of the philosophy of law in history is essentially focused on the discussion of the law of nature. Every philosophy of
law is part of a general philosophy which it either exemplifies or
implies. As such, it partakes of its problems and its limits.[3] It
would therefore be surprising if Polanyi's general philosophy did
not do the same. By asserting that his insistence upon the personal coefficient in all knowledge reconfirms certain premises of
natural-law doctrine and permits its restatement on a new and
more lasting basis, one has however only opened the door, so to
speak, to a labyrinth of difficult further questions. Not only the
multiplicity of meanings associated with the term, but also grave
issues of Polanyi's own views need consideration and possible
clarification.

It is now many years since Charles Grove Haines published his
well-known study on the revival of natural-law concepts.[4] High-
lighting German *Rechtsstaat* doctrines along with those of Duguit, Hauriu, Krabbe, and Gény among others, he subtitled his
book "A Study of the Establishment and of the Interpretation of
Limits on Legislatures with Special Reference to the Development of Certain Phases of American Constitutional Law,"
thereby suggesting that higher law notions had been implicit in
the American constitutional tradition. He buttressed this view by
an extensive review of past natural-law doctrines as they had
been developed in antiquity, in medieval Europe, and in early
modern times. The vast range of the spectrum of natural-law
conceptions can here be gleaned, as it reappeared in twentieth-
century versions.[5] Haines opened his discussion with a statement

2. Erik Wolf, *Das Problem der Naturrechtslehre* (Karlsruhe: C. F. Müller,
1955), p. 107.
3. Carl Joachim Friedrich, *The Philosophy of Law in Historical Perspective*
(2nd ed.; Chicago, University of Chicago Press, 1963, esp. chap. i).
4. Charles Grove Haines, *The Revival of Natural Law Concepts* (Cambridge, Mass.: Harvard University Press, 1930), *passim*.
5. Otto Gierke, *Natural Law and the Theory of Society, 1500–1800* (Cambridge: Cambridge University Press, 1934; 2 vols., trans. and ed. Ernest
Barker) which consists of lengthy extracts from the fourth volume of Gierke's
Das Deutsche Genossenschaftsrecht (Berlin: Weidman, 1868-1913) published
in 1913, as well as a lecture by Ernst Troeltsch on "The Ideas of Natural Law

which appropriately highlights the basic function of all the various doctrines of natural law. He wrote:

> The conviction that there are superior principles of right or higher laws to which the ordinary civil rules made by man must conform and which necessarily place limits on the operation of such rules, is one of the most persistent ideas in the evolution of legal thought.

It is indeed on this function of natural law that the various views converge. Natural law, by providing a measuring rod for man-made law, at the same time legitimates such law whenever it is found to conform to the higher norm. In order to fulfil this double function, natural law must be thought of as pre-existing and real, not merely a subjective and arbitrary standard, but something given, firm and unalterable.[6] The question which man *qua* man necessarily asks of any law is: Is it right?

It is the function of natural law to provide the grounds upon which the answer to such a question may be sought and framed. All those who have sought to discover such grounds have had to go beyond the experience of the law to accomplish the task. That experience may be religious, philosophical, or merely human and communal, it may be rooted in transcendental beliefs or in cultural customs, but it is invariably thought of as experience of something pre-existing and real, of something that can be shown to exist. It is the experience of justice or of the lack of it; the sense of injustice is perhaps the most powerful stimulus to a search for a law that transcends the humanly instituted rule. In this connection one might cite Polanyi: "All cultural life is based on the assumption that the standards set by our masters were right and hence the kind of truth or other mental excellence that

---

and Humanity" and an elaborate introduction by the late Professor Sir Ernest Barker, the third section of which (pp. xxxiv-l) deals with natural law. Tracing the notion back to Aristotle, Barker concludes that "social thought, as it operates in time, is indeed a basis of justice; but the mind of man will always demand that the core of justice shall be beyond time and space," and, speaking in the words of Gierke, "the undying spirit of Natural Law can never be extinguished." Cf. also Otto von Gierke, *The Development of Political Theory* (New York: W. W. Norton, 1939, trans. Bernard Freyd from the German work *Johannes Althusius und die Entwicklung der naturrechtlichen Staatstheorien* [Breslau: 1880]), esp. chap. vi.

6. Wolf, *Naturrechtslehre*, pp. 108-110.

they achieved is valid and capable of indefinite expansion."[7]
Polanyi wrote these lines primarily with scientific work in mind,
but they apply equally to the law and its expounders. This
statement forms part of his "critique of doubt" and his insistence
that beliefs are essential to everything we do and accomplish.
Such "critique of doubt" points the way to what appears to be
the heart or if one prefers the hard core of natural law doctrine:
it is necessary to believe that justice can be done, in order to have
any laws at all. Ancillary notions such as that a man should be
considered innocent until he is proven guilty are meaningless,
except on the presumption that it is only "fair" to consider all
men innocent—not morally, for "we are all sinners"—but under
the law. This presumption is rather extraordinary in many ways,
and it may cogently be doubted whether tax collectors and po-
licemen could perform their duties if they proceeded on such a
belief.[8] This paradox manifests the dialectic of the general belief
in the workability of justice, namely that it is also part of the
hard core of natural law to believe that justice, full justice, cannot be done. Laws only approximate natural-law standards, just
as judicial decisions only approximate legal rules, and yet only in
the process of striving for specification is the struggle for justice
won or at least forwarded.

At the center of all legal philosophy is the problem of the
relation of law to justice. For it is always and everywhere true
that legal rules are often believed not to be just, yet that they
ought to be so. Law is oriented toward justice and hence unjust
law is imperfect law, if law at all. Medieval thinkers, following
Cicero, were inclined to deny that an unjust law could be said
properly to be a law at all; but such a view is not in accord with
human experience. Especially prior to changes in the law, its
increasingly manifest injustice is the very lever which causes it to
be changed; yet surely before such change is accomplished, it is
still operative law. This patent experience has misled others,
notably Hobbes and his followers down to the present,[9] to make

7. *S.M.*, p. 61.
8. *P.K.*, pp. 277-279.
9. Among recent writers, H. L. A. Hart, *The Concept of Law* (Oxford:
Oxford University Press, 1961) is in this tradition; although refined and
distinguished by a skilful criticism of what Hart calls the "simple imperative

law the basis of justice, and thus to identify the two. Such a view
is also incompatible with experience; for men have always considered some laws unjust and in need of change. Hence it is the
change in law which requires us to recognize that law is oriented
toward justice, that it is intended to actualize justice, but that it
does do so but imperfectly.[10] The law is felt to embody justice
imperfectly in two different senses. First, no convivial order perfectly realizes the sum of all values upon which justice may be
founded. Secondly, given any constellation of values, legal reasoning, like all other reasoning, is never able to make wholly explicit
the relation between the values and legal traditions upon which
it relies and the particular piece of legislation or judicial decision
at which it arrives. The tacit component in knowledge which
Polanyi has stressed and to which we shall return below bears
heavily upon our sense of the imperfection of the law. For it is
this component which troubles and disturbs all reasoning on
justice.

What is justice? Or rather what is the characteristic of the

------

theory" (namely Hobbes's) and informed by a recognition of rival subjective
claims in the name of justice, he believes justice to be largely identical with
"fairness"; on pp. 154-155 we find this view elaborated in terms of the
proposition that most of the criticisms (of the law) made in terms of the just
and the unjust could almost equally well be conveyed by the words "fair" and
"unfair." The notion that "justice" is "fairness" has been explored more fully
by John Rawls, "Justice as Fairness," *Philosophical Review*, LXVII (1958),
164-194. The term manifests the "subjectivist" or "psychologist" slant of this
approach.

10. For this reason Polanyi says: "You cannot formalize the act of commitment, for you cannot express your commitment non-commitally. To attempt
this is to exercise the kind of lucidity which destroys its subject matter." *T.D.*,
p. 25. One could elaborate this general fact about the structure of feats of
knowing to show its peculiar bearing upon judicial decisions by observing
that you cannot give formal rules for integrating the particulars upon which
you commitally and acritically rely (and which are largely unspecifiable) into
the comprehensive entity: a judicial decision. That Polanyi clearly has this in
mind is shown in *P.K.*, p. 54: "In deciding a case today the Courts will follow
the example of other courts which have decided similar cases in the past, for
in these *actions* they see embodied the rules of the law. This procedure
recognizes the principle of all traditionalism that practical wisdom is *more
truly embodied in action than expressed in rules of action*. Accordingly, the
Common Law allows for the possibility that a judge may interpret his own
action mistakenly. The judicial maxim which sometimes goes by the name of
the 'doctrine of the dictum' lays it down that a precedent is constituted by the
decision of a court [the issue of its reliance upon largely unspecifiable clues],
irrespective of its interpretation implied in any *obiter dicta* of the judge who
made the decision. The judge's action is considered more authentic than what
he said he was doing." (Emphases and interpolations my own).

social event of which it may properly or is in fact conventionally said that it is a just act? And more particularly a just political or legal act? The answer which seems to come closest to observed reality is the following: to say that a legal or political act is just means that it accords with the values and beliefs of a given community, that such a judgment is essentially comparative and evaluates acts and persons by reference to the standard of rightness.[11] Such comparisons presuppose three essential conditions, and can only be in accord with the prevalent values if the facts on which they are based are not untrue, if the relation between facts and values is not arbitrary, and if the norms derived from such comparisons do not ask the impossible. In other words, a combination of the impossible, the arbitrary, and the untrue could never result in a just act. To put the preceding in yet another way, a legal act is just if it is based on a balanced evaluation of the persons it affects, comparing them on the ground of values prevalent in the political community.

But is the just then relative and changeable? Undoubtedly to some extent it appears to be so. But if there are universally valid values, values, that is, which all human communities share, the just would partake of such universality to that extent. This problem has been explored by Clyde Kluckhohn among others. In his *Mirror for Man,* he undertook to transcend the value relativism prevalent in anthropology by exploring the common elements in human culture. He showed that in spite of many significant differences there is a basic common core. The conviction that there is such a common core, he expressed by saying:

> As men of all nations struggle to adjust themselves to the new demands of the international situation, they steadily modify their conceptions of themselves and of others. Slowly but surely, a new social order and new personality trends will emerge in the process.[12]

11. Carl J. Friedrich, "Justice: The Just Political Act," American Society for Political and Legal Philosophy, *Justice,* Carl J. Friedrich and John W. Chapman, eds. (New York: Atherton Press, 1963 [*Nomos,* VI (1963), 24-43]), and Richard McKeon, "Justice and Equality," *ibid.,* pp. 44-61. Cf. for a further elaboration of the issue as well as other points in this essay, Carl J. Friedrich, *Man and His Government* (New York: McGraw-Hill, 1963), chaps. xiv and xv.

12. Clyde Kluckhohn, *Mirror for Man: The Relation of Anthropology to Modern Life* (New York: Whittlesey House, 1949), p. 227.

The same conviction we also find in Polanyi but with a distinctive emphasis on the freely choosing individual who partakes of culture by participating in its development. For he believes that the achievement of a free society is "man's cosmic calling."[13]

If there is one universal value, freedom, then other values will be universal also. For values are related. The illusion of relativity is the result of the many and varied judgments which men have formed in their search for what is right. The effort has been accompanied by ever renewed claims to have found the ultimate answer. Absolute justice is the corresponding illusion. It has been the child of religious passion. Where absolute truth is believed to have been revealed, ultimate values are believed to be known and hence absolute justice can be asserted. The faith in a transcendent justice has shaped the origin and the development of Western politics. Doctrines of natural law have been its most frequent expression. When the faith disintegrated, the belief in natural law went with it.[14]

But the function of natural law is so ineluctable that it reappeared in a new garb. This new garb is provided by the social sciences. What was once asserted as the patent universal law of reason whether based on philosophy or revealed religion, now presented itself as the "laws of human nature" as hypothetically formulated in anthropology, psychology, sociology, economics, and political science. All these and related fields have been engaged in discovering the valid generalizations about human relations and human behavior, the kind of basic standard by which to evaluate and assess the law. For inasmuch as law seeks to realize justice, and justice, as we have seen, presupposes that the comparisons between persons which determine the more or less of justice are in accord with prevailing values, the three criteria of "not impossible," "not arbitrary," and "not untrue" all set limits to what the law may provide. For the several sciences all produce knowledge which vitally affects prevailing values. They have been undergoing a rapid evolution as facts which used to be believed true have turned out not to be such, and consequently

13. *S.M.*, p. 97; Cf. also *L.L.*, esp. chap. vii, "The Perils of Inconsistency."
14. Cf. the works cited above, n. 4, and Carl Joachim Friedrich, *Transcendent Justice: The Religious Dimension of Constitutionalism* (Durham, N.C.: Duke University Press, 1964), esp. chap. i.

norms derived from them have been shown to ask the impossible. Hence the term "policy sciences" has been proposed to suggest their function in relation to law.[15]

These social sciences have until recently been inspired by an uncritical belief in the absolute validity of their findings; or perhaps it would be more correct to say that a good deal of their work aimed at such a science. At times it even allowed itself to be carried away to the point of denying the scientific value of other, e.g., institutional and legal, approaches to their respective subject matter. But the intrinsic nature of the sciences of man never made such an outlook appear particularly sensible. Aristotle's well-known dictum at the beginning of his *Ethics* that it is contrary to truly scientific method to seek a greater degree of precision in any field than the data permit remained the *locus classicus* for methodological caution. That truth is always only approximate and that truth-claiming propositions must allow for a wide margin of error remained the firm conviction of most social scientists. If true, it raises a central issue for the natural-law function of modern social science. Polanyi's insistence upon the continuity of the logical structure among all forms of knowing from physics to our knowledge of persons, his demonstration that all knowing issues from a tacit-explicit framework, such that without tacit knowledge there could never be any explicit knowledge and, finally, his attack upon the ideal of total formal explicitness because of the ubiquity of the personal coefficient—all

15. Daniel Lerner and Harold D. Lasswell, eds., *The Policy Sciences— Recent Developments in Scope and Method* (Stanford: Stanford University Press, 1951) ; in a review article of this important volume, "Policy—A Science," in *Public Policy*, IV (A yearbook of the Graduate School of Public Administration, Harvard University [Cambridge, Mass.: Graduate School of Public Administration, 1953], 269-281) , I pointed out that it is a characteristic of our time that policy has taken the place of law as the major focus of concern; how to convert such policy, when decided, into law is a technical task to be left to technicians. It is clear, however, that for the purposes of the discussion in this paper, in light of Polanyi's work, law and public policy are both manifestations of freely choosing man. As the authors themselves say: "The word 'policy' is commonly used to designate the most important choices made either in organized or in private life." It may be noted in passing that the word "policy" does not appear in Polanyi's index, nor does the problem play any significant role in his analysis of personal knowledge. This is curious, because his concern with a "post-critical" approach to knowledge is significantly related to the same issues as the shift from law to policy.

these may be considered valid elaborations of Aristotle's methodological *caveat*.

First let us explore the problem of the relation of truth and
justice a bit further. Truth is always an open question. Truth is
not given us, except as a task to be pursued. Because of its
dependence upon truth, justice is likewise an open question. It
can therefore never be certain in any absolute sense. The paradox
which was dealt with above does not, however, allow indefinite
postponement of a decision. Admittedly the search for truth takes
time; so does the search for justice. But beyond a certain point
the search for further facts becomes unjust. Some of the most
perplexing problems in judicial procedure are connected with
this need for bringing the argument to an end. In other words,
the acceptance of the imperfection of justice is part of its approximate realization. The imperfection of our achievement of justice, however, is not merely the result of the practical necessity of
coming to a decision; it is logically impossible to give an exhaustively explicit and formal justification of a judicial decision. As
Polanyi is usually at pains to point out with reference to all
human endeavors to know the truth, the personal coefficient
means that in the final analysis truth-claims with universal intent
can be upheld only by their authors' accrediting their own powers of judgment, subject always to the superintendency of the
convivial order *in* which they make this accreditation. This
means that the making of all such claims is inherently fraught
with risk. There is a very interesting, though brief, section in
Polanyi's work which deals with assertions of fact.[16] In it, we

16. *P.K.*, pp. 253-255. Polanyi elaborates his position by calling attention to
the fact that "an articulate assertion is composed of two parts: a sentence
conveying the content of what is asserted and a tacit act by which this
sentence is asserted." He adds: "Therefore, if '*p* is true' expresses my assertion
or reassertion of the sentence *p*, then '*p* is true' cannot be said to be true or
false in the sense in which a factual sentence can." Rather the statement is
one of personal involvement or commitment to the proposition contained in
p. Hence "the misleading form of the expression '*p* is true' which disguises an
act of commitment in the form of a sentence stating a fact leads to logical
paradoxes." But not only to logical paradoxes, but also to a misunderstanding
of what is meant by the relatedness of justice to truth; for the element of
commitment is vital to an understanding. The facts are never "mere" facts,
but always relevant facts, and this assertion of relevance is decisive. When a
judge rules out a certain statement by a witness, he does not mean to deal
with the factualness of the asserted fact, but with its relevance to the case in
hand.

learn that "an articulate assertion of fact must be accompanied by some persuasive feeling." He goes a step further and claims that "any attempt to eliminate this personal coefficient, by laying down precise rules for making or testing assertions of fact, is condemned to futility from the start." The student of law and justice is at first amazed at reading these statements; for the law of evidence in all the more highly developed systems of law is largely composed of such "precise rules" and the elaborate adversary procedure in English and American courts of law would break down without such precise rules. But on further reflection, one perceives that it is not the laying down of more or less precise rules which is condemned to futility, but the attempt to eliminate the personal coefficient by doing so. This indeed no legal system of evidence attempts to do; rather it pitches one personal coefficient against the other in the expectation that the judge (and hopefully the jury) will be able to glean from such a contrast a closer approximation to the truth than would otherwise be possible. Indeed, this adversarial practice affords the convivial setting for the appearance of largely unspecifiable clues upon which those may rely who have a decision to render.

We are face to face at this point with a phenomenon which has been called "situation sense." The late Karl Llewellyn wrote on this highly important aspect of the rendering of justice as follows:

> Situation sense will . . . indicate the type-facts in their context and at the same time in their pressure for a satisfying result, complete with whatever the judge or court brings and adds to the evidence, in the way of knowledge and experience and values. . . .[17]

Situation sense is clearly that experience-based apprehension of a totality, a *Gestalt* or configuration, which occupies so central a place in Polanyi's thought. It is interesting in this connection to recall that Polanyi himself is clearly aware of the relationship. "There is, therefore, strictly speaking no possible contradiction

17. Karl N. Llewellyn, *The Common Law Tradition—Deciding Appeals* (Boston: Little, Brown, 1960), p. 60; see also pp. 121 ff. The importance of "situation sense" is, of course, not limited to judges; cf. Friedrich, *Man and His Government,* pp. 465 ff. and throughout.

between the factual findings of a court of law and those of scientific and ordinary experience."[18] Hence, the possibility of relating law through considerations of justice to the findings of the social sciences as the modern equivalent of natural law. The ever-renewed questioning, the organized doubting which characterizes science is also the basis of judicial work, and hence Polanyi noted with special interest that "the procedure of the law courts prescribes the observance of strictly impartial agnostic doubt in respect to a specified range of topics."[19]

The situation sense of the experienced judge finds its most workmanlike tool in the "rule of precedent." It is of such crucial importance for dispute-settling in many jurisdictions, especially in stabilized regimes, that we must explore it further.[20] Precedent is, of course, a very general guide of action in all spheres of life. The *Oxford English Dictionary* tells us that a precedent is a previous instance or case taken as an example or rule for subsequent cases or as supporting or justifying some similar act or circumstance. The ground and reason for all precedent following was well put by Karl Llewellyn. "It takes time and effort to solve problems. Once you have solved one it seems foolish to reopen it."[21] The power of precedent is, to recall a great judge's remark, the power of the beaten track. However, the track is often not as beaten as is pretended, and an elaborate set of rules and distinctions has been developed for either applying precedent or escaping from it, as the situation seems to require. The "following of precedent" is preceded by discretionary selection of those precedents which are to be followed. The pleadings of opposed counsel cannot but heighten the judge's sense of free choice precisely in allowing to become manifest to his "situation sense," his tacit powers, those very unspecifiable clues upon which his decision relies. It would be foolish indeed to assume that a case can be decided on the basis of precedent alone; if it could, no counsel in his right mind would allow it to go before the court. This choice

18. *P.K.,* pp. 277 ff.
19. *P.K.,* p. 277.
20. Friedrich, *Man and His Government,* chap. xxiv, and Karl N. Llewellyn, *The Bramble Bush: Our Law and Its Study* (New York, 1930; Oceana, 1960), pp. 64-65. Cf. also his trenchant "Impressions of a Conference on Precedent," first published in 1940, and reprinted in *Jurisprudence,* X (1962), 116-127.
21. Llewellyn, *The Bramble Bush, loc. cit.*

of the judge is further restricted in terms of the hoary doctrine of *stare decisis*. This principle, while seemingly directed toward preventing change, actually often makes for it; its true purpose is to prevent arbitrary and casual change as well as to provide a basis for effective rationalization of the decision in terms of existing law. This is done by two sharply divergent interpretations of arguable precedents, namely a narrow and a broad one, called also the "strict" or "loose" view.[22] Such an alternative provides for a wide range of discursive reasoning and a decision based upon elaborate ratiocination will appear less arbitrary, especially if the reasons for a dissent are also made public. It has therefore been wisely said that "in such matters the thing that counts is not what I believe to be right. It is what I may reasonably believe that some other man of normal intellect and conscience might reasonably look upon as right."[23] It is at such points that the argument from natural law and justice becomes important.

Reasoning in terms of precedent also serves the vital function of maintaining not only the continuity of the legal system, but its more or less automatic enforcement, as men anticipate the probable outcome of controversies and adjust their conduct accordingly, if "the precedents are against them." Here, as in the selection of precedents by a judge, tacit knowing plays a decisive role. Polanyi's insistence that "there are vast domains of knowl-

---

22. *Ibid.*, pp. 60 ff., 63 ff., and *Praejudizienrecht und Rechtsprechung* (Leipzig: T. Weicher, 1933), pp. 44-46. According to the strict view, the judge must make certain just what it was that the precedent decided; he must confine the case to its particular facts and the reasoning focused on them. This view is applied to unwelcome precedents. It is the technique for freeing the lawyer and the judge of precedents. The loose or broad view maintains that the court has decided any or all points on which it chose to rest the case, no matter how broad the statement. This loose view accordingly provides lawyer and judge alike with a technique for making the most of welcome precedents. What is decisive for our discussion here is, of course, the term "welcome"; the question is: What determines that a precedent is "welcome"?

23. Benjamin N. Cardozo, *The Nature of the Judicial Process* (New Haven: Yale University Press, 1921), p. 89. Later in this study (p. 142), Cardozo observed: "Acquiescence in such a method has its basis in the belief that when the law has left the situation uncovered by any pre-existing rule, there is nothing to do except to have some impartial arbiter declare what fair and reasonable men, mindful of the habits of the life of the community, and of the standards of justice and fair dealing among them, ought in such circumstances to do, with no rules except those of custom and conscience to regulate their conduct."

edge that exemplify in various ways that we are generally unable to tell what particulars we are aware of when attending to a coherent entity which they constitute," while written with scientific experiment in the foreground of attention, applies equally to the law. Indeed, quite often the terms "justice" and "natural law" are mere shorthand expressions for that large domain of tacit knowing.[24] They hint at the situation-sense of a wise judge. Acquiescence in such general standards as justice and natural law is grounded in the belief that when the law does not quite fit the situation which the judge is called upon to handle, there is the urgent need for a metalegal framework of reference within which some impartial arbiter may declare what is just in terms of the community's values, interests, and beliefs.[25]

Particularly difficult issues arise when the argument involves the commission of a crime. The liberal age inclined to the view that the safest and soundest way out was to insist that no punishment (for a crime) could be imposed without antecedent sanction by express and formal law (nulla poena sine lege). This comfortable doctrine is placed into jeopardy when men commit hitherto unheard of crimes, or when the conflicting legal orders (in connection with a revolutionary transformation of society) clash on what is a crime. He who defends himself or another against a criminal accusation will in any case claim that either he did not commit the act, or that the act committed was no crime, or that there exist extenuating circumstances, such as insanity at the time of commitment. What is forbidden may be settled by customary law. All these issues came to the fore when it was decided that Hitler and his accomplices should be brought to the

24. Michael Polanyi, "Tacit Knowing—Its Bearing on Some Problems of Philosophy," *Review of Modern Physics*, XXXIV (October, 1962), 229-240.

25. Cardozo, *Judicial Process*, p. 142. At this point Llewellyn introduces a distinction, worthy of further exploration, between the philosopher's natural law and the lawyer's natural law; cf. *Jurisprudence*, pp. 111 ff. He says that "a *lawyer's* Natural Law is an effort to bring the philosopher's Natural Law to bear in lawyerlike actual regulation" on the particular legal problems of a specific society" (p. 112). It is obvious, then, that these are not two kinds of natural law, but one; and the lawyer's is the application of the other, the philosopher's. Thus the famous natural law triad of the Roman law, as stated by Gaius and Ulpian, finds its application, e.g., in the problems of slavery as handled in the *Corpus juris civilis*. I have discussed these issues at greater length in a review article in *Ethics*, LXXIV (April, 1964), 201-207, "Karl Llewellyn's Legal Realism in Retrospect."

bar of justice. Some of those who had been committed to the liberal outlook tried to construct a "positive" basis for considering the starting of a war of aggression by dwelling upon the provisions of the Briand-Kellogg pact. But apart from the fact that this pact did not contain any explicit provisions for the punishment of any violator, there were much better reasons for condemning the Nazi leadership, once natural law and justice were admitted to be relevant sources for a legal decision. There can be little doubt that the vigorous reassertion of natural-law doctrine after World War II was closely related to these problems. Reference to the conscience and the customs of humanity was needed to give the accusations an adequate rational foundation.[26]

To determine whether a given act violates such general norms calls for the highest ability as well as the greatest authority (in the sense of the capacity for reasoned elaboration).[27] There can be no recognition of a crime, in the communally convincing sense of "a violation of established values and beliefs," without a judge (*nullum crimen sine judice*). Otherwise, we are cast upon the turbulent sea of such totalist notions as the "healthy sentiment of the people" (Hitler) or the "inexorable laws of history" (Diamat). The category "crimes against humanity" has a cognate ring of purely emotional points of reference. Yet a reasonable judgment could be achieved, in spite of the fact that in several respects there was no settled law which dealt with the deeds committed by Hilter and his followers. They nonetheless could be considered crimes (and were generally so considered) because they violated customary (legal) rules which a court could, by a process of reasoned elaboration, firmly link to the values, interests, and beliefs of the community of nations for which it spoke. It is possible to argue thus because the Nazi regime by destroying the government according to law (*Rechtsstaat*) had itself eliminated the premise upon which the rule *nulla poena sine lege*

26. The literature on the philosophy of war crimes trials is very extensive. For a competent general review, see Wesley L. Gould, *An Introduction to International Law* (New York: Harper and Row, 1957), chap. xx, esp. pp. 606 ff. and notes.

27. Friedrich, *Man and His Government*, chap. xii; cf. also the volume (I) of *Nomos* entitled "Authority" (Cambridge, Mass., 1958).

rests. But it was, of course, essential that the judges should possess the aura of impartiality, for this is crucial where the rules are in doubt. It was very unfortunate that this essential condition was not fulfilled, and that instead judges of the warring victorious nations, even though men of the highest probity, were called upon to be "judges in their own cause."[28] Under United Nations auspices, in comparable situations, such an error would hardly be committed; arbitral bodies have invariably been drawn from "neutrals." At this point, a comment of Polanyi is apropos, namely that "to study the recurrence of the word 'justice' as a mere noise in its repeated occurrence in appropriate situations is *impossible,* for only the meaningful use of the term can indicate to us what situations we are to look at."[29] The dangers involved in not giving adequate attention to the problem as to who is to judge, that is to say who possesses the authority that goes with tacit knowing, the skilful exercise of "situation sense," the "connoisseurship" which relies tacitly upon judicial clues in order to attend to the formulation of a decision, was made manifest by the plan of a few literary men to "try" President Johnson as a "war criminal." Readily admitting that they were highly partisan and lacked all juridical experience or training, these men nonetheless believed that they were justified in "judging" a complex international situation. In doing so, they gravely violated the very natural law which it was their intention to vindicate.

This kind of perversion of justice is the obverse of the Fascist and Communist extremes of positivism which presume that the will of a ruling group, whether class or race, possesses unlimited capacity to determine the content of justice. They are secularized versions, however, of an older belief according to which justice is determined by a transcendent being whose will is revealed to persons with a special charisma or gift for interpreting the divine intentions for man. It is part of the dialectic of a natural law which is seen to be made manifest in the findings of social science inquiry that the belief in transcendent sources of justice gener-

28. Besides the reference in n. 26, cf. for the Eichmann case Yosal Rogat, *The Eichmann Trial and the Rule of Law* (pub. by the Fund for the Republic, Inc., Santa Barbara, California: Center for the Study of Democratic Institutions, 1961).
29. *P.K.,* p. 116.

ated the constitutionalist orders which alone provide the range of freedom for such inquiry. Thus, as the findings have served to undermine the belief, they have literally been sawing away at the branch they are sitting on.[30] Fortunately, counterfindings which may be able to halt this suicidal enterprise are being developed. There is nothing in the experience of mankind which excludes the possibility of certain constitutionalist principles being of universal validity, even though they arose in a contest which is no longer viable.[31] Polanyi has raised the question as to whether the age of science is not drawing to a close;[32] if it were, a recourse to older forms of natural law may be the only corrective which will allow man to evade the ever-present threat of a lapse into anarchy. To avoid such a lapse, a full understanding of the significance of polycentricity is vital; for exceeding the "span of central direction" which is manageable will inevitably produce a complete breakdown of the political order. As a consequence, a curious reversal of outlooks has occurred in our time. In response to the totalitarian extremes of centralization and autocracy, men of radically secular outlook have reverted to the more conventional kinds of natural-law thinking. In this connection, Polanyi observed:

> It would seem to me that on the day when the modern sceptic first placed his trust in the Catholic Church to rescue his liberties against the Frankenstein monster of his own creation, a vast cycle of human thought had come full swing. . . . The critical enterprise which gave rise to the Renaissance and Reformation, and started the rise of our science, philosophy, and art, had matured to its conclusion and had reached its final limits.[33]

Humean, if not Kantian, criticism of natural-law thinking is here revealed as the danger which eventually materialized in the totalitarian movements; for it, as much or more than Hegelian dialectics, paved the way for the cynical approach to natural law and

---

30. Carl J. Friedrich, *Transcendent Justice, passim,* but esp. chap. i.
31. Cf., e.g., V. O. Key, *The Responsible Electorate* (Cambridge, Mass.: Harvard University Press, 1966), and earlier Carl J. Friedrich, *The New Belief in the Common Man* (Boston: Little, Brown, 1942).
32. *P.K., passim; L.L.,* p. 67.
33. *L.L.,* p. 109.

justice which found its most telling expression in Marx's description of justice as "a bourgeois prejudice." Considering the fact that justice has been a focal point of human interest in every kind of political order, especially in the light of Marx's own passionate concern with social justice, this sort of cynical *bon mot* possesses only symbolical significance. Yet, in face of this challenge, liberalism is becoming conscious of its metaliberal roots, and hence "is forming an alliance with other beliefs," as Polanyi points out.[34] To put this another way, one can say that the "logic of liberty" carries beyond liberalism.

One of the key points at which this new "logic of liberty" becomes visible is the recognition of the universal value and function of natural law, as specified in the findings of the social sciences, provided it is realized that these findings are hypothetical and provisional and in common with all knowledge depend upon largely unspecifiable tacit elements, and hence for practical action in concrete situations need to be implemented by convictions transcending the known. Since any norm or rule raises the question as to its rightness (Kant's: What shall I do?), the perennial questions of natural law are part of the "human condition" in which man finds himself as a consequence of his very existence. Hence the "law of human nature" is seen as something which is there, which exists as an inescapable part of man's very being. Since that is so, the projection of such working norms in terms of an explicit belief in a higher, more demanding (ideal) order appears to be implied in their very existence. Such a projection may also be undertaken in strictly logical terms, by way of exploring what figures of thought are implicit in the existential and normative patterns of thinking. Basic concepts such as contract or obligation which recur wherever men have sought to develop a system of law can thus be distilled from the mass of legal data, whether actual or potential.[35] Beyond these realms of knowledge lies the issue of how to justify any or all of

34. For this point, the so-called neo-liberal movement stands witness. Cf. especially Alexander Ruestow, *Ortsbestimmung der Gegenwart* (3 vols.; Zürich: E. Rentsch, 1950-1957) and my review article "The Political Thought of Neoliberalism," *American Political Science Reveiw*, XLIX (June, 1955), 509-525.

35. A similar, though somewhat more metaphysical and religious presentation is found in Wolf, *Naturrechtslehre*, pp. 110-113.

them by transcendent belief. One of the most trenchant, albeit rhetorical statements of this dimension was given by Edmund Burke in his speech on the impeachment of Warren Hastings:

> There is one thing, and one thing only, which defies all mutation; that which existed before the world, and will survive the fabric of the world itself; I mean justice; that justice, which, emanating from the Divinity, has a place in the breast of everyone of us, given us for our guide with regard to ourselves, and with regard to others, and which will stand, after this globe is burned to ashes, our advocate or our accuser before the great Judge. . . .[36]

To my knowledge, Polanyi never says anything as radical as this. But by claiming that man is moved by moral and intellectual passions, having a universal intent, and bearing upon an inexhaustible reality, he is speaking of a "law of human nature" which "defies all mutation"; and to that extent is entirely in agreement with Burke.

We are closer to that burning to ashes Burke spoke of, but somewhat more perplexed about just how deeply justice is felt by every one of us. The work of the social sciences has given a more sophisticated meaning to "the calling of man." Polanyi put this more differentiated position very well, when he wrote: "Everywhere the potential operations of a higher level are actualized by their embodiment in lower levels which makes them liable to failure."[37] The true nature of law, as it seeks to actualize justice, partakes of this truth. It is not the content of the natural law which changes but the understanding of it.[38]

A return to the old natural law consisting of eternally valid principles is excluded. The very notion of nature upon which it rested is no longer tenable, and nothing shows this more strikingly than the work of men like Polanyi. The criteria for determining whether particular law is right law are very general rules of procedure, and such rules of procedure, including the reference to the findings of the social sciences as central, claim for

36. Edmund Burke, *Works* (Boston: Little, Brown, 1839), VIII, 572.
37. *S.M.*, p. 67.
38. Friedrich, *Philosophy of Law*, chaps. xvii and xix. There are also further references to Stammler and others.

themselves general validity in the sense of the old natural law. Thus the world of norms, the world of values, is understood as embedded in the world of being as a whole, as part of existence.

With these sketchy comments we hope to have indicated some of the points at which Polanyi's work bears upon the on-going discussion of the role of natural law and justice. There are others which it would have been interesting to explore. Polanyi's reasoned conviction that machines cannot think, but only regurgitate the thoughts built into them by man, is part of his searching critique of the "limits" of science—"limits," if that they be, common to all feats of knowing. The study of man discloses a freely choosing and creative being whose nature can only be gauged in terms of the logic of liberty. Such a view is part of the core of modern natural law, existent but only known in part, and forever evolving in harmony with man's calling.

PERSONAL KNOWLEDGE AND THE CRISIS OF THE PHILOSOPH- ICAL TRADITION

Helmut Kuhn

I. *Scope and Origin of Personal Knowledge*

Everything Professor Polanyi has written in philosophy reveals a hard core of relatively few basic concepts which, taken together, reveal a comprehensive vision of reality. They convey what Polanyi himself might call an image—an intuited whole rich in suggestive power. The particular area, however, within which this universal matrix originally took shape is natural science. The point of departure for Polanyi as a philosopher is a study of the methods of the sciences in which he is a master—in physics, mathematics, and biology. Branching out from there his ideas attain to the level of philosophical universality. At the same time they come in contact with a wider set of ideas of different origin. A place has to be assigned to them within that pattern of living ideas which has grown out of the philosophical tradition. The scientist, reflecting on science, transcends the scientific mode of thought and finds himself at the point of confluence of two different traditions—science and philosophy.

Polanyi is by no means a foreigner in the land whose border he crosses in the guise of an immigrant from science. He is keenly aware of the bearing of his ideas on the entire area of philosophical thought. In fact they furnish him the principles of a spirited critique of modern civilization. Nor is he unacquainted with the various strands composing modern philosophy. He hails Henri Bergson as a spiritual kinsman, and in his lectures on "Man in Thought," delivered at Duke University, he briefly sketches his position in relation to Husserl's phenomenology, Dilthey's *Gei-steswissenschaft,* and to existentialism as represented by Heidegger and Sartre. But evidently these statements, noting a parallelism of tendencies or a divergence of views, do not express a deeper indebtedness. The originality of Polanyi as a philosophical thinker is partly due to the fact that he, unlike the majority of philosophical writers, owes his inspiration to an immediate en-counter with facts, problems, and experiences rather than to a familiarity with the conflicting solutions offered by the record of past philosophical labors. As a result the acquaintance with his books comes as a challenge to the teacher of philosophy. In order properly to place the author's contribution he will have to survey philosophical tradition in its entirety. In the end he may find that even those of Polanyi's ideas which appear novel and daring are deeply rooted in the history of philosophical thought. Po-lanyi, though an original thinker, is not a revolutionary one. Far from subverting time-honored tenets, he is bent on reviving a metaphysical mode of thought by discovering its unexhausted potentialities.

In the sequel we propose first to focus on two elements of the doctrine of personal knowledge: its ontological import and its educational significance, i.e., its power of forming the mind of the knower; and we shall do so with a view to pointing out their function within the pattern of metaphysical thought as founded by Plato and Aristotle. In the second place, we shall relate personal knowledge, especially the idea of "indwelling," to the theory of historical understanding as it developed chiefly in Ger-many in the wake of Hegel's system—a development which has brought about a crisis of the philosophical tradition generally known under the title of "historicism." The question then before us will be whether and how the theory of personal knowledge can assist us in breaking the present deadlock.

II. *Personal Knowledge and the Classical Tradition*

In analyzing physical knowledge Polanyi rejects the utopian note that has insinuated itself into the enthusiastic appraisal of physics by physicists and which was expressed by Laplace in his

famous dream of a world formula.[1] For Polanyi, the object of
physics is not nature but a stratum of nature, and whatever the
height of perfection to which physics may rise, it will always
remain a theory about nature or reality—a reality of which we
shall continue to have knowledge previous to, and independently
of, physics. Why labor the obvious? one may retort. It is precisely
these obvious truths which are darkened by an elaborate and
popular theory substituting the whole of nature for its part, thus
raising physics, a science among other sciences, to the status of
Universal Science. In letting the object of physics be what it
actually is, Polanyi also restores the physicist to his real nature.
He sees him neither as the embodiment of a "transcendental
consciousness" nor as the robot who, like a living cog in the
research machinery, handles concepts in conformity with mathematically defined rules. In the first place the physicist, like every
scientist, is a human being in pursuit of truth—a particular kind
of truth. And as a member of the community of fellow scientists
he will be equipped for his research by both natural gifts and
special training. Accordingly science itself is not primarily a body
of clearly defined concepts, though this too belongs to its instrumental equipment. It is rather a joint enterprise of people scattered over various countries whose sole purpose is the furtherance
of the progress of knowledge on a particular subject matter. The
actualization of this purpose will then take place in the individual person through acts of discovery or comprehension (which,
for the most part, will actually be a rediscovery). Of course,
various motives may induce a person to become a scientist and to
engage in research of any kind or of this particular kind. But for
the actualization of science as such it is essential that the objective purpose and the personal motive coincide—that knowledge
is striven after for knowledge's sake.

A widely accepted theory affirms that the lust for power is the
hidden spring behind the tremendous creative energies responsible for the growth of occidental civilization, at least from the
Renaissance onwards. This attempt to cast an ideological tinge
on the great scientific achievements of the modern age is quietly

1. *P.K.*, pp. 139-141.

brushed aside by an analysis which distinguishes between the nature of science and its depravation. At the same time, this analysis safeguards the human significance and dignity of science. Nothing is more objective and impersonal than the aim of scientific endeavor. It is truth about some particular subject matter and nothing but truth. But this totally impersonal goal engages the highly personal dedication to the task of attaining it. Only passionate commitment enables man to discover significant truth. Every knowledge worth this name is *personal* knowledge.

This sketchy rendition of Polanyi's theory of knowledge has as yet failed to note one significant trait. Like every analyst of cognitive processes he is impressed by the constructive activity of the mind in achieving knowledge, and in describing this activity he does not shrink from occasionally speaking of entities being "produced" by the knower.[2] But not for a moment does he think of following the path of transcendental philosophy in regarding the creative process of the mind in pursuit of knowledge as constituting its object. There is no trace of the Kantian idea of the object having to conform to a rational faculty lodged in man. According to Polanyi the hallmark of genuine knowledge consists in establishing contact with reality. It is not made but discovered,[3] and in this respect his point of view is closer to that of common sense than to the idealist tendency which is characteristic of the bulk of contemporary philosophy of science.

Knowledge has an intrinsically ontological significance: it claims to reveal reality such as it is by itself. Polanyi undertakes to justify this claim by two propositions, the first of which may be called the argument from fecundity. In starting research in any field of knowledge one may put forward an idea which at first does not seem to him much more than a guess. Then, looking for corroborating evidence, he will assemble a number of further ideas which link up with the first one. Carrying on he may finally succeed in building up a well-balanced conceptual structure— nothing less than a theory. But does it bear on reality? This capital point remains in doubt. In fact we have, in describing the process of research, committed exactly that mistake which Po-

2. *Duke*, II, p. 2.
3. *P.K.*, pp. 64, 124, 130, 147; *Duke*, I, pp. 19, 20; III, p. 23.

lanyi warns us to avoid: we have overstressed the constructive activity of the mind. Starting afresh we may once more begin with a good guess, followed by a search for supporting evidence. But this search is not to be likened to the work of a bricklayer who piles brick onto brick till the wall stands. The first idea, once laid down, if it is actually a good idea, will have a mobility of its own. It will provide a lead for our further search. For no first idea will ever be first in the sense of abiding in a vacuum. From the beginning it will, in spite of its novelty, be part and parcel of a wider context of pre-existing notions, enriching and, at the same time, disrupting it. It will explain a number of known facts while clashing with others, and the contradictions will prove the most fruitful part of it. The attempt to overcome them will lead on to fresh surmises and these to discoveries which, in their turn, will cast a new light on the position from which we started. Eventually our experience will come to resemble that of a gold-digger who has struck a mine rather than that of an architect. The initial guess, an idea daringly posited by an act of will, develops into a process with a momentum and a direction of its own. And through this process the object, at first vaguely per- ceived, takes on sharp contours and discloses ever new aspects. Inexhaustible depths of truth open up to our quest, and we would run counter to its meaning should we try to see in it anything but a manifestation of reality.[4]

So much for the argument from fecundity. The second argu- ment in favor of a realist interpretation of knowledge—we may term it the "analogical proof"—yields an even deeper insight into the operations of the mind engaged in the pursuit of knowledge. Every kind of learning, Aristotle teaches, starts from pre-existent knowledge.[5] It proceeds from things known to things unknown, or from the better known to the little known. Aristotle was the first to formalize this procedure by defining the syllogism, and modern logic has refined on this pioneering analysis. However, logical or mathematic formalizations must fall short of elucidat- ing the process of discovery. This process, the very life of science, can be subjected to a structural analysis and made intelligible in

4. Cf. *Duke*, I, pp. 11 f., 19 f.; III, pp. 20, 23.
5. Aristotle *Analytica posteriora* 71a.

the light of methodological reflection. But no fixed rules can be set up which would enable us to control or produce it in an impersonal manner. The nature of cognition itself precludes the possibility of an *ars inveniendi,* a technique of discovering truths such as Raimundus Lullus and Leibniz had imagined it. This is the negation inherent in the affirmation of personal knowledge.

The phases of the movement from the known to the unknown can be thrown into relief by distinguishing between *proximal* and *distal* terms—a terminology borrowed by Polanyi from the language of anatomy.[6] In the act of knowledge we focus attention not on the things known but on what is to be known. We attend, as Polanyi puts it, *from* the proximal term *to* the distal term. "Think the unknown!" is the maxim which governs our search. The starting point, the proximal term, is for the explorer what the diving board is for the diver: it is an object of tacit knowledge only. And this concept of tacit knowledge in Polanyi's epistemology plays a rôle analogous to that of "horizon" in Husserl's phenomenology.[7] In both cases the focus of intelligent attention is conceived as shading off into a peripheral area. But the same scheme is of a more dynamic character in Polanyi's view: it depicts a process rather than a state of consciousness. In addition the dynamic relationship between proximal and distal terms takes on a semantic function. The proximal data signify that which is envisaged as a distal term, or the latter can be said to disclose the meaning of the former. The sight of printed syllables leads us to expect a meaning, and once we have grasped it, we see the syllables in the light of this disclosure. Similarly we perceive the features of a face, attending "from them" to the mood they express, and thus we come to read the features in the light of a psychological insight gained through them.[8]

This elementary analysis of cognition as a process reveals a dynamic pattern located within the sphere of consciousness. In considering this pattern we have been dealing with operations of

6. *Duke,* II, pp. 14 ff.
7. Cf. H. Kuhn, "The Phenomenological Concept of 'Horizon,' " in *Philosophical Essays in Memory of Husserl,* ed. Marvin Farber (Cambridge, Mass.: Harvard University Press, 1940) , pp. 106-123.
8. *Duke,* II, p. 16.

the mind, and the question of their bearing on reality, their ontological significance, has so far remained open. Only now do we enter upon a new phase of our inquiry by noting that the process under analysis extends beyond the closed sphere of reflective self-awareness, that, far from being solely an orderly sequence of inward events, it dovetails with certain structures of the outer world, thus enlightening us on principles which determine reality as such. This larger horizon opens up thanks to an analogical argument which shows that the relationship between proximal terms and distal terms is duplicated twice: first by the mind-body relationship and secondly by the stratification of reality.

Tacit knowledge, over and above characterizing the way in which proximal terms are known, encompasses that vast realm of mental operations in which the knowing and the doing are welded into a unified pattern. Skills of every kind exemplify this union. The skilled craftsman has a specialized knowledge bearing on the purpose of his work, the material in which he works, the tools which he uses, and the way in which the tools have to be handled. But only a fraction of this knowledge is known explicitly and objectively, i.e., in such a way that it could be expressed in speech or put down in writing. The craftsman's knowledge is essentially a "know-how"—a form of tacit knowledge. Polanyi rightly insists on the fundamental difference between technical and theoretical activity, between the art of making something and the art of discovering truth.[9] But this distinction does not blind him to the fact that science too as the methodical search for truth requires and develops skills of its own and a connoisseurship which defies every attempt to assimilate science to an impersonal machinery for the production of truths. Science, no less than the activity of the *homo faber*, testifies to the dominance of tacit knowledge. Overlooking the wide field of proximal terms used by science we may ask what the ultimate presuppositions are on which the entire conceptual architecture rests. The question, Polanyi asserts, is unanswerable and the simile leads astray. A search for these presuppositions is futile

9. *P.K.,* pp. 178 ff.

because the actual foundations of our scientific beliefs cannot be asserted at all. When we accept a certain set of pre-suppositions and use them as our interpretative framework, we may be said to dwell in them as we do in our own body.[10]

The comparison drawn between the scientist's dwelling in a framework of presuppositions and everyone's dwelling in his own body, far from being a mere metaphor, points to an analogy of immense scope. Underlying the function attributed to tacit knowledge in cognitive and technical life there is the wide area of basic experiences where the "unknowingly known" appears to have its proper habitat: human behavior regarded as involving not only the agent's mind but also his body. According to Aristotle, the hand is "the tool of tools."[11] Using a tool with our hand, lifting an object or pressing a button, we rely on our intimate acquaintance with the wide-ranging capacities of this organ of ours. But such innate acquaintance is no direct awareness: by focusing attention on the motion of our fingers we would not further but inhibit their purposeful operation. The immediate but indirect awareness which we have not only of our hands but of the whole of our organic body prefigures the scholar's personal familiarity with his field of competence or the statesman's intuitive grasp of the complex situation within which he has to act.

It is impossible to understand what it means to know something, without finding out about the meaning of "doing something." Again in order to study human action, we must take into account the person as mind-in-body. Yielding to a propensity inherent in the primal object of our analysis, the act of knowing, we have inadvertently slipped across the borderline hedging in consciousness as a self-contained entity, and we find ourselves at grips with external reality, represented by our body. Epistemology cannot remain true to its purpose unless it spills over into ontology. But the same propensity carries us still further. In relying on the analogy that links the pursuit of truth in the rarefied atmosphere of abstract science with the elementary acts

10. *Ibid.*, p. 60.
11. *De anima* 432a1.

of vital orientation we bridge the gulf which separates man from animal. We come to see "that all articulation is rooted in the kind of comprehension by which animals make sense of their situation."[12] And Polanyi draws on his intimate acquaintance with modern behavioral science to make clear what "bridging" in this case actually means, and it certainly does not mean for him a denial of the gulf. In a sense there is an unbroken ascending line of performances: "perception prefigures all our knowing of things, drive satisfaction prefigures all practical skills."[13] But there is also discontinuity: man alone is able to carry on processes of consecutive reasoning, an ability which is closely bound up with his freedom of rational choice. This, our intellectual superiority over the animals, "is almost entirely due to our powers of symbolic operations."[14] And this is tantamount to saying: Man's distinctive endowment is articulate speech.

Not only does the analogical analysis of knowledge succeed in inserting the knower into reality by identifying him as a member of the all-comprehensive ontological community of things that are, but it also assigns to him a place within the cognate realm of living beings. This is brought home to us by a formula which may be termed "the ontological equation."[15] Two sets of observations are placed side by side, the one relating to the process of knowledge, the other to the structure of reality. Our awareness of a complex entity (the distal term) depends on a tacit knowledge—a phenomenologist would say the "co-awareness"—of the particulars composing it (the proximal terms). The dependence here is mutual though not symmetrical. For once I switch attention from the whole to the particulars I lose sight altogether of the former. Again there is the parallel observation: a comprehensive entity, e.g., an animal, relies for its peculiar operations on the particulars and the laws governing their operations, for example, physicochemical laws. But by themselves these laws will never account for the organizing principles of the higher entity. Thus we arrive at an analogical formula which reads: The distal term in knowledge is to the proximal terms as a structured whole

12. *P.K.*, p. 250.
13. *Ibid.*, p. 99.
14. *Ibid.*, p. 257.
15. *Duke*, IV, p. 6.

is to its components or as a higher type of structure is to a lower one.

Summing up we find that knowledge and reality are tied together by a natural affinity of structure—by the bond of *connaturalitas,* as the Scholastics had it. Knowledge by its very nature is a process, better still an aspiration directed toward an anticipated goal and at the same time an orderly rise from one level of vision to a higher one. The meaning of this intellectual endeavor consists in the disclosure of reality. But reality, independent though it is of our knowing it, owns a peculiar fitness for becoming known by us. Its own hierarchical structure both parallels and renders possible the cognitive enterprise of man. His intellectual pursuit appears to be prefigured by the stratification of reality. From this point of view biology can be viewed as a propaedeutic to the theory of knowledge, and conversely we can regard the theory of knowledge as an extrapolation of biology. Finally the analogical insertion of knowledge into reality admits of a genetic interpretation: while reflecting by its dynamic structure the morphological scale of beings, reaching from molecular agitations and from photons to the highest forms of life, knowledge is at the same time the consummate achievement of the evolutionary drive to which the universe owes its origin.[16] However, evolutionism as Polanyi understands it does not submerge man in nature. With the genesis of man "a decisive break"[17] occurs in the continuous rise of higher and ever higher structures and performances. Purposive effort takes on the form of passionate commitment to an absolute demand. And this reflection at last clinches both the argument from fecundity and the analogical reasoning which together aim to fasten knowledge onto reality. In asserting the truth of an idea or a statement we express the conviction that it bears on reality. But the meaning of truth is intelligible only to one who acknowledges the absolute demand made on him by truth.[18] Only within a framework of commitment, i.e., only for

16. Polanyi follows Lloyd Morgan and Samuel Alexander in adopting the idea of "emergent evolution." By devoting the concluding chapter of *Personal Knowledge* to this topic, he acknowledges the fundamental importance of evolutionism for his point of view.

17. *P.K.,* p. 378.

18. *Ibid.,* pp. 308, 312, 379.

personal knowledge, does knowledge reveal its ontological significance.

Does the joint result of the preceding arguments amount to a proof of the existence of reality independent of our knowledge of it and therewith to a refutation of epistemological idealism? Does it lay once and for all the ghost of solipsism which haunted the minds of idealists and seemed frightening still to Edmund Husserl?[19] As a matter of fact, neither that proof nor this feat of exorcism is produced or even intended. Of course Polanyi, like every modern philosopher, is well aware of the possibility of a total internalization of experience which would reduce the whole world to "my representation of the whole world"—an idea, incidentally, which was not fully unknown even to the ancient philosophers.[20] But the implied conclusion which Polanyi draws from his premises seems to suggest that this possibility, though not meaningless, misses the point. It fails to take cognizance of that meaning of "knowledge" which alone is relevant to our query. For this query, aimed as it is at the actual process of the discovery of truth, the problem of solipsism as little arises as does that of subjective or transcendental idealism. Knowledge, wherever and under whatever form it be practiced, is invariably discovered at grips with reality. And that token of a truth grasped, the contact with reality is accomplished only within a framework of personal commitment which, in its turn, requires, over and above the personhood of the single knower, an acknowledgment of other persons as possible participants.[21] The risk of believing something to be real is of necessity a shared venture.[22]

Polanyi understands his own point of view as a move toward a "post-critical philosophy."[23] The adjective "critical" here denotes a philosophy which, in the manner of Descartes, adopts doubt as its heuristic principle. This principle, according to Polanyi,

19. E. Husserl, "Cartesianische Meditationen" in *Husserliana* (The Hague: Nijhoff, 1950) , I, 69 ff.
20. The idea "that everything might consist of thoughts" (ἐκ νοημάτων ἑκστου εἴυχι) is examined and dismissed as absurd by Plato, *Parmenides* 132c.
21. *P.K.*, p. 336.
22. *Ibid.*, p. 313.
23. Cf. the subtitle of Polanyi's *magnum opus* and the explanation of it, pp. 265-268.

opens the road toward the objectivism which he combats—an interpretation of reality which undertakes to discard the element of tacit knowledge and to transform science (including philosophy) into a completely formalized system, resting on doubt-proof, self-evident principles. By consistently centering our analysis on the ontological problem we may give this self-appraisal a slightly different turn. In referring to the theory of tacit knowledge as to a "postidealist" or "posttranscendental" approach we suggest an alternative way of determining the locus and function of Polanyi's thought in the present situation. In doing so we assume that Descartes, the initiator of critical philosophy, is also the father of modern idealism. Although he acknowledges space (*res extensa*) as a substance alongside with thought (*res cogitans*) he evidently fails convincingly to establish the substantial status of the former. In fidelity to his method of deductive reconstruction from indubitable principles he might have been satisfied with viewing space as an object of thought (*res cogitata*). Thus the anti-Cartesianism characteristic of much of contemporary philosophy suggests the surmise that the present crisis, source of a widespread sense of frustration, is due to the exhaustion of the potentialities of the idealist or transcendental approach.[24] Personal knowledge as advocated by Polanyi may then be regarded as both an evidence of the crisis and a successful attempt to break the stalemate by a revision of principles.

With all the daring novelty of its approach personal knowledge does not propose a revolutionary departure from traditional philosophy. On the contrary it is to a larger extent than Polanyi seems to realize a recovery of modes of thought at home in the pre-Cartesian tradition—that is to say, in classical metaphysics as founded by Socrates, Plato, and Aristotle.[25] The subject-object

24. In *Traktat über die Methode der Philosophie* (München: Kösel, 1966), I have tried to substantiate this interpretation.
25. Polanyi himself affirms: "we must now go back to St. Augustine to restore the balance of our cognitive powers"; "St. Augustine brought the history of Greek philosophy to a close by inaugurating for the first time a post-critical philosophy" (*P.K.*, p. 266). This is a paradoxical claim. Just as Descartes had to reaffirm the possibility of attaining truth in the face of Montaigne's scepticism, so Augustine before him was confronted with the universal doubt as propagated by the Academy. The very formulae with which Descartes warded off the attack by laying down the indubitable truths of self-knowledge were anticipated by St. Augustine (cf. the survey of the

relationship is of cardinal significance for every philosophical understanding of reality. But in admitting this much we do not commit ourselves to regarding this relationship as the axis around which the philosophical cosmos has to turn. Precisely this, however, is the view generally embraced by post-Cartesian thought. The knowing ego confronting the thing known—such is the crucial experience acknowledged and variously interpreted by the British Empiricists, by Kant and the Positivists, and finally by modern Phenomenologists. Personal knowledge, in this respect, resembling American Pragmatism and Bergson's Vitalism, marks a departure from this tradition. For Polanyi too, knowledge is the outgrowth of organic life, retaining the marks of this its origin even in its proudest achievements. But unlike Pragmatism, personal knowledge succeeds in inserting the cognitive process into nature without jeopardizing the transnatural significance of knowledge. Truth, through commitment, becomes the basis of a temporal event without being reduced to temporality.

In maintaining this position Polanyi does not adventurously strike out in an as yet untried direction. He rather regains the path of classical metaphysics, perhaps without being fully aware of the fact. There is, in the first place, the problem of method. Polanyi does not follow one of the established methods of contemporary philosophical research, an omission that redounds entirely to his advantage. It saves him from being led astray by an abstract idea of knowledge. With an open mind he focuses attention on the pursuit of truth such as it is familiar to him through his own scientific research, and thus he catches sight of it in action. Then, realizing that the scientific process cannot be adequately grasped in isolation, he gradually widens the scope of his analysis. By means of analogical internalization and extrapolation he achieves a comprehensive interpretation of cognitive life, of the life of the person of which cognition is an integral part,

---

relevant passages in E. Gilson, *Introduction à l'étude de St. Augustin* [Paris: Vrin, 1949], pp. 53-55) . If the recognition of doubt as a heuristic principle is considered the distinctive mark of a "critical" approach St. Augustine should rather be given the title of the initiator of critical philosophy. On the other hand, Polanyi is fully entitled to quote St. Augustine's *crede ut intelligas* in support of his concept of heuristic vision. But Augustine is more Greek—or the Greek Plato more Augustinian—than Polanyi seems to imagine.

and finally of the life of the universe which encompasses all forms
of life. Similarly, Plato and Aristotle, the founders of classical
philosophy, followed up the clue suggested to them by Socrates in
choosing art ($\tau \acute{\epsilon} \chi \nu \eta$) as their point of departure and as an analytic scheme—the art of the shoemaker, of the physician, or of the
farmer. Thereby they created a philosophical language modeled
throughout on the procedures of craftsmanship; and for two
millennia this language was to continue the idiom of the philosophical tradition.[26] In doing so they used their heuristic model,
art, in a way which is strictly paralleled by the use to which
Polanyi puts his model, which is science. They discovered the
peculiar rationality inherent in art: the artist knows how to
provide means toward an end, causes calculated to produce a
desired effect. Transcending the analysis of any one single art or
art as such they then reflected on the co-ordination of all the
various arts in life. Thus they came to see that the teleological
structure of art is duplicated by the rationality inherent in personal and political life. By this reflection the analogical resemblance and, at the same time, the radical difference which obtains
between goods and the Good was borne in upon them and
enabled them to face the problem of the possibility of an "art of
living" which would transform the passionate dedication to the
Good into a mastery over the rest of human velleities. Guided by
the same model, they developed an art of knowing. They noticed
that practicing any art involves knowledge, at least an implicit
one, and that, in addition to the rationality of its internal structure, art both reveals and relies upon the rationality of its objects: the shoemaker must know something about both the
human foot and the nature of leather, the physician about the
human body, the farmer about cattle and corn. Refining upon
this elementary observation and working out its implications,
Aristotle eventually arrived at his famous formula according to
which "art partly perfects what nature is unable to finish and

26. The paramount importance of $\tau \acute{\epsilon} \chi \nu \eta$ in Plato's philosophy has been
frequently enlarged upon. Cf. John Wild, *Plato's Theory of Man* (Cambridge,
Mass.: Harvard University Press, 1946) , pp. 45-87; H. Kuhn, *Sokrates: Versuch
über den Ursprung der Metaphysik* (2nd ed.; München: Kösel-Verlag, 1956) ,
pp. 17-35.

partly imitates nature."[27] Nature itself was viewed by Plato as well as by Aristotle as a likeness either of a work of divine craftsmanship or of craftsmanship itself divinely at work in living bodies. The heuristic model at the basis of this interpretation, art (or craftsmanship), was considered primarily a form of man's rational intercourse with nature rather than an instrument of dominion over nature. Hence there was no room in this vision for a Cartesian ego which would first internalize the real world and transfigure it into a totality of thoughts ($\nu o\acute{\eta}\mu\alpha\tau\alpha$) and then raise the question as to whether or not an outer reality exists. The unending grand dispute between idealism and realism would have seemed either irrelevant or absurd to Plato as well as to St. Augustine or to Thomas Aquinas. By removing this vexed problem from its central position Polanyi's postcritical philosophy falls into line with the approach of precritical or, as we might prefer to say, of pre-idealist philosophy.

The kinship of personal knowledge to classical philosophy extends even further. We remember how Polanyi's conception of cognitive life helps him elucidate the processes of life and the function of consciousness in general. The path he traces with these analogical observations was first charted by Plato, and the host of his followers, in fact the representatives of the philosophical tradition as a whole, had followed suit. The key term for Plato was the idea of "use." As the artist uses tools and materials for accomplishing his work, or as the products of his art are used by a superior art for its more comprehensive purposes, so the soul uses the organic body for the attainment of its ends. It is not the eye that sees nor the ear that hears, but I see with my eyes and hear with my ears. Implied in the idea of use is that of the ego as a center of spontaneous activity. In addition it is a principle of hierarchical order: that which uses ranks above that which is used. So the soul is superior to the body, and the superior entity, while using the inferior one, is bound to take care of it: "The soul in her totality has the care of inanimate being everywhere, and traverses the whole heaven in divers forms appearing."[28] The

27. Aristotle *Physica* 199a15.
28. Plato *Phaedrus* 246b (trans. B. Jowett).

"ontological equation," by means of which Polanyi establishes the idea of a stratified universe, is the revival of a Platonic argument.

The idea of a hierarchically ordered universe is more than a cosmological hypothesis. It is fundamental to the understanding of human nature and it confers upon the art of knowing its unique human significance. Within the frame of reference set by this cosmology the gradual acquisition of knowledge is an ascent of the soul rising from lower types of reality to more elevated forms. And this disclosure of ever more inclusive visions of reality and meaning is at the same time a cleansing of the eye of the soul. Progress of knowledge is inseparably one with the fashioning of the whole person. Intellectual enlightenment and moral growth, mutually dependent and also producing one another, appear as two aspects of one and the same process—man's assimilation to God within the bounds of human frailty. This, of course, is a Platonic interpretation of life and reality. From it stems the entire mystical tradition of the Western World, Christian, Jewish, and Islamic, and its principles are conceived of as not only admitting, but standing in need of, religious faith as their complement. It is one of the illuminating surprises awaiting the reader of *Personal Knowledge* to find that its author succeeds in restoring the ancient concept of ascent, robbed of its basis by Cartesian and Kantian physicalism, to a new lease of life. For him all knowledge is personal knowledge. Yet he recognizes degrees from a lesser to a more far-reaching participation of the knower, and he sees the evolutionary ladder co-ordinated with a corresponding series of rising scales on the side of the intellectual achievements.[29] Once again the decree of modern philosophy which divorces wisdom from philosophy is canceled and the desire to know truly may link up with the effort to do right.[30]

III. *Personal Knowledge and the Plight of Historicism*

Not physics but physicalism, not natural science but a mistaken interpretation of natural science inhibits the grasp of those

29. *P.K.*, p. 347.
30. *Ibid.*, p. 363 n.

fundamental truths on which the moral and religious life of mankind hinges. In correcting the error of physicalist or objectivist philosophy Polanyi finds himself at loggerheads with Neopositivism, that contemporary school of thought which claims "philosophy of science" for its rightful domain.[31] The refutation of this claim is implied throughout in the pages of *Personal Knowledge*, and the chapter on "The Critique of Doubt" is a brilliant attack on the sceptical and positivist strain in modern philosophy. In the present context, however, we are less interested in the antipositivist controversy than in another question relating to the place of personal knowledge in the modern scene.

In building up an antithesis to the positivistic point of view Polanyi joins a battle which has been raging for a long time. Especially in Germany, under the leadership of Wilhelm Dilthey, a philosophical movement developed which vigorously opposed the attempt to universalize methods borrowed from the natural sciences and above all from physics. In defense of historical knowledge, whose scientific value was questioned by the self-appointed champions of physics as the paradigm of all sciences, Dilthey worked out a theory of knowledge which, while acknowledging a duality of methods—the method of natural science set over against that of the humanities—assimilated philosophy to the latter. With him philosophy bade fair to become absorbed in the *Geisteswissenschaften*. The scientist, according to Dilthey, "explains" (*erklärt*) ; i.e., he discovers the causes of observed effects, thus arriving at general laws which, in the ideal case, can be expressed by a mathematical formula. The historian, on the other hand, or more generally the practitioner of a *Geisteswissenschaft* "understands" (*versteht*) . Through *Verstehen* he obtains an intuitive comprehension of a meaningful structure which, though of infinite variety, always conforms to a basic pattern expressive of personal life; and no analysis can push beyond this life in which the historian himself as a human person participates. This intuition of structure, far from reducing the event under consideration to the status of an object of detached speculation, is an act of intelligent participation through which the states of mind and the actions of the persons involved in that

31. *Ibid.*, pp. 269-298.

event are imaginatively re-enacted by the understanding observer. Knowledge, in other words, is here mediated by the knower's *Erlebnis,* and it thereby ceases to be impersonal knowledge.[32]

Undoubtedly personal knowledge as advocated by Polanyi has a certain affinity to Dilthey's theory of *Verstehen.* Like Polanyi the German followers of Dilthey as well as the adherents of Heidegger's "hermeneutics of existence" (a "radicalized" modification of Dilthey's *Verstehen*) emphatically reject an "objectivist" conception of knowledge. The understanding which they cultivate is not to be practiced by the indifferent observer looking at things, as it were, "from the outside." It rather is to grant an "inside view." The one who understands has to place himself, by an act of imaginative empathy, in the center of the experiential context (*Lebenszusammenhang*) in order intelligently to re-enact it (*nachzuerleben*) . The knowledge resulting from this act may very well be described as an "indwelling"—to Polanyi a concept of paramount importance,[33] in fact "the universal principle of knowing."[34] This indwelling is achieved through interiorization, the characteristic act of tacit knowledge which in its turn is "the sovereign instrument for establishing the existence of comprehensive entities and understanding their structure."[35] Instead of merely observing the entities which compose reality we must, according to Polanyi, dwell in them in order to know them.

The affinity of Polanyi's notion of indwelling to the theory of *Verstehen* is as evident as the fundamental difference between the two points of view. Dilthey aims at a "critique of historical reason." In the spirit of an idealist conception of the theory of knowledge he is anxious to secure a philosophical basis for historical knowledge, or more generally for the *Geisteswissenschaften,* as a counterpart to the philosophical foundations of natural science laid by Kant. Polanyi also develops a theory of knowl-

32. Cf. L. Landgrebe, *W. Diltheys Theorie der Geisteswissenschaften* (Halle: M. Niemeyer, 1928) ; H. A. Hodges, *The Philosophy of Wilhelm Dilthey* (London: Routledge and Kegan Paul, 1952) .

33. The concept occurs in *Personal Knowledge* (see the index) , but its full significance is developed only in *Duke,* especially in the Second Lecture, "The Structure of Tacit Knowing," pp. 21-25. Cf. *T.D., passim.*

34. *Ibid.,* p. 25.

35. *Ibid.,* p. 21.

edge, but one whose center of gravity is in the idea of reality or being. The incubus of an internecine warfare between natural science and historical knowledge does not trouble him. He can therefore carry on his analysis on the level of strict universality. With an impartial eye he views the diversification of sciences as reflecting a diversified reality. For the Dilthey School, *Verstehen* is basically uniform and its principal object is man in history. Polanyi's "indwelling," on the other hand, admits of a scale of modifications which correspond to the stratified order of reality. An elementary form of indwelling is already involved in the identification of the submicroscopic particles of matter, of cobblestones, or of stellar bodies; it attains to the higher form of conviviality in biological knowledge, to a still higher one where the object known is on the same ontological level with the knower—in psychology, sociology, or history. Finally, the apogee of indwelling is reached in the act of worship which constitutes religion. Here the affirmation by which we generally accept an object as existing is less sharply separated from its existence itself: the one who accepts is also the accepted one. Hence existence attributed to God has a meaning different from that generally intended by existential judgments.[36]

Knowledge through indwelling, in Polanyi's theory, includes Dilthey's *Verstehen*. At the same time it bridges the chasm between natural science and *Geisteswissenschaften,* so disturbing to philosophers of the Dilthey School, by a hierarchical vision of the universe. But the two interpretations of reality, in spite of the difference of scope as well as of origin, are animated by the same profound concern for man and his fate in the modern world. Natural science and its puissant offspring, modern technology, have multiplied and perfected the tools with which to ward off the evils besetting human life and to heighten its amenities. But man does not live on bread alone. He who uses these tools cannot learn from the tool-makers how to live his life. Not science but a philosophy which purports to interpret science threatens the truths which give meaning to life and provide principles for the guidance of action both individual and social. In fending off this

36. *P.K.*, pp. 279 ff. In this context Polanyi acknowledges his indebtedness to Paul Tillich's theological ontology.

menace to the humanity of man personal knowledge and German hermeneutic philosophy stand together. It is only natural that this particular ethos should develop in close association with a passionate interest in history. This interest, the source of the vitality of Dilthey's philosophy of Life, may be defined as the point of convergence of the three forms of historiography distinguished by Nietzsche: of monumental history, which discovers the timeless meaning in the deeds and achievements of the past; antiquarian history, which remembers the past as the basis of living tradition; and of critical history, which, in reviewing past life, distinguishes that which is living from that which is dead.[37] All three motives are at work in the Dilthey tradition. Its representatives care for history as such, at least for the history of ideas, no less than for the analysis of the historical method. But the primary object of their intellectual affection, with the master himself as well as with his disciples, is classical German humanism, the rise and flowering of German literature and philosophy at the turn of the eighteenth and nineteenth centuries, that creative movement which remodeled the German language, raised human hopefulness to a higher level by envisaging a lofty image of poetic and human perfection, and gave substance and meaning to the ideas of nationhood and humanity. When, after a positivistic interlude, Dilthey's historically-minded philosophy of Life took shape in the latter part of the nineteenth century, it appeared as a scholarly resuscitation of the golden era of German intellectual creativity, as a Third Humanism[38] of a somewhat academic deportment; and although the light of this philosophy was tainted with the melancholy hue of an afterglow, its contribution to the intellectual life of the decades preceding the World

37. F. Nietzsche, *Vom Nutzen und Nachteil der Historie für das Leben* (*Unzeitgemäße Betrachtungen,* II).

38. "Third Humanism" was originally the somewhat presumptuous title of an abortive attempt made in the twenties to reconquer for classical studies a dominant position in intellectual life. Its most important literary document was Werner Jaeger's *Paideia: the Ideals of Greek Culture* (2nd ed.; New York: 1945; Oxford: Oxford University Press; first German edition of Volume I, 1933). But by emphasizing the idea of education, Jaeger's Third Humanism struck the keynote of the larger movement of which it was a belated expression. It is a characteristic fact that almost all the more important representatives of paedagogy in Germany in the first half of our century belonged to the Dilthey School (Spranger, Litt, Flitner, Nohl, to mention only the best-known names).

War I can hardly be overrated. Yet there was a skeleton at the banquet of the philosophers feasting on historical erudition and indulging in dreams of humanistic grandeur. And this reminder takes us back to the idea of a crisis in contemporary thought and confronts us with the observation that, in the last analysis, there can be no alliance between personal knowledge and historicism. The name of the unbidden guest was relativism. "Philosophy is its time comprehended in thoughts."[39] This famous sentence in Hegel's *Philosophy of Right,* read in its proper context, did not involve relativism. Time, in Hegel's view, was that progressive unfolding of the Spirit whose grand scheme was traced by him in the philosophy of history—a novel discipline designed to reveal the plan of divine providence.[40] On the strength of his dialectic by which he construed world history as a duplicate of the ascending order of reality, Hegel affirmed the identity of the philosophical system with the history of philosophy. Hence understanding a philosophy as the expression of its time was for him tantamount to defining its contribution to the consummate system of Hegelian dialectic. This Hegelian view of history was, as it were, the pound entrusted to the Dilthey School by the master dialectician, and the use to which they put it proved to be gain as well as loss.

The exponents of modern historicism reject the untenable idea of history constructed a priori as a dialectical progress, and by the same token they surrender the identification of the history of philosophy with the philosophic system. They still speak of historiography as *Geisteswissenschaft,* a term reminiscent of Hegel's view of history as a progressive manifestation of the Absolute. But in point of fact they replace *Geist,* which is rationality itself *(absolute Vernunft)*, with *Life,* an irrational power. The Hegelian dictum about philosophy as "its time comprehended in thoughts" is still considered valid. More than that, it becomes the maxim for the interpretation of philosophical writings of the

39. "Was das Individuum betrifft, so ist ohnehin jedes ein *Sohn seiner Zeit;* so ist auch die Philosophie *ihre Zeit* in Gedanken erfaßt." Hegel, *Grundlinien der Philosophie des Rechts,* Vorrede. Jubiläumsausgabe, ed. H. Kurtz (Stuttgart: Fr. Frommans Verlag, 1928), VII, 35.
40. G. W. F. Hegel, *Die Vernunft in der Geschichte* (5th ed.; Hamburg: J. Hoffmeister, 1955); F. Meiner *(Sämtliche Werke. Neue kritische Ausgabe,* Vol. XVIII A, pp. 39-43).

past. But there is no longer that background of meaning which originally supported it—the vision of an ultimate truth progressively unfolding through the history of philosophy. So the formula simply expresses a surrender to relativism. But accepting relativism actually means to relinquish the idea of philosophy. Philosophy in the singular is superseded by a numberless host of philosophies, each one of them reflecting its own time, all of them presuming to be true and none of them entitled to this presumption. The disillusioned observer, on the other hand, the representative of *Geisteswissenschaft,* who surveys the field of variegated frustration as which the history of philosophy must appear to him, is not engaged in philosophy either. He can, it is true, make intriguing observations and enrich his acquaintance with human nature. Following Dilthey's example he may try to distinguish certain basic types of philosophy which used to fight each other all through history in vain attempts at justification and refutation. In fact they are irreducible to each other, and only the obsession with an unverifiable principle blinds them to the futility of their disputes. But this reporting on a battle in which the reporter refuses to take sides forfeits the title of philosophy and deserves to be styled metaphilosophy or "philosophy of philosophy" instead.[41]

From the epistemological point of view a division of labor takes place. On the side of the multiple philosophies under analysis, knowledge is personal knowledge indeed, but in a sense which obliterates the distinction between personal and subjective; on the side of the analyst, knowledge claims to be objective and impersonal, but its objects are philosophies irreconcilable with each other. With this distribution of rôles knowledge is either personal, relevant, and untrue or impersonal, irrelevant, and true. But knowledge devoid of truth ceases to be knowledge, and irrelevant knowledge is not desirable. A devastating conclusion, and Dilthey was not blind to it. He found himself confronted with the "wreckage of philosophy" and saw men who shared his convictions look upon the great idealist systems of the

---

41. The title chosen by the editor for Volume VIII of Dilthey's *Gesammelte Schriften* (2d ed.; Stuttgart: B. G. Teubner, 1960) reads: *Weltanschauungslehre. Abhandlungen zur Philosophie der Philosophie.*

past as a "chain of aberrations" resembling a nightmare.[42] But as
a scholar and a man he withstood the temptation of indifference
by "dwelling in" the infinitely suggestive recollection of past
achievements—a resignation which proved inimitable to most of
his followers. Hence historicism, the philosophy of resignation,
had to be succeeded by existentialism, the philosophy of despair.
Historicism, brought face to face with its own principles, must
annihilate itself. Rising to a greater intellectual honesty the
existentialist philosophers dared to envisage the nothingness
underlying historical relativism. So they rediscovered in their
own way the personal character of knowledge, realizing that life
without passionate commitment spells despair. But they did not
know to what they ought to commit themselves; or, presuming to
know it, they nevertheless felt that choices of this sort should not
and could not be justified by reasons. So they fell an easy prey to
political ideologies, Martin Heidegger turning National Socialist,
J.-P. Sartre, Communist. Certainly it is no exaggeration to speak
of "a crisis in philosophy."

By recognizing knowledge in all its forms as a personal achievement Polanyi opposes the grand alliance, highly effective in the
past and yet philosophically unsound, between natural science
and an objectivist and technologically minded philosophy. By
this critique he safeguards the metaphysical and religious verities
whose foundations are sapped by post-Cartesian, "critical" philosophy. In his insistence on the personal character of knowledge as
well as in his solicitude for man's metaphysical and religious
needs he may find his efforts paralleled by German historicism,
and especially the idea of indwelling may be regarded as a link
between the theory of tacit knowledge and hermeneutic philosophy. However, this is an *entente* of strictly limited validity. The
followers of the Dilthey tradition in both its original and its
existentialist form fail to define the border line which separates a
personal knowledge from a subjective one. By succumbing to
historical relativism they destroy the basis of their own advocacy
of traditional values. H.-G. Gadamer, at present the leading
representative of the Dilthey tradition as modified by Heidegger,

42. Cf. Dilthey's inaugural lecture in Bâle 1867 (*Gesammelte Schriften*, 2d
ed.; V, 12-27).

makes an energetic effort toward overcoming relativism by rendering to historical interpretation its objective dignity. He regards it as a *"Geschehnis"* (a happening), outcome of the contact of the interpreter's mind with its historical object and, at the same time, perpetuation of the tradition which embraces and supports both the knower and its object.[43] Is this a way to surmount the quandary of historical relativism? At any rate it is not the way suggested by Polanyi. History as happening is history looked at from outside. Personal knowledge is knowledge viewed not as happening but as an achievement, i.e., as something to be performed by us. And this difference is of decisive importance.

Philosophy is personal life transformed into thought. But this transformation can mean two different things. Thought is either "direct thought," which, while wholly absorbed in the object to be known, continues to be a function of life: the quest of truth is included in the quest of the good life; or else it is "indirect thought," i.e., detached awareness of the pursuit of truth as a process, in other words, reflection. The two, direct knowledge and reflective knowledge, are never to be separated from each other. Reflexiveness is an inextinguishable feature of human thought, and our awareness of objects is invariably accompanied by a critical awareness of this awareness. *"Das: Ich denke muß alle meine Vorstellungen begleiten können."*[44] But only as long as direct thought is in the lead can philosophy remain what it should be: personal life in search of its goal rather than a mere mirroring of this life. Whenever reflection usurps leadership, philosophy degrades into *Reflexionsphilosophie.* This regularly happens when philosophy, forgetful of its unique mandate, borrows its principles from one of the specialized forms of knowledge, be it natural science or historical scholarship. Polanyi's work stands in our time as a great reminder of this distinction and an urgent invitation to authentic philosophy. In addition it reconciles what tends to fall apart, at any time and especially in the present crisis of philosophy: the proud firmness of conviction on the one hand and the humble awareness of the fallibility of all

43. H.-G. Gadamer, *Wahrheit und Methode* (Tübingen: Mohr, 1960); cf. H. Kuhn, "Wahrheit und geschichtliches Verstehen," *Historische Zeitschrift* (1961), pp. 376-389.
44. Kant, *Kritik der reinen Vernauft,* 2d ed., pp. 131ff.

our reasoning on the other. Thus personal knowledge acquires an educational and political significance. Speaking in terms of a Platonic simile:[45] it helps to weave together into an enduring web the harsh and courageous skeins of human nature with the filaments of a stuff both gentle and meek.

45. Plato *Statesman* 307 a-c.

POLANYI AND WITTGENSTEIN

C. B. Daly

I

Professor Polanyi himself would not seem to suspect any notable affinity between his thought and that of Wittgenstein, or to
expect much sympathy for his ideas from the Wittgensteinians.
In *Personal Knowledge,* he mistakenly, as I believe, connected
Wittgenstein's "language game" slogan with nominalism and
regarded Waismann's "open texture" theory as incompatible
with the thesis of the personal ingredient in knowledge.[1] He
seemed to think that Wittgenstein's linguistic approach to philosophy in *Philosophical Investigations* was overtly a grammatical
rather than a strictly philosophical exercise. "The purpose of the
philosophic pretence of being merely concerned with grammar,"
he wrote, "is to contemplate and analyse reality, while denying
the act of doing so."[2]

I shall argue, however, that there is much more affinity than
Professor Polanyi realized, between Wittgenstein's methods and
results, especially in the period of *Philosophical Investigations,*
and the central insights of the author of *Personal Knowledge.*

It is necessary first to show that Wittgenstein's appeal to ordinary language and the use of words had nothing to do with
lexicography or with grammar. It was a deliberately chosen philosophical method for dispelling peculiarly philosophical errors.
Wittgenstein was impressed by the frequency with which, in
philosophy, people are led astray by the monistic tendencies of
the human mind, the monopolistic propensities of language. He

1. *P.K.,* pp. 113-114, 253; cf. p. 95.
2. *Ibid.,* p. 114.

became convinced that the errors which he subsequently came to recognize in the *Tractatus* had their origin in this unifying urge of thought and language. The paradox is that language succeeds by unifying the mutiple, the diverse, and the complex; but this very success becomes its peril. It "makes everything alike."[3] It ignores differences. It can create a kind of compulsive drive towards monolithic definitions and monistic metaphysics. Wittgenstein uses the vocabulary of disease and therapy to describe this condition. The unifying urge is like a "bewitchment"; we become "dazzled," "fascinated," "calloused," "cramped," "tormented."[4]

Malcolm quotes from a lecture of his in 1946:

> What I give is the morphology of the use of an expression. I show that it has kinds of uses of which you had not dreamed. In philosophy one feels *forced* to look at a concept in a certain way. What I do is to suggest or even invent other ways of looking at it. I suggest possibilities of which you had not previously thought. You thought that there was one possibility or only two at most. But I made you think of others. Furthermore, I made you see that it was absurd to expect the concept to conform to those narrow possibilities. Thus your mental cramp is relieved, and you are free to look around the field of use of the expression and to describe the different kinds of uses of it.[5]

Wittgenstein himself described his philosophy as "a battle against the bewitchment of our intelligence by means of language."[6] The strategy of this battle is the return to ordinary language in its endless variety, and thereby to the facts in their diversity. In the *Blue Book* he warned of the "craving for generality," which could equally be called "the contemptuous attitude towards the particular case."[7] Since philosophical errors arise

3. *Philosophical Investigations*, trans. G. E. M. Anscombe (Oxford: Blackwell, 1953), II (p. 224e).
4. *Ibid.*, secs., 109, 115, 116, 309, 348, 393.
5. Norman Malcolm, *Ludwig Wittgenstein, A Memoir* (Oxford: Oxford University Press, 1958), p. 50.
6. *Op. cit.*, p. 109. Compare *The Preliminary Studies for "Philosophical Investigations," Generally Known as the Blue and Brown Books* (Oxford: Blackwell, 1960), p. 27: "Philosophy, as we use the word, is a fight against the fascination which forms of expression exert upon us."
7. *The Blue and Brown Books*, p. 18.

from myopic concentration on one definition, one meaning, one linguistic pattern, we can correct them only by reminding ourselves of others. Hence the celebrated phrases:

> The work of the philosopher consists in assembling reminders for particular purposes.[8]
>
> A main cause of philosophical disease—a one-sided diet: one nourishes one's thinking with only one kind of example.[9]
>
> A main source of our failure to understand is that we do not *command a clear view* of the use of our words.—Our grammar is lacking in this sort of perspicuity. A perspicuous representation produces just that understanding which consists in 'seeing connexions.' Hence the importance of finding and inventing *intermediate cases*.[10]

Both rationalist metaphysicians and positivist antimetaphysicians were clearly among those seen by Wittgenstein as guilty of typically philosophical error. He writes:

> Thus we may say of some philosophizing mathematicians that they are obviously not aware of the difference between the many different usages of the word "proof"; and that they are not clear about the difference between the uses of the word "kind" when they talk of kinds of numbers, kinds of proofs. . . . Or, we may say, they are not aware of the different *meanings* of the word "discovery" when in one case we talk of the discovery of the construction of the pentagon and in the other case of the discovery of the South Pole.[11]

Now it seems to me that it is illuminating to look at Polanyi's researches in the light of these programs and methods of Wittgenstein. A broad but valid characterization of Polanyi's whole work is that it is a battle against the positivist interpretation of science and of human experience. Positivism can be helpfully described in Wittgensteinian terms as a "bewitchment of our intelligence"

8. *Philosophical Investigations*, sec. 127.
9. *Ibid.*, sec. 593; cf. *The Blue and Brown Books*, pp. 149-150, 170.
10. *Philosophical Investigations*, sec. 122.
11. *The Blue and Brown Books*, pp. 28-29; cf. pp. 25-26.

by means of restricted senses imposed on a range of words in our language. Words such as "knowledge," "truth," "proof," "explanation," "verification," "cause," "reason" are first of all restricted to the specialized meaning they are alleged to have in science; and, next, their use in science is further restricted to special definitions assigned to them by positivist philosophers. The latter purport to be defining these terms as science uses them, and claim to be speaking for scientists in so doing. The greatness of Polanyi's work lies in this: that in it, almost for the first time, a scientist refutes positivism by showing that this is not in fact how scientists do use these terms. Polanyi shows that positivist interpretations are simply not adequate to the experience of scientists, to the reality of the community of scientific research workers, or to the history of science.

In examining Polanyi's monumental opus, one is continually reminded of Wittgensteinian slogans. With wide-ranging erudition Polanyi "assembles reminders" which show that discovery in science is much more "the intuition of rationality in nature" than the collection of observational or experimental facts; and that validation of scientific hypotheses depends as much on personal and community judgments of rightness and relevance as on empirical verification. He "nourishes our thinking" with many kinds of examples of creative insight, personal commitment, moral conviction, in the making of science, so as to correct the "one-sided diet" positivists provide of fact-gathering and hypothesis-verifying. Polanyi does more than any predecessor to "command a clear view" of the multiplicity and diversity of pursuits, methods and procedures which is covered by the term science. He is prolific in the "finding of intermediate cases" which show unsuspected resemblances between scientific thinking and moral judging, metaphysical reasoning, aesthetic evaluation, religious believing. He thus contributes powerfully towards the "perspicuous representation," producing the "understanding which consists in seeing connexions" between science and other forms of human experience, from which positivists had dogmatically separated it.

Wittgenstein had spoken of the language-based errors of philosophy as deep-seated.

The problems arising through a misrepresentation of our forms of language have the character of *depth*. They are deep disquietudes; their roots are as deep in us as the forms of our language and their significance is as great as the importance of our language.[12]

He liked to speak of language as part of "the natural history of human beings."[13] "An expression," he said, "has meaning only in the stream of life."[14] I shall return to these notions later. Here I simply want to call attention to the coincidence that Polanyi sees parts of our difficulty in escaping from positivism as residing in the fact that positivism has entered so deeply into our culture as to become almost a compulsive need of our thinking.

> . . . the prevailing conception of science, based on the disjunction of subjectivity and objectivity, seeks—and must seek at all costs—to eliminate from science such passionate, personal, human appraisals of theories. . . . For modern man has set up as the ideal of knowledge the conception of natural science as a set of statements which is 'objective' in the sense that its substance is entirely determined by observation. . . . This conception, stemming from a craving rooted in the very depths of our culture, would be shattered if the intuition of rationality in nature had to be acknowledged as a justifiable and indeed essential part of scientific theory. That is why scientific theory is represented as a mere economical description of facts; or as embodying a conventional policy for drawing empirical inferences; or as a working hypothesis, suited to man's practical convenience—interpretations that all deliberately overlook the rational core of science.[15]

Elsewhere he writes:

> The decisive reason why such obviously inadequate formulations of the principles of science were accepted by men of great intellectual distinction lies in a desperate craving to represent scientific knowledge as impersonal.[16]

12. *Philosophical Investigations*, sec. 111; cf. secs. 109, 340, 387, 664.
13. Cf. *ibid.*, secs., 25, 415.
14. Malcolm, *Ludwig Wittgenstein, A Memoir*, p. 93.
15. *P.K.*, pp. 15-16; cf. pp. 5-6.
16. *Ibid.*, pp. 168-169.

Polanyi is aware, as Wittgenstein was, of the persuasive power of positivistic definitions or redefinitions of terms. Positivists attempt, he points out, to escape from the full implications of "rationality" in science by redefining it as "simplicity." Polanyi's technique for rebutting this move is, in effect, a Wittgensteinian technique, an appeal to "look" at the facts of our usage of the term "simplicity."

> . . . simplicity in science can be made equivalent to ration-
> ality only if 'simplicity' is used in a special sense known
> solely by scientists. We understand the meaning of the term
> 'simple' only by recalling the meaning of the term 'rational'
> or 'reasonable' or 'such that we ought to assent to it,' which
> the term 'simple' was supposed to replace. The term 'sim-
> plicity' functions then merely as a disguise for another
> meaning than its own. It is used for smuggling an essential
> quality into our appreciation of a scientific theory, which a
> mistaken conception of objectivity forbids us openly to
> acknowledge.[17]

Polanyi goes on to say that the same considerations apply to the positivist use of such terms as "symmetry" and "economy." He concludes:

> I shall call this practice a pseudo-substitution. It is used
> to play down man's real and indispensable intellectual pow-
> ers for the sake of maintaining an 'objectivist' framework
> which in fact cannot account for them.[18]

It is interesting to find Polanyi quite independently operating a linguistic-analytic critique of positivism which recalls C. L. Stevenson's "persuasive definitions" analyses in ethics,[19] which were themselves anticipated by Wittgenstein.[20]

17. *Ibid.*, p. 16.
18. *Ibid.*, pp. 16-17.
19. C. L. Stevenson, *Ethics and Language* (New Haven: Yale University Press, 1945) ; *Facts and Values, Studies in Ethical Analysis* (New Haven: Yale University Press, 1963) . See C. B. Daly, "C. L. Stevenson: Morals as Persuasion," in *Philosophical Studies* (Maynooth, Ireland) , XIII (1964) , 89-126.
20. See *The Blue and Brown Books*, pp. 48, 57; *Philosophical Investigations*, sec. 88.

II

Polanyi's method of establishing the personal, passionate, committed, and communitarian components of knowledge, by appealing to historical and contemporary examples of knowing, and specifically of scientific knowing, seems at first sight quite remote from Wittgenstein's linguistic technique. But closer examination reveals surprising parallels.

Part Two of *Personal Knowledge,* entitled "The Tacit Component," especially its long chapter on "Articulation," contains valuable reflections on language which resemble Wittgenstein's methods while frequently surpassing his results. Polanyi demolishes the notion that language is based on denotation and denotation itself reducible to what philosophers have called ostensive definition. He gives abundant evidence that "the process of denotation is itself unformalizable."[21] Denotation, he says, is an art. It contains personal, inarticulate, tacit elements which go far beyond the observation and naming of present facts.[22]

Naming is not the essence of meaning. Mathematical symbols "do not refer to particular things and may be altogether empty categories, well defined, but applying to nothing . . . [They] may tell us something which is important, without primarily referring to anything outside themselves."[23]

Within the sciences we can discern a sequence, ranging from the descriptive sciences through the exact to the deductive and mathematical sciences, in which terms have decreasing factual content with increasingly higher degrees of formalization and symbolization.[24] Thus any theory of science which attempts to reduce its logic and its meaning to empirical verification and falsification, is refuted by an appeal to the diversity of ways in which scientific statements do in fact have meaning.

The positivists are indeed affected by the same sort of error as that which Wittgenstein came to see as imputable to Russell and to his own *Tractatus,* that of seeking to explain language in

21. *P.K.,* p. 87; cf. pp. 81 seq.
22. *Ibid.,* pp. 81-95.
23. *Ibid.,* p. 86.
24. *Loc. cit.*

terms of unique names for unique individual objects.[25] Wittgenstein's remedy for this error is, of course, to invoke the multiplicity of *uses* of names or words, the diversity of "language games," the existence, not of identity of meaning so much as of "family resemblances" between words in different "language games."[26]

Polanyi remarkably parallels the Wittgensteinian appeal from "meaning" to use in his study of the "operational principles of language." These he distinguishes as (1) principles which control the process of linguistic *representation;* (2) principles which control the *operation* of symbols to assist the process of thought. He goes on to derive from the principles of representation the Laws of Poverty and Grammar, of Iteration and Consistency; and in the description of these we can discern affinities with well-known Wittgensteinian themes concerning "language games" and the overlapping and criss-crossing of the members of "families" of linguistic uses.[27]

But the similarity between Polanyi's and Wittgenstein's approach can best be brought out by juxtaposing paragraphs from each. Polanyi writes:

> . . . we must *use* the word 'justice,' and use it as correctly and thoughtfully as we can, while watching ourselves doing it, if we want to analyse the conditions under which the word properly applies. We must look, intently and discriminatingly, *through* the term 'justice' at justice itself, this being the proper use of the term 'justice,' the use which we want to define. To look instead *at* the word 'justice' would only destroy its meaning. Besides, to study the recurrence of the word 'justice' as a mere noise in its repeated occurrence in appropriate situations is *impossible,* for only the meaningful use of the term can indicate to us what situations we are to look at.[28]

It is scarcely necessary to point out that, in this passage, *looking "at* 'justice' itself" is no exercise of inspection of a "Platonic," "separate" idea or essence of justice. It is instead an appeal to our

25. *Philosophical Investigations,* sec. 38; cf. secs. 23-28, 380, 444; *The Blue and Brown Books,* p. 172.
26. *Philosophical Investigations,* secs. 23-24, 65-67.
27. *P.K.,* pp. 77 *et seq.; Philosophical Investigations,* secs. 23-24, 67-68.
28. *P.K.,* p. 116.

experience of situations in which we *know* it is proper to use the term "justice." This passage is, to my mind, a perfect instance of the effectiveness of the Wittgensteinian slogan: "Don't think, but look." Polanyi seems to me to be fulfilling here Wittgenstein's injunction:

> This is the position you are in if you look for definitions corresponding to our concepts in aesthetics or ethics. In such a difficulty always ask yourself: How did we *learn* the meaning of this word ("good" for instance)? From what sort of examples? in what language games?[29]

Polanyi warns us not to look *at* the word "justice"—for this would only destroy its meaning—but *through* it to its uses. Compare Wittgenstein:

> This is connected with the conception of naming as, so to speak, an occult process. Naming appears a *queer* connexion of a word with an object.—And you really get such a queer connexion when the philosopher tries to bring out *the* relation between name and thing by staring at an object in front of him and repeating a name or even the word "this" innumerable times. For philosophical problems arise when language goes on holiday.[30]
>
> When philosophers use a word—"knowledge," "being," "object," "I," "proposition," "name,"—and try to grasp the *essence* of the thing, one must always ask oneself: Is the word ever actually used in this way in the language-game which is its original home?[31]
>
> The confusions which occupy us arise when language is like an engine idling, not when it is doing its work.[32]

Polanyi's reflections lead him to abjure the idol of "clarity." Wittgenstein had classically proclaimed in the *Tractatus*:

---

29. *Philosophical Investigations*, sec. 77. In *The Blue Book* Wittgenstein warned of the difficulties that arise "when, in philosophising, we contemplate what we *say* about things": see *The Blue and Brown Books*, p. 23. The idea is the same as Polanyi's—that we must look *through* the word to its uses.

30. *Philosophical Investigations*, sec. 38.

31. *Ibid.*, sec. 116.

32. *Ibid.*, sec. 132; cf. secs. 136, 291, 413.

Everything that can be thought at all can be thought clearly. Everything that can be said at all can be said clearly.[33]

Whereof one cannot speak thereof one must be silent.[34]

Polanyi, on the contrary, concludes:

. . . strictly speaking nothing that we know can be said precisely; and so what I call 'ineffable' may simply mean something that I know and can describe even less precisely than usual, or even only very vaguely. It is not difficult to recall such ineffable experiences, and philosophic objections to doing so invoke quixotic standards of valid meaning which, if rigorously practised, would reduce us all to voluntary imbecility.[35]

But Wittgenstein had himself come to the same conclusion, repudiating as a typically 'philosophical' malady the requirement of "complete exactness."[36] It arises from a *"preconceived idea* of crystalline purity,"[37] and is really a demand for the unattainable, which would make actual thinking or communication impossible.

The more narrowly we examine actual language, the sharper becomes the conflict between it and our requirement [for the crystalline purity of logic was, of course, not a *result of investigation:* it was a requirement]. The conflict becomes intolerable; the requirement is now in danger of becoming empty.—We have got on to slippery ice where there is no friction and so in a certain sense the conditions are ideal, but also, just because of that, we are unable to walk. We want to walk: so we need *friction.* Back to the rough ground![38]

The "rough" ground, for Wittgenstein, is "the subjects of our everyday thinking,"[39] the "everyday use" of words, as distinct

33. *Tractatus Logico-Philosophicus* (London: Routledge and Kegan Paul, [1922] 1955) , 4. 116.
34. *Ibid.,* 7.
35. *P.K.,* pp. 87-88; cf. pp. 95, 251, 259.
36. *Philosophical Investigations,* sec. 91.
37. *Ibid.,* sec. 108.
38. *Ibid.,* sec. 107.
39. *Ibid.,* sec. 106.

from the artificial uses imposed on them by philosophers doing metaphysics by mistake.[40] We could say that the "rough ground" offered by Polanyi as an escape from the slippery sophisms of positivists, is the "tacit component" of language, the "ineffable domain" which is presupposed to all speaking but is not itself spoken. Instances of this are the personal interpretation of meaning which underlies all reception or communication of information; and which implies a whole unspoken context of previous experience and theory;[41] again, the personal and incommunicable elements involved in "connoisseurship," whether in art, taxonomy, medical diagnosis, surgery, or in a wide variety of creative insights, classificatory and verificatory procedures in science itself.[42]

Above all, thought and language embody an element of transcendence towards the future: they exceed both our present evidence for their truth and our present understanding of their import. The history of science, he shows, offers plenty of examples of "the oddity of our thoughts in being much deeper than we know and in disclosing their major import unexpectedly to late minds." Our conceptions make "sense beyond any specifiable expectations in respect to unprecedented situations."[43]

III

But the most striking similarity between Polanyi and Wittgenstein in their philosophy of language is that both see language as meaningful only within the wider context of culture, tradition, and ways of human living. Once again, there seems no better way of bringing out similarities between these two apparently dissimilar philosophers than to juxtapose passages from their writings.

Wittgenstein wrote:

There are *countless* kinds (of sentence) : countless different kinds of use of what we call "symbols," "words," "sen-

40. Cf. *Ibid.*, sec. 116.
41. *P.K.*, pp. 90-95.
42. *Ibid.*, pp. 88-95, 347-368. Compare *S.M.*, pp. 22-27, 44-46. See also "The Logic of Tacit Inference," *Philosophy*, XLI (1966) , 369-386; and "The Modern Mind, Its Structure and Prospects," *Encounter* (May, 1965) , 1-9.
43. *P.K.*, p. 104. Compare *S.F.S.*, pp. 10 *et seq.*, 33 *et seq.*

tences." And this multiplicity is not something fixed, given
once for all; but new types of language, new language
games, as we may say, come into existence, and others
become obsolete and get forgotten. (We can get a *rough
picture* of this from the changes in Mathematics).

Here the term "language-*game*" is meant to bring into
prominence the fact that the speaking of language is part of
an activity, or of a form of life.[44]

Ask yourself whether our language is complete;—whether
it was so before the symbolism of chemistry and the notation
of the infinitesimal calculus were incorporated into it; for
these are, so to speak, suburbs of our language.[45]

He called attention to: "The fluctuation of scientific definitions:
what today counts as an observed concomitant of a phenomenon
will tomorrow be used to define it."[46] What in Wittgenstein are
little more than hints of where to look for evidence of the living
growth of language, find their fulfilment in Polanyi's quite independent researches. Polanyi gives instance after instance of scientific discoveries or of semantic decisions by scientists which mod-
ify the use of language whether in a correct and fruitful sense or
in a wrong and misleading one.[47] Polanyi is, in effect, showing, to
use a Wittgensteinian phrase, how scientific language is altered
and the progress of scientific research modified by the "linguistic
recommendations" of scientists.[48]

But ordinary non-scientific language too is a living and constantly changing activity. Polanyi writes: ". . . since every occasion on which a word is used is in some degree different from
every previous occasion, we should expect that the meaning of a
word will be modified in some degree on every such occasion."[49]

The affinity between the two philosophers' theories of language
is, however, masked by the fact, to which we have called attention
already, that Polanyi thinks Wittgenstein's theory "originates in

44. *Philosophical Investigations,* sec. 23. Compare *The Blue and Brown
Books,* pp. 25-28.
45. *Philosophical Investigations,* sec. 18.
46. *Ibid.,* sec. 79.
47. *P.K.,* pp. 107-110, 134-142, 274-275, 292-294. Compare *S.F.S.,* pp. 85-96.
See also Polanyi, *L.L.,* pp. 10-15.
48. See *The Blue and Brown Books,* pp. 56-59, 65, 70. Compare *Philosophical Investigations,* secs. 401-402, II xi (pp. 202-203).
49. *P.K.,* p. 110.

the tradition of nominalism," and that his "language game" slogan implies that "language is a set of convenient symbols used according to . . . conventional rules."[50]

That this is a misunderstanding is sufficiently shown by the fact that Wittgenstein's examples of "language games," as we have just seen, are frequently taken from the fields of mathematics and science from which Polanyi's own illustrations come. Wittgenstein's doctrine is the antithesis of conventionalism. Its whole purport is the same as Polanyi's, to prove that the restrictive theories of language and of meaning advanced by logicians of a positivist persuasion are inadequate to the facts of language as an ongoing activity.[51]

This is the force of the well-known phrases: "To imagine a language means to imagine a form of life. . . .[52] "What has to be accepted, the given, *is*—so one could say—*forms of life*."[53] But Polanyi has done much more than Wittgenstein did to give content to the concept of "forms of life." It is indeed one of the most important of Polanyi's achievements to have shown that all our language has a tacit, unspoken reference to the culture, the intellectual communities and traditions whose presuppositions and standards provide the implicit norms for both our everyday and our scientific languages. He writes:

> In learning to speak, every child accepts a culture con-
> structed on the premises of the traditional interpretation of
> the universe, rooted in the idiom of the group to which it
> was born, and every intellectual effort of the educated mind
> will be made within this frame of reference. Man's whole
> intellectual life would be thrown away should this interpre-
> tative framework be wholly false; he is rational only to the
> extent to which the conceptions to which he is committed
> are true.[54]
>
> We assimilate most of these pre-suppositions by learning
> to speak of things in a certain language. . . . Our language
> includes the numerals and elements of geometry, and it
> refers in these terms to laws of nature whence we can pass

50. *Ibid.*, p. 113.
51. See *Philosophical Investigations*, sec. 23.
52. *Ibid.*, sec. 19.
53. *Ibid.*, II xi (p. 226e).
54. *P.K.*, p. 112.

on to the roots of these laws in scientific observations and experiments.

The curious thing is that we have no clear knowledge of what our presuppositions are and when we try to formulate them they appear quite unconvincing.[55]

There have been in philosophy few more sustained refutations of rationalism and positivism, with what Waismann called their "clarity neurosis,"[56] than Polanyi's patient probing into the pararational and metarational roots of all our reasoning, and, in particular of scientific reasoning. He provides overwhelming corroboration of H. H. Price's challenge that "Clarity is not enough."[57] He abundantly illustrates Waismann's dictum that "the living spark of rationalism is irrational."[58] Polanyi's writings are an impressive contribution to what Merleau-Ponty has called "the philosophical mission of the twentieth century," namely to "explore the irrational and to integrate it into an enlarged reason."[59]

IV

A characteristic contribution of Polanyi in this connection is his stress on the fiduciary character of all knowledge and language, and the interpersonal quality of all verification and particularly of scientific verification.

"The Fiduciary Programme" of knowledge includes our commitment, by and in it, to a vision of reality which subtends our language but surpasses our speech.

. . . personal knowledge in science is not made but discovered, and as such it claims to establish contact with reality beyond the clues on which it relies. It commits us, passionately and far beyond our comprehension, to a vision of

55. *Ibid.*, p. 59.
56. F. Waismann, "How I See Philosophy," in *Contemporary British Philosophy*, ed. H. D. Lewis (London: Allen and Unwin, 1956), pp. 464-465.
57. See the paper with this title by H. H. Price in *Clarity Is Not Enough*, ed. H. D. Lewis (London: Allen and Unwin, 1963), pp. 15-41.
58. F. Waismann, "Verifiability," in *Logic and Language*, First Series, ed. Antony Flew (Oxford: Blackwell, 1952), p. 143.
59. M. Merleau-Ponty, "L'Existentialisme chez Hegel," in *Sens et non-sens* (Paris: Nagel, 1948), p. 125.

reality. Of this responsibility we cannot divest ourselves by setting up objective criteria of verifiability—or falsifiability, or testability, or what you will. For we live in it as in the garment of our own skin. Like love, to which it is akin, this commitment is a 'shirt of flame,' blazing with passion and, also like love, consumed by devotion to a universal demand. Such is the true sense of objectivity in science. . . . I called it the discovery of rationality in nature, a name which was meant to say that the kind of order which the discoverer claims to see in nature goes far beyond his understanding; so that his triumph lies precisely in his foreknowledge of a host of yet hidden implications which his discovery will reveal in later days to other eyes.[60]

Intellectual commitment is a responsible decision, in submission to the compelling claims of what in good conscience I conceive to be true. It is an act of hope, striving to fulfill an obligation within a personal situation for which I am not responsible and which therefore determines my calling. This hope and this obligation are expressed in the universal intent of personal knowledge.[61]

Polanyi's assimilation of scientific knowledge to moral knowledge is original and crucial. It illuminates both the nature of science and the nature of morals, both of them distorted by arbitrary modern separations of descriptive from evaluative expressions. The objectivity of science is safeguarded both by Polanyi's insistence on the objectivity of morals and by his stress on the community character of scientific commitment.

The latter doctrine is developed in his chapters on "Conviviality," on "The Logic of Affirmation," on "The Critique of Doubt," and on "Commitment," in *Personal Knowledge*, as well as throughout the monograph *Science, Faith and Society*. He gives copious illustration from the history of science of how the direction of research, the interpretation of experimental findings, the acceptance, retention or abandonment of scientific theories, have been affected by the prevailing consensus of the international community of scientists.[62] This consensus has, of course, in

60. *P.K.*, p. 64.
61. *Ibid.*, p. 65.
62. *Ibid.*, pp. 137-138, 274, 292-294.

turn been shaped by the discoveries and creative insights of scientific geniuses; but even this shaping has been effected through the personal example and person-to-person influence of the master as much as by any logically formulable procedures.[63]

Science as lived is therefore formed by factors which are in principle unstatable in positivist logics of science and which have in practice been ignored in positivist theories of science. Polanyi has unanswerably shown that positivism can account for everything in science except discovery and verification—which are nearly everything in science! By positivists, he protests:

. . . we are given an account of the scientific method which, having left out the process of discovery on the grounds that it follows no definite method, overlooks the process of verification as well, by referring only to examples where no real verification takes place.[64]

Polanyi pursues his relentless critique of positivism by showing that science cannot be isolated from other forms of human knowing, living, loving, valuing.[65] He shows that science cannot be understood apart from the "form of life" of the scientific community, and indeed of the rational human community in general. Positivists had distinguished science sharply from all other "unscientific" forms of human knowledge. Science was given a monopoly of rationality, verification, proof, objectivity, even meaning; while other types of experience were held to be irrational, emotive, subjective, devoid of "literal meaning." This antithesis can no longer be sustained in face of Polanyi's evidence. Rationality in science is not unique. It is akin to rationality in ethics.[66] It is akin to rationality in politics, in jurisprudence and law.[67] Creative thinking in science is not dissimilar to intuition in art and literature.[68] Formal intellectual beauty is a criterion of truth

63 *Ibid.*, pp. 53-54, 120-131, 182-183, 187-194, 311-312, 374-380; cf. *L.L.*, pp. 26-31; *S.F.S.*, p. 44. See also *Duke*, V, pp. 8-16.
64. *P.K.*, pp. 13-14.
65. See *ibid.*, p. 133: "In teaching its own kinds of formal excellence science functions like art, religion, morality, law and other constituents of culture."
66. *Ibid.*, pp. 63-65, 132-134; compare *L.L.*, pp. 4-5, 28-30, 39-40, 45-46; *S.F.S.*, pp. 34-35, 38-41, 81-84.
67. *P.K.*, pp. 133-138, 214-215, 380.
68. *Ibid.*, pp. 214-215, 300-303, 350-354.

in science, as it is of excellence in aesthetics.[69] Scientific theory
rests on scientific belief, which, in turn, is comparable with
religious belief.[70] The criteria of verification for scientific hypotheses are not totally dissimilar to the norms of orthodox belief
in a Christian church.[71]

It must be noted that Polanyi is comparing science with other
types of human conviction, not so as to detract from the rationality of science but so as to show that its rationality is not unique.
His case is that non-scientific certitudes too can be rational; and
their ways of being rational help us to understand the rationality
of science. Science can be passionate, because there are intellectual passions. Science can be like ethics because ethics is moral
reasoning and practical knowing. Science is verified by consensus
in so far as consensus is achieved by rational processes, defined by
rational criteria.[72] Science can resemble religion because religion
too is belief that leads to understanding.[73] The reverse, of course,
also applies: morals and religion, because they resemble science,
cannot be merely subjective and non-rational.[74]

It seems to me that all this research can be interestingly described in terms of Wittgenstein's technique. Wittgenstein would
call it giving scientific expressions meaning in "the stream of life"
of science, or seeing science as "a form of life,"[75] part of the
"natural history of human beings."[76] It is a process of attending
indirectly to what science cannot say about itself directly; for
science exhibits, exercises, but does not found or justify, its own
rationality.

Polanyi strikes a quite Wittgensteinian note when he writes:
. . . if I cannot speak except from inside a language, I may at

69. *Ibid.*, pp. 145-150, 166, 283, 311.
70. *Ibid.*, pp. 264-268, 283, 286.
71. *Ibid.*, pp. 207-209, 279-283. In *L.L.* he writes: "Science has a most closely
knit professional tradition; it rivals the Church of Rome and the legal
profession in continuity of doctrine and strength of corporate spirit" (p. 39).
Comparison with the Protestant churches is made in *S.F.S.*, pp. 56-59.
72. The rational character and empirical reference of scientific consensus
are argued in *P.K.*, pp. 145-150, but are shown to be consistent with the
criteria of "elegance and beauty."
73. See *P.K.*, pp. 199-202, 266-268; compare *S.F.S.*, pp. 44-45.
74. *P.K.*, pp. 214-215, 267-268, 311-312.
75. *Philosophical Investigations*, sec. 19.
76. *Ibid.*, sec. 415. Compare *The Blue and Brown Books*, pp. 102-103.

least speak of my language in a manner consistent with this situation."[77]

Wittgenstein in the *Tractatus* was mystified by the fact that language cannot "express" but can only "show" its mirroring of the world.

Propositions can represent the whole reality, but they cannot represent what they must have in common with reality in order to be able to represent it—the logical form.[78]

Propositions cannot represent the logical form: this mirrors itself in the propositions. That which mirrors itself in language, language cannot represent.

That which expresses *itself* in language, *we* cannot express by language.[79]

What *can* be shown *cannot* be said.[80]

This was one main source of Wittgenstein's "mysticism" in the *Tractatus*.[81]

He came to see, in the *Philosophical Investigations*, that this sort of mysticism was a mistake, and he "showed the way out" from it by "turning [the] whole examination round."[82] He now saw that language "doing work" breaks the mystical spell cast by language "idling."[83] The impossible search for the single ineffable insight is abandoned in favor of attention to the countless uses of language. These countless uses can express indirectly what they cannot express directly. They can show, first, negatively, that there is no one single "logic of the facts,"[84] no one single meaning of "meaning" or sense of "sense." They can show, positively, the various logics of different sorts of discourse, the varieties of criteria of meaning and of sense, of reasons and of proof

77. *P.K.*, p. 253.
78. *Tractatus*, 4.12.
79. *Ibid.*, 4.121.
80. *Ibid.*, 4.1212.
81. See G. E. M. Anscombe, *An Introduction to Wittgenstein's Tractatus* (London: Hutchinson University Library, 1959), pp. 161-171; Erik Stenius, *Wittgenstein's Tractatus* (Oxford: Blackwell, 1960), pp. 207-209, 218-226.
82. *Philosophical Investigations*, sec. 108. I have examined this and other aspects of Wittgenstein's development from the *Tractatus* to *Philosophical Investigations* in two articles entitled "New Light on Wittgenstein" in *Philosophical Studies*, X (1960), 5-49 and XI (1961-1962), 28-62.
83. *Philosophical Investigations*, sec. 132.
84. Cf. *Tractatus*, 4.0312.

and of truth. This, it seems to me, accurately describes also what Polanyi has done about science.

The objection has been made to Wittgenstein—it could be made to Polanyi—that this procedure compromises the rationality of science. I have argued that Polanyi's enterprise is not a diminution but an *enlargement* of the notion of rationality. His thesis is not a mere anti-empiricism but a plea for the enlargement of empiricism.

Wittgenstein himself anticipated the objection of conventionalism that might be raised against his method. He writes: "So you are saying that human agreement decides what is true and what is false." He replies:

"It is what human beings *say* that is true and false; and they agree in the *language* they use. That is not agreement in opinions but in form of life."[85]

Treating of induction, he writes:

Whether the earlier experience is the cause of the certainty depends on the system of hypotheses, of natural laws, in which we are considering the phenomenon of certainty. Is our confidence justified?—What people accept as a justification—is shown by how they think and live.[86]

This is not other than Polanyi's "fiduciary programme," expressed, for example, in the passage:

We must now recognize belief once more as the source of all knowledge. Tacit assent and intellectual passions, the sharing of an idiom and of a cultural heritage, affiliation to a like-minded community: such are the impulses which shape our vision of the nature of things on which we reply for our mastery of things. No intelligence, however critical or original, can operate outside such a fiduciary framework.[87]

V

Another area in which fruitful comparison can be made of Polanyi and Wittgenstein is that of our knowledge of mind and

85. *Philosophical Investigations*, sec. 241. Compare II xi (pp. 225-226).
86. *Ibid.*, sec. 325; cf. sec. 326 and II xi (pp. 225-226).
87. *P.K.*, p. 266; cf. pp. 53-54, 216-219, 264-268, 374-379.

mental processes, our own and other people's. Both have important things to say in relation to the problems of behaviorism and solipsism; and their approaches are notably similar.

Regarding the philsophy of mind, Wittgenstein's deepest determination is to oppose the idea that philosophy is introspection, analyzing private experiences, trying to isolate and identify the "hidden essence" of mental states and processes. This he calls a "dead-end in philosophy."[88] It is based on a "misleading parallel," that "psychology treats of processes in the psychical sphere, as does physics in the physical."[89]

Wittgenstein insists that mental processes, such as knowing, sensing, intending, willing, etc., are not *two* distinguishable things, a public thing and a private thing, an overt physical and a "hidden" mental thing. To determine what knowing is, therefore, we must not look *in* to detect some "occult process," a sort of "gaseous medium."[90] We must instead look *around* at the various situations in which I can rightly say "Now I know," "Now I understand," "Now I know how to go on."[91]

Thinking "is not an incorporeal process which lends life and sense to speaking, and which it would be possible to detach from speaking, rather as the Devil took the shadow of Schlemiel from the ground."[92] Naming evinces the ability to deploy a whole range of vocabulary and grammer: "a great deal of stage-setting in the language is presupposed if the mere act of naming is to make sense."[93] Intending "is embedded in its situation, in human customs and institutions."[94] So it is also with believing, hoping, expecting, wishing.[95] It is what we *say* and what we *do* in these situations which is mental or rational.[96] The mental is *in* the behavioral, the rational *in* the physical, the spiritual *in* the material. The test of knowing, understanding, is "knowing how

88. *Philosophical Investigations,* sec. 436; cf. secs. 91-92, 106, 645; II xi (p. 225).
89. *Ibid.,* sec. 571.
90. *Ibid.,* secs. 36, 38, 109, 152-154, 608-609.
91. *Ibid.,* secs. 152-154; II xi (p. 219).
92. *Ibid.,* sec. 339.
93. *Ibid.,* sec. 257; cf. sec. 649.
94. *Ibid.,* sec. 337; cf. 591.
95. *Ibid.,* secs. 437-441, 574-592.
96. *Ibid.,* secs. 156-165, 167-168, 547-557. Compare *The Blue and Brown Books,* pp. 78-79, 100-104, 110-116, 150-152, 172-173.

to go on."[97] No "hidden process" occurs when I know, or understand, or when I rationally solve a problem. Simply there are the
"particular circumstances which justify me in saying I can go
on."[98]

"Meaning" is not a single mental thing but many things, all of
them embodied things. Wittgenstein ends his reflections on mental processes on the sharp note: "Nothing is more wrong-headed
than calling meaning a mental activity. Unless, that is, one is
setting out to produce confusion."[99]

Wittgenstein was conscious that he could be suspected of behaviorism. He rejects the charge. He insists that he is simply
excluding wrong ways of speaking. He is merely correcting wrong
concepts of soul or mind, wrong philosophical theories of soul-
body relationship. It is a self-negating, soliloquistic, "private-
language" theory of the self which he is combating. But the
alternative is not behaviorism.[100] Wittgenstein implicitly rejects,
by anticipation, what has been called the dispositional behaviorism of Ryle.[101] It is not without significance that the last word of
The Blue Book is: ". . . we can't substitute for 'I' a description
of a body."[102] While denying that a body *has* a soul, he affirms
that "the human body is the best picture of a human soul."[103]

Wittgenstein's doctrine of embodied rationality can be interestingly correlated with many of Polanyi's reflections. An important
theme in *Personal Knowledge* is the distinction between focal
and subsidiary awareness. This appears in Polanyi's later writings
as the distinction between focal and distal awareness. Attention
to this has enabled Polanyi to explore ways in which intelligence
is embodied in skills, in the use of tools, in the adoption of
methods or techniques of problem-solving. In such cases we attend focally to an immediate sequence of tasks, acts, or movements; but our performance of these is inhabited by a skill or

97. *Philosophical Investigations*, secs. 152-154, 179.
98. *Ibid.*, sec. 154.
99. *Ibid.*, sec. 693.
100. For relevant texts indicating Wittgenstein's anti-behaviorist position,
see my article, "New Light on Wittgenstein, II," in *Philosophical Studies*, XI
(1961-1962), 28-38. See also Peter Geach, *Mental Acts* (London: Routledge
and Kegan Paul, 1957), pp. 107-123.
101. See *Philosophical Investigations*, II x; cf. secs. 350, 591.
102. *The Blue and Brown Books*, p. 74.
103. *Philosophical Investigations*, II iv.

sense of fitness or of reasonableness of which we have only a subsidiary or distal awareness.[104] We cannot articulate the presuppositions of our skills and methods; but it is their presence that makes our performances successful and rational.[105]

Polanyi makes an important application of this analysis to the sphere of language itself, showing that linguistic achievements, such as reading, naming, interpreting, meaning, are dependent on a subsidiary or distal awareness of language. We could express Polanyi's thought by saying that language is something "known in" or "known from" rather than explicitly known.[106] Science itself incorporates personal skills, 'hunches,' 'flairs,' and commitments which cannot be articulated or logically formalized, yet are part and parcel of its rationality.[107] Polanyi writes:

> . . . the supposed presuppositions of science are so futile because the actual foundations of our scientific beliefs cannot be asserted at all. When we accept a certain set of presuppositions and use them as our interpretative framework, we may be said to dwell in them as we do in our own body. . . . They are not asserted and cannot be asserted, for assertion can only be made *within* a framework with which we have identified ourselves for the time being; as they are themselves our ultimate framework, they are essentially inarticulable.
>
> It is by his assimilation of the framework of science that the scientist makes sense of his experience.[108]

Polanyi returns frequently in later writing to the theme of knowledge as "dwelling in" its presuppositional sources and reaching out from them to cognitive objects which we in turn come, by knowing, to "indwell."[109] The first presuppositional

104. *P.K.*, pp. 49-65; cf. *S.M.*, pp. 29-39, 44-47; "The Logic of Tacit Inference," *Philosophy*, XLI (1966), 369-386; "The Modern Mind, Its Structure and Prospects," *Encounter* (May, 1965), pp. 1-9.

105. *P.K.*, pp. 55-58.

106. *Ibid.*, pp. 87-131; cf. p. 57.

107. *Ibid.*, pp. 54-63, 120-131.

108. *Ibid.*, p. 60. This could be interestingly compared with Collingwood's thesis about metaphysics as the uncovering of the "absolute presuppositions of science" which cannot be rationally justified because they are the (provisionally) ultimate foundations of all rational justification.

109. See "The Logic of Tacit Inference," *Philosophy*, XLI (1966), 369-386; "The Modern Mind, Its Structure and Prospects," *Encounter* (May, 1965), pp. 1-9; *Duke*, II, pp. 19-25.

source of all our knowledge is our own body, and it is known only tacitly, as "dwelt in," as that *from* which we attend *to* other things.[110] These reflections have, as Polanyi recognized, much in common with the reflections of existentialists and phenomenologists.[111] But the resemblances with Wittgenstein are also sufficiently evident from what has been said above.

Polanyi's approach to the problem of knowing other minds is set in the same context of the distinction between focal and subsidiary awareness. He writes:

> Practical skills and practical experience contain much more information than people possessing this expert knowledge can ever tell. Particulars that are not known focally are unspecifiable, and there are vast domains of knowledge, relating to living things, the particulars of which are largely unspecifiable. . . . We know a face without being able to tell, except quite vaguely, by what particulars we recognize it. And this is also how the mind of man is known. A man's mind can be known *only comprehensively, by dwelling within the unspecifiable particulars of its external manifestations.*[112]

Polanyi's answer to behaviorism is similar to Wittgenstein's:

> The mind is a comprehensive feature of man. It is the focus in terms of which we are subsidiarily aware of the play of a man's features, utterances and whole behaviour. A man's mind is the meaning of these workings of his mind. It is false to say, as Ryle does, that these workings *are* his mind. To say this is to commit a category mistake (to use Professor Ryle's term) of the same kind as we should commit if we said that a symbol *was* its own meaning. . . . It is always the mind itself that we know primarily; any knowledge of its workings is derivative, vague and uncertain.[113]
>
> *We experience a man's mind as the joint meaning of his actions* by dwelling in his actions from outside.[114]

110. *P.K.*, pp. 58-60, 321-324; *S.M.*, pp. 31-33; *Duke*, II, pp. 19-22.
111. *Duke*, III, pp. 9-12. He refers to Dilthey and Lipps, Husserl and Heidegger.
112. *S.M.*, p. 33.
113. *S.M.*, p. 65.
114. "The Logic of Tacit Inference," *Philosophy*, XLI (1966), 14.

Polanyi's refutation of solipsism is in the same direction of thought. We have already noted his insistence on "conviviality," community, and consensus as integral constituents of all knowing.[115] For Polanyi, as for Wittgenstein, "private language" about "private sensations" is meaningless. His reflection leads to a philosophy of encounter which resembles the contemporary existentialist and phenomenological meditations on the theme of interpersonal relations. He writes:

> . . . when we arrive at the contemplation of a human being as a responsible person, and we apply to him the same standards as we accept for ourselves, our knowledge of him has definitely lost the character of an observation and has become an encounter instead.[116]

The parallel with Wittgenstein here too is remarkable. Wittgenstein declares that:

> . . . "sensation" is a word of our common language, not of one intelligible to me alone. So the use of this word stands in need of justification which everybody understands. . . . A sound is an expression only as it occurs in a particular language game, which should now be described.[117]

He claims, as Polanyi does, direct and proper knowledge of another's mind:

> I can know what someone else is thinking, not what I am thinking.
> It is correct to say "I know what you are thinking," and wrong to say, "I know what I am thinking."
> (A whole cloud of philosophy condensed into a drop of grammar.) [118]

For Wittgenstein, as for Polanyi, it is not a question of meeting other bodies and inferring that they have minds or souls. Souls are not inferred, they are encountered.

---

115. *P.K.*, pp. 150-171, 203-223, 264-268.
116. *S.M.*, pp. 94-95.
117. *Philosophical Investigations*, sec. 261; cf. secs. 246, 258, 286, 290-293, 322, 398.
118. *Ibid.*, II xi (p. 222e) .

My attitude towards him is an attitude towards a soul. I am not of the *opinion* that he has a soul.[119]

Can I not say: a cry, a laugh are full of meaning?[120]

Pity is a form of conviction that someone else [to wit, not some *body*] is in pain.[121]

The following passage from *Philosophical Investigations* would be equally at home in *Personal Knowledge*:

Is there such a thing as 'expert judgment' about the genuineness of expressions of feeling?—Even here, there are those whose judgment is 'better' and those whose judgment is 'worse.'

Correcter prognoses will generally issue from the judgments of those with better knowledge of mankind.

Can one learn this knowledge? Yes; some can. Not, however, by taking a course in it, but through 'experience.'—Can someone else be a man's teacher in this? Certainly. From time to time he gives him the right *tip*.—This is what 'learning' and 'teaching' are like here.—What one acquires here is not a technique; one learns correct judgments. There are also rules, but they do not form a system, and only experienced people can apply them right. Unlike calculating rules.[122]

VI

An important similarity between Polanyi and Wittgenstein is the philosophical importance they both attach to Gestalt psychology. Polanyi finds in it evidences of the "tacit components" in knowledge, whether in the form of perceptual mechanisms only "subsidiarily" known, or of the latent interpretative frameworks whereby we perceive wholes as more and other than collections of parts.[123] Wittgenstein adopts the Gestalt language of "perceptual shift" to describe that "noticing of an aspect" which he regards as characteristic of philosophy.[124]

119. *Ibid.*, II iv (p. 178e).
120. *Ibid.*, sec. 543.
121. *Ibid.*, sec. 287.
122. *Ibid.*, II xi (p. 227e).
123. *P.K.*, pp. 55-61, 97-98, 340-342; cf. *S.M.*, pp. 27 *et seq.*
124. *Philosophical Investigations*, II xi (pp. 193e-214e).

Others working in the Polanyi manner have explored further the implications of Gestalt psychology for the interpretation of scientific knowledge. One of these, Thomas S. Kuhn, in independent research into the history and espistemology of science, provides remarkable confirmation of Polanyi's interpretations and, at the same time, unexpected support for my comparison of Polanyi with Wittgenstein. Kuhn, for example, stresses the role of tradition, consensus, authority, within the scientific community as important determinants of research and results in science.[125] He stresses the "tacit" character of demarcatory rules and methodological principles in science.[126] He calls attention to the place of intuition, personal insight, in scientific discovery.[127] He describes the importance of trained perception in scientific observation, in terms that recall Polanyi's frequent analyses of "connoisseurship" in science.[128] He finds an important place in scientific verification for aesthetic categories and for "faith."[129] He shows how science is modified by the high-level "quasimetaphysical commitments" with which it is associated in different periods and from which it can only with difficulty be distinguished.[130]

His chief contribution, however, is to interpret revolutions of scientific theory in terms of "perceptual shift" or "paradigm shift."[131] He invokes in this connection Wittgenstein's celebrated simile of the figure that can be seen alternately as a rabbit's head or as a duck's.[132]

After referring to the scientific revolutions associated with Einstein and Copernicus, Kuhn writes:

> Practising in different worlds, the two groups of scientists see different things when they look from the same point in the same direction. . . . Both are looking at the world, and

125. *The Structure of Scientific Revolutions* (Chicago: International Encyclopaedia of Unified Science, University of Chicago, 1962), pp. 4-6, 18-20, 103, 148-151, 157-158, 163-165, 167-169.
126. *Ibid.*, pp. 46-49, 54-55, 110.
127. *Ibid.*, pp. 121-122, 131-134.
128. *Ibid.*, pp. 110-111.
129. *Ibid.*, pp. 156-157.
130. *Ibid.*, p. 41; cf. p. 4.
131. *Ibid.*, pp. 84-85, 117-119.
132. *Ibid.*, pp. 85, 110-111. Compare Wittgenstein, *Philosophical Investigations*, II xi (pp. 193 *et seq.*).

what they look at has not changed. But in some areas they
see different things, and they see them as different relations
one to the other. That is why a law that cannot ever be
demonstrated to one group of scientists may occasionally
seem intuitively obvious to another. Equally, it is why,
before they can hope to communicate fully, one group or
the other must experience the conversion that we have been
calling a paradigm shift.[133]

This process is simply not verifiable or falsifiable by empirical
tests or decidable by logical procedures: "the competition between
paradigms is not the sort of battle that can be resolved by
proofs."[134] Positivism totally fails as an explanation of how science works.[135]

This is closely parallel to Polanyi. I have quoted earlier, for
example, the passage in which he declares that science commits us
to "a vision of reality" for which we can invoke no criteria of
verifiability or falsifiability or testability.[136] Elsewhere he shows,
with reference to the Copernican and other scientific revolutions,
that such disputes "do not appear as scientific arguments, but as
conflicts between rival scientific visions."[137] He writes:

We can now see, also, the great difficulty that may arise in
the attempt to persuade others to accept a new idea in
science. . . . To the extent to which it represents a new way
of reasoning, we cannot convince others of it by formal
argument. . . .[138]

This seems to me to have a very far-reaching implication,
which is not developed by Kuhn nor, explicitly, by Polanyi. This
implication concerns the nature and validity of metaphysics.
Wittgenstein himself, as we have seen, regarded the effecting of a
"perceptual shift" as the aim of philosophy.[139] After him, linguistic philosophers have tended to apply this schema particularly to
metaphysics. G. J. Warnock, referring to Berkeley as typical,

133. Kuhn, *The Structure of Scientific Revolutions,* p. 149.
134. *Ibid.,* p. 147.
135. *Ibid.,* pp. 97, 147-148.
136. *P.K.,* p. 64.
137. *Ibid.,* p. 152.
138. *Ibid.,* p. 151.
139. *Philosophical Investigations,* II xi; cf. secs, 109, 122, 125-126, 435, 559,
600, 654-655.

writes that "the [metaphysician's] doctrines consisted rather of a kind of re-description, a shift of view-point, a modification of modes of thought. He saw the same world that the rest of us see, but saw it from a rather different angle."[140]

But this is exactly how Polanyi and Kuhn have taught us to describe scientific thinking! In this light, it will be no longer plausible to separate science rigidly from metaphysics, as the meaningful from the meaningless, the way logical positivism did in Professor Ayer's confident youth. It will not even be repentance enough to say that metaphysics may "express an interesting and challenging attitude to life" though it is not "capable of stating facts," as Professor Ayer puts it in his somewhat chastened prime.[141] It is not simply that former logical positivists have to rethink their whole attitude to metaphysics; they have to rethink their whole attitude to science too. For science and metaphysics can no longer be separated in the old pre-Polanyi ways. John Passmore has pointed out "the dilemma in which the logical positivists, like Hume before them, constantly found themselves—throw metaphysics into the fire, and science goes with it, preserve science from the flames and metaphysics comes creeping back."[142]

VII

There is at least one instance in which an explicit adoption of a Wittgensteinian linguistic technique would, I think, have helped Polanyi to develop more effectively an insight of his own. It is in the field of ethics. Polanyi has treated repeatedly of the paradox of contemporary morals whereby scepticism about moral standards is allied with exorbitant moral exigencies to produce the typical revolutionary fervors and fanaticisms of our time. He calls it a process of "moral inversion."[143]

140. "Analysis and Imagination," in *The Revolution in Philosophy*, ed. Gilbert Ryle (London: Macmillan, 1956) , p. 122.
141. "The Vienna Circle," p. 74.
142. *A Hundred Years of Philosophy* (London: Duckworth, 1957) , p. 392.
143. See *P.K.*, pp. 227-237; cf. pp. 142, 180; *L.L.*, pp. 105-110, 198-200; *Beyond Nihilism*, The Thirteenth Eddington Memorial Lecture (Cambridge: Cambridge University Press, 1960) ; "The Modern Mind, Its Structure and Prospects," pp. 7-9; *Duke*, V, pp. 3-8.

Polanyi has here uncovered a feature of modern morals which is of the first importance but which few have studied. The morality of anti-moralism or immoralism, the ethics of angry protest, the morals of man in revolt, are among the most distinctive features of modern culture from Nietzsche to Camus, from Kierkegaard to Péguy or from Marx to Sartre. Polanyi refers chiefly to Marx, though he instances also Freud.[144]

It seems to me that it would be valid and illuminating here to examine how far the "anti-moral" moralists are, in Wittgensteinian terms, taking words like "authenticity," "sincerity," "justice," "brotherhood" out of their place in the "stream of life" which is human moral living, and in the "language game" which is human moral discourse, and "subliming" them into unattainable absolutes.[145] The result can be that everything we ordinarily mean by "sincere" is condemned as hypocrisy in the name of an unattainable and inhuman absolute of authenticity; or genuine practical efforts at creating just structures of society are derided in the name of an absolutist theory of abstract justice. If ethical terms were kept situated in their human context the excesses of moral fanaticism would be seen as philosophical errors.

Polanyi comes curiously close to this type of analysis, though moving in another direction, when he says that moral inversion results from the tensions introduced into human society by the conflict between the unlimited moral expectations and demands of Christianity and man's disillusioned experience of their unattainability. He thinks the phenomenon can be explained as due to the secularization of Christian morals, with a consequent transference of its inherent tensions into the sphere of secular society.[146] But here again one could argue in Wittgensteinian terms that Christian moral concepts get their proper interpretation from the "stream of life" of Christian experience and the "language game" of Christian teaching. Here justice is reconciled

144. *P.K.*, pp. 233-234, 309. His criticism of Freud, pointing out his inconsistency both with himself and with ordinary experience, is not unlike the criticism of Freud by Wittgenstein. See Wittgenstein, *Lectures and Conversations on Aesthetics, Psychology and Religious Belief*, ed. Cyril Barrett (Oxford: Blackwell, 1966), pp. 41-52, 23-24. Cf. Malcolm, *Memoir*, pp. 44-45.
145. Compare *Philosophical Investigations*, secs. 38, 89.
146. *L.L.*, pp. 103-110.

with mercy, sincerity with charity, sanctity with repentance, perfection with humility, in a natural and supernatural history of human beings, constituting a fellowship of sinners under the judgment but also the compassion of God. The explanation of moral inversion is scarcely that "since no society can live up to Christian precepts, any society professing Christian precepts must be afflicted by internal contradictions";[147] but rather that Christian precepts, torn from their context in Christian faith and life, cannot but be distorted, as any moral precept, torn from its setting in the moral life of man, cannot but be inverted. It is an old Christian adage that heresies are truths wandering away from the truth, and that this is precisely why they are strong and destructive. Wittgenstein's diagnosis of philosophical diseases is not wholly dissimilar to this description of heresies.

It might be argued that Wittgenstein's therapy could usefully be applied also to some of Polanyi's attempts to assimilate science to religious faith, attempts which leave at least the present writer unhappy. It is one thing to call attention to the fiduciary element in science and to stress the dependence of science on belief or faith—faith in the rationality of the cosmos, the uniformity of nature, or the value of science. This aspect of science is ignored by positivist dogmatism. It needs to be affirmed. But it is quite another thing to confuse the faith of science with religious faith or even the Christian Faith, and to extend to science the application of the Augustinian formulae: *Fides quaerens intellectum* and *Nisi credideritis, non intelligetis*.[148] Faith in the religious and above all in the Christian sense has a specific meaning, to be learnt only from Christian theological vocabulary, Christian tradition and experience. Wittgenstein's injunctions are relevant here too: "the meaning of a word is its use in the language."[149]

VIII

If one were to attempt a general description and assessment of Polanyi's work in Wittgensteinian terms, one could say that

147. *Beyond Nihilism*, p. 4.
148. *P.K.*, pp. 266-267; *S.F.S.*, pp. 44-45.
149. *Philosophical Investigations*, sec. 43.

Polanyi eminently achieves what Wittgenstein regards as the characteristic function of philosophy, the re-vision of the whole field of science, of scientific knowing and of knowledge in general. He makes us "notice aspects" which current orthodoxies were concealing, makes us "look" at what our "thinking" was "calloused" into ignoring, shows us "doors" of escape from logical prisons of positivism.[150] He "dissolves" errors that arose from "looking at the facts through the medium of a misleading form of expression."[151] All this is inestimable, and it is the lot of few philosophers to have achieved so much.

Polanyi's work may be seen as the antithesis which negates the thesis of positivism. This Hegelian analysis has been revived in a different form, under Wittgensteinian influence, by John Wisdom, who speaks of philosophy as progressing through paradox to discovery. Antithetical theses, he suggests, each affirming in turn what the other had denied and denying what the other had affirmed, bring cumulatively into view opposed but complementary aspects of reality. Philosophy, in this view, succeeds precisely by being paradoxical and provocative.[152]

This is, perhaps, itself a paradoxical view. More soberly, one might suggest that Polanyi's thought, having triumphantly reinstated against positivism the non-logically-formulable aspects of scientific reasoning, might be developed in the direction of showing how the non-logical in science is reconciled with the logical, the creative with the inductive, the subjective with the objectifiable, "personal" knowledge with "critical." Having shown the non-truth in positivism and the non-positivistic in truth, he might complete his service by helping us to see in synthesis the truth in positivism and the positivist element in scientific truth. This, too, would be good Wittgensteinian practice; for, if it is necessary to show how like non-scientific forms of knowing sci-

---

150. Compare *Philosophical Investigations,* secs. 108, 109, 123, 309; Malcolm, *Memoir,* p. 51.

151. *The Blue and Brown Books,* p. 31.

152. See "Philosophical Perplexity" and "Metaphysics and Verification," in *Philosophy and Psycho-analysis* (Oxford: Blackwell, 1957), pp. 36-50 and 51-101. See also *Paradox and Discovery* (Oxford: Blackwell, 1965), especially pp. 114-138.

ence is, it is also necessary to show how unlike them it is, and why. Both likenesses and differences between various "language games" are relevant in philosophy.[153]

IX

Polanyi's writings had when they first appeared the stance of a brave, lone protest against established orthodoxies in British philosophical thinking. Its affinities lay rather with continental existentialist or personalist thought, with Marcel's "methodology of the inverifiable,"[154] with Husserl and Heidegger and Jaspers. In the probing of the metarational sources of science, one could see parallels with Bachelard and with Lévi-Strauss. Among English philosophers, kinship was evident only with thinkers out of the "main stream" of contemporary British philosophy. Thus the resemblance is striking between Polanyi's reflections and John Macmurray's efforts to found a post-Kantian, postcritical philosophy on "the form of the personal."[155] Similarities exist also with the work of C. A. Campbell[156] or with the impressive efforts of E. E. Harris[157] to reinstate some unduly discredited truths of the idealist tradition.

But it is notable—and is, for the present writer, an endorsement of the theme of this paper—that, under the influence of Wittgenstein, even "main stream" British linguistic philosophy today shows some signs of some movements towards Polanyi's themes. Some of these are the subject of other contributions to this volume. In addition, one could instance recent studies of

153. Dr. Drury reports that Wittgenstein once thought of using as motto for *Philosophical Investigations* a quotation from King Lear: "I'll teach you differences." See *The Listener*, January 28, 1960.
154. This is the title of a study of Marcel by Pietro Prini, *Gabriel Marcel et la méthodologie de l'invérifiable* (Paris: Desclée de Brouwer, 1953).
155. See the two series of Gifford Lectures, 1953 and 1954, published as *The Self as Agent* (London: Faber, 1957), and *Persons in Relation* (London: Faber, 1961). Compare *The Boundaries of Science* (London: Faber, 1939).
156. See the Gifford Lectures, 1953-1954 and 1954-1955, *On Selfhood and Godhood* (London: Allen and Unwin, 1957).
157. See *Nature, Mind and Modern Science* (London: Allen and Unwin, 1954); *The Foundations of Metaphysics in Science* (London: Allen and Unwin, 1965).

intention,[158] attention,[159] the embodying of thought and rationality in action and in free choice.[160]

But it is perhaps in the enigmatic writings of John Wisdom that we will find *more suo* most resemblance to Polanyi's topics. I cannot better express my final tribute to Polanyi's method and my concluding statement of his affinity to Wittgenstein than by borrowing words from Wisdom's paper on "A Feature of Wittgenstein's Technique":

> If we now . . . think of more normal enquiry directed upon the actual events in nature, in life, we shall find on occasion questions which cannot be answered, statements which cannot be tested, either by experiment and observation or by reasoning in general terms. . . . Thought too will fail us here if we think that all thought which carries us to the truth must be thought on lines as definable or at least as conventional as the thought of an accountant who assesses a firm's financial position, and forget how much it may be a matter of giving our minds to incidents and incidents, whether they be as familiar as the fall of an apple or as recondite as the Michelson-Morley experiment, or the disorder of a man like poor Dr. Schreber.[161]

Wisdom said about Mace, and I should like to apply the words to Polanyi: He "is one of those who, whether they are doing philosophy or not doing philosophy, combat our inclination to allow habits of thought and talk to confine our efforts to see better than we have before what things are like."[162]

158. E.g., G. E. M. Anscombe, *Intention* (Oxford: Blackwell, 1957) .
159. E.g., A. R. White, *Attention* (Oxford: Blackwell, 1964) .
160. E.g., Stuart Hampshire, *Thought and Action* (London: Chatto and Windus, 1959) ; *Freedom of the Individual* (London: Chatto and Windus, 1965) ; A. I. Melden, *Free Action* (London: Routledge and Kegan Paul, 1961) ; Anthony Kenny, *Action, Emotion and Will* (London: Routledge and Kegan Paul, 1963) ; compare Bernard Mayo, *Ethics and the Moral Life* (London: Macmillan, 1958) .
161. *Paradox and Discovery*, pp. 102-103.
162. *Ibid.*, p. 166.

POLANYI AND J. L. AUSTIN

Ian Ramsey

It would be generally agreed that Michael Polanyi's most distinctive contribution to contemporary thought has been (in his own words) to elucidate "some essential features of the process of knowing which are disregarded by the modern conception of positive scientific knowledge."[1] Starting "by rejecting the idea of scientific detachment"[2]—an ideal which, while false, is perhaps harmless because disregarded in the exact sciences, though it "exercises a destructive influence in biology, psychology, and sociology"—he regards "knowing as an active comprehension of the things known." In this way there is, he says, a "personal participation of the knower in all acts of understanding."

J. L. Austin, in his turn, is critical of 'scholastic' theories of perception, and especially of their attendant sense-data, those supposedly hard, independent, bare, atomic 'facts' which for long—at least since Russell—have been taken to supply the philosophical presupposition of scientific thinking, and to justify scientific detachment. Further, while welcoming the recent "revolution" in philosophy as "salutary,"[3] Austin's own original contribution has largely come from his being concerned not just with words, but with "speech-acts," with what a speaker does with his words. Is there anything here akin to Polanyi's "personal participation"?

What I shall do in this article is to suggest that despite the

1. Michael Polanyi, "Faith and Reason," *The Journal of Religion*, XLI, No. 4 (Oct., 1961), 237-247.
2. *P.K.*, p. vii.
3. J. L. Austin, *Philosophical Papers*, ed. J. O. Urmson and G. J. Warnock (Oxford: Oxford University Press, 1961), pp. 221-222.

more obvious differences in their approaches, and in the topics with which they are concerned—Austin is the more analytical and critical, Polanyi is the more synthetic and constructive; Austin is the more professional linguistic philosopher, nurtured in the classical tradition; while Polanyi, nurtured in the sciences, develops his philosophical interests within that background, and the background of social studies—there are, nevertheless, interesting and significant similarities between M. Polanyi and J. L. Austin. As our comments will already have indicated, they share a critical attitude towards the ideal of scientific detachment. Both Polanyi and Austin are critical of the view that the world consists of a number of atomic objects or bare facts, of the view on which knowledge is paradigmatically descriptive information about these 'objective' facts. Further, M. Polanyi, with his themes of personal participation and commitment, and J. L. Austin with his doctrine of performatives, of speech-acts, of words having "illocutionary force," resemble each other at least in their recognizing that many assertions have a self-involving character which an over-simple empirical view overlooks as much as the attitude of scientific detachment. I shall suggest, however, that Austin was so nervous of metaphysical blunders that he failed to see the wider implications of his views, and more positively I shall argue that my own concept of disclosure can be used to interpret the insights of both Austin and Polanyi in a way that avoids the crude metaphysics which Austin rejected, while clarifying and developing Polanyi's discussion at certain crucial points. We might say, alternatively, that both Austin and Polanyi are critical of an oversimplified, stereotyped empiricism, and its associated ontology. In this way they each point to the need for a broader empiricism. What I hope to do is to show that such a broader empiricism needs and benefits from the concept of disclosure.

My discussion will fall into two parts. In the first part I shall discuss their treatment of the view, characteristic of a simple empiricism, that to every word or phrase or assertion there belong exactly specifiable criteria which provide the 'meaning' or 'verification.' In the second part we shall see how far Austin's elucidation of performative utterances as a form of words by means of which one, while saying something, *does* something resembles Polanyi's insistence upon all knowing as a special form of personal doing, and I shall suggest that there are various advantages in using the concept of disclosure for the further interpretation of both.

First then, let us compare Polanyi and Austin in their views about the relation of assertions to verifiable criteria, about the relation of words to observable facts. On a simple empiricism every assertion or word will be used with its own exactly specifiable criteria, so that the meaning of any assertion is given by enumerating these criteria which verify it, these being the "facts" to which the assertion (if true) corresponds. Polanyi and Austin are both concerned to show the limitations of such a view, and in this way, (as I have said) both point to a broader empiricism.

We may begin with an example which Polanyi gives in the article on "Faith and Reason" to which I have already referred. He tells how:

> A few years ago a distinguished psychiatrist demonstrated to his students a patient who was having a mild fit of some kind. Later the class discussed the question whether this had been an epileptic or a hystero-epileptic seizure. The matter was finally decided by the psychiatrist: "Gentlemen," he said, "you have seen a true epileptic seizure. I cannot tell you how to recognize it; you will learn this by more extensive experience."[4]

Polanyi comments:

> The psychiatrist knew how to recognize this disease, but he was not at all certain how he did this. In other words, he recognized the disease by attending to its total appearance and did so by relying on a multitude of clues which he could not clearly specify. Thus his knowledge of the disease differed altogether from his knowledge of these clues. He recognized the disease by attending to it, while he was not attending to its symptoms *in themselves*, but only *as clues*. We may say that he was knowing the clues only by relying on them for attending to the pathological physiognomy to which they contributed.[5]

4. Michael Polanyi, "Faith and Reason," p. 239.
5. *Ibid.* (Italics mine.)

The conclusion is that there are no exactly specifiable criteria, e.g., for the recognizing of a particular disease. We do not recognize an epileptic seizure, and we do not verify the assertion: "This is an epileptic seizure" by scanning some definitive group of necessary and sufficient criteria. Something more is needed; what Polanyi calls 'understanding' or 'comprehension,' and such 'knowledge of the disease' emerges in a way to be discussed from a knowledge of the observable 'clues,' as something altogether distinctive. For Polanyi, an 'understanding' or 'comprehension' of some object is only possible when the awareness of some set of particulars is transformed into an awareness of the 'entity as a whole.' "A subsidiary awareness of the particulars" must give place to "our knowledge of the whole."[6] Indeed there is an oscillation between these two kinds of awareness or knowledge. As he says:

> We may successfully analyze the symptoms of a disease and concentrate our attention on its several particulars, and then we may return to our conception of its general appearance by becoming once more subsidiarily aware of these particulars as contributing to the total picture of the disease,[7]

and he continues: "such an oscillation of detailing and integrating is the royal road for deepening our understanding of any comprehensive entity."[8]
It is such 'comprehension' which, he says:

> is the cognitive faculty cast aside by a positivistic theory of knowledge, which refuses to acknowledge the existence of comprehensive entities as distinct from their particulars; and this is the faculty which I recognize as the central act of knowing. For comprehension can never be absent from any process of knowing and is indeed the ultimate sanction of any such act. What is not understood cannot be said to be known.[9]

6. *Ibid.*
7. *Ibid.*
8. *Ibid.*, pp. 239-240.
9. *Ibid.*, p. 240.

For Polanyi then, knowledge in the sense of this comprehensive attention is "a kind of knowledge which we must acquire by becoming aware of a multitude of clues that cannot be exhaustively identified."[10] But how does this kind of knowledge arise from our awareness of the multitude of clues?

At this point, however, let us leave Polanyi for a moment and turn to J. L. Austin to see what he in his turn has to say about the relation of criteria to words and assertions. In *Philosophical Papers*[11] Austin is concerned with the question, asked (say) of us when we have said of a bird seen on the branch of a tree that it is a goldfinch—"How do you know it's a goldfinch?" Suppose we answer, "Because it has a red head." Here, says Austin, is an answer which is "dangerously definite" for it

> implies that *all* I have noted, or *needed* to note, about it is that its head is *red,* (nothing special or peculiar about the shade, shape, etc. of the patch) : so that I imply that there is no other small British bird that has any sort of red head except the goldfinch.[12]

In other words it is dangerous to be too definite, to have too stereotyped an empiricism, to have criteria too closely tied to assertions. For it tempts us, and our hearers, to suppose that here is something capable of knock-down proof; it tempts us to take a rigid, ossified view of language and facts, which fails to take account of the subtleties and flexibilities, of the open texture or "saving vagueness" of language as she is used. As Austin says:

> Whenever I say I know, I am always liable to be taken to claim that, in a certain sense appropriate to the kind of statement (and to present intents and purposes) , I am able to prove it. In the present, very common, type of case, 'proving' seems to mean stating what are the features of the current case which are enough to constitute it one which is correctly describable in the way we have described it. . . . Generally speaking, cases where I can 'prove' are cases where we use the 'because' formula.[13]

10. *Ibid.,* p. 240.
11. J. L. Austin, *Philosophical Papers,* pp. 52-53.
12. *Ibid.,* p. 53.
13. *Ibid.,* pp. 53-54.

But, as Austin points out, there are other possible answers to
the question, "How do you know it's a goldfinch?" We might say,
for example, "*From* its red head." Here's an answer which (he
says) "differs materially"[14] from the other answer. In this case,
when we say that we "know" or that we can "tell" it is a
goldfinch "from its red head," we are claiming, says Austin, "to
recognize" the bird as a goldfinch.[15] The important point is that
"this that we see, or otherwise sense" on such occasion "is not
necessarily *describable* in words, still less describable in detail,
and in non-committal words."[16] Austin continues:

> Nearly everybody can recognize a surly look or the smell of
> tar, but few can describe them non-committally, i.e. other-
> wise than as 'surly' or 'of tar': many can recognize, and 'with
> certainty,' ports of different vintages, models made by dif-
> ferent fashion houses, shades of green, motor-car makes
> from behind, and so forth, without being able to say "how
> they recognize them," i.e. without being able to 'be more
> specific about it'—they can only say they can tell 'by the
> taste,' 'from the cut,' and so on. So, when I say I can tell the
> bird 'from its red head, or that I know a friend 'by his nose,'
> I imply that there is something peculiar about the red head
> or the nose, something peculiar to goldfinches or to him, by
> which you can (always) tell them or him. In view of the
> fewness and crudeness of the classificatory words in any
> language compared with the infinite number of features
> which are recognized, or which could be picked out and
> recognized, in our experience, it is small wonder that we
> often and often fall back on the phrases beginning with
> 'from' and 'by,' and that we are not able to say, further and
> precisely, how we can tell. Often we know things quite well,
> while scarcely able at all to say 'from' what we know them,
> let alone what there is so very special about them. Any
> answer beginning 'From' or 'By' has, intentionally, this
> saving 'vagueness.'[17]

So there are answers which, in some way or other, sit loose to
any particular set of criteria. When we talk of goldfinches, and in

14. *Ibid.*, p. 52.
15. *Ibid.*, p. 52.
16. *Ibid.*, p. 52-53.
17. *Ibid.*, p. 53.

particular of knowing that something is a goldfinch "from its head," we make an affirmation which, while it is based on one criterion or, maybe, a number of related criteria, is not restricted to those criteria as it would be in the "because" case. Rather, as Austin says—and we may recall Polanyi's phrase "a multitude of clues"—in such cases there are an "infinite number of features which are recognised, or which could be picked out and recognised."[18] In such cases it is 'recognition,' rather than proof by descriptive assertion, which is the point at issue. In other words, there is no limit to the number of observable features that 'recognition' involves; recognition is never a mere surveying of observable criteria. What happens in such cases, I shall suggest, is that one or another feature characterizing (say) the head of the goldfinch, brings to mind a sequence of features, few or many, and less or more discriminated, and that we recognize the bird as a goldfinch when around this sequence of features a disclosure occurs. Only then, I shall argue, can we talk of recognizing a goldfinch as that to which the pattern of criteria *refers,* as that which our assertion is *about.* But that is to anticipate.

It will now be readily seen how similar Austin's "recognition" of the goldfinch is to Polanyi's "comprehension" of the epilepsy. For Polanyi, as for Austin, there is the need to survey particulars, be they few or many. But, for both Polanyi and Austin, this "detailing" is only part of the story, though it is that part of the story which "a positivistic theory of knowledge," when it has been restrictive and oversimplified, has taken to be the whole story. Such particulars, such criteria, are 'clues' pointing, Polanyi would say, to a 'whole' which we 'comprehend,' pointing, I would say, to a disclosure. There are parallels to such a situation whenever the 'light dawns' around a multitude of clues, as when a series of regular polygons, constructed so that their vertices are always equidistant from a fixed point disclose a circle; or when we 'see' a person as more than the observables which meet the professional eye of a doctor, psychiatrist or sociologist.

Polanyi makes the same point in an article on "The Creative Imagination":

18. *Ibid.,* p. 53.

Our knowledge of reality has . . . an essentially indeterminate content: It deserves to be called a vision. . . . This
vision, the vision of a hidden reality, which guides a scientist in his quest, is a dynamic force. At the end of the quest
the vision is becalmed in the contemplation of the reality
revealed by a discovery; but the vision is renewed and
becomes dynamic again in other scientists and guides them
to new discoveries. I shall now try to show how both the
dynamic and the static phases of a scientific vision are due
to the strength of the imagination guided by intuition. We
shall understand then both the grounds on which established scientific knowledge rests and the powers by which
scientific discovery is achieved. I have pursued this problem
for many years by considering science as an extension of
ordinary perception. When I look at my hand and move it
about, it would keep changing its shape, its size, and its
color, but for my capacity for seeing the joint meaning of a
host of rapidly changing clues, and seeing also that this
joint meaning remains unchanged. I recognize a real object
before me from my joint awareness of the clues which bear
upon it. Many of these clues cannot be sensed in themselves
at all. The contraction of my eye muscles, for example, I
cannot experience in itself. Yet I am very much aware of the
working of these muscles indirectly, in the way they make
me see the object at the right distance and as having the
right size. Some clues to this we see from the corner of our
eyes. An object looks very different when we see it through a
blackened tube, which cuts out these marginal clues. We
can recognize here two kinds of awareness. We are obviously
aware of the object we are looking at, but are aware
also—in a much less positive way—of a hundred different
clues which we integrate to the sight of the object. When
integrating these clues, we are attending fully to the object
while we are aware of the clues themselves without attending to them. We are aware of them only as pointing to the
object we are looking at. I shall say that we have a subsidiary awareness of the clues in their bearing on the object to
which we are focally attending.[19]

Polanyi's "focal attention," "comprehension," what he also calls
(less happily I think) "tacit awareness," is clearly a kinsman of

19. *Chemical and Engineering News,* XLIV (April 25, 1966) , 86.

Austin's "recognition" which goes beyond the features which may be separately described. In this way both point to what I have called a disclosure, a cognitive situation which breaks in on us as we survey a series of verifiable criteria, many or few.

Now as the extract just quoted makes clear, both Polanyi and Austin want to talk of an 'object,' an 'object' being comprehended, or attended to, an 'object' to which the clues point, something (e.g., a goldfinch) being recognized. It is at this point that I believe that the accounts of both Polanyi and Austin are inadequate, and where I am bold enough to suggest that by an appeal to the concept of disclosure, as I have introduced it above, by the addition of this to their already broadened empirical epistemology both will discover a supplement which each needs.

To argue this conclusion let us first relate Austin's position here to his discussion with Strawson about facts.[20] Austin claims "that to say that something is a fact *is* at least in part precisely to say that it is something in the world." For Austin, to talk about 'fact' is, at least in part, to make some kind of existential, referential claim, to talk about something 'out there.' As he says a little later: "One might say that 'fact' resembles 'person': 'persons' are not, of course, facts, and facts are not persons, but to say so-and-so is a person or a fact is, in part at least, to say so-and-so is real." So Austin wants to say that the mange on a cat is a fact, is real, is something 'in the world,' that the draughtiness of a kitchen is a state of affairs, again something in the world. As he has said earlier:

> . . . things and persons are far from being all that the ordinary man, and even Strawson, would admit to be genuinely things-in-the-world whatever exactly that may mean. Phenomena, events, situations, states of affairs are commonly supposed to be genuinely-in-the-world, and even Strawson admits events are so.[21]

But this merging and muddling of "facts" and "being-in-the-world" conceals I fear for Austin the reference question which Strawson is doing his best to clarify and to highlight.

20. "Unfair to Facts," in *Philosophical Papers.* The discussion relates to an old symposium in *Proceedings of the Aristotelian Society,* Supplementary Volume XXIV.
21. *Ibid.,* p. 104.

Strawson, distinguishing what sentences are *about* from what they *state,* does not mind calling the latter "facts"—facts thus being features of the world talked about in statements—but above all else he wants to clarify those cases where there is a genuine objective reference, where assertions are *about* something, about some object, thing or person. He is, in other words, alert to the reference question when Austin seems almost oblivious of it. Has Austin, indeed, done any justice to the reference claim?

I suggest that for Austin, justice *will* only be done to his reference claim if we agree that the objective reference of a word or phrase or assertion, where there is one, is given—self-disclosed—in those disclosure situations to which a survey of the relevant states of affairs, or features of the world, or criteria leads. Such disclosures will occur around those states of affairs which are not only in an obvious sense 'in-the-world,' but *of* something. Here is a suggestion which might well reconcile Austin's position with Strawson's position. It seems to me an essential development of Austin's view if he is to deal adequately with the reference problem. As for Strawson—on Strawson's view certain states of affairs characterize persons or things, and my suggestion would be that they do so as and when these states of affairs, in one way or another, generate a disclosure. Strawson says in effect that such a disclosure will occur only around persons or things. To take an example, if we ask: What is it which is draughty, facing north, labour saving . . . the answer which comes at a moment of disclosure when the features being surveyed 'fit' together is: *This* kitchen. The reference, the object is disclosed in this way as and when the criteria, the clues together enable a disclosure. We can of course agree with Austin, as we have done, that "phenomena, events, situations, states of affairs" are all in some obvious sense "in the world"; but the matter of reference which Strawson is rightly anxious to clarify is another, second-order, issue, and it is only settled, I am suggesting, if and when the phenomena, states of affairs, features of the world give rise to a disclosure.

Returning now to our earlier discussion of Austin, my suggestion is that we can only speak of knowing a goldfinch from its head, if around the "infinite number of features which are recognised, or could be picked out and recognised" a disclosure occurs which discloses that object of which the features are features. Only then may we speak of an 'object,' e.g. a 'goldfinch' being recognized. In this way, then, the matter of reference, which it seems to me that Austin neglects, requires an appeal to disclosure to do justice to it; the infinite number of observable features that provide the criteria for an assertion must evoke a disclosure for them to be said to be features *of something*.

Let us now see how, for Polanyi, a similar appeal to disclosure is needed, if he is to claim the comprehension of an 'object,' that the clues point to an 'object.' Further, the appeal to disclosures is absolutely necessary in Polanyi's case in order to make it abundantly clear that Polanyi is making more than merely a psychological point, though his acknowledgment of similarities to the Gestalt psychologists may encourage that mistaken interpretation. I think it would do an injustice to the importance and far-reaching character of Polanyi's insights to think of his theory as being 'purely psychological,' and I suggest that an appeal to disclosures is necessary to scotch that particular misunderstanding, as well as, at the same time, to establish the objective reference as in Austin's case.

So far as the reference problem goes, if we are to comprehend not only what "a true epileptic seizure" is, but to comprehend a true epileptic seizure belonging to and characterizing a person, then the relevant features, the clues must generate a disclosure, giving the seizure its necessary anchorage in a person along the lines we have already indicated.

It seems to me that Polanyi intends to go thus far; that here is the full fruition of Polanyi's position; and my point is that in this full development, the concept of disclosure is implied as that in which the reference claim is grounded, as well as that which makes it evident that this is no 'merely psychological matter.' The justification for saying this will, I hope, be evident when we look again at Polanyi's notion of 'comprehension' which he exemplifies and further discusses in the article we have already mentioned.

Comprehension as he points out, is not only involved in recognizing a true epileptic seizure as distinct, for example, from a hystero-epileptic seizure. It is also involved, he says, if I may quote a passage whose conclusion we have already quoted,

> in the identification of the species to which an animal or a plant belongs. An expert who can identify 800,000 species of insects must rely on a vast number of clues which he cannot identify in themselves. This is why zoology and botany cannot be learned from printed pages, any more than medicine can. This is why so many hours of practical teaching in the laboratory have to be given in many other branches of the natural sciences also. Wherever this happens, some knowledge of the comprehensive aspect of things is being transmitted: a kind of knowledge which we must acquire by becoming aware of a multitude of clues that cannot be exhaustively identified.[22]

He gives the further example of skills, about which he remarks that:

> A performance is called skilful precisely because we cannot clearly identify its component muscular acts. The craftsman's cunning consists in controlling these component acts jointly with a view to a comprehensive achievement. Such also is the sportsman's and the musical performer's art. Neither can tell much—and mostly can tell very little—about the several muscular acts he combines in accomplishing his art.

In this way comprehension is some total, self-involving, cognitive attitude which matches, as it occurs in response to, so I have suggested, a disclosure, a disclosure which itself arises around and goes beyond the criteria or components ("component muscular acts") which it contains. This 'going beyond'—in this sense 'transcendence'—is evidenced when we recall, as Polanyi does, that we can never "direct our attention to an object as mere object while relying on it as the tool of a skilful performance."[23] As he says:

> You must keep your eye on the ball, and if you look at your bat instead, you inevitably lose the stroke. Any skilful per-

22. "Faith and Reason," p. 240.
23. *Ibid.*

formance is paralyzed by attending focally to its particulars, whether these are the dexterous movements of our body or the tools which we employ.[24]

He further exemplifies comprehension by reference to speech. "Listen," he says, "intently to the sound of your own words, disregarding *their meaningful context* which is the *comprehensive entity that they should subserve,* and you will be instantly struck dumb."[25] Signs, symbols, and gestures must be subordinated to the act of comprehension which incorporates them. His final example is sensory perception. "It is sensory perception," he says, "and particularly the way we see things, that has supplied Gestalt psychologists with material for their fundamental discoveries which I am expanding here into a new theory of knowledge."[26] The merit of Gestalt psychologists is to have shown

> that our seeing is an act of comprehension for which we rely, in a most subtle manner, on clues from all over the field of vision as well as on clues inside our body, in the muscles controlling the motion of the eyes and in those controlling the posture of the body. All these clues become effective only if we keep concentrating our attention on the objects we are perceiving.

Here, then, without a doubt, Polanyi believes that comprehension is a cognitive attitude, which goes beyond clues, to secure reference to the objects we are identifying, using in a skilful way, talking about[27] or perceiving. My point has been that for an adequate understanding of "comprehension" the concept of disclosure is involved. Comprehension occurs when a survey of the clues gives rise to a disclosure in which a person attends fully to an object.

This disclosure basis becomes very plain, I believe, when we see what Polanyi says of comprehension later in the article. He

24. *Ibid.*
25. *Ibid.,* pp. 240-241. (Italics mine.)
26. *Ibid.,* p. 241.
27. It might be said that the 'objects' here are no more than the particular word-tokens being used. But this I think would be to misinterpret Polanyi. The words are like tools of communication (cf. L. Wittgenstein) and the "comprehensive entity that they should subserve" is "their meaningful context," i.e., what we are talking about.

invites us to recall the examples I have just mentioned, and he comments on the comprehension that they all exemplify. "More often than not we comprehend things in a flash."[28] More often than not, in other words, there are disclosure situations, for a metaphor such as "in a flash" is indigenous to and indicative of disclosures.

Yet, rather surprisingly, Polanyi continues:

> But it is more illuminating to think of the way we struggle from a puzzled incomprehension of a state of affairs towards its real meaning. The success of such efforts demonstrates man's capacity for *knowing the presence of a hidden reality* accessible to his understanding. This capacity is at work in all our knowing, from the dawn of discovery to the holding of established truth. *Our active foreknowledge of an unknown reality* is the right motive and guiding of knowing in all our mental endeavours. Formal processes of inference cannot thrust toward the truth, for they have neither passion nor purpose. All explicit forms of reasoning, whether deductive or inductive, are impotent in themselves; they can operate only as the intellectual tools of man's tacit powers reaching toward the hidden meaning of things.[29]

My difficulty, and it recalls my nervousness lest Polanyi's insights should be regarded as "merely" psychological, is that here he *seems* to be giving us dubious psychology masquerading as metaphysics, and in a way which, to some degree, confuses logical and temporal sequence. What are these "tacit powers" or this "active foreknowledge of an unknown reality" or "comprehensive entities"? My suggestion is that we can avoid these curious and perhaps puzzling phrases, we can avoid this puzzling mixture of psychology, epistemology, and metaphysics when we recognize that the point—or so I am suggesting—of all these remarks is that the disclosures which "comprehension" involves may well precede, even if they more often follow, their spelling out in terms of some particular features or clues, and that this may often be the case in scientific discovery. Beyond this I do not think we need attach much importance to the temporal sequence.

28. *Ibid.*, p. 243.
29. *Ibid.* (Italics mine.)

Perhaps then the only point at issue here is that a disclosure will not always have the spectacular character of a "flash," it may just be a "becoming aware" in some rather more decisive way, what Polanyi aptly calls in a passage I have already quoted "focally attending." But nothing of this need presuppose, I would say, a prior and tacit awareness.

All that on one side, however, I think that whatever the *temporal* sequence, the *logical* relation of knowledge of particulars or clues to comprehension is by far the more important issue; and that, I suggest, is illuminated by the concept of disclosure. In brief, I do not think that Polanyi relates at all clearly enough tacit knowledge and knowledge of particulars, and I suggest that this is precisely what the concept of disclosure could enable him to do. It is when "knowledge of particulars," attention to details or clues, leads to a disclosure that comprehension occurs, something which is not "merely" psychological, and something which by its disclosure character safeguards the objective reference of what discloses itself to us. Further, the reference of each disclosure, the 'object' which discloses itself, need not be given such misleading descriptions as 'the whole' or 'an unknown reality.' True, when the object reveals itself and is given in a disclosure situation there is a characteristic unity—a 'whole'—of disclosure and response; and this disclosed 'object' is not known as the particulars or clues are known, for such an 'object' discloses its objectivity. But we need not be metaphysically more extravagant than that.

It is now time to turn to the second theme[30] on which we shall compare Polanyi and Austin—the self-involvement which Polanyi would say characterizes all knowledge, and which Austin originally suggested characterized some knowledge, though later he, too, seems to have thought of it as a more universal feature, so that all assertions would have some illocutionary force. Here I shall argue that Austin was not metaphysical enough, and that again the concept of disclosure can help them both.

Let us begin by recalling Austin's early remarks on performa-

---

30. The reader will notice that the first and second themes cannot be kept entirely distinct, but it makes (I hope) for easier reading to separate the themes as much as possible.

tive utterances which are printed in *Philosophical Papers*.[31] "I want to discuss," he says,

> a kind of utterance which looks like a statement and grammatically, I suppose, would be classed as a statement, which is not nonsensical, and yet is not true or false. . . . They will be perfectly straightforward utterances, with ordinary verbs in the first person singular present indicative active, and yet we shall see at once that they couldn't possibly be true or false. Furthermore, if a person makes an utterance of this sort we should say that he is *doing* something rather than merely *saying* something. This may sound a little odd, but the examples I shall give will in fact not be odd at all, and may even seem decidedly dull. Here are three or four. Suppose, for example, that in the course of a marriage ceremony I say, as people will, 'I do' (sc. take this woman to be my lawful wedded wife). Or again, suppose that I tread on your toe and say 'I apologize.' Or again, suppose that I have a bottle of champagne in my hand and say 'I name this ship the *Queen Elizabeth*.' Or suppose I say 'I bet you sixpence it will rain tomorrow.' In all these cases it would be absurd to regard the thing that I say as a report of the performance of the action which is undoubtedly done—the action of betting, or christening, or apologizing. We should say rather that, in saying what I do, I actually perform that action. When I say 'I name this ship the *Queen Elizabeth*' I do not describe the christening ceremony, I actually perform the christening; and when I say 'I do' (sc. take this woman to be my lawful wedded wife), I am not reporting on a marriage, I am indulging in it. Now these kinds of utterances are the ones that we call *performative* utterances.[32]

He then faces a possible misunderstanding: At this point, he says:

> One might protest, perhaps even with some alarm, that I seem to be suggesting that marrying is simply saying a few words, that just saying a few words is marrying. Well that

31. Pp. 220-239.
32. *Ibid.*, p. 222.

certainly is not the case. The words have to be said in the appropriate circumstances, and this is a matter that will come up again later.[33]

But he then rejects one possible account of where the significance of performatives lies. "The one thing we must not suppose," he says,

> is that what is needed in addition to the saying of the words in such cases is the performance of some internal spiritual act, of which the words then are to be the report. It's very easy to slip into this view at least in difficult, portentous cases, though perhaps not so easy in simple cases like apologizing. In the case of promising—for example, 'I promise to be there tomorrow'—it's very easy to think that the utterance is simply the outward and visible (that is, verbal) sign of the performance of some inward spiritual act of promising, and this view has certainly been expressed in many classic places. There is the case of Euripides' Hippolytus, who said, 'My tongue swore to, but my heart did not'—perhaps it should be 'mind' or 'spirit' rather than 'heart,' but at any rate some kind of backstage artiste. Now it is clear from this sort of example that, if we slip into thinking that such utterances are reports, true or false, of the performance of inward and spiritual acts, we open a loop-hole to perjurers and welshers and bigamists and so on, so that there are disadvantages in being excessively solemn in this way. It is better, perhaps, to stick to the old saying that our word is our bond.[34]

It is perfectly evident that Austin is suspicious of any metaphysical overtones, and in particular is very critical of such a phrase as "inward and spiritual acts."

With this explication of performative utterances, and keeping in mind this note of caution which Austin sounds in a metaphysical direction (for I shall return to it presently), let us now pass to a later section of the chapter where Austin considers the question: How can we be sure whether an utterance has to be

33. This point is not discussed in the present article. It relates to Austin's specifying conditions under which the utterance of words may be infelicitous and so on.

34. *Ibid.*, p. 223.

INTELLECT AND HOPE

classed as a performative? Are there, he asks, any criteria, e.g., of
verbal form, to guide us? We would obviously very much like, he
says, to discover some grammatical criterion for performatives,
"some grammatical means of deciding whether an utterance is
performative,"[35] and it might seem as if he had found one—that
all performative utterances are in the first person singular present
indicative active:

> All the examples I have given hitherto do in fact have the
> same grammatical form; they all of them begin with the
> verb in the first person singular present indicative ac-
> tive—not just any kind of verb of course, but still they all
> are in fact of that form. Furthermore, with these verbs that
> I have used there is a typical asymmetry between the use of
> this person and tense of the verb and the use of the same
> verb in other persons and tenses, and this asymmetry is
> rather an important clue. For example, when we say 'I
> promise that . . . ,' the case is very different from when we
> say, 'He promises that . . . ,' or in the past tense 'I prom-
> ised that . . . .' For when we say 'I promise that . . .' we do
> perform an act of promising—we give a promise. What we
> do *not* do is to report on somebody's performing an act of
> promising—in particular we do not report on somebody's
> use of the expression 'I promise.' We actually do use it and
> do the promising. But if I say 'He promises,' or in the past
> tense 'I promised,' I precisely do report on an act of promis-
> ing, that is to say an act of using this formula 'I promise'—I
> report on a present act of promising by him, or on a past act
> of my own. There is thus a clear difference between our first
> person singular present indicative active, and other persons
> and tenses.[36]

But, argues Austin, this is not a necessary condition. For there
is, he claims, at least one other standard form. It is "every bit as
common" as the first person present indicative forms, and it is
one

> where the verb is in the passive voice and in the second or
> third person, not in the first. The sort of case I mean is that

35. *Ibid.*, p. 228.
36. *Ibid.*, pp. 228-229.

of a notice inscribed 'Passengers are warned to cross the line by the bridge only,' or of a document reading 'You are hereby authorized' to do so-and-so. These are undoubtedly performative, and in fact a signature is often required in order to show who it is that is doing the act of warning, or authorizing, or whatever it may be. Very typical of this kind of performative—especially liable to occur in written documents of course—is that the little word 'hereby' either actually occurs or might naturally be inserted.[37]

The matter, he argues, is in fact more complicated still:

Unfortunately, however, we still can't possibly suggest that every utterance which is to be classed as a performative has to take one or another of these two, as we might call them, standard forms. After all it would be a very typical performative utterance to say 'I order you to shut the door.' This satisfies all the criteria. It is performing the act of ordering you to shut the door, and it is not true or false. But in the appropriate circumstances surely we could perform exactly the same act by simply saying 'Shut the door,' in the imperative. Or again, suppose that somebody sticks up a notice 'This bull is dangerous,' or simply 'Dangerous bull,' or simply 'Bull.' Does this necessarily differ from sticking up a notice, appropriately signed, saying 'You are hereby warned that this bull is dangerous?' It seems that the simple notice 'Bull' can do just the same job as the more elaborate formula. Of course the difference is that if we just stick up 'Bull' it would not be quite clear that it is a warning; it might be there just for interest or information, like 'Wallaby' on the cage at the zoo, or 'Ancient Monument.' No doubt we should know from the nature of the case that it was a warning, but it would not be explicit.[38]

On the other hand he suggests that perhaps all the various forms might after all be so rewritten as to become one or other of the two standard forms—and I suggest that the reader notes some of the phrases which occur in the following passage viz: "There is a good deal in this," and "To some extent" there's "justification for this hope," phrases which indicate perhaps a reluctance to get

37. *Ibid.*, pp. 229-230.
38. *Ibid.*, p. 230.

to closer grips with the point, still more to recognize that it might
have wider, even metaphysical implications:

> In view of this breakdown of grammatical criteria, what we
> should like to suppose—and there is a good deal in this—is
> that any utterance which is performative could be reduced
> or expanded or analyzed into one of these two standard
> forms beginning—'I . . .' so and so, or beginning 'You (or
> he) hereby . . .' so and so. If there was any justification for
> this hope, as to some extent there is, then we might hope to
> make a list of all the verbs which can appear in these
> standard forms, and then we might classify the kinds of acts
> that can be performed by performative utterances.[39]

Whether Austin was reluctant or not, at any rate I myself will
not hesitate to go further, and I suggest that it was Austin's lack
of interest in, or perhaps aversion to, any possible metaphysical
implications, that prevented him from seeing that the grammatical diversity—even duality—was not ultimate; and that indeed
the first person present indicative active is characteristic of all
performative utterances, which are in this way peculiarly and
manifestly self-involving.

Consider, for example, the cases which Austin gives of second
or third person passive utterances, e.g., "Passengers are warned to
cross the line by the bridge only" or, on some document, "You
are hereby authorized to . . . .' All such sentences or phrases,
despite their grammatical appearance, occur in a first person
frame, and it is the important function of 'little' words like
"hereby," or 'little' phrases like "By order," to point to this first
person setting which is needful to give the utterance its performative character, to make it e.g., a warning. Like many other little
words they are logically crucial, and express a whole social and
verbal setting. For example, "By order" on a railway notice board
is equivalent to saying "Here I am, the Secretary of the British
Transport Commission, warning you . . . ," and if time and
health and practical possibilities allowed, the notice could be
replaced by the Secretary himself standing there warning each
passenger. "Hereby" on a particular document can again be

39. *Ibid.*

replaced by a first person frame originating in (say) the Controller's office of some Atomic Energy Research Authority.

In short, there are not two standards of performative utterance as Austin seems to think. The first person present indicative active is the logical paradigm, and performatives, precisely because they have this logical character, are important for the self-involvement they express;[40] indeed their logical interest and the self-involvement factor stand (or fall) together. In this connection it is very significant from my argument that this element of self-involvement becomes very evident even for Austin when, earlier in *Philosophical Papers*[41] he considered the particular performative utterance "I promise."

> When I say 'I promise,' a new plunge is taken: I have not merely announced my intention, but, by using this formula (performing this ritual), I have bound myself to others, and staked my reputation, in a new way. Similarly, saying 'I know' is taking a new plunge. But it is *not* saying 'I have performed a specially striking feat of cognition, superior, in the same scale as believing and being sure, even to being merely quite sure': for there *is* nothing in that scale superior to being quite sure. Just as promising is not something superior, in the same scale as hoping and intending, even to merely fully intending: for there *is* nothing in that scale superior to fully intending. When I say 'I know,' I *give others my word*: I *give others my authority for saying* that 'S is P.'[42]

Notice that, in Austin's phrases, when I perform this 'ritual' of promising, I "stake my reputation," "bind myself to others," "give others my authority" or "my word"—where obviously to "give others my word" is *not* here just to make noises at them, or even merely to communicate. Promising involves, as Austin says, a "new plunge,"[43] which is precisely what we do when we respond

40. Dr. D. D. Evans has explicated some of the theological implications of this self-involvement in his *Logic of Self-Involvement* (London: S.C.M. Press, 1963).
41. And some ten years earlier in time.
42. *Philosophical Papers*, p. 67. (Italics in the original.) It is interesting that in a footnote on pp. 66-67, Austin again explains the importance of the first person present indicative.
43. Here is another phrase indicative of disclosure.

to the challenge of a disclosure, to an obligation disclosed around the circumstances which become the subject of a promise.

We may now broaden the picture even further. We may well ask: Are there ever any non-performatives, any utterances in which I am not in any way 'involved'; are there any utterances which are in no way self-affirming? Have not *all* utterances *some* illocutionary force, as Austin later came to call this doing-in-saying characteristic? Do any assertions *merely say*—at least any assertions which are *personally* uttered as distinct from being mouthed or uttered by some answering service? Does not Austin's concept of speech-act itself suggest the contrary? As he himself says in *How to Do Things with Words*, "the more we consider a statement not as a sentence (or proposition) but as an act of speech (out of which the others are logical constructions) the more we are studying the whole thing as an act."[44] In such a case (I suggest) every sentence (or proposition) is in one way or another self-involving. My own supplementary suggestion would be that it is the logical constants in an assertion that ensure, for all utterances, that we *do* something more than merely *say* the words.[45] Of course I readily grant, as this reflection itself makes evident, that we involve ourselves in our utterances in vastly different ways, and the performative force of utterances like "I promise" or "I take thee to my wedded wife" or "I name this ship the *Maurotania*" is of far more crucial importance than it is in, say, "The angle of incidence is equal to the angle of reflection."[46] But even this utterance of a law of reflection is an utterance which becomes a performative in my saying it in a context where I am teaching. For it then becomes what W. Zuurdeeg called "convictional language,"[47] which brings us very conveniently to Polanyi, who, I shall argue, in his concept of 'personal knowledge' shows many similarities to Austin's position.

Polanyi, in his *Personal Knowledge*, speaks of 'assertions' in ways very reminiscent of Austin's 'speech-acts.' For example, he remarks that "a sincere allegation is an act that takes place in

44. Ed. J. O. Urmson and G. J. Warnock (London: Oxford University Press, 1962), p. 20.
45. Following the suggestion of Berkeley, who shrewdly saw that verbal "particles" were closely linked with his doctrine of notions.
46. *Vide,* William Poteat's essay in this volume, pp. 198 ff.
47. *An Analytical Philosophy of Religion* (London: Allen & Unwin, 1959).

speaking or in writing down certain symbols. Its agent is the speaking or writing person."[48] Here is a view of assertions as self-involving, and the element of personal commitment which is not to be contained in any 'impersonal' logic of 'strict criteria,' is made even more evident later in the book when he remarks that

> only a speaker or listener can mean something *by* a word, and a word *in itself* can mean nothing. When the act of meaning is thus brought home to a person exercising his understanding of things by the use of words which describe them, the possibility of performing the act of meaning according to strict criteria appears logically meaningless. For any strictly formal operation would be impersonal and could not therefore convey the speaker's personal commitment.[49]

He develops his view of assertions a little later, and relates it to his concept of comprehension or tacit knowledge when he remarks that "an articulate assertion is composed of two parts: a sentence conveying the content of what is asserted and a tacit act by which this sentence is asserted"[50]—here is the distinction again between knowledge of particulars or 'clues,' and a full comprehension—and he recalls that this distinction has some similarity to R. M. Hare's distinction between the "phrastic" and "neustic" components of an assertion.[51] He remarks, of course, that

> The act of assertion itself does not, of course, consist of two parts—one tacit, the other articulate—of which the first can be cancelled while the second, now unasserted, can be tested by confrontation with the facts. It is an act of tacit comprehension, which relies altogether on the self-satisfaction of the person who performs it. It can be repeated, improved, or cancelled, but not tested, or said to be true, in the same sense in which a factual statement can be tested and said to be true.[52]

48. *P.K.*, p. 27.
49. *Ibid.*, p. 252.
50. *Ibid.*, p. 254.
51. R. M. Hare, *The Language of Morals* (Oxford: Oxford University Press, 1952), p. 18, where phrastic relates to the features of the world that a sentence indicates, and neustic relates to that "nodding assent" by which we make the sentence our own.
52. *P.K.*, p. 254.

He continues:

> Therefore, if '*p* is true' expresses my assertion or reassertion
> of the sentence *p*, then '*p* is true' cannot be said to be true
> or false in the sense in which a factual sentence can. '*p* is
> true' declares that I identify myself with the content of the
> factual sentence *p*, and this identification is something I am
> doing, and not a fact that I am observing. The expression '*p*
> is true' is therefore not itself a sentence but merely the
> assertion of (an otherwise unasserted) sentence, the sen-
> tence *p*. To say that '*p* is true' is to underwrite a commit-
> ment or to sign an acceptance, in a sense akin to the
> commercial meaning of such acts.[53]

By thus regarding "p is true" as declaratory and self-involving,
registering an act of commitment though it has the form of a
sentence stating a fact, Polanyi realizes that his position is reminiscent of Max Black's "No truth theory of truth," and Strawson's critique of the semantic theory: but he also realizes that he
differs from both in so far as he is attempting to "accredit the use
of 'truth' as part of an a-critical act of affirmation."[54] It is in these
ways that tacit comprehension for Polanyi leads at once to a
theory of knowledge as 'personal' and to the view of 'truth' as a
commitment word, a word registering a self-affirmation.

As Thomas A. Langford remarks in an essay on "Michael
Polanyi and the Task of Theology":

> Polanyi . . . not only talks about the role of tacit compre-
> hension in knowledge, he makes it an integral part of his
> theory of knowing. He does not simply allow for it, as a
> maverick intrusion, he argues that it must be given a basic
> position in the comprehension of reality. Tacit knowledge
> is primary because it *establishes coherence* by the powers of
> perception, conceptualization, speculative imagination, and
> skilful effort. To take Polanyi seriously is to recognize a
> forthright challenge to the usual and 'official' understand-
> ing of scientific-intellectual enquiry. Empirical investiga-
> tion has now been taken into a context that insists upon the
> dimension of personal decision and commitment.[55]

53. *Ibid.*
54. *Ibid.*, p. 255 n.
55. *Journal of Religion*, XLVI, No. 1, Part 1 (Jan., 1966), 47.

He "insists that all thinking involves the total person in relation to his appropriated context."[56]

So both Austin and Polanyi recognize the ultimacy for epistemology of the personal act of affirmation, of the speech act. But what Austin does not recognize, while for Polanyi it is of great importance, is that such personal participation in talking and knowing eludes interpretation in terms of empirical 'impersonal' data. In this sense there is involved for Polanyi, in talking about the self-involving character of knowledge, a metaphysical claim; and from his view personal participation is presupposed by, and is never reducible to the scientific, factual "content" or "clues" which only point to the full, personal comprehension which transcends them.

As I have said already, Austin seems to me to neglect these metaphysical implications of his doctrine of performatives, of words used with illocutionary force; Polanyi, on the contrary, relishes them. On any view of knowledge, he says, other than the one which highlights the need for personal participation, "Man dominates a world in which he himself does not exist. For with his obligations he has lost his voice and his hope, and been left behind meaningless to himself."[57] This is the case, for example, with "the ideal of scientific detachment,"[58] which, as we saw earlier, he rejects. As Langford expresses it, Polanyi

> has argued that we have no more reliable grounds for our knowledge claims than these acts of personal discrimination, whether they are our own or those to which we happen to subscribe personally, since appeals to 'objective fact,' 'empirical data,' or 'formal rules of explicit inference' are, at bottom, no more than what a community of inquiry accepts them to be (that is, when members of this community are acting as persons making claims having universal intent). Hence, logically, these appeals have the same sort of backing and are no less precarious than other types of personal decisions. Far from altering the procedures by which we would know and do scientifically, this is merely a description of the means by which we have, in fact, worked

56. *Ibid.*, p. 48.
57. *P.K.*, p. 380.
58. *Ibid.*, p. vii.

and prospered in science, notwithstanding the regnancy of a general misdescription. The first result of this investigation is, then, the assertion of the primal place that personal expectation, hope, and commitment have in every act of knowing.[59]

The "false ideal of scientific detachment," he says, "exercises a destructive influence in biology, psychology, and sociology, and falsifies our whole outlook far beyond the domain of science."[60]

At this point we may, I think, usefully take up again the theme of disclosures, and see how it can be used further to illuminate Austin's account of performative utterances and Polanyi's account of personal knowledge, and at the same time show more clearly the point where metaphysical claims may arise. Turning first to Austin, are not promises a way of articulating our response to the claims, disclosure-given, of some person to whom we made our promise in the setting of a particular kind of situation? More broadly, are not all speech-acts responses to the claims, disclosure-given, of our environment? The environment, ceasing to be dead, formal, 'impersonal,' discloses a claim and we cease to be tongue-tied, we come alive and respond in some appropriate speech-act. Only in this way, I suggest, as a response to some disclosure do we make self-involving assertions, participate in the world, respond to some claim, and so on. It is when a situation 'takes on depth,' 'comes alive,' becomes the occasion of a disclosure that we respond characteristically with some form of self-affirmation or self-involvement; it is then that we, too, 'come alive' in a self-disclosure, to initiate a speech-act, a promise and so on.

Further, if, as Polanyi argues, such self-disclosure transcends the impersonal criteria which are its objects—and this I would say follows from the fact that self-disclosure discloses our subjectivity—which can (logically) never be reduced to third person 'objects,'[61] there arises the possibility of our associating chastened

59. Op. cit.
60. P.K., p. vii.
61. For a fuller discussion of this crucial point see, e.g., my paper in Biology and Personality, ed. I. T. Ramsey (Oxford: Blackwell, 1965); esp. pp. 178-186. The same point I believe lies behind Polanyi's contention which we noticed above, that 'impersonal,' 'strict criteria' cannot do justice to personal commitment.

metaphysical claims with self-involving assertions—whether Austin's performative utterances or Polanyi's personal knowledge. It need not be the crude metaphysics which Austin rather laughs aside. The point is rather that here in performative utterances or personal knowledge is a self-involvement, a personal 'inwardness,' 'spiritual' at least in the sense of not being reducible to impersonal criteria or objects, the distinct perception of Hume. This is why performative utterances are the significant utterances they are. They belong to personally significant situations going beyond "observables." Can they not still be spoken of, albeit with logical or ontological circumspectives, in terms of words like "inward" or "spiritual"?

At any rate, Polanyi with his claim for personal participation and involvement, Austin with his doctrine of performatives and speech-acts are similar in seeing that many—and perhaps all— assertions have a self-involving character which an oversimplified empiricism, traditional scientific theorizing and much traditional philosophical speculation overlooked. My point has been that this self-involving character, and all that it implies, can be further elucidated by interpreting both Austin and Polanyi in terms of the concept of disclosures, which in this way supplements both their views. That it further permits of some metaphysics is for me no disaster, and even words like "inward" and "spiritual" might be rehabilitated in this context.

But there remains one issue which Polanyi's exposition explicitly raises, and it is an issue which takes us back to our first theme. It is an issue which Austin's narrower concerns do not explicitly raise. The issue is this. If there is self-involvement in knowing or speaking, if there is this personal factor in knowledge, do we not make knowledge 'subjective'? Has 'objectivity' to be analyzed merely in terms of the agreement which exists between those who make assertions? Polanyi is quite clear about his own answer. In the Preface to *Personal Knowledge* he says of his view that there is a *"personal participation* of the knower in all acts of understanding," that it

> does not make our understanding *subjective.* Comprehension is neither an arbitrary act nor a passive experience, but a responsible act claiming universal validity. Such knowing

is indeed *objective* in the sense of establishing contact with
a hidden reality; a contact that is defined as the condition
for anticipating an indeterminate range of yet unknown
(and perhaps yet unconceivable) true implications.[62]

But how *does* this knowing establish "contact with a hidden
reality," how can it claim to be objective? We are back with the
reference problem with which we began.

My answer now, as before, is that we do not ourselves make
contact with, establish our hold on some 'hidden reality.' To
suppose that is to make a myth-eaten error. Rather does the
'hidden reality' establish contact with us by disclosing itself to us.
For, as I argued earlier, comprehension is grounded in a disclosure. 'Tacit knowledge' is certainly not tacit in being the passive
acceptance of some 'empirical data'—this is one reason why I am
less than happy with the adjective "tacit." Precisely because tacit
knowledge (so called) arises disclosure-wise, being knowledge of
what discloses itself to us as other than ourselves, Polanyi's theory
can make sense of objectivity. Even though knowledge is personal
it is not subjective. I suggest, then, from various directions that
the concept of disclosure can give to Polanyi's view a greater
coherence, as well as helping it to face more adequately problems
which are implicit in its very novelty and audacity. My suggestion is that we might summarize his position by saying that all
comprehension, all assertions, arise in a disclosure situation
where objectivity, objective reference, is safeguarded precisely in
so far as something other than ourselves discloses itself to us;
comprehension and personal knowledge arise as a matching response.

What I have suggested then is that the self-involving character
of knowledge implied both in Austin's doctrine of performatives
and in Polanyi's account of personal knowledge points back to
and can be illuminatingly interpreted in terms of disclosures,
which can also assure Polanyi of the objectivity he needs as well
as relating more adequately comprehension and tacit knowledge
on the one hand, and knowledge of criteria or particulars on the
other. I have further suggested that because Austin was so critical

62. *P.K.,* pp. xiii-xiv. (Italics in the original.)

of metaphysics of the old brand he did not see that what was significant about performatives was their first-person logic, pointing to their grounding in self-disclosure, which then allows for and involves, I would say, some metaphysical claims in so far as the personal subjectivity given in self-disclosure and affirmed in performative utterances cannot be reduced to 'objects,' to impersonal criteria.

Disclosure theory, then, can provide for both Polanyi and Austin a supplement which, in the case of Polanyi, makes his view the more coherent as well as meeting more satisfactorily his difficulties—first or last—over reference and objectivity: and in the case of Austin, it clarifies his epistemology and draws out the significance—even the metaphysical significance—of his doctrine of performatives. I am far from supposing that Austin, if he were alive, would readily agree with, still less rejoice in, such suggestions; but perhaps they will be more welcome to Michael Polanyi. At least they are offered in that hope.

MYTHS, STORIES, HISTORY, ESCHATOLOGY AND ACTION: SOME POLANYIAN MEDITATIONS

William H. Poteat

I

In this essay I shall talk about man and language from a perspective opened up for me by the writings of Michael Polanyi.[1] I am concerned first to show some modalities of my relation to my spoken and written words; how these issue in more or less tacit forms—among them: myths, stories, and histories; how each form may afford different ways of indwelling the ambience of my world (or of participating in the many different levels of Reality). Then I shall suggest that displaying these helps us to see something of the many forms of personal existence open to me. I shall conclude by suggesting the bearing of this new perspective upon some of the notorious perplexities over the meaning of myths, stories, and history; and of the language of theology and of religious performances generated by the lingering ethos of positivism.

A

Being-in-the-world and moving from within my own body towards its many horizons of thought-action goes on most of the time without my having explicitly to attend to the process of

1. It is impossible to give specific references in the Polanyi corpus which, thus examined out of context, could yield the views I am here developing. It is the impact of the corpus as a whole which has educed these meditations.

integration which, taken globally, *is* my being-in-the-world. Some of the modalities of my being-in-the-world are the differing relations I may have to the more or less tacit articulate systems of language. In general, most of the time, integration among *these* occurs in a fashion analogous to that in which somatic particulars are tacitly integrated into even the simplest bodily movement. Indeed, movement, expressive gesture, ritual, speech, reflection, and wonder are all modes of my being-in-the-world.

No formal or explicit—or at least exhaustively explicit—specification of the integration among the varying logical neighborhoods of articulate speech or among the strata of Being within which, as a person, I quite unproblematically live most of the time is possible. Yet my existence is on the whole more or less personal and most of the time moderately integral because an integration is constantly going on in tacit ways.

First, I take it for granted that we all use words, that once upon a time each of us did not, and therefore that we all at some time had to learn to do so. Giving an account of how we do and how we did, I believe, would take us to the very prelingual ground of human intelligence. The wonder of it all is obscured by the fact that this initiation into speech and its skilful use is always going on all about us; and also by the fact that if we do start wondering about it, the closer we draw to the prelingual ground of human intelligence the more difficult it becomes to say what it is we see, until finally it becomes impossible to say.

When I am speaking more or less skilfully and unselfconsciously, my words are in my body somewhat as a musician's performance is in his before he has performed it, making their way toward the tip of my tongue, each bearing its still indeterminate intimations of its own propriety which only become somewhat more determinate at that moment when, letting it loose into the world, I discern and acknowledge this propriety, however tacitly. This active-passive quality of my relation to my own utterances is, I believe, primitive and irreducible. It parallels Polanyi's tacit-explicit, subsidiary-focal, proximal-distal, attending-from—attending-to dichotomies and suggests as well the vectorial relation of the terms of the dichotomy: *given—the received.*

Paul Cézanne said: "I wait until the landscape thinks itself in me." And when I see his landscapes, I believe he very often did and that *it* very often did. To believe this is of course not at all to believe that Paul Cézanne was somehow disingenuous to sign "P. Cézanne" in the corner of "The Quarry at Bibemus" instead of signing it, say, "Q. at Bibemus!" Speaking too is like this. Learning to speak is perhaps also like this. The word speaks itself in me and having spoken itself in me, I speak it; having intimated its propriety to me, I greet it as my own—often with a feeling of surprise, occasionally with something stronger.

It is for this reason, no doubt, that each word, the propriety of which I come tacitly to acknowledge as I launch it into the world after its companions, already there, and just ahead of those waiting in their time to be noticed, seems at once both absolutely new and pre-existent: absolutely new as a unique doing in a recognizably unique but indeterminate context; pre-existent as an indeterminate intimation of its own propriety; pre-existent also in the legacy of my native tongue.

Second, I shall assume, what seems to me not only consistent with but actually entailed by my first assumption, that each of us emerges from a prereflective, anonymous background into the increasingly personal existence of bearing a proper name and reflexively using the pronoun in the first person. We move out of a prepersonal, prehistorical background which is an indeterminate ground-meaning and ground-being from which we are projected into history and a more fully personal existence, while nevertheless always bearing within ourselves roots that reach into this anonymous background—even as Cézanne's landscapes bear within them their rootage in his body in its landscape.[2]

Every significant configuration, whether the mere orderly mo-

2. One might put the matter so: When I notice what it is like to be a person and try to say, among the many possible things I might say are: 1. "I exist as a person because I have emerged from a prereflective background into the reflective existence of having been *given* a proper name and of having been *enabled* to answer to it and of having been *given* my native language with the pronominal resources in it for making reflexive references to myself." When I talk this way, if I attend to what I say, I will be inclined to notice the sense in which personhood is a *gift*, that I am not my own author. It is this I think that issues in the many forms of the ontological 'argument'! 2. On the other hand, I may say, "I exist as a person because I have *received* this gift, appropriated it as my own, thereby becoming the author of deeds [if asked: 'Who did this?,' I reply: 'I did!'] the agent of very particular acts, the integration of many intentions."

tility of my body, a spontaneous expressive gesture, an impromptu dance, 'choreographed'[3] by nothing more reflective than the affects that inspire it and the body's limits which embody it, a religious rite, a declaration of love, a Petrarchan sonnet, a general theory of the universe as it is for macrophysics—all these are importantly alike (they are rooted in my body) and importantly different (the last in the series seems abstract and distanced from its somatic origins as the first does not.) The last therefore may seem equivocal and dubitable as to its vectorial relation to my world as the first does not.

I do not in fact hold the view that as we move over the range from the first case to the last we move from what is immediate and indubitable (some people have a most equivocal and tentative relation to their own motility) towards what is mediated and hence inherently dubitable. It serves my purpose here, however, to pretend that this is so invariably in order to suggest that to the many significant configurations which comprise my world I bear very different relations ranging from some which are immediate, unequivocal, and manifestly and indubitably bound into that world, to others which are mediated (through, e.g., reflection), equivocal, and having a dubitable vectorial thrust towards and anchorage in something other than the configuration itself.

This brings me to the third and final presupposition to which it seems important to call particular attention: that, namely, having to do with the relation between language (or articulate speech) and Reality. Obviously, the making of it is already clearly foreshadowed in the foregoing.

When we have achieved that modality of being-in-the-world which is articulate personal utterance, we also are reflective in the highest degree—given thereby at once our highest powers of articulate affirmation and our most sophisticated forms of equivocation. Only highly developed languages have the explicit grammatical resources for distinguishing among moods—or modes: indicative, subjunctive, optative, vocative, etc. Don Giovanni hesitates not at all—"purchè porti la gonella voi sapete quel che fa!" Faust's and Hamlet's inner life in their worlds is not to be

3. Throughout I shall use single quotation marks to call attention to an odd, equivocal or, in context, logically heterogeneous use of a word or concept; and I shall use double quotation marks where I mean to be directing attention *to* the word or concept rather than using it to another end.

compared with his; reflection—especially in its subjunctive mood—forces its way in upon them.

How then can we always be sure? The answer of course is that we cannot be. But if we *never* were, if there were no prelingual, prereflective Eden in which we confidently moved outward toward the limits of the world, the memory of which, be it ever so tacit, we bear within us at every moment, then there would be no reflection and we could not reflectively entertain our hesitations.[4]

4. This is really to say that if the self were ever a wholly deracinate and absolutely lucid for-itself then, paradoxically, the conditions for the existence of such an entity would not be fulfilled and there could therefore equally be neither a self nor another. The import of this for the existence of an articulate framework such as one's natural language is that only on condition that *it* has its roots in an inarticulate and, to that language, opaque somatic intimation of itself in prepersonal configurations (upon which we tacitly rely) can there be such natural languages. The notorious history of our doubts about the bearing of language upon something other than itself (which perhaps extends as far back at least as Occam) results from the insistent belief that language is *not* prefigured in prelingual somatic intimations of itself. This has its significance for moral philosophy as well. Even those human acts which are entered upon with utmost lucidity have their origin in and retain their relation to my prereflective presence in the world (upon which I tacitly rely) and issue in consequences which I not only cannot foresee, but which in fact remain forever opaque. Whatever it is that bears my name therefore cannot be affiliated *only* with or exhaustively assimilated to these *lucid* volitions. (This insight I owe to Professor John Silber). Also cf. M. Merleau-Ponty, *The Phenomenology of Perception,* trans. Colin Smith (London: Routledge and Kegan Paul, 1962) : "The other person is never quite a personal being, if I myself am totally one . . . ," p. 352, *et passim.* Finally this means that I cannot explicitly say what it is to be a self (person) because it is always an integration of the particulars of my body-in-the-world with (from the natural standpoint) its many different levels of reality and the principles governing the integration of each level through the determination of the boundary conditions left open by the principles governing the particulars in themselves at the next lower level. Also it is an integration of all my skills—motor and intellectual—of my formalized, reversible, and articulate as well as my unformalized and largely unformalizable intellectual, moral, and aesthetic powers of discrimination to a firmament of values and obligations. And, finally, it is an integration of all these to anticipatory, heuristic powers. This integration is paradigmatically achieved in the act of comprehendingly using, with its always reflective force, the pronoun in the first person singular—within the context of our language and all its personal pronominal resources.

Any attempt to specify the nature of this comprehensive entity (to which reflexive reference is made) through the detailing of the particulars by relying upon which I perform this feat of integration must result in its destruction, in some measure; on the other hand, any attempt to assimilate the self to the mere act of uttering the first personal pronoun, be it ever so lucid, is to make the self less than an integration of the particulars of my being-in-the-world with its past, present, and future.

However, I must recognize both that, on one hand (from the natural standpoint), there is a stratification of organismic structures, skills, and

The subjunctive mood is, ontologically, parasitical upon a primordial indicative.

In all our personal acts of articulate assertion, whether of propositions concerning particular matters of fact, of general theories, of a comprehensive view of the universe, or even in more tentative heuristic explorations of the as yet unarticulated, we are relying proximally upon our inarticulate, tacit, and always incorrigible commitment to the privileged and paradigmatic reality for each of us of our own bodies in a world. This commitment, which we hold acritically, inarticulately, and tacitly, operates proximally as the token of the bearing upon Reality of our distal assertions of particular propositions which, if we do indeed *assert* them, we hold to be true.

Now, since assertions of particular facts are explicit and are made within an articulate framework, we do not hold either them or their bearing upon Reality (which is a question of a logically different order) acritically. Even so, because of our tacit, acritical commitment to Reality in our being-in-our-own-bodies-in-a-world, we cannot in good faith *assert* as true a particular articulate proposition concerning a matter of fact without *in the very same* act tacitly asserting its bearing upon Reality. The tacit-explicit poles are primitively, acritically given.[5]

---

formalized intellectual powers which provides the ground conditions for some measure of continuity through time or for personal identity; and, on the other, that each new feat of integration is unique, an achievement, and therefore was, before its achievement, liable to failure.

I cannot explicitly say, then, what the self is because when I am performing that feat which is the ultimate mark and norm of its reality, namely, reflexive self-reference, I am dwelling in an integration by relying upon largely unspecifiable particulars. To *attend from* the integration in which I dwell in order to *attend to* the particulars which jointly constitute it is to lose the ultimate focus which enables me to avoid identifying myself either with my body *simpliciter* or alternatively with the mere act of lucid choice or reflexive self-reference.

The making of promises, the putting of my personal seal upon a decision by saying, "I promise," "I have decided," is merely the final and highest act of integration in a hierarchy of integrations and, as such, may be called my subscription to myself. Through this subscription, at once tacit and explicit, I lay claim and come to have a relation to the particulars of my-body-and-its-past-in-the-world which is a *personal* one. (*Vide* n. 21 below for the bearing of these observations upon some Christian theological claims.)

5. Cf. ". . . we are dealing with an urge towards an affirmation—yet an affirmation which it seems impossible to make, since it is not until it has been made that I can regard myself as qualified to make it. It should be noted that this difficulty never arises at a time when I am actually faced with a problem

How is it plausible to make such a claim?

All propositions which are asserted *can* be noncommittally *stated*—formulated, if you like in a subjunctive modality. The bearing of such a noncommittally stated proposition upon Reality *can be*—one is tempted to say, in the light of the philosophic tradition since Descartes, *more than likely will be*—noncommittally evaluated. When, however, a proposition is *asserted*, its bearing upon Reality can only be committally evaluated; which is to say, in the light of our precritical and proximal reliance upon our own bodies as the primordial and indubitable token and paradigm of Reality, with the consequent conviction that all propositions held by ourselves to be true are disclosures of that Reality.[6]

Such are some of the relations among personal acts of assertion, the claims of truth for them and claims of their bearing upon Reality.

B

But before going further with these words about words, I wish to enter a general *caveat* concerning concern with words. In a

---

to be solved. In such a case I work on the data, but everything leads me to believe that I need not take into account the *I* who is at work—it is a factor which is presupposed and nothing more. Here, on the contrary, what I would call the ontological status of the investigator assumes a decisive importance. Yet so long as I am concerned with thought itself I seem to follow an endless regression. But by the very fact of recognizing it as endless I transcend it in a certain way: I see that this process takes place within an affirmation of being—an affirmation which I *am* rather than an affirmation which I *utter*: by uttering it I break it, I divide it, I am on the point of betraying it." Gabriel Marcel, *The Philosophy of Existentialism*, trans. Manya Harari (New York: The Citadel Press, 1963), pp. 17-18. There are striking parallels between Polanyi's tacit-explicit, proximal-distal dichotomies and Marcel's problem-mystery dichotomy, especially in their use for ontological analysis.

The reader is also referred to the very different but cognate findings of the student of human development, Erik Erikson, whose "psychological" reflections upon our ways of being-in-the-world are of great import. See Erik Erikson, *Childhood and Society* (2d ed.; New York: W. W. Norton and Co., 1963), pp. 247 ff.

6. This elucidation must strike non-philosophers as at best an ingenious feat devised to triumph over a difficulty which common sense would never allow to arise. This is in fact the case. But philosophy in the modern period and the sciences and even theory-laden common sense which get their own theories about knowing and doing *from* this philosophic tradition are so ubiquitously infected by this "subjunctivitis" that only a more radical form of reflection can overcome it!

way, once the subject is brought up, it almost immediately becomes a dangerous and profoundly misleading preoccupation.
We find ourselves trying to talk our way into and out of different
ways of being in the taken-for-granted world of our existence.
And this easily leads to our coming to believe that our ways of
being-in-the-world are primitively and primarily formed and
maintained by various tissues of words—words sighed, words
asserted, declaimed, invoked, performed, and uttered straight, or
uttered in quotes, or with exclamation marks and question
marks—whether written out or implied in our inflection, in our
raised eyebrows, or whatnot. And while I do not wish to say that
this may not be so, or so often or so sometimes, I want to insist
that many things that are not in any sense words or tissues of
words and that bear very few analogies with them are nonetheless
bearers of meanings and significances and hence are conveyors of
order by means of which or 'in' which we have our several ways
of being-in-the-world: things like colors—alone or in combination; sounds, alone or combined, either simultaneously or successively—or both—with a tempo-relation varying variously with
our pulse rate and hence with our stride, our gait, and our
gestures; linear configurations which reproduce or vary from the
archetypal horizontal or vertical axes of that radical locus in the
world for each of us, our own body, or which are the actual traces
of the gestures of that body or those of some other like it; things,
too, like masses, large in relation to the primitive mass which is
our own body, or small; or hard, powerful, overwhelming, like
Stonehenge or St. Peter's; or grand, intricate, rational, humane,
but numinous like Chartres; or soft, minute, delicate, rare.

All these have an integrity of their own as presences in the
world we are in, like Cézanne's shapes—apples and pears or
Mont St. Victoire we call them—independent of the universe of
words. And no less than with the words we depend upon for our
meanings, they usher us into ways of being-in-the-world.

C

Novelists, critics, poets, theologians, and ordinary human
beings are pretty well out of business, in their critical moments, if
"person" and "action" come under a cloud. Ayer's *Language*

Truth and Logic was a cloud which nearly everyone saw. The need for common cause was clear. But too much of the counterattack has been bemused by an *idée fixe* that the terms of the discussion about language had been definitively set for all time by A. J. Ayer or the logical positivists. It is merely a curiosity that in spite of all that has been written in this area by "ordinary language analysts" in and out of Oxford for nearly twenty years one still encounters in some of the things they write—especially about literary meaning and religious meaning—the ghost of A. J. Ayer. It is scandalous, however, how often he turns up in a quite unghostly fashion in the discussion of these questions by critics and theologians.

The special proprietary interest of both theology and of the language of religious performances in the concept "person" in literature, while obviously taken quite for granted by critics, has been singled out for attention by at least two latter-day so-called linguistic analysts, themselves by no means logical positivists nor by any means of the same persuasion between them. For both, "person" has a logically primitive role to play in works of literary art.

John Wisdom observes: "Novels which I have mentioned could be called studies of acts, but clearly they are better called studies of persons. A person is an exceedingly complex pattern in time."[7]

Gilbert Ryle, in a different context, in, that is to say, his widely read and widely misunderstood *The Concept of Mind*, which has been called, wrongly I believe, an exercise in linguistic behaviorism, says: "Where logical candour is required from us, we ought to follow the example set by novelists, biographers and diarists, who speak only of persons doing and undergoing things."[8] And he goes on to add: "Men are not machines, not even ghost-ridden machines. They are men—a tautology which is sometimes worth remembering."[9]

7. *Philosophy and Psychoanalysis* (Oxford: Blackwell, 1953), p. 225.
8. Gilbert Ryle, *The Concept of Mind* (London: Hutchinson, 1949), p. 168.
9. *Ibid.*, p. 81. Though they have not made explicit reference to the bearing of their findings upon the elucidation of the peculiar logical requirements of literary-artistic discourse, theological argumentation and exposition of religious performances, two other Oxford Philosophers—again of very different

But if Ayer's empirical verificationist view of meaningful language took a single form of discourse and made it paradigmatic for all speech to which we could give a cash value, perhaps Wittgenstein's alternative view of the realm of speech being comprised of a variety of language games, governed by constantly changing and seldom specified, sometimes unspecifiable rules, played with ever-evolving counters, and among which the only relation which obtained was that of a "family-resemblance," has led those who took the notion from Wittgenstein either to concern themselves narrowly with what they have called ordinary language; or, alternatively, to fail to notice the special proprietary interest—at least the presumption of it—in certain concepts or in certain tokens for certain language games—and also to fail to notice the inescapability of certain games. When Laplace said of God: "I have no need of that hypothesis," he was in a way making an important Wittgensteinian remark. The language games "physics" and "chemistry" have no use for the concept "God."

The token "God" is not the peculiar property of theological discourse or of religious performances, nor is even the token "Thou." Nor need it be so that the token "molecule" be copyrighted for exclusive use by chemists. Logicians have made excellent use of it. And obviously "hearts" no more belongs to poker than to bridge; nor does it belong exclusively to cardiology.

But even so, the token "God," having that use it has when governed by the logical context of theological argument or religious performances—which is to say when its meaning is a function of a particular and specifiable conceptual environment—*does* belong, as a concept, peculiarly to theology or religious performance; just as "molecule," in a yet similar case, is a proprietary interest of chemistry; just as also "hearts" in a game when it is "trumps" is a purely bridge-like concept.

---

persuasion as between them—have reckoned with the peculiar logical status of person-words. P. F. Strawson, in *Individuals: An Essay in Metaphysics*, argues to the logical unanalyzability and hence, in his terms, the metaphysical indispensability of "person." In a quite different form of argument, but still largely in terms of the linguistic method, Stuart Hampshire, in *Thought and Action*, makes out a similar case; one which is doubly interesting for being closer than hailing distance to the sort of thing one hears so-called existentialists saying.

There are many tokens in our speech which may have a use in many different games, just as many different ball games may be played with a ball designed primarily for tennis. But if we possessed no token of a certain sort and no special way of using it in a special conceptual environment, then there would be one game less to be played.

And of course I am suggesting that both theological discourse and the language of religious performances on one hand and that of literary art on the other are impossible without the common token "person," and the analogous *use* of that token, and that in this sense they both have a proprietary interest in this token and in this concept.

What we have been calling language games, after Wittgenstein, and sometimes call universes of discourse, if they have no tenses and no demonstratives, can be *distinguished* from one another. For example, we can easily start out playing bridge and end up with a very new game we have improvised as we play without having planned it and without having codified its rules as we went along. It would be odd to suggest in such a case that we should not come to entertain a number of important different beliefs and expectations about the world which usually result from such improvisations upon familiar universes of discourse when we are talking about the world. Poets perform such feats; metaphysicians do. They bewilder us and themselves. Often they edify us.[10]

Unlike an exercise in mathematics in which, lacking demonstratives, no references to the world and therefore to the many different language regions in our speech about the world are made, in a treatise on sociology or psychoanalysis or history or theology, however given any of these latter may be to the use of special sociological, psychoanalytical, historical, or other tokens, inevitably a reference to the world and hence to the many different language regions in our speech *about* the world will soon or

10. Cf. Wisdom, *op. cit.*, p. 263: "To gain a new apprehension of any part of reality we have to shake off old habits of apprehension crystallized probably in a well-known mode of presentation." And p. 270: "So does it come about that new facts give us a new apprehension of old ones and a new apprehension of old facts new freedom in looking for new ones. The metaphysician doesn't even remind us of things we had forgotten."

late be made. This being so, we cannot think of these language games or universes of discourse as hermetically sealed off from one another. Even if we can spot with ease the other side of the *linguistic* tracks, rarely do we have to pass through any explicit border checkpoint.

In all languages by means of which, at some point, it is possible to make an extranotational semantic reference to the world, one inevitably, at some point also converges upon the contingent helter-skelter of our ingenious and bewildering improvisations with the 'other' languages we find being used by others and by ourselves to make that same or similar or analogous kinds of extranotational reference.

It may be useful to speak here of logical neighborhoods, of linguistic topographies, of certain conceptual sets which normally seem quite familiar but which can easily be altered beyond all recognition, or can be recognizably altered in such a way as to induce laughter—say, by leaving out, misusing or using in an odd way tokens or concepts that have hitherto been quite familiar features of the landscape—misuses like puns or malapropisms, like *Alice in Wonderland,* or like a child's drawing or a painting by Cézanne or one by Georges Mathieu. Our first impulse is to say: "Oh no, that won't do at all! That's not the way it goes." But then, if we only look again we may want to say: "Well, by George, I never noticed!"

Freud took a concept like "sexuality"—and then "repression," "unconscious," "neurosis"—and shifted them about on the landscape of our talk about minds and suddenly we felt confused, even a little alarmed—but also often pleasantly surprised—about "reasons," "causes," "responsible."

What I am trying to suggest by this is just that while in a given generation "physics," "psychology," "history," "theology" or whatnot may be quite recognizable logical neighborhoods because of their proprietary interest in certain concepts, they still can all become very strange to us overnight.

So much, for the moment, for languages, language games, universes of discourse—and hence for theological language, the language of religious performances, and the language of literary art. Unfortunately there are still other preliminary warnings to

make—and this next is to be a most important one. There may
be a Wittgensteinian fly-bottle waiting behind his own illuminating injunction "Don't look for the meaning of a word, look for
its use" into which we may heedlessly fly.

D

So far we have had a few words about words. Let us now say
something about saying.

In all our preoccupation with words as tokens or tools, as
having this or that "use" according to the rules—specified or only
implicit—like balls, rackets, bats, cue sticks, or chessmen, playing
cards or kernels of corn in an improvised game of bingo—or as
occupying this logical neighborhood, having this or that place in
a conceptual topography, we are in danger of being misled by the
notion of meaning as use—*when this is taken exclusively in
conjunction with the language-game model*—misled, that is, into
overlooking the user, a *conditio sine qua non* of something's
having a use! The kinds of relations I may have to the words I
may use cannot be exhaustively displayed in terms of the language-game analogy, or any other single analogy.

Perhaps the point is more concretely displayed if I observe that
when we begin to think of "saying" we begin to see that flirting is
not only different from love-making as poker is different from
twenty-one; it is different in at least one importantly different
way: with regard to flirting and love-making my ways of abiding
in my words and acts, the degree and nature of my personal
backing they receive, the question of "good faith"—all these are
important in contemplating the differences between *them* as they
are *not* in contemplating those between poker and twenty-one.
And seduction is, of course, yet *another* case—as Kierkegaard
saw! Even to the point, I think, of implying that seduction is not
merely a more advanced case of flirtatious advances.

In short, if we speak of logical neighborhoods, conceptual
topographies, we must remark the most important fact about
them: They are *inhabited*—and through them *sayers*—to keep to
the metaphor—stride, dance, sneak, stalk, march, hide, jump out
to surprise, and even pronounce benedictions, maledictions, in-
terdictions, and sing the *Nunc Dimittis*. And these things they do

joyfully, soberly, seriously, mockingly, absent-mindedly, entreat-
ingly, hopefully, prayerfully, lovingly, deceitfully, dogmatically,
diffidently, performatively, and mindlessly—like a recorded announcement.

Our personal backing is behind our acts and our uttered words
in many different ways. Sometimes we mean what we do and say,
and saying is what we have done; sometimes we mean them, but
not quite; sometimes we believe we mean them and are taken to
mean them, but if we are asked, we are not sure; sometimes we
don't mean them at all—and say so, with our eyes; sometimes we
don't mean them and don't by any means say. And it is difficult,
now that you think about it, to say what exactly it is to say.

One might quite unproblematically say: "He played his ace
rather absentmindedly, indeed, almost irresponsibly." We might
even say: "There was something equivocal about his last stroke,"
though this surely begins to sound more like literary criticism
than sports writing, more like Cleanth Brooks than even the
elegant Allison Danzig, or at most like W. H. Auden sending a
dispatch from Wimbledon! But the game analogy begins to show
strain when we try to imagine saying: "On the fairways his game
is open and straightforward, but on his approaches to the green
his irons become hopelessly ironical." It becomes almost but
never quite bankrupt when we try to imagine wondering to
ourselves: "It is true, he has moved his bishop, but is he serious or
is he just pretending?"

The environment of words, as we all know quite well, is not
only other words, and the uses to which their resourcefulness
permits them to be put. It is also the many different kinds of
personal backing they may receive, the various ways of saying
that there are—including hardly saying at all, and even *not*
saying at all.

Making sense out of what has been said is, we all know quite
well, a function not only of the sorts of things we find in diction-
aries, grammars, logic books; nor is it a function only of pointing,
gestures, facial expressions, and tones of voice; nor yet is it a
function only of speech habits and usages. It depends also upon
the skills of speakers and hearers; upon the confidence of each in
the other, upon the *bona fides* of both. Above all, it depends

upon concrete elements of which we are not even aware, even less have codified, including elements of which we *could* not become aware, hence *could* not codify.

To realize the extent to which this is the case, one need only contemplate the many ways we *fail* to make sense, and how amusing, because how surprising we find (when we do find them) the causes of these failures to be. If some of the causes of our failures are a surprise, then some of the causes of our successes go unnoticed. Indeed, the surest way to frustrate every attempt to "make sense" would be to keep our attention ever alert to the ways in which we *do*.

Speech, let us not forget, is something *done* with words (which suffer themselves thus to be used) ; and every action not only can be modified adverbially, but speech as action is a saying, a backing by someone of the words he uses in some one or another way.[11] Along with seeing the logical environment of words, that is to say, their ways of being used, we have also to attend to the kind of personal backing they receive from their users.

Merely sounding words is not 'uttering' them; mere uttering is not 'saying'; and saying is not one but many things.

Now, we all know this quite well—that is why I feel obliged to enlarge upon it still further.

There are not only "Stages on Life's Way"—aesthetic, ethical, and religious ways of being in the world. There are ways, too, of *saying*: aesthetic, ethical—perhaps religious.

We are likely to know quite well what we mean when we observe: "He *says* he loves her, but does he really?" It seems like a different case, however, to reflect to oneself: "I say I love her, but do I really?" Different, but not absurd.

When we are "joking" are we saying what we have uttered? And what of "teasing?"

---

11. The most acute and imaginative analysis of language in the Analytic tradition of Wittgenstein (II) which takes seriously the notion of speech as an action, while focusing upon the "performative" and later what he comes to call the "illocutionary" force of language, is found in J. L. Austin's *How To Do Things With Words*, ed. J. O. Urmson (Oxford: Oxford University Press, 1962) . E.g., ". . . the more we consider a statement not as a sentence (or a proposition) but as an act of speech (out of which the others are logical constructions) the more we are studying the whole thing as an act," p. 20, *et passim*.

Suppose you are Walter Mitty, acting out a fantasy in imagination in which you depict yourself telling a story to an audience of one—to yourself—and suddenly you hear yourself say in imagination, voice full of reassurance, "The Captain will get us through; the Old Man will see us through." What kind of personal backing have the words you silently tell yourself; what kind have the bits of dialogue you hear? Would the case be different if you were to blurt them out, so as to be heard by a passer-by?

Imagine you are an actor playing Hamlet in the classic style, as written in a definitive text of Shakespeare, what kind of *saying* would "Hamlet's" words be, what kind of personal backing would you be giving them? How would it be different if you played a "method" Hamlet?

When we flirt, we use words, and other things. And I think we would be inclined to say that it is a game, and a delightful one at that, even though it sometimes leads to much gamier stuff and hence stops being a game altogether—or becomes a very different sort of game. But if we use words when we flirt, are we saying them, and if so how? It's true that we can raise the question of "good faith" about flirtation. But it does seem very queer to wonder whether X's flirtations are serious or whether he is "only playing at it." Though many a woman must have half-wondered: "Is he flirting seriously, or merely putting me on?"

Courting, of course is a different case—as when we use a rhetoric of either a high or a low style to win the heart—or at least the favors—of a woman. To say: "I am courting in earnest" tells you nothing as to whether I am courting her favors or her heart. And, if I wonder myself whether it is her favors or her heart I am courting, a tape recording of what I have uttered to the lady won't tell me what I've *said*, where my heart is, where my personal backing stands, or lies—or 'lies.'[12]

12. W. H. Auden has raised some of these questions with characteristic wit in "Dichtung und Wahrheit (an unwritten poem)," *Homage to Clio* (New York: Random House, 1960), pp. 35 ff. How can I *say* "I love you," Auden wonders, and then he imagines: " 'My Love,' says the poet, 'is more wonderful, more beautiful, more to be desired than . . .' "—there follows a list of admirable natural objects and human artifacts—(*more wonderful*, I should like to say, *than Swaledale or the coast of North-West Iceland, more beautiful than a badger, a sea-horse or a turbine built by Gilkes & Co. of Kendal, more*

Or take the case of my recounting a dream to my analyst. Where is the personal backing here? It is not like recounting barely remembered past events where we are inclined to be equivocal in our backing because of our uncertainties. It is rather that giving a backing to the saying of our dreams is a queer kind of backing because the dream-world is a queer kind of world. And while we're on the subject, why is it supposed that 'saying' my fantasies to another has a kind of therapeutic value for me? Discoveries may be made. But is not the different kind of 'saying' than that of my merely saying them to myself quite as important?

Or what of my describing my childhood to my analyst? What of my personal backing here? Am I misremembering or inventing the story? I may not know. My analyst will not care at first about the difference—though he may suspect. But the judge and jury? They will care.

We can remark, too, the kinds—different kinds—of saying involved in barefaced, sophisticated, and premeditated lying; unpremeditated, perhaps, in a way, 'unintentional' lying—as when I give myself a dramatically more interesting role in a narration of events in which I have been involved; or "making a good story better."

Or again, let us compare telling stories, bearing witness, testifying under oath.

Or let us imagine my signing my name to a confession exacted of me under extreme duress of an old-fashioned sort; 'signing my name' to a confession after being brainwashed; 'forging' my signature to a draft of 'my' bank account, while suffering from amnesia.

---

to be desired than cold toast for breakfast or unlimited hot water . . .). What do such comparisons provide? Certainly not a description by which *you* could be distinguished from a hundred possible rivals of a similar type," pp. 47-48. And again: " 'I will love you whatever happens, *even though* . . .'—there follows a list of catastrophic miracles—(*even though,* I should like to say, *all the stones of Balbek split into exact quarters, the rooks of Repton utter dire prophecies in Greek and the Windrush bellow imprecations in Hebrew, Time run boustrophedon and Paris and Vienna thrice be lit by gas . . .*). Do I believe that these events might conceivably occur during my life-time? If not, what have I promised? *I will love you whatever happens, even though you put on twenty pounds or become afflicted with a mustache: dare I promise that?,*" p. 48.

What does it mean to say: "X says he believes in the Creed, but does he really?"

What is it to be "as good as one's word (s) "?

All these questions point to different ways of formulating a general phenomenology of saying, an enterprise which would, I fear, prove both boring and unedifying.

What has been concerning me in all this is the curious relation of man to words; how through some poignant mystery we have occasionally the courage just to say something; and yet how even then—indeed especially then—it comes to us—this courage—unbidden, as a gift, but a gift which paradoxically, it may seem, if faithfully received, puts us into bondage: as if giving ourselves out of our prehuman silence into the realm of speech and saying is an act first of hope, then of love and thanksgiving for the world, but also an act by which everything becomes forever ambiguous and equivocal.

II

So far I have sought to view the phenomena of speech in terms of new possibilities afforded by Polanyi's work. I now wish to show the bearing of these general facts upon literary artistic languages on one hand and the languages of theology and of religious performances on the other; and to do this by attending particularly to the concepts "myth," "story," "history," "act," and "person."

A

In his *An Empiricist's View of the Nature of Religious Belief*, R. B. Braithwaite, accepting the empirical verification theory of meaning, goes on to remark the analogies between certain religious statements and certain ethical ones. "The kernel for an empiricist of the problem of the nature of religious belief," he says, "is to explain, in empirical terms, how a religious statement is used by a man who asserts it in order to express his religious conviction."[13]

He goes on to suggest that the primary element in this use is

13. (Cambridge: Cambridge University Press, 1956) , p. 11.

that the religious assertion is used as a moral assertion. For him, a religious assertion is, then, an assertion of a general policy for action, of an intention to live a life of a certain sort.

Now, this suggestion is so patently simple-minded, in view of my earlier warnings as to the actual logical heterogeneity of languages, that you may well wonder why I have taken it seriously at all. And the answer is that it is an interesting and, as we shall see, revealing bit of simple-mindedness—because, without explicitly saying so, even Braithwaite doesn't believe it.

First, he says: ". . . the difference between religious and purely moral principles is that, in the higher religions at least, the conduct preached by the religion concerns not only *external* but also *internal* behavior. The conversion involved in accepting a religion is a conversion, not only of the *will,* but of the *heart.*"[14] Now, the distinctions between *external* and *internal* and between *will* and *heart* have a great deal of analogy with different ways of saying and doing, of giving my personal backing to my words and deeds, of investing myself in what I do and what I say.

Of much greater interest is Braithwaite's tacit admission that there is an element in religious discourse which is not at all just declarations of policies for living a certain kind of life. He says: ". . . the intentions to pursue the behaviour policies, which may be the same for different religions, are associated with thinking of different *stories* (or sets of stories) ."[15]

Again, let us overlook the simple-mindedness in order to take note of two things: (1) Braithwaite suggests here that, even if one need not have "stories" in order to complete the meaning of merely *ethical* policy statements, one *does* need them or at least one does in fact *have* them as parts of religious discourse; and that, if we did not have them as parts of religious discourse, it would be difficult to tell one religion from another. (2) Perhaps we shall discover that Braithwaite's important distinction between the "external" and the "internal," between the "will" and the "heart" (and my distinction between different kinds of personal backing) are themselves functions of the particular stories

14. *Ibid.,* p. 21. (Italics mine.)
15. *Ibid.,* p. 23. (Italics in the original.)

such that without *these* stories not only would the distinction between one religion and another disappear, but that between religion and ethics would disappear as well.

For all his attempts to assimilate religious utterances to declarations of life policies, Braithwaite very much believes in stories. Indeed, he believes, it turns out, in Christian stories, in a far more logically primitive sense, with a far greater range of logical efficacy than even he has realized. He believes in these stories *necessarily*, in a way; for even just as a moral philosopher, "action," "person," etc. have their meaning in their locus, for him, in a logical topography which is supplied by these stories. Like all of us, he is, if only in a cultural sense, a *de facto* Christian.

He believes in these stories and we may well ask: "Why?"

And I think the answer is just that policy-statements of a very general sort—like "I have decided to live an agapeistic life"—though *story-neutral* in appearance, when viewed and elucidated by a moral philosopher of a verificationist turn of mind, are seen in fact to be nothing of the sort. Such statements, when they are responsibly analyzed macrologically, are intelligibly interpretable at all only if their implicit "stories" are explicated. The need of stories (and I deliberately use the term vaguely at this point) then lies precisely in the fact that policy-statements are about intentions to act in certain ways, and action is inconceivable apart from stories. It is stories which display how the concepts "action," "person," "will," "heart," "inner," "outer" are used. The precise meaning of and hence the differences between Confucian policy-statements and Christian policy-statements are entirely a function of their differing stories.

Anyone who makes a declaration of a general policy for action in good faith has at the same time committed himself to some story or set of stories apart from which such a declaration would be unintelligible, even though the subscription to the stories be only tacit and becomes explicit only when someone ingenuously asks: "Whatever do you mean?" And this is so whether one is a Christian declaring an agapeistic policy, a Marxist declaring a socialistic policy, or a moral philosopher of a Kantian persuasion declaring a rational deontological policy.

"Action," hence a "policy for action," is logically incomplete without "stories." A universe in which the "saying of stories" is logically impossible is a universe in which the concepts "action," "person," "decision," "choose" have no use; and is therefore also a universe in which "right," "wrong," and "good" have no use.

But if I have made sport with Braithwaite's verificationist simple-mindedness, it has been done by using the concept "stories" in so vague a way as to subsume under it concepts having as heterogeneous uses as do the concepts "myth," "folktale," "autobiography," "biography," "story" (in the sense of a narrative of events), "story" (in the sense of a conscious work of the art of fiction), "drama" (in the sense of a conscious imitation of an action), "ritual" (in the sense of a paradigmatic enactment), and "history."

The time has come for some sorting out among these—and since my concern here is mainly with that of "person" (as a concept that literary art, theological discourse, and the language of religious performance have in common and without which none of them would be possible), I shall consider mainly "myth," "history," "story," "person," "action."

In what follows I shall try to do three things.

First, I shall suggest that there are at least two conceptions of "myth": one I associate with its origin in primitive ritual, primitive cosmology and with its fulfilment and near destruction in the great conscious works of tragic poetry of Greek antiquity; and in which there are, from our point of view, no persons—but only gods, heroes and "proto-persons," and in which there are, in consequence, no actions, in our sense, a sense yet to be displayed. The other view of "myth" is one which is clearly associated with "stories," in which, risking oversimplifications, I am tempted to say, there are "persons" and "heroes," but no "gods"; and with "history" in which there are certainly "persons" and perhaps some "heroes." To remark a second use for the concept "myth," as I shall be developing it, in no way diminishes its importance for us; but I shall hope to show that its meaning and use are dramatically altered in the new logical affiliations I wish to establish for it.

While "myth" in this second sense is neither "story" nor "history," it is a necessary extension of them which has to do with the beginnings and especially with the endings of actions and therefore shares with "stories" and "histories" references to persons. Indeed, it is myth in this sense which refers me to the logically heterogeneous "events" attending my emergence from my prelingual, prepersonal, prehistorical anonymous background into which reach roots from my present personal existence and which therefore do in this irreducibly equivocal way make references to a person insofar as I see myself personally in their light. By means of them I grasp myself as both *given* and as *the receiver*. Further, not only do myths in our second sense *make references to persons*, in the full sense; insofar as the concept "action" is a necessary affiliate of "person," and, insofar as an action which cannot be regarded from the standpoint of its completion is not an action, in the full sense in which our tradition has for a very long time understood it; and finally, insofar as it is myth (in our second sense) alone which permits such a view of action, "myth" is a necessary affiliate of "person."

Secondly, I shall try to display the peculiar way of 'saying' one has in the art of fiction—in stories, in other words—hoping to underscore their differences from both myth, in both of our senses, and from history.

Finally, I shall suggest something about some overlooked aspects of the notion "history."

Before I can embark upon these perilous seas I must distinguish between mere "narrative" on the one hand and "history" and "story" on the other; and I shall have in turn to distinguish between "history" and "story"—where in the latter case we have in mind chiefly a conscious product of the art of fiction.

It is obvious that "myths," "histories," "stories," and "narratives" are not and could not be conveyed in mathematical notations or in logical calculi—because (though not only because) there are no tenses or tense surrogates as parts of their logical grammar, as there are in all our natural languages.

However, though the suggestion, I know, ignores some common usage, there is, among the above cases, one form of discourse which takes place quite normally in our natural languages and therefore makes frequent use of the tense distinctions that are found there, but for which tenses have a different use, or at least, a different value from that they have in "myth," "story," and "history." I mean, of course, "narrative."

I do not wish to make great play with this point. I only suspect that an important contrasting feature of the role of tenses and other time-words when affiliated with "myth," "story," and "history" can be elucidated by remarking their characteristic uses in "narrative"—though I shall also want to suggest that their use is not identical among the former three.

It is clear from the *Oxford English Dictionary* that "narration" has an intimate historical connection with courts of law; that to *narrate* is to give a recital of facts (not of events—which, when we tell of them, have an organic connection); that a narrative is such a recital. Reciting a set of facts seems to be a temporal affair in a way different both from deducing conclusions from premises and from giving an historical account—although they both consume time in the doing, and though the latter very much depends upon tense distinctions.

But a narrative as *mere narrative* (and not as an important part of "history" which is a concept without use apart from that of "the facts") simply recites a list of facts. Think, for example, of the prosecution narrating the facts of his case, even if only by means of examining a witness; "On or about August 25, Poteat was proceeding down West Franklin Street . . ." etc.

Now, in due course, no doubt it becomes the function of the prosecution to show beyond a reasonable doubt to reasonable men, that temporal and therefore perhaps causal connections (or the presumption of them) do obtain among the recited facts. But as a mere recital of facts—though this takes time and times are fixed within the words in which the recital is given and so on—this narration (though to claim this may require a rather esoteric distinction) is not a "story" nor is it "history"—*as mere narration*. It is the job of the prosecution, having done this much, then to show that the stuff composing what has been recited in the narrative as the facts can be so construed as to be seen as having 'organic' connections of the sort which would lead reasonable men to say: "These facts, if that is indeed what they are, do seem to add up to the crime cited in the indictment." In short, it leads reasonable men to construe the components of a narrative as so 'organically' related as to deserve to be called history.

Notice, we can quite coherently say: "Yes! No doubt about it! X happened. Y happened and so did Z. But did the crime claimed in the indictment happen?" If we can sometimes wonder whether the crime did occur, while having no doubts about X, Y, and Z, then sometimes concluding that the crime did happen is not logically on all fours with accepting X, Y, & Z, as narrated, for facts. And, if they are not on logical all-fours, a simple narrative need not, indeed, cannot be equivalent to what we ordinarily mean by "history."

In a court of law, testimony is designed not only to establish what did or did not happen, but also to discover if all these things taken together have an 'organic' connection entitling them to be relevantly and meaningfully connected in such a fashion as will enable reasonable men to say: "Yes, this is a reliable history; the crime, as claimed in the indictment, *was* committed."

And when opposing counsel rises to object during direct-examination that a question is *argumentative*, one thing he often means to claim is that (in the terms of my analysis) 'historical connections' are being prematurely made.

That which distinguishes a mere narrative of facts from what adds up to a crime, and that also which distinguishes one type of crime from another—first degree murder, manslaughter—is precisely questions about there being *intent* and about the nature of the *intent*—often notoriously difficult to establish and certainly established, if at all, in a logically very different way from establishing 'the facts.' A narration of the facts becomes judicially material only when intent, that is, a *person* personally *behind* 'the facts,' an agent, an actor more or less giving his acts a personal backing, enters the account of events. For it is only then that the narrative becomes more; it is then that it may add up to a crime.

Recitals of facts then—in the above sense—though they are, in two different senses of fact, necessary conditions of both stories and of histories, are not the same as stories and histories.

Let me now drop this overrefined distinction, since I trust that it has by now done its work.

The most distinctive characteristic of myth in the classical sense to remark for present purposes is that though, like a story it unfolds in time, so that in one perfectly good sense we may say there are 'events' recounted (though I warn you, they are of a logically most peculiar sort) and we may say that these 'events' are laid out in time, so that, in one sense, we want to claim that Y was *after* X and *before* Z (as we are not tempted to say of the relations stated in a tenseless mathematical notation), it is not a report of unique events, and, in *our* senses of these notions, has neither a beginning nor an end—as a circle has neither beginning nor end. Myths, in this classical sense, look very like stories and histories because the notation in which they are presented has tense distinctions, and because something seems to *happen* in them—in our sense of "happen." But in fact they are at least as much like what is given in tenseless mathematical notations, since what is given in them is eternal, or given eternally.

Their origin seems to have been associated with the ritual enactment of the passage of the cosmos through the course of its finite order. Being finite, as is, say, a circle, one could say both that from any given point in this course one could view the entire course as already given, eternally given, eternally repeated (if it were not absurd, one is tempted, for the sake of logical accuracy, to say "eternally 'peated' ") and that therefore nothing (new) ever happened on nothing (really) new ever happened; and also say from that same given point that there were things—familiar, eternally repeated things yet to happen.[16]

In myth construed in this way, the first of the two ways I wish to display, there are no events, no novelties, no decisions, and

16. When I awkwardly characterized as finite the order of the cosmos, as ritually and mythically conceived, and when I speak of the passage of the cosmos through this course as one in which, in our own quite uncontroversial sense, nothing (new) happens, some of what I mean may perhaps be elucidated by aspects of the following model. With a pair of ordinary gaming dice, it is possible to compute with mathematical exactness the finite number of possible combinations and permutations of turned-up die sides. One could specify, if one wished, each single possible combination of such turned-up sides; and one could also specify the finite number of such possibilities. Let this case now stand for the cosmos as Classically conceived. If one knows of it what one would know as the result of the computations and know it quite apart from actually observing any exhaustive run-through of its possibilities *all* that is logically possible in that cosmos (one could say, *all* that eternally *is* in it), then *from that standpoint,* one would regard the contingent possibility of actually making an exhaustive run-through of combinations as a fact of small or of no importance and would regard the "time" consumed in an actual course of an exhaustive run-through as "time" in which, in a way, nothing happens.

MYTHS, STORIES, HISTORY . . .

therefore no actions and no persons—in our sense of these notions (yet to be deployed).

It is in the great conscious works of tragic poetry by Sophocles, Aeschylus, and Euripides, which in fact presuppose the elements of these myths as they have come down to them from ritual, the oral tradition of folklore, and finally the epic, that the peculiar logic of these myths is best seen, for it is precisely in these works of conscious art that the ultimate pressure upon the logical limits of the ancient myths is brought to bear.

In these plays, ancient myth, even with its now attenuated hold upon the notion of a finite course for the cosmos, survives, as is well attested by the great sigh of ritual-magic relief that one hears from the final chorus at the end of *Oedipus Tyrannus*:

> ". . . see him now and see the breakers of
>   misfortune swallow him!"[17]

But in them we do begin to see heroes and guilt and salvation and therefore intimations of acts and persons; therefore intimations too of stories and of histories.

Now, the strain under which myth, in the first of our senses, is put is related to the fact that tragic poetry, as is not the case with ritual, folk-myth, and even the oral antecedents of epic, is a conscious work of art.

Saying myth and saying tragic poetry are importantly different kinds of saying. The kind of personal backing we find in one is crucially different from that we give the other. The extent to which we abide in the words of one is not the same as in the other. We are serious in the one as we are not serious in the other. The Eucharist may be dramatic, but for the true believer it is not a play. To say that art gains some kind of autonomous life of its own is to say it loses the seriousness of ritual and the seriousness too of myth. It becomes *play* when it becomes conscious of itself.

W. H. Auden has said: "There is a game called Cops and Robbers, but none called Saints and Sinners."[18]

Art, and hence the art of the story (as I wish to understand it)

17. Translated by David Grene (Chicago: University of Chicago Press, 1954).
18. *Poets at Work*, ed. Charles D. Abbott (New York: Harcourt Brace, 1948), p. 170.

are absolutely necessary to our life as persons, but not merely because they are serious, but rather because they are, at the same time, play.

I must now briefly discuss art as play.

St. Augustine, in his reflections upon his youthful wilful act of stealing pears, which he did not want, expresses one of the profoundest impulses of the human spirit—the impulse to author an absolutely gratuitous act, decisively, and with impunity, to assert man's independence of all necessity. The act whereby one wilfully disobeys the law is seen by Augustine as a perverted image of God's transcendence of the world. He says: "And wherein did I, even corruptedly and pervertedly, imitate my Lord? Did I wish, if only by artifice, to act contrary to Thy law . . . so that . . . I might imitate an imperfect liberty by doing with impunity things which I was not allowed to do, in obscured likeness of Thy omnipotence?"[19]

It was the nineteenth century which particularly explored the interesting logical alliances among "art," "crime," "play," "sanctity," the "acts gratuite" and "personhood."

A successful ultimate transcension of necessity such as was sought by Kirilov was unimaginable in terms of Greek myth alone. But in their great conscious works of tragic poetry, the Greeks depicted the penultimate transcension by man of necessity. This contributed importantly to their view of man as distinct from everything else there is. Since the tragedy was a play, that is, a conscious work of art, the spectator could indwell the action being imitated with less than ritual or mythic seriousness, and thereby vicariously depict and enjoy the freedom of the hero, the while retaining amnesty from the retribution which befalls him. He could both dwell in and not dwell in the imitated action.

Literary art, precisely because it is play, a let's pretend, enables us to have a certain detachment, to come into some sense of what is reflexively named by the pronoun first person singular. By being fictive, literature divorces us from the world of what, in any given age, we soberly choose to call reality. It is precisely by this means that we discover what it is to transcend the world as a self.

19. *On the Trinity*, Bk. XI, chap. v.

In saying: "Let's pretend," we perform an act of freedom from the world of necessity.

Now, it is only when art and existence are so distinguished as to enable us to *pretend* that we achieve this freedom from the world of necessity. At the same time, it is only when, having made the distinction, we do not go on to mistake art for existence that we can remain human. Existence is serious and dreams are not; existence can fully engage our personal wills and art cannot; history we are fully engaged in, by fiction we are not.

Those for whom this distinction has not yet become clear are either primitives or children; those for whom it has vanished are madmen.

Even, however, when one has said all this, one must concede that if we achieve an attitude of irony toward what is serious by our aesthetic indwelling of a story, we also achieve some substantive view of our own personhood because even an aesthetic indwelling is nevertheless a *genuine indwelling*. Even stories are things in which I after all do, in a sense, believe. The fiction I read of which I want to say: "That is *my* story, in a way," is a form of words to which I may be said to give a high degree of personal backing. And insofar as this is true, it is appropriate to say that it is in terms of such a story that I understand who I am and what I am doing when I act.[20]

B

It remains now to suggest some differences among uses of the concepts "story," "history," "myth" (in our first sense), and

20. Hannah Arendt has commented with great beauty upon this. She says: "The scene where Ulysses listens to the story [at the court of the King of the Phaeacians] of his own life is paradigmatic for both history and poetry; the 'reconciliation with reality' . . . came about through the tears of remembrance. The deepest human motive for history and poetry appears here in unparalleled purity: since listener, actor, and sufferer are the same person, all motives of sheer curiosity and lust for new information . . . are naturally absent in Ulysses himself, who would have been bored rather than moved if history were only news and poetry only entertainment." "The Concept of History," *Between Past and Future* (New York: The Viking Press, 1961). Though Miss Arendt's way of sorting out the concepts "history" and "poetry" (or "story," as I say) is far from precisely congruent with my own in this essay, I find her way illuminating and congenial, and elucidatory of matters which are not here at the center of my concern, but which in another setting might well be.

"myth" (in what I shall henceforth call the eschatological sense).

The best way to round off this already overprotracted analysis is to consider the above concepts in the light of the concept "action."

A *story* is a temporal deployment of events which differs from myth, in the Classical sense, in that it requires the concept "happen" in a logical environment other than that afforded by ritual re-enactment, the passage of the cosmos through its finite course and eternal return; it requires the concept "person"; and it requires that of "action." In a sense which can be made clear only at the very end of this inquiry, it requires "beginnings" and "endings"—but "beginnings" and "endings" such as are appropriate to a conscious work of *art* to which our relation is aesthetic, in the 'saying' of which our personal backing is at least equivocal, in which the indwelling of our words is not confused with a commitment to existence as such.

History is a similar temporal deployment of events, bound to what we question-beggingly, but unproblematically, and, I think for present purposes, benignly call 'facts.' It too requires the concepts "happen," "person," and "action"—as well as many others that are of small concern here. It too speaks of "beginnings" and "endings." But, since our 'saying' of history is serious as our 'saying' of stories is not; since we make history our *own* as with a mere story we do not, since our personal backing of it is not equivocal, and our indwelling of our words is precisely a commitment to existence; our saying of the 'beginnings' and 'endings' of our own history are serious in the way appropriate to a person, and yet, these 'beginnings' and 'endings' of my history, about which I am serious, are not themselves parts of that history—except as logical extensions of it that are *mythical*, in the eschatological sense.

I may be the agent of my own acts, or at least of some of them—including the 'act' whereby I claim a particular deployment of events clearly rooted in facts, as being my very own story, even if perchance some or even much of this 'act' of claiming and indwelling my own story occurs on the psychiatric couch. I may, indeed I must, be also the agent of the tacit 'act' of claiming the logically problematic mythical account of 'beginnings' and 'endings' without which the history which I claim as my very own would be incomplete. Without these 'accounts' of radical beginnings and radical endings, the concepts "person," "action," "happen" will not function as they must if history is not to become either a mere *story* or a mere *myth*, in the Classical as opposed to the eschatological sense.

In the nature of the case, I cannot be both the agent of particular acts which make up my history and also the 'agent' of its logically heterogeneous 'beginnings' and 'endings'—not, anyhow, agent in the same sense. To do so would require that I should be a God, an "author and finisher"; it requires me to be both unproblematically *in* my history and also *outside* of it. If I were such a being as this, I could not also be an agent and a person in history, in those senses of these notions we have developed.

Let me now briefly analyze certain aspects of the concept "action."

What is an action? I want to say in the first place that the universe of action is necessarily *dramatic*. But then this does not get us very far.

What do I mean? I mean that such a universe is one in which the concepts "person" and "moral discrimination" have logical autonomy. Neither "person" nor "moral discrimination" can be regarded as assimilable to or analyzable into other concepts without remainder. "Person" cannot be analyzed as "dynamic biochemical system" or as "animal"; "moral discrimination" cannot be reduced to "instinct," "desire," "organic" or "biochemical system seeking to remain in homeostasis" or to their sum.

No concept is logical-topography-neutral. In some sense, it would be appropriate to use the concept "agent" of Oedipus, Orestes, Hamlet, Job, and William H. Poteat. It would be misleading in the extreme to suppose that "agent" as a concept could have the same use in all five cases—or, indeed, in any two. Let me bring this out by using a somewhat outlandish analogy. Imagine at one extreme a victim of schizophrenia in a state of complete catatonia. At the other, conceive an electronic computer more sophisticated than any now in existence.

In the one, we have a case of a recognizable member of our own species of whom we might hesitate to use the concept "person." In the other, an electronic machine of which we seem increasingly willing to say that it "solves problems," "makes decisions"—even perhaps that it "acts."

I think most of us recognize that in the latter case we are using a rather extended analogy.

In the former, however, our hesitations over using the concept "person" are more real and certainly more poignant. (Why, by the way, is that?) I think we are inclined to hesitate over the use of "person" because it is unimaginable that any 'intentions' will ever be made 'public.' We may even wonder over the propriety of using "intentions" in such a setting.

A member of species *Homo sapiens* who never says anything or does anything verges towards the limits of the applicability of "person." We recognize this even in the most ordinary ways. We say things like: "He is very much of a person"; "He really doesn't seem human."

Now, remembering all the warnings already issued, I will define an action as a public occurrence that is intended by a person. Someone who bears a proper name and has a unique spatio-temporal existence and of whom if it is asked: "Why did X happen?," can answer: "I was trying to Y," is properly called the agent of an action.

Another way to put this would be: an action is an occurrence which we have good reason to believe derives its meaning from the fact that the occurrence was opted by Jones *as Jones.* This means of course that an actor (in the sense of one who professionally plays parts on a stage) is not *as actor* the agent of actions except those required by his profession.

I am aware of difficulties here, and aware that what I have just said runs counter to a good deal of common usage. Yet it is precisely these divergencies I need to bring out.

The actor in a play is not, in the presently relevant sense, the agent of actions, because what occurs on the stage derives its meaning (comes to be acts at all) not from *his* intentions, *his* story, but from the text of the play.

Hamlet intends to kill the king. If asked: "Why did Hamlet

kill Polonius?," we do not answer: "Because Sir John Gielgud
intended to kill the king and made a mistake." Even less are we
likely to say: "Because Sir John Gielgud intended to kill Sir
Ralph Richardson."

Now, this yields the distinction between an occurrence which
derives its meaning from a play and one which derives its meaning from a personal intention. It also underscores one of the
differences between art and history; between play actions and
'serious actions.'

But even this does not take us far enough.

Everyone who says of me: "Poteat is reading in order to pass his
exams," has in mind a particular story—the story of Poteat.

Not only so. When I say of myself: "I am reading because I
intend to pass my exams," I have in mind a story—or more
properly, a minute tract within a story—which I would call *my*
story. This again yields the distinction between a play-story and a
serious story. A serious-story is the story of at least one bearer of a
proper name, having a unique spatio-temporal existence, who
sees his own action as deriving from this story; and who, if asked:
"What are you doing?," would answer by recounting some tract
of that story. Or to put the matter less awkwardly but more
vaguely: what is for a person a serious story is history.

There can be no action without a story; there can be no history
without the serious and unique intendings of existent persons.

C

A story becomes a history because the deployment in time of
events which we see to be the products of "actions" or "persons"
in the light of this story is claimed by someone as his very own.

I suggested above that "history" in this sense, with which
"person," "action," and "intention" function unproblematically,
remains incomplete unless it is possible for me to *say, indwell,
give my personal backing* to references to radical beginnings and
endings which cannot be on logical all-fours with the story I have
made my very own. I cannot claim to be both the "author and
the finisher" of my own history.

I want to conclude now by saying that those references to
radical beginnings and endings comprise the substance of escha-

tological myth (a usage which has no hint of the pejorative in it) ; and that far from being mere adornments of history, as we understand it, they are absolutely essential conceptual conditions for "action," "person," and "history" having that use which we by now are incapable of abandoning.[21]

III

What then are we to make of all of this?

We may say, I think, (1) that eschatological myths, stories, and histories, though they constitute a small fraction of the many articulate forms in use among men, though they are logically heterogeneous in their uses and are variously indwelt by their users, *are* peculiarly and irreducibly affiliated with the articulation of personal existence, intention, and action, as we have for a very long time understood these; (2) that they all enjoy, their heterogeneity notwithstanding, the same kind of legitimacy in relation to that understanding; and (3) that they are only upheld and integrated into a complex though stratified logical topography through the personal backing and subscription 'from within' of those persons whose modalities (among others) of being-in-the-world they are.

All this means, finally, that uses of, or references to, eschatological myths in theological argument or in religious performances— myths like the creation, the fall, the resurrection—are not *in principle* more problematical than each and every articulate form in use—though each and every such form is not problematical in the same way; nor, indeed, is any given form in the same way differently problematical from all others at every time.

21. A Christian theologian might well say at this point: "The self to which I subscribe but cannot know [see note 4 above] is to be known only in hope and through faith, whereby I see myself as one already known." (Cf. " 'By relating itself to its own self and by willing to be itself, the self is grounded transparently in the Power which constituted it.' And this formula again, as has often been noted, is the definition of faith." S. Kierkegaard, *The Sickness Unto Death,* trans. Walter Lowrie [Princeton: Princeton University Press, 1941], p. 216.) And, he might continue: "In the present time we do indeed see only through a glass darkly, yet in terms of eschatological myth, as St. Paul has put it definitively for the Christian, even now in hope by faith we know ourselves as creatures who also always have been known." Of this I should be inclined to say: it is this claim which has often given such intensity and depth to the view of personal existence within the history of our own sensibility.

Every such form depends upon and has no stronger legitima-
tion than its grounding in its living use among men. If the use of
any language requires justification, then the use of each and
every language requires it—an absurd and impossible program,
since at least *one* language will always have to be acritically used
All that can be reasonably required is the disclosure of analogies
and disanalogies obtaining among the heterogeneous forms actually in use.

Such a fiduciary grounding cannot be explicitly prescribed; nor
is there any sure protection against its eventual erosion.

After three centuries of a quest for, if not an assurance of,
certainty we must contritely confess that we in the Western
world have lived by nothing more substantial than hope, recognizing nevertheless that hope has always been rewarded by unexpected knowledge and that speech, made bold by hope, has
always disclosed to us more than we could explicitly anticipate
and than we can ever fully say.

> "What the dead had no speech for, when living,
> They can tell you, being dead: the communication
> Of the dead is tongued with fire beyond the
>   language of the living."[22]

22. T. S. Eliot, "Little Gidding" in *Four Quartets* (New York: Harcourt,
Brace and Co., 1943) .

POLANYI'S INTERPRETATION OF
SCIENTIFIC INQUIRY*

Chaim Perelman

The thesis concerning the personal character of knowledge so profoundly and so brilliantly defended by Michael Polanyi is, along with other parallel efforts, part of the antipositivist reaction which has developed through the years after World War II. Positivism, following a Western tradition which continues Cartesianism and Anglo-Saxon empiricism, has accentuated the opposition between an impersonal science which announces objective and universal truths, and the totality of our value judgments which only express subjective opinions that are variable, if not in opposition to one another, as well as irrational. In science, universal agreement about objective truths is not only possible, but effectively realizable. In the realm of human action we are pulled in different directions by feelings, interests, and passions of a subjective nature which are at the origin of all the conflicts which assail humanity. Science can contribute to the establishment of unanimous agreement in matters of knowledge; on the other hand, human action, which does not tend to describe that which is, but tends to realize a future conforming to our wishes and desires, thereby escapes from reason and the universal agreement which could be established under its rule. The dislocation of the unity of culture which results in a dichotomy opposing science to all other aspects of human activity delivers a fatal blow to philosophy and its age-old ideal of practical reason. For—let us not forget it—philosophy since the time of the Greeks has been the

---

* Translation by Donald W. Millholland.

love of wisdom, a rational knowledge leading to happiness and virtue.

The enterprise of Polanyi is, in a sense, revolutionary, for it reverses a trend which has characterized the evolution of Western humanity since Descartes; but in another sense it is counterrevolutionary, and goes back to an ancient tradition against which Descartes and Cartesianism fought with acknowledged success. According to the conception generally held prior to Descartes, which everyone accepted without questioning, all knowledge is based on a tradition, transmitted by the master to his students, and reserved to an elite of the initiated. This is a point of view shared by all the schools of antiquity, as well as those of the Middle Ages. The idea that each human being is endowed with reason, that it is sufficient to deliver reason from the prejudices that encumber it, so that it may reach truth with evidence, is implied in Saint Augustine, but its most paradoxical consequences have been expressed by Rousseau, after being uncovered by Duns Scotus and Descartes.

Duns Scotus affirmed the existence of propositions evident in themselves:

> A proposition will be called self evident when it is known as true in virtue of the terms which it contains: "ex suis termins ut sui sunt." Hence it is not self-evident because it is actually perceived as true by some intellect, but because it can be apprehended by any intellect which understands the proper meaning of the terms and which sees that the predicate is essentially contained in the subject.[1]

The idea of a truth, and even of evidence, that is impersonal is thus neatly affirmed. We all possess the faculty of reason, Descartes would say, which would permit us to observe evident truths, but "because we are all children before being men, and because it was necessary for us to be governed for a long period of time by our appetites and perceptions,"[2] our judgments are neither so pure nor so solid. There is, therefore, only one remedy for

1. Duns Scotus, *Opus Oxoniense,* in *Opera Omnia* (Paris, 1891-1895), IX, 836 V. See also Chaim Perelman, "On Self-Evidence in Metaphysics," *International Philosophical Quarterly,* IV, No. 1 (New York, Feb., 1964), 8-9.
2. Descartes, *Discours de la Méthode,* 2e partie, in *Oeuvres* (Paris: Editions de la Pléiade, 1952), pp. 133-134.

this situation, and it is Rousseau who furnishes it to us. One must keep the child from all contact with prejudices of a social origin. One must never teach him anything under the guise of any authority whatever:

> Let him [your student] learn nothing because you have told it to him but because he has understood it himself; let him not learn science, let him invent it. If you ever substitute authority for reason in his mind he would no longer reason he would be no more than the toy of the opinion of others.[3]

Rousseau would not like a child to study the sciences, but to discover them by himself and, according to Rousseau, in order to arrive at this, it is sufficient to observe facts, for they speak for themselves to each unprejudiced mind.

The entire tradition of the Enlightenment presupposes that science has been completely fulfilled; this could only take place in the mind of God. The role of man in that case is not therefore to invent explicit formulas, nor to elaborate a world view; it is, rather, not to deceive oneself in unveiling that which has been known by God throughout eternity. That is the reason why the rationalists first, and the positivists later (even if the latter are unaware of the presuppositions implied in their attitudes) have so strongly insisted upon the method of verifying scientific utterances, without paying attention to the problems posed by their elaboration. For Descartes it was a question, thanks to his method, of retrieving with certainty the divine truths thought by God, in a perfectly adequate language. But in order for the empiricists to adopt the same attitude, it is necessary for them deliberately to neglect the problem of expressing our sensible impressions in a particular language, as if all languages were conventionally interchangeable. But if, as Whewell convincingly showed us more than a century ago, all language is structured by the theories which elaborate it, there is in all language, as in all theories, an aspect by which they surpass the sense-data. A theory can be affirmed or invalidated only to the extent to which, in surpassing a past experience, it becomes applicable to a future experience: past experience *alone* is incapable of a parallel extrapolation without the intervention of the creative spirit.

3. J. J. Rousseau, *Emile* (Paris: Firmin-Didot, 1898) , p. 181.

The greatest reproach that Polanyi addresses as much to the rationalists as to the empiricists is that in their attempt to elaborate a scientific methodology they have neglected the problem of invention, scientific creativity, which he puts at the center of his concerns. Because they have failed to consider scientific creation, relegating it to the domain of psychology and subjectivity[4] (about which scientific methodology had nothing to say), the positivists have been able to conceive of scientific activity as impersonal, as foreign to the tradition in which the scientist was formed, to the authorities he has followed, to the masters who have served him as models. But if one elaborates a methodology of the sciences, taking account of the central place which creative minds occupy in this field, the new perspective permits a critique of positivism which is both penetrating and ruthless.

In his work *Personal Knowledge* Polanyi clearly shows how at each step in the scientific process, experience, talent, and the technical skill of the scientist intervene, for neither the perception of the object nor the elaboration of hypotheses, nor even their verification, can be done in an entirely formal or mechanical fashion. How many times have the conclusions of experience been put aside or held to be negligible? The judgment of the scientist, formed through contact with an experienced tradition, his flair, and even his intuition play an indispensable role. According to Polanyi,[5] this personal, unformalizable character of knowledge is due to the fact that all perception focused on an object (focal awareness) is accompanied by a subsidiary awareness of which we do not take account in the same way, but upon which we rely for our perception of the whole. On the other hand, as he remarks,[6] if we focus upon the particulars, we lose the perception of the whole that these particulars constitute or express. If we pay attention to each sound in isolation the melody which they compose tends to escape us, at least partially; and, conversely, we do not notice the individual notes if we focus attention on the melody.[7]

The result of this, Polanyi shows us, is that analytical thought, concerned as it is with immediately perceptible particulars,

4. Cf. *P.K.*, p. 14 n. 1.
5. *Ibid.*, p. 55.
6. *Ibid.*, p. 57.
7. *Ibid.*, p. 58.

makes us lose sight of the perception of the whole, and prevents us from attaining, in turn, a knowledge of a higher level—a fact which has been brought to our attention by the Gestalt theories. Thus if interest is focused only on the physicochemical aspects of living organisms, the specific character of biology is left out of account, that is, its concern with beings whose functioning is either normal or disturbed, which explains the implied teleology of this discipline, somewhat embarrassing to its practitioners. For, let us not forget, it is the role that each organ must fulfil in the functioning of an organism which makes it possible for us to distinguish between a well-developed living being and a sick or monstrous organism. The laws of physics and chemistry cannot account for the construction of a technical object (although they can explain its failures); nor can they help us understand the structure of a living being.

In putting the stress upon the creative inventive aspect of scientific activity, Polanyi shows to what extent this activity depends upon the personal decisions of the scientist and his intellectual involvement, thereby coming close to other forms of culture such as law, religion, art, morality, etc.[8] The development of the sciences would therefore be attuned to the world-view of those societies in which they have their origin. The sciences develop only because of the commitment of the scientist to an intellectual passion analogous to that aroused by the cult of beauty or by the struggle for a noble cause.

> Our vision of reality, to which our sense of scientific beauty responds, must suggest to us the kind of questions that it should be reasonable and interesting to explore. . . . In fact, without a scale of interest and plausibility based on a vision of reality, nothing can be discovered that is of value to science; and only our grasp of scientific beauty, responding to the evidence of our senses, can evoke this vision.[9]

Personally, I cannot but subscribe to this critique of positivism and of the objectivistic conception of science. Like Polanyi, I think that the concept of absolute doubt leads nowhere, and that all scientific research is founded upon presuppositions in which

8. *S.F.S.*, pp. 58-59; *P.K.*, pp. 308-309.
9. *P.K.*, p. 135.

the scientist places his trust, at least for the time being, that the mind of the scientist is inspired by considerations of beauty and rationality which lead him in his quest for yet undiscovered aspects of reality. In this way the scientist may resemble the artist and the mystic, the prophet and the philosopher. There is hardly anything more significant in this regard than the famous passage where Kepler, in the introduction to the fifth book of his *Harmonia Mundi*, extols his discoveries. However, I wonder if, in stressing the creative aspect of scientific activity, Polanyi has not underestimated that feature which nevertheless distinguishes the sciences from other activities of the mind.

It is an undeniable fact in the history of science that, at each epoch, there is a set of propositions about which the scientific community is in accord, for the time being. Even if one speaks of these propositions with scorn as of "dead science," even if one is not entirely in agreement in enumerating them, even if they are only provisionally considered as true, even if several are expected to be called in question by some future great discovery, the existence of a body of accepted truths constitutes a fact whose importance must not be overlooked. One could possibly oppose one or another of these propositions, but only on condition of showing their incompatibility with other propositions that are more firmly established. In any case they must be presumed true until proof is offered to the contrary. In contrast, it should be noted that such a body of accepted truths does not exist in philosophy or in law, or in the domains of art, morality, or religion—at least when one crosses the boundary of a particular community. This situation cannot be explained without the existence of techniques of proof and verification, of prediction and experimentation, which are proper to the sciences, and for which there is no equivalent in the other disciplines. This is certainly not to say that verification in the natural sciences can be made entirely formal and impersonal; for the process of verification is carried out within a discipline whose presuppositions must not be taken for granted, with the help of instruments, by means of a terminology elaborated by a particular theory, and by making skilful use of techniques. When a scientific theory takes account of all the facts in a specific domain without neglecting facts left unexplained by an earlier theory, and when it permits predictions which the earlier theory did not support, it takes very little time before it imposes itself on the world of science. It is only when no theory is entirely satisfying that several hypotheses are able to share the favor of specialists. In this context one must moreover recognize that the arguments considered relevant by the partisans of one theory may be considered irrelevant by the partisans of another. This divergence may be due to rival world views or philosophies. But in that case, one seeks, as far as possible, to eliminate disagreement in the domain of science by relegating it to the field of philosophy.

Because of this existing body of scientific truths, all past science is truly out of date. This is not the case with the other branches of culture. Just because an artistic, philosophic, or religious conception is an attractively new one, it does not disqualify works of art, philosophy, or religions from past centuries. But the science of today dispenses with the science of yesterday, however much it owes to it in terms of its language, its methods, and its problems; but our artistic, philosophic, and religious past is always present in our culture; it does not cease to contribute to its actual life. A theory of science must take account of this peculiar situation, for if it were to neglect this aspect of things, it would be as lame as that theory which neglects the creative aspect of the scientist.

More than all other disciplines, science requires invention and verification. It is not because the scientist has such a penetrating vision of reality that he cannot be mistaken. Rather, to the extent that this vision is ample and fertile, there is risk that—at least partially—it may not conform to reality. Moreover, experience may well disprove the most attractive hypotheses. Indeed, the creative activity of the scientist is not simply perception of a hidden structure; it is very often an attempt to provide an explanatory hypothesis which, by going beyond the actually perceived data, incurs the risk of being at least partially falsified by the facts. Indeed, the activity of the scientist is not simply perception of a "Gestalt"; it is an extrapolation, more or less bold, passing the boundaries of experience. Polanyi himself recognizes[10] that scientists spend their lives making correct guesses. But

10. *Ibid.*, p. 143.

how would they know that their guesses were correct if they did not admit some criteria that would indicate when they had erred? They certainly expect that their hypotheses may be amended or sometimes even entirely abandoned. It is in this respect that the explanations of the scientists differ essentially from those of the Azande to which M. Polanyi compares them.[11] There is a nucleus of undeniable truth in the claims of K. Popper according to which scientific activity is characterized by the capacity of the scientist to benefit from his mistakes and gradually to correct them.

Precisely because scientific activity is indissolubly linked with the techniques of prediction and verification, there is a dialectical relationship between the two levels so aptly distinguished by Polanyi, the level of the simple elements and the level of the whole which they condition. To be scientific, a comprehensive view must provide for the prediction of details; and these details must be actually observed, in order to corroborate the over-all hypothesis.

Moreover, even ordinary perception, which Polanyi takes as a model for the view of the scientists,[12] is not immediately given: J. Piaget has proved, in his outstanding studies on child psychology, how the adaptation of perception is formed slowly by a process of correcting a number of hypotheses that are abandoned one after another. The same applies to the scientist's view of reality where, in the elaboration and testing of hypotheses, submission to the real plays a more important role than in art, philosophy, and religion; in these latter, the creator is able to *decide*, though not arbitrarily, about the superiority of one point of view over another. His decision is in fact as much an expression of his personality as of the elements he seeks to organize. This is not the case, in any comparable manner, with the natural sciences.

The scientist who studies reality must bow before the results that he obtains; he is not their master. True, these results are correlated with a theory, a language, a methodology, a technique of measurement; but all these are part of the framework of our scientific enterprise and belong to the presuppositions which

11. *Ibid.*, pp. 287-288, 284.
12. *Ibid.*, pp. 57-58.

condition our research. As to these presuppositions, we may perhaps some time call one or another in question, but this will never happen without good reason. To abandon them, it would be necessary to show their incompatibility with others that are considered less doubtful or more fundamental. Further, one cannot discard a doubtful particular without disqualifying it in terms of a new theory, a new approach which ought in turn to be submitted to the test of experience. Now in art, philosophy, law, and religion a variety of incompatible points of view can be put forward without there being any generally accepted criteria which would permit discarding all other points of view in favor of one only.

Hence the difference which I am trying to establish between truth and rationality.[13] In virtue of the principle of non-contradiction, a proposition and its negation cannot be simultaneously true; from this follows out rejection of pluralism in scientific matters. But when it is a question not of describing the real but of putting it in perspective, of evaluating it, of elaborating an ontology (and *not* a natural science), then different points of view may confront one another without any one of them imposing itself on the others; each of them may lay claim to rationality—that is to say to a universality analogous to that demanded by Kant's categorical imperative.[14] Each philosopher may present his point of view as universally valid, at least ideally, without this point of view necessarily being admitted by all. The same holds of that kind of legislation which claims to be the only just one, but which nevertheless must be imposed by a legitimate authority in order to become obligatory. When generally admitted criteria do not permit a choice between antagonistic claims, and yet practical problems must be solved, the recourse to authority is inevitable. Hence the recourse to the judges while the legislative power has authority to decide about the obligatory character of the rules. But in a science that is independent of all

13. Cf. Chaim Perelman, "Désaccord et rationalité des décisions," *Archivio di Filosofia* (*Logica e Analisi*) (Roma, 1966), pp. 87-93.
14. Cf. "La Quête du rationnel" in Chaim Perelman and L. Olbrechts-Tyteca, *Rhétorique et Philosophie* (Paris: Presses Universitaires de France, 1952), pp. 110-120.

political and religious power there is no authority capable of saying what is true and no need for such authority.

This is the main criticism I would make concerning Polanyi's theory of science. To my mind, it likens the personal involvement of the scientist too much to that of the artist or the philosopher.[15] I believe there are essential differences. Even if, like Polanyi, I am a partisan of personal knowledge integrated with a cultural tradition, I should still like to stress the particular place of science in our culture. For, in science, the techniques of proof and verification make it possible to bring about agreement in essentials, an accord inaccessible in other domains. It is in this sense that I would like to see Polanyi's ideas developed. Their depth and interest are undeniable; they make a major contribution to the critique of the foundations of contemporary positivism.

15. *P.K.*, p. 133.

THE GENTLE RAIN—A SEARCH
FOR UNDERSTANDING

William T. Scott

Throughout the ages the gentle rain has slaked man's thirst and watered his crops. It has brought rejoicing and misery, life and death. Man has speculated upon the causes of rain and sought to control it by means ranging from witchcraft to cloud seeding. Yet how rain occurs, what aery mechanisms generate raindrops out of the tenuous fog of a cloud, remains a puzzle of extraordinary difficulty which atmospheric scientists are just now beginning to solve.

In our search for understanding of the causes and behavior of the gentle rain, we must study the natural history of clouds and their internal structure. We need to investigate clouds in their environment, to learn how they come to be formed, whence they draw their water, and how they interact with each other. We also need to know more than we do about the sizes and numbers of droplets they carry, the sort and quantity of ice crystals they develop, the values of temperature and humidity that occur, the speed of updrafts and the kind of turbulent mixing of damp and dry air that goes on.

In efforts to unravel some of the mathematical aspects of this puzzle and in my sharing in the wider cloud physics program of the University of Nevada's Desert Research Institute, I have been struck by the way Michael Polanyi's theory of knowledge[1] illuminates our efforts. Polanyi serves both as interpreter and guide in a

1. See especially his *P.K.*; also *S.M.* and *T.D.*

field where many answers are beginning to appear and new methods are fast developing.

Since little effort has thus far been made to formulate the underlying assumptions and principles of research in the physics of precipitation,[2] it is stimulating to use Polanyi's interpretation and guidance in developing such a formulation, six aspects of which are presented in this article.

The two central intertwined themes of Polanyi's philosophy are epistemological and ontological: the personal involvement of the knower in his knowledge and the many-leveled structure of reality. In each section I discuss one or both of these themes. I begin with the *Scales of Organization* of the atmosphere, which illustrate the many levels of reality, as well as the part-whole character of all perception. We apprehend each phenomenon of the atmosphere as a thing in itself, but we also perceive it to be both constituted of particulars belonging to smaller scales and as being itself a part of a larger whole.

The *"part-whole"* or *"from-to"* character of perception involves a large degree of tacit knowing. From the fact that we know things we cannot tell may be derived a consideration of several *Unspecifiable Arts* in cloud physics, which are the subject of my second section.

The high degree of personal judgment implied by the existence of unspecifiability in scientific method appears in sharp contrast to the usual scientific ideal that aims at exactness of measurement and prediction. In section III on the *Laplacean Ideal* I examine this ideal of exactness and give reasons why I consider it misplaced.

The discovery and validation of good theories involves personal judgment based on a vision of reality which these theories promise to reveal to us. The question of *What Is a Good Theory?* in cloud physics and a characterization of models used in trying to find one are taken up in section IV.

2. I speak of the rain as gentle out of appreciation and respect, but of course rain is not always gentle. The scientist who explores its puzzles must reckon with the violence of electrical storms and the vast strength of hurricanes. For the purposes of this article, however, it is sufficient to consider the simpler and less dramatic aspects of steady rains, intermittent showers, and clouds that do not rain at all.

In any field each person doing research can become expert and make a contribution only in a small corner of it. He must rely on his colleagues throughout the rest of the field for the knowledge he builds on. The mutual personal involvements of *Cloud Physicists and Their Colleagues* are considered in section V.

The most personal element of all in the search for knowledge is commitment to the reality we seek and to the discoveries we make, a commitment that implies faith. *Commitment and Faith* form the subject of the concluding section.

I. *Scales of Organization*

The entire field of atmospheric science, from cloud physics to global circulation, resolves itself into activities focused on several different levels of reality, or scales of organization. An account of these scales and their interactions will provide an opportunity to introduce the reader to some of the main features of clouds and the rain process as we currently understand them[3] and to illustrate the character of Polanyi's outlook as a Gestalt philosophy.[4]

A single cloud may be described as a particular eddy or bubble in the ever-changing motion of air in a particular valley or plain or mountain region. The conditions that lead to cloud formation in a given region involve the motion of large parcels of air as they interact with the local terrain, in the scale of motion which is called the *mesoscale*. The mesoscale serves as the basis for short-range judgments of what the weather is about to do.

Beyond the mesoscale lies the *macroscale*, which involves the circulation of air over continents and oceans, in fact, all around the planet. The major feature of motion on this scale involves the rising of warm air in the tropics, its spreading out north and south as gravity impedes its rise, and its tendency to generate the prevailing westerlies by maintaining the high speed of the earth's rotation at the equator as it moves to temperate zones. On this

3. For an introductory account of clouds and processes within them, see Louis A. Battan, *Cloud Physics and Cloud Seeding* ("Science Study Series," Garden City, New York: Doubleday, 1962).

4. See William T. Scott, "Polanyi's Theory of Personal Knowledge—A Gestalt Philosophy," *Massachusetts Review*, III (Winter, 1962), 349-368.

scale of motion, the irregular generation of large cyclonic storm systems is of especial importance for the weather.

Even the macroscale is not comprehensive enough for a complete description of the behavior of the atmosphere, for the relation of the earth to the sun and to the intervening medium governs the basic "fuel" for the whole process—solar heat. Atmospheric science at its highest level of organization is thus contiguous to astronomy.

On the other hand, the problem of how the gentle rain occurs involves a succession of ever smaller scales from the mesoscale downward. An isolated cumulus cloud has a life of its own during which it is relatively independent of the larger scales of motion. For twenty minutes or so it maintains a clearly recognizable though constantly changing form. We recognize the *Gestalt* of the cloud by merging together the particulars of shape, contrast with background, texture, and relation to other clouds.[5]

If we replace our focus of attention on a whole cloud with consideration of the parts or components of the cloud, we come immediately to consider its myriads of tiny droplets, usually ranging from a ten-thousandth to a thousandth of an inch in diameter. These droplets are so fine that even a slowly rising column of air can easily support them. It takes a million or so droplets coalesced together to form a corpuscle big enough to fall to the ground and be counted as a raindrop. Therein lies our central problem: How does this coalescence happen and what circumstances control it?

The *microscale* of cloud physics includes droplets and their interactions, the dust particles or other so-called *condensation nuclei* on which droplets form, the ice crystals into which some of the droplets freeze in the cold upper parts of the clouds, and the environment of air and water vapor.

A still smaller scale, that of molecular processes, is also relevant to cloud physics. The passage of water molecules in and out of water-drop surfaces and ice-crystal faces is a basic process which influences the happenings in a cloud but only partially controls them. While the main feature of these physicochemical phenomena are well enough understood for applications to cloud

5. *P.K.*, p. 57.

processes, more research is needed in particular areas, such as the role of certain of the dust particles in a cloud in stimulating the formation of ice crystals.

These several scales illustrate Polanyi's ontological structuring of reality into levels,[6] differing both in the spatial dimensions of the objects involved and in the complexity of organization of the relevant processes. Comprehension at each level requires the recognition of organizing principles appropriate to that level, principles which cannot be derived from those governing subordinate levels. In *The Tacit Dimension* Polanyi illustrates the logical independence of the principles of a higher level or scale from laws of lower levels in terms of language:

> The operations of a higher level cannot be accounted for by the laws governing its particulars forming the lower level. You cannot derive a vocabulary from phonetics; you cannot derive the grammar of a language from its vocabulary; a correct use of grammar does not account for good style; and a good style does not provide the content of a piece of prose. We may conclude then quite generally . . . that it is impossible to represent the organizing principles of a higher level by the laws governing its isolated particulars.[7]

A larger scale or higher level exercises control over lower levels involved in it by determining shapes or forms of action, or more generally by determining boundary conditions left open by the laws of the lower level. Polanyi calls this relation of upper level to lower the "Principle of Marginal Control."[8] Numerous illustrations can be given of the principle of marginal control in cloud physics. The molecular processes of evaporation and condensation govern the rates of growth for water droplets in given circumstances of temperature, humidity, and character and number of condensation nuclei. The dynamics and structure of the whole cloud and the surrounding mesoscale determine which particular circumstances for droplet growth will occur. The behavior of a cloud and its mesoscale environment is in turn dependent on heat and evaporation in the nearby terrain and the

6. *Ibid.*, pp. 381-382; Michael Polanyi, *S.M.*, p. 46.
7. *T.D.*, p. 36.
8. *Ibid.*, p. 40.

motion of large air masses into the given region as determined on the macroscale.

The effect of lower levels on operations on the higher levels is to set limiting conditions for them. For example, no cloud process can violate the physical principle of conservation of energy. It is important to note that setting *conditions* on a given level is not the same as *accounting* for operations at that level, for such conditions cannot even define these operations. No principles drawn from the microscale can define the organization of a cloud or even of the eddies that form it. It is also impossible for the larger scales to define operations at the lower levels. The mesoscale cannot define or determine the principles of condensation, coalescence, and other processes that constitute the mesoscale.

The scales of organization in the atmosphere are also interrelated by a process peculiar to the motions of gases and liquids, the formation of turbulent eddies. Fluids, both gas and liquid, can move in regular streamlines only if their particles travel slowly enough. As soon as motion is speeded up in a water pipe or in a wind, whirls and eddies appear in random fashion. At high speeds, the entire motion is turbulent, with an average flow that appears smooth only if not closely examined.

Along with myriads of small eddies, fluid flow involves large vortices, rising plumes and bubbles, and other features which can be recognized as separately existing entities for short periods of time. Their initiation appears to be a random process, but once they have appeared, their future behavior and final disappearance can be approximately predicted.

Individual cumulus clouds are often best described as eddies arising in this way. They usually occur in an environment that is unstable because the hot air that wants to rise is close to the ground underneath layers of colder air at moderate heights. Winds along the surface can start bubbles of warm air rising, which form clouds by carrying water vapor to a sufficiently cool height. We have here an example of how large-scale fluid motions tend to generate within themselves structural features that we recognize as belonging to a smaller scale. Such acts of recognition of structural features are central elements in Polanyi's epsistemology. They arise "by an act of comprehension which consists in merging our awareness of a set of particulars into our focal awareness of their joint significance."[9]

Let us consider some of the problems of knowledge in regard to levels in cloud physics. There are times when the microscale predominates in the researcher's attention, as when he is trying to study the rate at which small droplets collide and make larger ones. The operational principles of this process need to be made clear before its influence on the cloud as a whole can be determined.

On the other hand, there are times when the scientist obtains evidence showing that a larger scale of motion is to a considerable degree independent of occurrences on a smaller scale. For instance, the rates at which towers rise out of a cumulus cloud or the degree to which dry air may be entrained by turbulent motion at the sides of a cloud can be analyzed without having more than a quite rough idea of the rate at which water condensing into droplets releases its latent heat and adds to the buoyancy of air within the cloud. Or we can study the interactions of a group of clouds competing for the available moisture even if we scarcely understand what goes on inside each one.

There are other times in rain studies when two or more levels appear with equal importance—as when the scientist treats the formation of large rain drops and the way in which they drag substantial amounts of air down with them as they fall, or when he explores the relation of the temperature and speed of winds aloft to how high a cloud can grow and what its probability is to rain.

Polanyi's vision of an "essentially stratified world,"[10] perceived in a *Gestalt*-like way, receives confirmation from the roles that scales of organization play in the atmospheric sciences.

II. *Unspecifiable Arts*

The recognition of entities, such as cloud systems, separate clouds, individual bubbles of heated air inside a cloud, and so on, is but one of many unspecifiable arts that form the basis for our

9. *S.M.*, p. 44. Such acts of comprehension are treated in Gestalt psychology, but Gestalt psychology deals with their automatic character in contrast to Polanyi's emphasis on the intentional effort involved.

10. *P.K.*, p. 382.

present comprehension of atmospheric phenomena and our hope for new discoveries in the behavior of rain and weather. The existence of such arts and other tacit forms of knowing is fundamental to Polanyi's theory of knowledge,[11] and gives us further grounds for applying his theory to the problem of the gentle rain.

There are innumerable examples of unspecifiable art in the study of clouds and weather. The weather forecaster relies on thousands of reports by observers around the world who must exercise skill in describing clouds, rain, snow, "gustiness," and other features which are not subject to purely quantitative measurement. The weather-map maker needs special skills in correlating these reports and putting them in graphical form, and finally the forecaster himself must combine artful judgment with skilful use of maps and computational results.

The team of cloud experimenters[12] needs to select clouds that are alike in certain respects believed to be essential, in spite of the obvious individual differences of each cloud from every other. The scientific group making such judgments has to combine a tacit integration of visual clues, both conscious and subliminal, with the arts of choosing and executing appropriate measurements of temperature, humidity, wind speed and so forth. These observations may be taken from balloons that rise through the cloud or the the air nearby,[13] or from aircraft that fly through the clouds at predetermined levels. The team must put together many clues obtained from these observations in determining whether a given cloud is appropriate for the given experiment. The resulting comprehension they attain is an entity that exists on a higher level of organization than the clues which are its parts, in striking parallel to the structure of the entities being comprehended.[14] The arts of knowing what measurements should be taken, what degree of precision is needed or tolerable, how to

11. Michael Polanyi, "Tacit Knowing: Its Bearing on Some Problems in Philosophy," *Reviews of Modern Physics*, XXXIV (Oct., 1962), 601-616; *S.M.*, Lecture 1; *T.D.*, Lecture 1.
12. Such as the Project Hailswath group in 1966 at Rapid City, South Dakota, testing out possible means of hail suppression or the Project Stormfury group in 1963 and 1965 seeding clouds in the Caribbean and watching their subsequent growth.
13. Giving results called "soundings" by analogy with deep-sea observations.
14. *T.D.*, pp. 33-34.

interpret the results, and how to integrate measurements with visual observations all involve tacit skills that cannot be articulated precisely.

We know that in our research operations we require specialized skills, but we usually cannot recognize rules by which these skills are performed, much less formulate them: *". . . the aim of a skilful performance is achieved by the observance of a set of rules which are not known as such to the person following them."*[15] Knowledge obtained in this way is clearly *personal,* in Polanyi's use of the term.

Even the articulable part of our knowledge requires the tacit art of using language that correctly describes what we believe is really going on in a system.[16] Confusions are often cleared up by a skilful introduction of new terms[17] which allow us to recognize and affirm hitherto unrecognized aspects of reality. For instance, the ice crystals in the cold upper parts of many clouds have long been thought to form in two ways. Some relatively bare or dry cloud nuclei may receive water molecules from the surrounding vapor and allow these molecules to arrange themselves directly into ice crystals. Such nuclei are called *sublimation* or *deposition nuclei.* Other ice crystals are formed by the freezing of droplets of water that have risen into the cold region, and contain within them small insoluble grains of crystalline material that start the water molecules freezing. Without such grains, called *freezing nuclei,* droplets may have to cool down all the way to −40°F. before freezing spontaneously.

These two terms, deposition nucleus and freezing nucleus, were inadequate to account for certain cases in which a small amount of liquid water had first to be absorbed or adsorbed on the nucleus before freezing could occur. Controversies over this process were resolved and a fresh view of the situation was obtained when L. Randall Koenig introduced the term *sorption nucleus* to describe the third class of particulate matter in clouds.[18]

Similarly, thought about mesoscale and macroscale motions as

15. *P.K.,* p. 49.
16. *Ibid.,* chap. v; *S.M.,* p. 25.
17. *P.K.,* pp. 107-112.
18. H. R. Koenig, "Ice in the Summer Atmosphere: Structure, Genesis, and Metamorphosis" (Ph.D. Thesis, University of Chicago, 1962).

relevant to weather forecasting really began when Tor Bergeron introduced the term "air mass" for a large mass of air of relatively homogeneous properties which moves over the earth to influence weather.[19] The imprecision of this term in no way hindered its usefulness. Instead it has called forth efforts which not only added to its precision—for instance, when C.-G. Rossby introduced the further concept of the jet stream[20]—but provided new insights into atmospheric phenomena, thus giving evidence that the original term had a genuine bearing on reality.

Great efforts have been made to achieve more precision and objectivity in science by the use of computers. However, personal tacit skills are inescapable in recognizing correct usage of a computer and in interpreting the meaning of its results. Computers may even be used to assist and improve skilful personal activity in an experimental program, in contrast to their usual supposedly more impersonal use. A recent development of great promise is the combined use of radar, telemetry, and on-line computing for guiding aircraft experiments in clouds. This plan, a cooperative effort of several institutions that was originally developed at the Desert Research Institute in Nevada, involves a telemetering radio link between instruments in the airplane and similar ones on the ground so that the latter keep step with the former. Radar sets follow the speed and position of the plane, as well as the location of the larger drops and ice crystals in the cloud. The telemetered data and the radar signals are fed into a computer which prints out on a map the flight path of the plane and pertinent information, such as wind speeds and directions, temperature, water content of the cloud, acceleration of the airplane, etc. The scientists in the control station can read all this information directly. As their skill increases in integrating the many clues provided by this scheme, they can direct the plane crew over the radio as to how to set their course for getting the

19. Tor Bergeron, "Über die dreidimensionale verknüpfende Wetteranalyse," *I. Geofys. Publ.,* V (1928), 111.
20. C.-G. Rossby, "On the Distribution of Angular Velocity in Gaseous Envelopes under the Influence of Large-Scale Horizontal Mixing Processes," *Bulletin of the American Meteorological Society,* XXVIII (1947), 53-68. See also H. Riehl, M. A. Alaka, L. L. Jordan, and R. J. Renard, *The Jet Stream* (*Meteorological Monographs,* Vol. 2, No. 7; Boston: American Meteorological Society, 1954), pp. 1-3.

most useful data. For instance, research into the problem of rain calls for data on the distribution of droplet sizes at different positions in a cloud. A properly executed sequence of flights with an air-borne droplet sampler may reveal some of the presently unknown details on droplet concentration and growth.

Personal guidance by a skilled staff using these tools of modern technology can make the difference between the collection of meaningful data and wasted flights with little or no results of importance. The particulars relied on for such personal guidance are to a considerable degree unspecifiable, for three interconnected reasons: (1) The particulars are seen by pilot, crew, and controlling staff in far too rapid a sequence for specification to be possible, even if individual elements could be specified when given enough thought and attention; (2) many of the features of cloud structure, wind pattern, instrumental fluctuations, radar-screen echoes, and the like are observed only subliminally and are unconsciously merged into focal awareness of the experimental situations by skilled observers; and (3) focal attention on some of the details could lead to a complete destruction of an awareness of the over-all situation—the observer would lose control and the pilot would have to rely only on his and his crew's observations at altitude.[21]

Tools used in this unspecifiable way, to provide particular clues on which we rely for focal attention to the experiment in progress, act as extensions of our bodies, as Polanyi describes for simpler instruments:

> Our subsidiary awareness of tools and probes can be regarded now as the act of making them form a part of our own body. The way we use a hammer or a blind man uses his stick, shows in fact that in both cases we shift outwards the points at which we make contact with the things that we observe as objects outside ourselves. While we rely on a tool or a probe, these are not handled as external objects. We may test the tool for its effectiveness or the probe for its suitability, e.g. in discovering the hidden details of a cavity, but the tool and the probe can never lie in the field of these operations; they remain necessarily on our side of it, form-

21. See *S.M.*, pp. 44-45, for Polanyi's description of unspecifiability.

ing part of ourselves, the operating persons. We pour ourselves out into them and assimilate them as parts of our own
existence. We accept them existentially by dwelling in
them.[22]

Polanyi describes four structural elements of tacit knowing, the
functional, the *phenomenal,* the *semantic,* and the *ontological,*[23]
which have a direct application in the use of tools for research.
Our reliance on the tool to attend to an object being probed is
the functional aspect. Our awareness of the tool in the background of our perception of the object constitutes the phenomenal aspect. In the fact that the clues furnished by the tool form
together the meaning of the object lies the semantic aspect. Our
experience of meeting a real object by use of the tool provides the
ontological aspect.

Finally, our "dwelling in" a tool is a form of commitment. It
expresses our anticipation of many further unpredictable insights
about nature to be obtained as we continue to use this tool in
research. The unspecifiability involved in the use of tools and in
all the other arts of research may appear to those used to exact
descriptions of methodology to be a basic if unavoidable defect.
On the contrary, it is the personal pole of such operations that
gives us contact with reality, allowing us to become convinced or
to doubt in accordance with our best judgment. In the final section we shall return to a further consideration of the element of
commitment in science.

III. *The Laplacean Ideal*

In most discussions of physical theory, impersonal objectivity
and exactness of measurement are held up as scientific ideals.
The personal components of scientific investigations that we have
just discussed appear to contradict these ideals. If we were to
accept the objectivist ideals, we could assume that the apparent
contradiction is purely a matter of human limitations which
future developments will progressively eliminate. Then we could

22. *P.K.,* p. 59.
23. *T.D.,* pp. 11-13.

envisage arriving at a time when cloud systems would be fully predictable in the sense of Newtonian Mechanics,[24] and the ideals of objectivity and exactness could be effectively pursued. I do not believe that such a time could ever come. I shall try to show why by phrasing Newtonian determinism in the form proposed by Laplace and then contrasting this form with the present situation in cloud physics, a situation which involves a combination of partly deterministic and partly statistical methodology. I shall also show how personal judgment—the basic element of the so-called human limitations—underlies whatever degree of success we can achieve in either a mechanistic or a statistical approach.

The Laplacean ideal proceeds from the assertion of Newtonian mechanics that the future behavior of a system of particles can be completely predicted if the laws of force are known and if at a given instant one knows precisely the positions and velocities of each individual particle.[25] If this theory is strictly upheld, it not only asserts that the motion of a system of particles is completely determined, but it offers us as the ideal program of science (1) an ever-improving accuracy of measurement of the initial states of the particles, (2) as precise as possible a computation of their motion by Newtonian laws, (3) and a verification of the computation by repeating the measurements at a given time later.

Although this threefold program may appear to be a sound approach to atmospheric science, it fails for several reasons. In the first place, it is totally impossible to obtain initial information on all the molecules in a given mass of air. We must resort to averages by the method of treating parcels of air as if they were portions of a continuous fluid. The particle equations of Newton are then replaced by field equations for the motions of a contin-

24. Newtonian determinism has, of course, been modified by the introduction of quantum-mechanical indeterminacy. However, this limitation operates at the atomic level and seems irrelevant to the levels from the microscale up to those of atmospheric motions in general. Quantum effects are important for the absorption and re-emission of the sun's heat in the atmosphere, but do not in this respect involve indeterminacy.

25. The Laplacean ideal and its difficulties are discussed carefully and at length by Ernst Cassirer, *Determinism and Indeterminism in Modern Physics* (New Haven: Yale University Press, 1956), chap. i. See also Henry Margenau, *The Nature of Physical Reality* (New York: McGraw-Hill, 1950), chap. xix, and *P.K.*, pp. 139-142.

uous fluid, the so-called Navier-Stokes equations. While these equations are themselves deterministic, they are approximate by their very nature so that the laws of force expressed in them may no longer be considered to be exactly known. Furthermore, the problem of measuring initial conditions still cannot be solved in practice although it is no longer absurdly impossible. We can get only approximate initial values which we smooth out in some idealized fashion, knowing thereby that here too we are losing precision in representing nature.

In the second place, the possibilities of numerical solution of the Navier-Stokes equations are severely limited even with the best computers. The equations must be further approximated in order to fit a computer, and then every computer has a limit of error to which it works. Its errors cumulate as more steps, representing more intervals of time, are calculated, so that computer solutions generally have the property of "blowing up"—giving numbers obviously far too large or otherwise in gross error after a sufficiently large number of time steps have been evaluated. This difficulty does not occur when processes that do not last long are being considered, for instance the motion of droplets from bottom to top through a small cloud in the order of a few minutes, but this exception only serves to illustrate the point. For longer duration processes, considerable improvements are being made in keeping computer solutions well behaved, but the very success of these improvements upsets the original Laplacean ideal. The way solutions are kept in bounds is to introduce dissipative and stabilizing effects that are known from micro- and mesoscale observations to play important roles.[26] Then, in fact, numerical computations begin to resemble observations from nature, *but they no longer derive their results solely from particles, laws of force, and initial conditions.* Furthermore, the use of stabilizing factors cannot overcome the third difficulty that the particular time and place where an eddy will appear in an otherwise steady flow of air may well be determined by imperceptible differences in initial conditions. Since an eddy may become a cloud or a

26. See J. Simpson, R. H. Simpson, D. A. Andrews, and M. A. Eaton, "Experimental Cumulus Dynamics," *Reviews of Geophysics*, III (Aug. 1965), 390 for an account of computer difficulties. Polanyi discusses frictional and stabilizing influences in *T.D.*, pp. 88-89.

hurricane depending on its size, we see that long-range predictability is severely limited in scope.

The limitations of predictability were concretely expressed at a conference on long-range weather prediction in Boulder, Colorado in 1964.[27] The conclusion was generally accepted that the best hope for the foreseeable future was to predict the weather accurately for a period of one week and to give significant probability estimates for one week more. Estimating the occurrence of small-scale effects is much harder than predicting regional weather. No less an authority than F. H. Ludlam of the University of London asserts that we cannot hope to predict individual showers more than one hour in advance.[28]

There are still more troubles with the Laplacean ideal. Even successful calculation of the motions of individual particles or parcels will fail to give the insight we seek. In the first place, we are concerned with clouds and their droplets. As molecules or parcels of air go in and out of droplets and clouds, we find our interest centered in the persisting organized wholes of our open systems, rather than in the particles that go in and out of them. The entities on which we focus attention change their boundaries and may be said to include more or fewer particles as they grow or decay. The Laplacean ideal provides no mechanism for distinguishing such wholes as the particles move in and out.[29] It takes highly trained personal skill to assess entities of this type. If one watches a group of small cumulus clouds for half an hour, one can readily observe the continual growth and decay of individual clouds of the group. However, the average person would find it very hard to decide what collection of white wisps in a blue sky to denote as belonging to a particular cloud.

Besides the use of computers for so-called "field-of-motion" studies based on approximate forms of the Navier-Stokes equations with effects of turbulence superimposed,[30] there is another

27. See especially a paper given at this conference by B. Ericksson, *World Meteorological Organizations,* Tech. Note No. 66 (1965), pp. 126-129.
28. Frank H. Ludlam, "Weather Forecasting," *Science Progress,* No. 161 (Jan., 1953), 91.
29. *P.K.,* pp. 139-142; the Laplacean ideal treats only a single level of reality, the very lowest!
30. Examples are given by Douglas K. Lilly, "On the Numerical Simulation of Buoyant Convection," *Tellus,* XIV (1962), 148-172; and Y. Ogura, "Convection of Isolated Masses of a Buoyant Fluid—A Numerical Calculation," *Journal of the Atmospheric Sciences,* XIX (1962), 492-502.

way in which numerical calculations are made, the so-called "entity" approach. In this approach, an entity in the form of a vortex ring, bubble, or rising plume is postulated and equations derived for it from properties of motion on the micro- and mesoscales. Models of this sort compute the rate of rise and expansion of the entity, its thermal behavior, and the behavior of its water content.[31] In several respects such models appear to be more fruitful than the field-of-motion type in providing insight into cloud behavior, but it is likely that the two types will come closer together in usefulness as research proceeds.[32]

A large part of the success of present methodology in atmospheric physics depends on the use of probability theory. Randomness as the basis for probability theory emerges, as Polanyi says, from efforts to focus on specific entities and submerge the details of background.[33] If many cases of a given entity are observed, or even just conceived, most of the details of the environmental background appear random. Stated another way, the entities appear to arise randomly from the environment. Random events such as eddies and vortices, or the appearance of momentarily stable open cloud systems, are subject to probability theory. Proper application of probability theory unfortunately requires large samples, which are almost never obtained in cloud physics. However, comprehension of observed entities as potential members of a large statistical class justifies their joint analytic treatment by the approximate entity type of model.

The statistical nature of atmospheric entities may be considered to arise from deterministic behavior which is simply beyond calculation,[34] or (if we imagine calculating initial conditions to a great extreme of accuracy) it may be ascribed to the basically indeterministic character of atoms and molecules as described by

31. See, for instance, Joseph Levine, "Spherical Vortex Theory of Bubble-Like Motions in Cumulus Clouds," *Journal of Meteorology*, XVI (1959), 653-662; and P. Squires and J. S. Turner, "An Entraining Jet Model for Cumulo-Nimbus Updraughts," *Tellus*, XIV (1962), 422-434.

32. This likelihood is indicated in unpublished lecture notes kindly furnished to me by Dr. Joanne Simpson.

33. *P.K.*, pp. 390-393.

34. The way in which eddy development in turbulent yet deterministic fluid flow simulates randomness is described by L. D. Landau and E. M. Lifschitz, *Fluid Mechanics*, trans. J. W. Sykes and W. H. Reid (Reading, Mass.: Addison-Wesley, 1959), pp. 102-107.

quantum indeterminacy. Our conception of the origin of this probabilistic character of nature is not the convincing fact about it, however. What is convincing is that ascribing probabilistic laws to atmospheric phenomena provides insight into the reality with which we are trying to deal.

The question of whether personal elements in scientific research can be ascribed to human limitations of observation and calculation can be answered in the negative by reference to our earlier discussion of unspecifiable arts and by other personal components to be discussed in the rest of this article. Limitations of both man and apparatus in accuracy of observations are, of course, quite important. Establishing limits to our confidence in experimental conclusions involves a special application of probability concepts in the well-established statistical theory of errors. Sampling methods are applied to cloud observations and reliability and precision estimates are made for instruments.

But even for these relatively objective situations, personal judgment is required. Instrument limitations are almost always estimated by those intimately acquainted with the operation of the instruments. They make such estimates with considerable confidence since the precision of most instruments is greater than the reproducibility of the atmospheric variables—temperature, wind, speed, humidity, water content—that are measured.

The smallness of statistical samples used in cloud physics calls for the exercise of considerable skill in drawing reliable conclusions since there is a large degree of error in results computed from such samples. A more subtle way in which personal judgment is required for error analysis is in decisions as to whether an unusually large or small value of some variable is a true random occurrence or an anomaly resulting from special causes. Take for example the sampling device which catches cloud droplets in soft plastic where they leave replicas to be counted.[35] If an unusually large number of droplets approaching raindrop size should be recorded, is the reason that the type of cloud that has been sampled can occasionally develop such drops, or that an unusual puff of industrial smoke came drifting by? Every unusual value in

35. Paul B. MacCready, Jr., and Clement J. Todd, "Continuous Particle Sampler," *Journal of Applied Meteorology,* III (1964) , 450-460.

a statistical survey must be examined and judged either to belong to the sample or to be irrelevant and hence to be rejected.

Numerical and statistical methods of research bear a close resemblance to laboratory investigation in that unspecifiable personal acts of operation, appraisal, and judgment underlie all the more objective specifiable components and are essential for success.

IV. What Is a Good Theory?

We cannot use Laplacean determinism as an ideal for a theory of cloud phenomena. What standard can we raise in its place?

Shall we say that a good theory is one that fits the facts within the limits of skilled judgment? The answer is both yes and no. It is correct to say that we aim for a situation in which facts and theory agree. However, the establishment of a fact—e.g., that certain types of rain arise from the ice-crystal process, or that the droplets at the base of a certain kind of small cumulus average two ten-thousandths of an inch in diameter—depends heavily on the acceptance of theory.[36] Measurements depend on the theory of operation of instruments and theoretical statements concerning which data are extraneous and which are meaningful. The various cloud types are distinguished by knowing which features are relevant. Facts in cloud physics are recognized as such only by persons who dwell within a range of theory of the sort just mentioned, "interiorizing" the theory as parts of themselves and using it like a tool. Thus we cannot say that facts exist either logically or chronologically prior to the theory by which they are affirmed and for which they furnish evidence. A close interaction of theory and fact is one reasonable criterion for the worth of a theory, but mere fitting of supposedly independent facts is meaningless.

Shall we say that a good theory is one that allows reasonably accurate prediction? Successful prediction of future events is surely good evidence for the validity of a theory, and is in fact

36. Karl R. Popper makes this point in his book that deals only with explicit logical elements in science, *The Logic of Scientific Discovery* (New York: Basic Books, 1959), p. 423.

one of the underlying aims of cloud physics research. But what of a theory that claims only to provide probabilities for many events or requires for those cases that it can predict with accuracy a set of data that are almost never obtainable? This is just the character that emerging theories of the gentle rain seem to have.

These theories specify elements of structure which a group of clouds may have in common and which will on the average lead to certain effects. Many other details, which may differ from cloud to cloud, are classed as irrelevant. The statistical results of a series of observations of these central elements are claimed to be independent of the secondary details. Thus the success or failure of prediction in the strict sense could not be used to test such theories. It is possible that in certain rare cases of considerable symmetry and freedom from extraneous influences a reasonably accurate prediction could be made on the basis of initial data, but obtaining such data—e.g., the wind velocity and nucleus concentration at points all over the underside of a cloud—requires far more sophisticated, extensive, and costly apparatus than is now available. We cannot even be sure that apparatus extensive enough to get all the input data we need would not seriously interfere with the system under test and render void our experiments.

Statistical testing is of course a form of verification of prediction, but the use of predictability as a criterion hinges upon the acceptance of skilled judgments about the selection of samples and the evaluation of results. Such a criterion is of limited usefulness as a test of a good theory, and clearly needs to be supplemented by other considerations.

Shall we say that a satisfactory criterion is the success of the theory in suggesting new experiments or in telling which new measurements are worth making?[37] The answer is partly yes, for the development of theory in interaction with experiment is an essentially creative process. A simple example of a theory suggesting a new experiment is that of the wave-cloud experiment being

37. The difference between a successful new experiment or significant measurement and a successful prediction is that the latter deals only with *expected* results, whereas the results of a new investigation may be completely unexpected and yet affirmed as successful, yielding valid information. See *T.D.*, p. 82.

carried out at the University of Nevada. The theory of air-motion over a mountain range into valleys beyond shows that a steady wave of air will arise beyond the edge of the mountains and, if conditions are right, will maintain a cloud at the peak of the wave. This wave cloud, a common sight east of the Sierra Nevada, is predicted by the theory to contain a continually generated set of droplets that move regularly through the cloud from front to back. According to the theory, several droplet-growth processes must go on in these streams of droplets, so that even though no rain is produced, a situation is provided in the field for studying microscale processes that cannot be carried on in the laboratory.

We can say, then, that fitting facts, predicting observations, and suggesting new experiments are meaningful but limited criteria for a good theory in cloud physics. The most adequate account of success in theory construction is essentially that given by Polanyi in *Personal Knowledge*.[38] A good theory is one that gives quantitative and qualitative insight into the processes and structures that function in a given system, such as a precipitating cloud. The theory must satisfy our standards of (1) coherence with accepted knowledge, such as the physics and chemistry of the microscale and the meteorology of the mesoscale, (2) agreement with observed facts obtained by using elements of the theory as a guide, as in the growth of a cumulus when latent heat in supercooled regions is released on cloud seeding, (3) logical and mathematical consistency, as when the equations describing a cloud as a rising plume are tested against the detailed Navier-Stokes equations to which the former is asserted to be a good approximation, and (4) ability to make clear the relevant features of a range of interesting situations in a rational, insightful way.

The formulation and critical examination of a theory in the light of these criteria involves an explicit integration of details that takes much of our knowledge out of the range of the tacit into the area of articulation. However, this process of integration must be understood as *complementing* tacit knowledge, acting partly in parallel with it and partly in alternation to it, but not as *superseding* the tacit. An extreme degree of detailed criticism

38. Pp. 134-139; see also *T.D.*, pp. 63-70.

may upset or even destroy our tacit understanding, but it often happens that skilled operations of explicit theory-making may result in deeper and wider ranging tacit knowledge as we come to dwell in the theories we accept on criteria we have already adopted.

A successful theory of the gentle rain will describe the circumstances under which cloud droplets grow by condensation, by coalescence, and by going through the ice-crystal stage. It will account for the influence of updrafts, vortex motion, turbulent mixing, and other features of cloud dynamics that the theory itself will declare to be relevant. The assertions will be quantitative to the extent that satisfyingly accurate predictions, including probability calculations, can be made.

In short, a good theory will satisfy standards we set ourselves for rationality and the accurate reflection of reality, including success in prediction and agreement with facts. Such a theory will provide us with satisfaction in the simple act of observing particular clouds and being able to answer the basic question of science "What is going on here?" Finally, it will open the way to our experiencing many new and unexpected consequences, in observation of events in the weather we have never seen before but yet can comprehend, in the invention of fruitful new ways of doing experiments in clouds, and in new theoretical insights into other levels of atmospheric phenomena on which the theory will have a bearing. It is success in these respects which will give us confidence that such a theory indeed describes reality.[39]

A theory of this type will have an objectivity we could not accord to any single fact, much less to any set of data.[40] Theories can be discussed, interpreted, reformulated, and otherwise examined, and inferences derived from them in innumerable ways by all sorts of persons. A widely accepted theory will have survived the criticism of many competent scientists, far more than could judge any particular set of facts with the specialized skills needed to appraise the taking of data and the inferring of results.[41]

39. *T.D.*, pp. 68-69.
40. *P.K.*, p. 4.
41. In addition to the specialized skills needed for the appraisal of a particular set of data, measurements are always subject to possible unsus-

The usual non-Polanyi view of objectivity puts the order just the other way: direct observation is considered the most objective, inferred facts next, and personally appraised theories are ranked quite low on the scale. This view leads to the treatment of data as good in themselves. It commonly happens in science that we preserve carefully recorded measurements which have no relevance to features of interest or significance and so are quite meaningless. The same objectivist attitude leads in some quarters to a suspicion of theory making, even to the absurd degree of insisting that every published paper contain empirical results.[42]

Let us turn now to specific features of current efforts at theory construction in cloud physics. These efforts center on the development of models. A model is an ideal conception of a physical situation that can be formulated in mathematical and physical terms, including both an organizing principle and specifiable details. A cloud model does not purport to represent any cloud precisely, but to represent the key features of a class of clouds with an accuracy sufficient to distinguish the behavior of this class from any other. For instance, one model of a small cumulus specifies a rising conical body of air that starts generating droplets throughout its cross section at a certain height and continues to rise with a specified amount of mixing of dry air entrained at the edges. Equations are given for the angle of the cone, the buoyancy and rate of rise of the body of air, its temperature and moisture variation, the mean droplet size, its growth, and other variables. The model assumes symmetry around an axis and uniform conditions across the cloud. Actual clouds that the model may fit will not be symmetrical or uniform, and will yield measurable values that only roughly fit those of the model. Nevertheless, valid conclusions may be possible as to whether the model describes the important processes that go on in the cloud.

Justifying a model is a form of verification. What does verification mean in the atmospheric sciences? Since precision cannot be hoped for, considerable judgment is required. Karl Popper's de-

---

pected instrumental failures or incomplete assessment of the circumstances (cloud type, etc.) being examined. A large fraction of published meteorological data appears to suffer from the last-named defect.

42. *P.K.*, p. 156.

scription of the method of subjecting a theory to possible falsification is reasonable for a model, provided the large element of judgment is provided for—the process cannot be reduced to pure logic.[43] The model we have just described asserts that the updraft velocity in the cloud will change rapidly with height. If observations show little or no variation, as they often do, the theory is to this degree falsified. If they show variations which are roughly of the right magnitude, the theory is tentatively valid and other observations are selected that might falsify it. It must be reiterated that neither conclusion can be significant without skilled appraisals that the cloud situation being observed is indeed that which the model tries to describe. We can say, paraphrasing Polanyi,[44] that the whole process of using a model involves the tacit powers of understanding a cloud situation, representing it correctly, performing correct computations (often by machine) to an appropriate degree of accuracy, and interpreting the results correctly in terms of available data and recognizable features. However, it must be recognized that direct verification in the sense just mentioned is not the whole story, for consistency of the theory with the laws of fluid motion and of droplet behavior is also required.

It might be noted in passing that cloud models generally embody concepts that cannot be tested operationally. A certain theoretical model asserts, for instance, that proportionately 1 out of 100,000 droplets is initially formed around an unusually large salt nucleus and becomes a large enough drop to fall and collect others, thus growing to raindrop size before leaving the cloud. Unfortunately, droplet sampling is extremely difficult. No one has yet found out how to capture a large enough sample of these rare droplets to allow a test of whether the number is 1 in 10,000, or 1 in 1,000,000 or any number in between. On the other hand, the model may conceivably be tested by consideration of type and frequency of rain produced, variation of initial nucleus concentration, and so on, thus indirectly testing for the presence of unobservable elements.

I have mentioned symmetry as a characteristic of simple mod-

43. Popper, *op. cit.*, chap. iv.
44. *P.K.*, pp. 115-117, 257-261.

els. Polanyi emphasizes the role of elegance and symmetry in theory construction for atomic and nuclear physics, cosmology, and other highly mathematical sciences.[45] In cloud physics, beauty and symmetry have more often led us astray than served as clues to success.[46] Some models are indeed elegant, but evidently much oversimplified. Many experiments, especially rain-making and similar efforts, have been based on simple symmetrical models, producing results that carry little conviction and generate much controversy. The extent to which simplification can actually produce fruitful results is a subtle and difficult question, and continues to be a source of serious debate.[47]

V. Cloud Physicists and Their Colleagues

Knowledge in cloud physics, as in every other area of culture, resides in a community of persons. Small groups of cloud physicists in Australia, Japan, England, Canada, the United States, and a few other countries—about a hundred persons all told—constitute the community that can be said to know cloud physics in its present state. Together they form the arena within which both development and debate are carried on. Polanyi's account of the structure of the scientific community as a whole and of the functioning of segments within it fits the cloud physics situation very well indeed.[48]

An active researcher in atmospheric science may be acquainted with most of the accepted theories, facts, and methods of his field, but outside his own specialization, his knowledge is bound to be incomplete and peripheral. In particular, he has little chance of acquiring the tacit components of knowledge held by his colleagues. Everyone in the field is dependent on others for knowledge outside his special area, relying on trusted authorities, professional meetings, and an accepted body of literature. The

45. *Ibid.*, pp. 15, 43-46, 134-135.
46. *Ibid.*, p. 149.
47. Panel on Weather and Climate Modification, *Weather and Climate Modification: Problems and Prospects* (Washington, D.C.: National Academy of Sciences—National Research Council, 1966), II, 8-9.
48. M. Polanyi, "The Republic of Science," *Minerva*, I (Autumn, 1962), 54-73; *P.K.*, sections 7.3 and 7.7; *T.D.*, pp. 70-74.

recognized authorities in any part of a field are not hard to identify. For instance, some years ago when I was interested in the question of which type of droplet sampler should be installed on the Desert Research Institute airplane, I found it easy to determine from a few colleagues the names of those I should visit in order to get acquainted with the current state of the droplet-measuring art.

At professional meetings a great deal of formal and informal interchange of opinion occurs, which both transmits knowledge between individuals and rearranges this knowledge into clearer and more rational form. This interchange sometimes creates genuinely new understandings. Always it reinforces the authority of the more convincing speakers and reduces the authority of others. Since cloud physics involves a rather small number of persons, scientific meetings are ideal opportunities for convivial sharing of thoughts and results.

The great body of articulable knowledge in cloud physics is to be found in the literature. But it is only available as knowledge to the people who are competent to read it, appraise it, and discard the out-of-date and unsound. Fortunately, a worker in the field can exercise critical faculties over a considerably wider range than that in which he can act as an authority. Review articles and textbooks written by such persons are especially helpful in presenting distillations of original articles so that everyone in the field, including students, can have access to the articulate knowledge of a portion of the field at a particular moment of time.[49]

Even more important than the judgment of readers is the judgment of editors and their referees. Journal editors generally send articles they receive to recognized authorities, and rely on the comments of these authorities to judge whether the articles have been competently prepared, follow accepted methods of the field, and will interest their readers. The wide readership among

49. S. A. Goudsmit, "Is the Literature Worth Retrieving?," *Physics Today*, XXIX (Sept., 1966), 52-55. Examples of review articles in cloud physics are given in footnotes 26 (*supra*) and 62 (*infra*). Currently reliable textbooks are B. J. Mason, *The Physics of Clouds* (Oxford: The Clarendon Press, 1957); N. H. Fletcher, *The Physics of Rainclouds* (Cambridge: Cambridge University Press, 1962); H. R. Byers, *Elements of Cloud Physics* (Chicago: University of Chicago Press, 1964).

atmospheric scientists of such periodicals as the *Journal of the Atmospheric Sciences* or the *Quarterly Journal of the Royal Meteorological Society* is a measure of the confidence felt in the editorial and refereeing policies of these journals. This confidence underlies the way most of us approach the articles in these journals which have a bearing on our own research.

Another way in which the community of atmospheric scientists acts as a holder and critic of knowledge is in the administration of governmental research funds. Panel discussions are set up to provide guide lines, boards of referees are selected to pass on the merits of specific proposals, and individuals are appointed to administer the making of decisions on fund granting. For instance, in November, 1963, a distinguished panel of scientists on weather and climate modification was asked by the National Academy of Sciences "to undertake a deliberate and thoughtful review of the present status and activities in this field, and of its potential and limitations for the future."[50] This panel held meetings with invited experts on a total of thirty-four days over a two-year period, and produced a detailed and careful document on the status of weather modification efforts and the underlying scientific problems as of November, 1965. This report has had—and is still having—enormous influence on federally supported research. It serves as well as an authoritative summary of the present state of knowledge in the field.

Persons chosen as administrators by granting agencies—e.g., the National Science Foundation, the Environmental Science Services Administration, the Bureau of Reclamation, and certain branches of the military—are themselves atmospheric scientists, or at least have been close to the field for some time. They are constantly in touch with current research, attend panel meetings and other conferences that set new directions in theory and experiment, confer with individuals seeking support, and keep in position to evaluate the interests of their agencies. The decisions made by panels, boards of referees, and administrators reflect judgments on the valid knowledge of the field and so help both to determine and to communicate this knowledge.

The way in which knowledge lies in the community and not in

50. Panel on Weather, *Weather and Climate Modification,* I, vii.

any one person is seen in the network character of all judgments involved. One reader or referee can judge only the material in his own field and in fields very near it, yet the combination of many overlapping critical competences adds to a continuous network of judgment operating on a principle of mutual control that is the basis of our confidence.[51] The current knowledge of clouds and the processes that seem to bring about the gentle rain transcends the competence of any individual in the community of those seeking understanding. It fits Polanyi's description of superior knowledge[52] and is capable of objective examination and criticism, just as is any particular theory contained within this body of knowledge. Thus, for each scientist, the search is not primarily to get knowledge for oneself, but to add to the store of superior knowledge to which we are all devoted.

The existence of the scientific community has a bearing on the so-called verifiability criterion of meaning. We consider an experimental result to be *meaningful* if it is by its nature repeatable—i.e., verifiable. We consider it *valid* if it has been sufficiently verified. But since each technique, especially in a small field like cloud physics, can be carried out by only a very few skilled workers, the only sense we can give to verifiability is to assert our belief that a result obtained by one skilled worker could be verified by one of the others who is similarly capable. It would be foolish for me, for instance, to think of verifying Patrick Squire's and Sean Twomey's observations of cloud droplet spectra in marine clouds,[53] for not only do I not have their skills, but I would become a different person with a different outlook if I went through the long process of acquiring it. But I can make sense of an assertion that Clement J. Todd at the Naval Research Facility in Norfolk, Virginia, could verify these results if he wished. Even further, I believe that Todd or any other skilled worker could determine whether Squires' and Twomey's results (1) are so well established as not to need verifying, or (2) are tentative and yet interesting so that a verification would be worth

51. *P.K.*, p. 217; *T.D.*, p. 72.
52. *P.K.*, pp. 374-379.
53. S. Twomey and P. Squires, "The Influence of Cloud Nucleus Population on the Microstructure and Stability of Convective Clouds," *Tellus*, XI (1959), 408-411.

the time and money, or (3) are unsatisfactory because of the primitive instruments used, so that adequate data on cloud droplet sizes in such locations should not be sought until better instruments are developed, or (4) represent information that can best be obtained in quite another way.

We see that if we wish to give meaning to a result by saying it *could* be repeated, we can refer only to repetition by the appropriate specialists. If we wish to discuss *actual* verification, we have to rely on the judgments of the same specialists as to whether adequate verification has been made or is worth making. Furthermore, experiments are rarely repeated exactly. Some experiments may be approximate duplicates of each other, but may use modified techniques which according to accepted theory will lead to the same numerical values or indications of structural features or whatever is at issue. Observations of droplet sizes in clouds are, in fact, generally checked by the use of several different types of sampler.

Any field in which research involves a great deal of judgment about what and how to measure and calculate is found to generate strong differences of opinion, in spite of the critical network of overlapping judgments that tends to bring about consensus. Some of the controversies that arise in cloud physics involve what valid arguments can be drawn from seeding experiments, such as those of Project Stormfury in which Joanne Simpson and her coworkers seeded large cumulus clouds in the Caribbean and induced almost explosive growth in several of them.[54] Other controversies involve the use of statistics in judging rain-making efforts.[55]

A continuing area in which a variety of opinions conflict is the question of how much basic scientific work must be done on the problem of rain, gentle or otherwise, before significant attempts can be made to develop weather modification techniques. Part of

54. Simpson, Simpson, Andrews, and Eaton, n. 26 (*supra*) ; comments by L. J. Battan in *Journal of Applied Meteorology*, IV (1965) , 426-429, with a reply; and comments by B. Vonnegut and R. E. Mottern in the same journal, V (1966) , 134-136, also with a reply.
55. D. L. Gilman, J. R. Hibbs, P. L. Laskin, *Weather and Climate Modification: A Report to the Chief, United States Weather Bureau* (Washington: U.S. Dept. of Commerce, 1965) , pp. 11-13; Panel on Weather, *Weather and Climate Modification*, I, 27.

the disagreement here is between those who believe that presently available simple models are adequate as a basis for rain-making efforts and those who argue that clouds are more complex and a much better descriptive "taxonomy" of them is needed before modification experiments can become meaningful.

Differences of opinion tend to arise and to be maintained because of different scientific backgrounds, different ways of looking at reality, or different observational experience. Persons may be brought up primarily as meteorologists and weather forecasters or primarily as physical chemists. They may tend to look at nature mathematically or experimentally or artistically. They may have spent long periods of time collecting hail from violent storms, or studying droplet behavior in the laboratory, or using computers for macroscale motion studies. Such differences lead scientists to dwell in reference frames that differ in important ways, although there remain regions of agreement that make it possible for them to work together.

At this point we can notice the role of doubt in helping to establish truth.[56] Each side of a controversy doubts some of the assumptions and procedures of the other. But many theories and facts are accepted by both sides and cannot be doubted, for they form the frame of reference out of which the doubts come and within which the debate can be carried on. Similarly, we cannot doubt all of our own assumptions and concepts, for as Polanyi says, we dwell acritically in the frame of reference out of which we try to criticize and improve our own assumptions.[57]

If the scientific community to which one belongs is divided, how does a person choose which part is right? Here is where the most personal act of all enters. Each person has to decide for himself who are the authorities he most trusts. Each of us has teachers and colleagues whose judgment he respects in determining what traditions, theories, and procedures are on the track of reality and what workers in the field are the most competent. Our personal adherence to a particular school of thought is a commitment, made out of our intellectual passion for truth. We each dwell within a frame of reference on which we rely for the

56. *P.K.*, pp. 274-277.
57. *Ibid.*, pp. 266-268.

pursuit of knowledge and to which we are committed; within it we believe we may come to satisfy the standards we have set ourselves for truth and beauty.

VI. *Commitment and Faith*

Participating in a particular branch of the scientific community and dwelling within its frame of reference is one aspect of the commitment of a scientist. Our commitment is to a set of *beliefs*, more or less specifiable, and to an underlying faith which is largely tacit.

Cloud physicists believe in the validity of the physics, chemistry, meteorology, and astronomy on which they rely for application to the study of clouds. They believe in the appropriateness of certain observational methods and of established model-making procedures. They believe that certain entities—such as clouds, plumes, air-flow patterns—can be correctly recognized by skilled persons, and so on.

A common view about science is that scientists give prior commitments to methods (i.e., premises, procedures, and such) and are dispassionately open-minded about resulting facts and the theories they use to account for them. This view is in contradiction to the realities of scientific investigation. Our commitment to methods is not prior to our other beliefs. Methods keep changing as new results appear. For instance, the discovery of the importance of especially large initial droplets leads to the search for methods designed to measure them. The further discovery that such measurement cannot be done (at present) in a satisfactory quantitative way initiates a search for indirect methods of testing models incorporating the large initial droplet concept. The development of new radar techniques leads to adoption of these methods in research, but also leads to controversy as to whether the data read from the instruments has any significance for the rain process or whatever is being studied—new technology sometimes is of assistance, but not necessarily.

Atmospheric scientists not only believe in many particulars that they consider already well established, they also believe in a broader way that meaningful new results will be found and new conceptions discovered to describe them. The beliefs they hold have a considerable degree of indefiniteness,[58] for these beliefs assert an expectation of continual readaptation to unpredictable new experience. This readaptation is an irreversible process, involving the jumping of conceptual gaps from the other side of which we look back in surprise at our earlier ignorance.

This gap-jumping aspect of problem solving, which Polanyi has described so well,[59] can be illustrated in many ways from the study of clouds. For instance, L. M. Hocking demonstrated with careful use of hydrodynamic theory that in the absence of electrification, no droplet smaller than about 20 microns (or so) could possibly coalesce with any still smaller drop, for in the rush of air as they approached, the smaller would be swept completely around the larger.[60] Thus it was believed that droplets must grow by condensation past this 20-micron barrier before the coalescence process could set in, and much thought has been expended to fit theory to this fact. However, J. D. Sartor of the National Center for Atmospheric Research and M. H. Davis of Rand Corporation examined Hocking's calculations and found that although the theory seemed quite properly worked out, the computed results had larger errors than expected. Something was wrong. Then Davis on still closer examination and comparison with other similar work in the literature discovered in Hocking's argument a subtle and unsuspected mathematical flaw which takes away the 20-micron barrier.[61] Now cloud physicists are open to the possibility in theory construction of including at least a small amount of small-droplet coalescence. Those of us working in coalescence theory have had our thinking considerably changed.

As another example, the presence of salt particles in the air near the oceans had been known for a long time, but it was generally thought that these particles could get into the atmosphere only from spray thrown up on rocky shores or from violent

58. *Ibid.*, p. 317.
59. *Ibid.*, pp. 123-130; *T.D.*, pp. 21-25.
60. L. M. Hocking, "The Collision Efficiency of Small Drops," *Quarterly Journal of the Royal Meteorological Society*, LXXXV (January, 1959), 44-50.
61. M. H. Davis, "Collisions of Very Small Cloud Drops," *Journal of Geophysical Research*, LXXI (1966), 3101-3104.

storms out at sea. Theories to account for or estimate the number of these particles naturally were based on these beliefs. When, however, it was shown that every tiny bubble of foam that collapses on the sea surface sends up a tiny jet in its middle and leaves three or four salty droplets to dry up in the air and be carried aloft as nuclei,[62] it became evident that special sources of salt are not needed—the sea can be treated as a steady producer regardless of storms and the proximity of a rocky coast. Again our considerations of experimental design and theories of nucleus distribution were altered.

A further aspect of commitment is to the possibilities of still further discoveries as a consequence of an acquisition of knowledge:

> It appears, then, that to know that a statement is true is to know more than we can tell and that hence, when a discovery solves a problem, it is itself fraught with further intimations of an indeterminate range, and that furthermore, when we accept the discovery as true, we commit ourselves to a belief in all these as yet undisclosed, perhaps as yet unthinkable, consequences.[63]

Changes in our conceptions that result from discoveries are changes in our mental existence. It is not only theories and their future implications in which we believe, it is ourselves. We commit ourselves to ourselves as competent within the areas in which we work, whether it is field work with aircraft, laboratory experiments with streams of colliding droplets, numerical computations, or entity-model developments. Our commitment is an expression of our responsibility to our passion for knowledge and our self-set standards for accuracy, consistency, and relevance.

The personal element of our commitment goes still further, for our reliance on the scientific community is not just with respect to the frame of reference in which we dwell and to the ideas and skills of the authorities that define it, it is on these persons themselves. When the names of Ludlam or Squires or other

62. A review of the evidence is given by D. C. Blanshard and A. H. Woodcock, "Bubble Form and Modification in the Sea and Its Meteorological Significance," *Tellus*, IX (May, 1957), 145-158.
63. *T.D.*, p. 23.

outstanding authorities are mentioned, those who know them put trust in them beyond the articulable matters that can be explicitly credited to them. They are not trusted as idols, but in terms of reliance on their competence, judgment, and common sense, along with an awareness of particular points of view and predilections that seem to their critics and admirers to produce blind spots and other limitations. Without this quite personal commitment, our convivial sharing in the creative and unpredictable adventure of seeking the key to mysteries of the atmosphere could not be carried on.

Consider finally our commitment to Nature. We do not yet know quantitatively which processes co-operate to produce the gentle rain. But as we proceed in our study, we continue to find new facts and to develop new conceptions that open our vision further, that affirm over and over that we are dealing with a reality, a reality that with all its own changing creativity nevertheless has a regularity and constancy that calls us to its study.

Belief in prior knowledge, responsibility to our conceptions, trust in ourselves and in others, commitment to reality, all together can be described as faith. Without faith, the search for understanding of the gentle rain would make no sense.

PERSONAL KNOWLEDGE AND CONCEPTS IN THE BIOLOGICAL SCIENCES

Sir Francis Walshe

The achievements of our century in biology in general and in the physiology of the nervous system in particular have been so remarkable that they need no eulogy from me. Those now in the seventh decade of life have seen the biological scene change beyond all expectation, though not so radically as has the realm of theoretical physics.

Here it is not my present purpose to review all these achievements, but to consider the ideas now dominant in biology and especially in neurophysiology; that is, what they tell us of the nature and content of scientific thinking in this field, the meaning of the discoveries within it and their interpretation by neurophysiologists in terms of the nature and status of life and mind.

The careful student of current opinion on these matters cannot fail to suspect that the greatness of the achievement in terms of knowledge is not matched by a comparable development of a generality of understanding. Of necessity the neurobiologist must be interested in the status of life and of mind, and of the nature of the relationship between brain and mind. Are these new dimensions transcending the known laws of physics and chemistry, or are they not? This is the debate with which we shall be concerned in this article, and with the contribution towards an answer that is to be found in the writings of Michael Polanyi. As a neurologist, it is appropriate that I should conduct it in the field of neurophysiology, as we find this discipline at the present time.

We live in an age that may be said to have inherited from more than a single 'genetic' source mechanistic concepts of life and mind, and in respect of the relation of the nervous system to both has developed increasingly atomistic ideas and techniques of research.

Two main factors have contributed to this: the first, an historical one that has influenced thought in the natural sciences since the time of Galileo, and the second, peculiar to neurophysiology and to what is sometimes called 'neuropsychology,' an almost exclusive preoccupation today with the intrinsic electrical activity of the nervous system which has channeled research into deep but somewhat narrow grooves.

Galileo conceived of a world of quantities without qualities; Descartes, of a body which was an assemblage of machines ruled by a mind that required nothing but itself in order to exist.

The ideas of Locke and of Hume fortified this outlook; and, nearer to our own time, the Natural Selection school of evolutionists finding, as they believe, in random mutations the basis of evolution, has been a further potent influence in the direction of a mechanistic biology.

From this it is a short step to the abolition of the concept of mind proposed by the linguistic analysts, now appropriating the garb of philosophy, and to the reduction of the ideas of life and mind, which Whitehead wrote of as "nature alive," to the language and ideas appropriate to the study of what he called "nature lifeless"; that is, physics, chemistry, and mathematics.

A philosopher of today, Marjorie Grene, has said that

> It is an article of faith with many, if not most, biologists that their science is really not biological at all but is only chemistry and physics writ large. And when they get the writing small and precise enough, they say it *will* be chemistry and physics.[1]

Again:

> The parts of an organism are chemical molecules: specify these and you need worry about 'life' no longer.[2]

1. *The Knower and The Known* (London: Faber and Faber, 1966), p. 206.
2. *Ibid.*, p. 208.

Many biologists now see in the 'cracking' of the genetic code, as their forefathers thought they saw in the synthesis of urea in 1832, a step towards the reduction of biology to biochemistry; to what might be called an *in vitro* biology in which everything can happen in a test tube or some other form of apparatus, rather than an *in vivo* biology of the living organism. In effect biology shrinks to the status of a special language, describing in its quaint old-fashioned way what are really chemical and physical processes all capable of formulation in mathematical equations.

To the minds of some of its more physicalist exponents psychology seems bent on the same fatal journey.

I. *The Evolution of Modern Neurophysiology*

Since we are here essentially concerned with the implications of current concepts in neurophysiology, a brief sketch of their development over the past hundred years is necessary for no truly critical survey of them is available.

In the 1850's the standard and representative textbook of physiology in the English language was Carpenter's once popular work.[3] In it the author speaks of the cerebral hemispheres as being "in complete physiological separation" from the rest of the brain, and as being concerned with ideas, emotions, will, and the guidance of reason. These functions were described as "unconscious cerebration," and the sole seat of conscious states was thought to be provided by the basal and sensory ganglia. Here all the activities of the hemispheres reached consciousness, and this was true also of sensation. While, finally, these ganglia controlled what Carpenter called "the automatic apparatus."[4]

It is submitted that the true birth of modern neurophysiological thought, at least as far as the higher levels of function of the nervous system are concerned, may be found in the writings of Hughlings Jackson (1835-1906). His papers began to appear

3. W. B. Carpenter, *The Principles of Human Physiology* (4th ed.; London: Churchill, 1853).
4. A replica of this apparatus is to be found in Penfield's "centrencephalic integrating system," with some elaborations and modifications, still fulfilling the role of the master mechanism in the brain, but now located in the brain stem.

in 1864,[5] antedating the opening of the modern era of experimental neurophysiology by some four years. In 1870 Fritsch
and Hitzig and in 1873 Ferrier opened this stage of development of the subject when they discovered that the mammalian
cerebral cortex was electrically stimulable and could be made
to evoke muscular movements in these circumstances. Hitzig
(1900) and Ferrier (1881) both acknowledged their debt to
Jackson and their confirmation in animals of his findings in man.

A third line of development derives from the comparative
neuroanatomists and the zoologists to whom we owe the first
explicit suggestions of equipotentiality as a primordial quality of
nervous systems.

Conceptually the work of Jackson and the zoologists has been
the most fruitful of these three separate developments in respect
of our understanding of the operational principles of the nervous
system, though today their influence is minimal.

For many years after 1870 experimentalists were mainly concerned with the electrical stimulation of the cerebral cortex and
with the results of ablations of small cortical foci. It is only since
the 1920's with the advent of electronic recording devices that
these have taken pride of place as a research technique and have
been centered upon basic neuronal processes: the genesis and
nature of the nerve impulse and of the phenomena of excitation
and inhibition, the nature of synaptic transmission, the passage
of nerve impulses within the nervous system by the eliciting and
recording of action potentials: in sum, the intrinsic electrical
activity of the nervous system in the single neuron and in massed
neurons in action patterns.

Inevitably this has been predominantly an analytic search
rather than one leading to general ideas about the operational
principles of the nervous system or to its levels of activity, and the
immense ingenuity of neurophysiologists has scarcely been
matched by the development of such ideas, but has tended to a
mechanistic and a reductionist point of view.

Jackson thought of the nervous system as one "for the coordi-

5. All references are to Vols. I or II of *The Selected Writings of John
Hughlings Jackson*, ed. J. Taylor (2 vols.; London: Hodder and Stoughton,
1930-1931; reprinted, New York: Basic Books, 1962).

nation of impressions and movements" and he eschewed the language of psychology whenever possible, adopting purely *as a methodological postulate* the idea of psychophysical parallelism, or concomitance.

It has been said that Jackson accepted this postulate as providing an adequate account of the brain-mind relationship, but more than once he stated explicitly that this relationship was a problem in metaphysics and beyond his range. Thus, to quote but one example, he writes:

> The doctrine of concomitance will seem unsatisfactory to those who seek an explanation of mental states. But no explanation is intended in any part of this paper. . . . I then ask that the doctrine of concomitance be provisionally accepted as an artifice in order that we may study the most complex diseases of the nervous system easily.[6]

O'Leary criticizes clinical neurologists for accepting this view of Jackson's in preference to "more erudite" doctrines.[7] Yet where are these to be found in the relevant literature? The dualism of Sherrington,[8] favored also by Adrian,[9] is not acceptable to these critics, and nothing is left but to follow Jackson's method, or to fall in with the purely mechanistic and reductionist view which Jackson described as an attempt to solve a difficult problem by "solidifying the mind into a brain," and then proceeding to equate the latter with a machine, or to reduce the brain further to a problem in chemistry and physics. This solution is indeed pressed upon us under pain of being called unscientific, or according to Lorenz, believers in miracles.[10]

It will be submitted that reductionism of this kind is logically unacceptable.

6. *Ibid.*, II, 84.
7. J. O'Leary, "Cerebral Universe," *Journal of Mental and Nervous Diseases* CXLI (1965), 1-15, and 135-154.
8. C. S. Sherrington (with Grünbaum), "Observations on the Physiology of the Cerebral Cortex," *Proceedings of Royal Dpc.* LXIX (1901), 206.
9. Lord Adrian, "Sir Charles Sherrington," *Notes and Records, Royal Society*, XII (1956), 225.
10. K. Z. Lorenz, "The Role of Gestalt Perception in Animal and Human Behaviour," *Aspects of Form*, ed. L. L. Whyte (London: Lund Humphries, 1951), pp. 176-178.

II. *Jackson and the Concept of Levels in the Nervous System*

A full account of Jackson's findings and ideas is not here possible. In brief, he established the plan of localization (or representation) of muscular movements in the cerebral cortex, finding that this was based on synergies involving two or many muscles in co-ordinated action. The individual muscles of the anatomist's nomenclature were not represented as such. Since any muscle lends itself to many synergies in different degrees and orders, the loss of any synergy might still be followed by unimpaired activity of its constituent muscles in other and similar synergies, thus allowing a high degree of "compensation" for lost movements. In this plan we can see the first adumbration of what has come to be called equipotentiality.

Again in focal ("Jacksonian") motor convulsions three main sites of onset are found; namely, the face, hand, and foot. In each instance the fit spreads in a specific march over the musculature from the focus of onset, and is not a simultaneous and generalized convulsion of all muscles involved.

The movements of the three 'leading parts' show the greatest variety and the widest regions of overlapping representations.

It is of interest to note that only as recently as 1950, Liddell and Phillips in stimulation experiments on the baboon cortex succeeded in reproducing this pattern of functional localization, or representation, of movements, and thus in confirming in an animal the conclusions drawn from man by Jackson, one not earlier accepted by experimental physiologists.

Further, from the observation of developing and receding disorders of cerebral function from focal lesions, Jackson first glimpsed the presence of a hierarchy of levels of function in the central nervous system; each level from the lowest to the highest showing, in the ascent, a wider range and greater flexibility of control over movements. The lowest level corresponding to those elements of co-ordination later described by Sherrington, namely, reciprocal and double reciprocal innervation, restricted in range and relatively fixed in pattern. His middle level, equated with the excitable motor cortex and its projection system, controlled a vast system of complex and widespread synergies, while his highest level, which he equated with the frontal region of the cortex, allowed all possible synergies in the active life of the resourceful and responsible subject.

Jackson's levels did not include the basic physicochemical level of nerve impulses and synaptic transmission. Of this level so little was known in Jackson's active years that he was not exposed to the fallacy of trying to account wholly for high level organization in the living organism in terms of chemistry and physics. His primary concern was with the operational principles of that comprehensive entity the nervous system, and this in effect is what has always separated his thinking from that of the schools of experimental neurophysiology that have arisen since his time, with the notable exceptions of those of Sherrington and, much later, of Lashley.

Multiple representation was inherent in Jackson's views. This proved to be the antithesis of what will later be discussed as the 'cortical mosaic' idea of functional localization in the cerebral cortex which, with the exceptions named, continued to dominate discussions on functional localization in the cortex for about fifty years after the 1870's amongst experimentalists.

III. *The Evolution of Modern Experimental Neurophysiology*

Here we have a story very different from that just sketched, and the differences of techniques and of thought are apparent. It shows also a preoccupation with the intrinsic electrical activity of the nervous system, and a lack over the years of any consistently applied principles in the interpretation of experimental results.

In the era of cortical stimulation and excisions, the electrical stimuli applied to the brain surface varied in strength, duration, and character from one experiment and from one experimentalist to another, strengths of current far exceeding those of the intrinsic electrical activity of the nervous system being employed. Also, the experimental animal was commonly anaesthetized, and thus the excitability of its brain diminished and its musculature rendered inert: in other words, the conditions of experiment were very remote from those of the life of the intact animal under natural circumstances.

Yet in 1894 Max von Frey had pointed out that electrical stimulation of the brain surface was something "nicht vorgesehen" in the economy of the brain and was grossly unphysiological, while even earlier Claude Bernard had commented that to destroy an organ did not suffice to reveal its functions. Never did cogent warnings fall upon more stony ground, or produce less effect. As a result there have been almost as many hypotheses of cortical organization as there have been experimentalists.

In fact, electrical stimulation unless of convulsive strength produces simple twitches, or what have been called "discrete movements," that is, restricted movements against the background of an inert musculature.

This finding led to the idea of the motor cortex as a mosaic of contiguous and fixed localizations of single muscles or small movements, and this concept, with the mysterious viability of the false, reigned supreme until comparatively recent times, and this, despite the fact that Sherrington's work with Grünbaum-Leyton (1906, 1917—but carried out at the turn of the century) had revealed the instability of responses from cortical points, and had analyzed the factors underlying this, thus destroying the validity of the mosaic idea, which was not given its final quietus until 1950 when Liddell and Phillips, as already stated, found in the baboon cortex a pattern of localization conforming to Jackson's idea, one implicit in the Sherrington work, and demanded by the facts of clinical observation in man.

Finally, we have to recognize the concept of an operational principle in the interpretation of experimental results[11] by which every experimental finding must be viewed in relation to the stimulus or other operation used to evoke it. If, in the Sherringtonian sense, a stimulus is 'inadequate,' that is, abnormal, *the experimental result must of necessity reflect the abnormality of the stimulus*. This principle has not prevailed in the field of experimental neurophysiology, and the neglect of logical analysis has vitiated much good experimental work.[12]

11. Percy Bridgeman, "The Operational Aspects of Meaning," *Synthese*, VIII (1950-1951), 257.
12. F. M. R. Walshe, "On the Interpretation of Experimental Studies of Cortical Motor Function, with Special Reference to the 'Operational View' of Experimental Results," *Brain*, LXXIV (1951), 249.

Only very recently has a contemporary neurophysiologist explicitly recognized this, Burns commenting that "the common habit of exciting cortex by superficially applied electrodes carries little chance of imitating physiological events."
In another equally revealing passage Burns writes:

> It is probably wise to admit at the outset that less is known about the functions of normal cerebral cortex than any other organ in the body. The great volume of experimental results carefully collected during the last century enables us to make many statements which *define the details of cortical reaction to particular forms of excitation*. Nevertheless, no one has succeeded in constructing from the individual known properties of the cerebral hemispheres an intelligible picture of normal function.[13] (Italics added.)

He attributes this to the immense complexity of the anatomy of the cortex, and it is true that compared to what remains to be discovered about the functions of this structure our present knowledge is small, but the passage just quoted reveals, and not for the first time, what a *terra incognita* to the experimental neurophysiologist the clinical physiology of the cortex still remains.

Clinical physiology employs different methods and is carried out on sentient and, for the most part, co-operative human beings, all of which is so unfamiliar as to be suspect. Nevertheless, clinical contributions to cerebral physiology have been considerable and have provided much information on cortical organization.[14]

Thus the gaps in our knowledge do not stem solely from anatomical complexity, but also from a special exclusiveness of thought that has led physiologists to "drink running water only out of their own wells," a custom virtuous enough in its original Biblical connotation, but in science an inhibiting influence upon ideas.

13. D. B. Burns, *The Mammalian Cerebral Cortex* (London: Arnold, 1958), p. 1.
14. Cf. F. M. R. Walshe, "The Contributions of Clinical Observation to Cerebral Physiology," (Ferrier Lecture, Royal Society), *Proceedings of the Royal Society*, B, 142 (1953), 208.

Perhaps the rigidity of thought here criticized has been responsible for the lack of response to Jackson's concept of functional localization in the cortex and to the concept of equipotentiality first adumbrated by him and developed over many years by zoologists, but brought into mammalian physiology by Lashley.

Lashley was one of the last of the "integrating neurophysiologists." He early rejected the mosaic concept with its subjection of function to imaginary structural arrangements. He came from psychology into physiology and thus had a wider background and a wider range of experimental methods than those prevailing in the electrical investigations of the nervous system by academic neurophysiologists.

This brief summary indicates both the achievements and the limitations of technical and intellectual method which have made the modern era of neurophysiology at once so impressive and so disappointing. The growing acceptance of physicochemical explanations of biology and psychology has inhibited any adventures of ideas beyond these narrow confines, as we shall find when we come to consider the problems of memory and of consciousness as conceived by experimental neurophysiologists today.

It is submitted that the vast mass of information as to the basic physicochemical processes which underlie all neuronal activity has issued from an investigation of parts largely for their own interest and without due recognition that parts are meaningless except in relation to the whole of which they are the parts. Analysis without synthesis provides a neurophysiology which is only the propaedeutic of an integrating neurophysiology that can hope to achieve an understanding of the nervous system as a comprehensive entity.

O'Leary, concerned with the future of neurophysiological knowledge, writes that

> Considering today's diverse and sophisticated technologies and the obvious bankruptcy of mentalistic thinking, only the physical sciences offer the potential necessary to open new avenues of exploration. The returns would be substantial if we could discover in neural mechanism the wellspring of behavior, define its meaning in physical lan-

guage, and apply the results in correcting the many faults that arise out of man's competitive nature.[15]

We must sympathize with this ideal, even while recognizing the ambitious nature of the program, and the danger that the more sophisticated the techniques the greater the demands they make upon judgment and the greater the possibilities of erroneous interpretation. A technique can become an end in itself and a yardstick by which everything must be measured,[16] accepting the existence of such an entity the methods of the physical sciences are quite inadequate to its discernment and understanding. The idea of the perfectibility of man by advances in science expresses the triumph of hope over experience, and presents us with the converse of Rousseau's fiction, the "noble savage," who was virtuous by reason of his lack of sophistication.

IV. *Mechanistic Accounts of Memory and the Engram*

The problem of memory and the idea of a memory trace or engram was first debated over two thousand years ago, but only for the past century has neurophysiology begun the search for the memory trace and the discernment of its nature.

The relevant literature, philosophical, psychological, physiological, and physical, is too vast even for enumeration.

But there are available to us two recent general reviews of the subject: an exhaustive critical review by Gomulicki[17] and a more recent and searching critique of modern theories by a clinical

15. J. O'Leary, "Matter and Mind: Pursuit of Inaccessibles," *Brain,* LXXXVIII (1965) , 777.

16. In his critical survey of some thirty current hypotheses about memory which the past century has produced, Gomulicki (*vide infra*) comments that "the replacement of *a priori* philosophical reasoning by experimental and clinical methods has not led . . . to a coalescing of the various divergent views into a unified basically acceptable body of theory. . . . If anything, the increase in knowledge has widened the gap between the various points of view." In seeking an explanation for the joint 'bankruptcy' of philosophy and physiology in regard to memory, he cites as one potent reason "the comparative lack of cross-fertilization of the relevant sciences." No one can acquit the physiologists of a heavy share of the responsibility for this.

17. Bronislaw R. Gomulicki, *The Development and Present Status of the Trace Theory of Memory* (Cambridge: Cambridge University Press, 1953) .

psychologist, E. Straus.[18] Two main views compete for acceptance: the notion of the 'trace' as a physical entity imprinted on
the neural ultrastructure, and the idea of a physiological 'disposition' or schema, an unlocalizable and ineffable state subject to
modifications in space and time.

Head and Holmes used the latter in their analysis of the sensory
functions of the cerebral cortex,[19] but on the whole physiologists
have preferred the physical trace, located in the cerebral cortex,
the temporal lobe cortex being the preferred location.

This physical trace is envisaged by some as of the order of a
tape recorder in which perceptions and ideas lie in chronological
sequence, with no explicit provision for their interaction or modification by the course of events lived through by the subject.

Having failed to locate the engram by his experiments, Lashley
rejected this mechanical idea,[20] and in his final paper[21] wrote as
follows:

> The billions of neurons in the cerebral network are organ-
> ized into a large number of systems. Each system consists of
> the traces of a number of habits or memories. Knowledge of
> the moves and games of chess would constitute one such
> system: memories of neural anatomy another; and so on
> through all the individual's varied interests. The traces or
> engrammata in any system are more closely connected with
> one another than with other systems.
>
> The systems are not anatomically separate, and the same
> neurons, in different permutations, may participate in
> many systems. I shall call these 'trace systems.'[22]

The student of Jackson's writings will recognize in this a close
but unwitting paraphrase of his concept of functional localization in the cerebral cortex independently reached by Lashley. A

18. E. Straus, in *Phenomenological Psychology* (New York: Basic Books,
1966) , p. 77.
19. Henry Head and G. M. Holmes, "Sensory Disturbances from Cerebral
Lesions," *Brain*, XXXIV (1911-12) , 102-271.
20. Karl Spencer Lashley, "In Search of the Engram," Society of Experimental Biology Symposium No. 4: *Physiological Mechanisms in Animal Behavior*
(Cambridge: Cambridge University Press, 1950) , pp. 454-482.
21. K. S. Lashley, "Cerebral Organization and Behavior," *Proceedings* of the
Association for Research in Nervous and Mental Disease, XXXVI (1958) ,
1-18.
22. *Ibid.*, p. 67.

more widely accepted version of the engram is Fessard's, as follows:

> Any conscious experience is at the beginning of a nmemonic recording, and any trace left by a conscious state is capable of engendering it anew. Thus it seems difficult to suppose that the ultimate basis of 'experience' in the physical world could be of another nature than that admitted (*sic*) for the storage of memories; i.e. a more or less durable modification imprinted on a plastic ultrastructure of the neuron.[23]

Eccles accepts Lashley's view, just cited, adds that "the remembered thought appears in consciousness as soon as its specific space-time pattern is replayed in the brain," and admits that this account does not bridge the "unbridgeable gulf between the matter-energy system of the brain and the non-sensual concept of the mind." It is not clear that these two comments are really informative. Like Fessard, Eccles seems to have a juke box concept of remembering and recollecting, not truly derived from anything that physiological research has provided.[24]

It was Aristotle who first bent his mind to this problem in the following proposition:

> We have to look on that which originates through perception in the soul and in the enveloping part of the body as at a portrait; an affection, the lasting disposition of which we call memory.
>
> For the act of perceiving imprints so to speak a scheme of the perceived, as if we seal with a signet ring. . . . When we remember, is it this impressed affection that we remember, or is it the objective thing from which this was derived? If the former, it would follow that we remember nothing that is absent, if the latter, how is it possible that, though perceiving directly only the impression, we remember the absent thing which we do not perceive.[25]

23. A. Fessard, "Mechanism of Nervous Integration" in *Brain Mechanism and Consciousness*, ed. J. F. Delafresnaye (Oxford: Blackwell Medical Publications, 1954) , p. 234.
24. J. C. Eccles, *The Neurophysiological Basis of Mind* (Oxford: Clarendon Press, 1953) , pp. 261-267.
25. Quoted by Straus, *op. cit.*, p. 77.

It seems that Aristotle has taken the matter as far as the two examples just quoted, and with a greater insight into the difficulties of the problem than these authors whose hypotheses tell us nothing more about the possible nature of the trace, or of how it comes to be 'replayed,' or what precisely is meant by the 'storage' of memories. They leave a host of unasked questions, such for example as: Does the replaying take the same span of physical time as the perception or event took to complete itself; thus, do the experiences of an hour, a day, or a week or longer take these various times in the replaying? Are successive replayings always identical in their items and their sequences; that is, does memory really conform to the juke box pattern, or to the 'playing back' of a tape recorder?

Also, is a trace really a portrait as Aristotle suggests and physiologists seem now to propose? Traces are by definition fragmentary. For example, does a trail of footsteps in the snow, or the scars on a chopping block, provide portraits of the persons and events involved in their formation? They are traces only and not portraits.

Further, common experience reminds us that memories 're-called' in speech or in writing are in many instances not reliable, but may be defective, distorted, or elaborated, and varying from one retelling to another. Also, when we recall, how can we tell that our "memory" is a true reproduction of what it purports to relate? We remember only what we remember and not what we may have forgotten. While, as for forgetting, what has become of the "imprint" on the plastic ultrastructure which is the postulated concomitant of every perception or idea?

The *Hixon Symposium*[26] was also the occasion of a discussion on memory and memory traces, and it was here that Lashley made his confession of *faith* that "the phenomena of behavior and of mind are ultimately describable in the concepts of the mathematical and physical sciences."[27] As we have seen, he rejected the fixed physical memory trace, and in his final paper he went so far as to remind his hearers that "these assumptions

26. *Hixon Symposium,* ed. J. L. Jeffress (New York: Wiley and Sons, 1951).
27. *Ibid.,* p. 112.

concerning cerebral organization are, of course, purely speculative and mainly inferences from psychological events."[28]

On this occasion, McCulloch made what might be called a "multidisciplinary" contribution to the subject,[29] upon which a fellow symposiast later commented as follows:

> While the negative entropy of this article is high, the author, doubtless in virtue of his diverse academic roots, writes as a psychiatrist about neurophysiology in the jargon of the mathematical physicist with all the crisp lucidity of the neo-Kantian philosopher.[30]

McCulloch's peroration ended as follows: ". . . through the cortex pass the greatest inverse feedbacks whose function is the purposive life of the human intellect. The joy of creating ideals, new and eternal, in and of a world, old and temporal, robots have it not. For this my Mother bore me."[31]

Köhler alone amongst the symposiasts uttered a cautionary word against this confusion of categories and languages,[32] but what they were all talking about was not the remembering, recollecting, and forgetting we all experience, but about imagined models of how the nervous system works as the necessary condition of these activities.

Perhaps the great William Harvey had a point when he advised his young friend, John Aubrey, as the latter recounts in his *Brief Lives*, "to go to the Fountaine head and read Aristotle" and not to heed the "neoteriques." Surely, analogies with tape recorders, filing cabinets in the basement, or the juke box type of memory are not promising starters in any quest for a cerebral basis of memory. That there must be some mode of physiological process as the substratum of memory cannot be disputed, and

28. K. S. Lashley, "Cerebral Organization and Behavior," *Proceedings of Association for Research in Nervous and Mental Disorders*, XXXVI (1958), 1-18, at p. 8.

29. *Hixon Symposium*, pp. 42-57.

30. This delightful critique was passed on to me by Lashley in 1953. Its author was unnamed.

31. This dithyrambic utterance apparently does not represent McCulloch's current view of the basis of the human intellect, for he now invokes a chemical process for memory; namely, that the engram "certainly involves ribose nucleic acid and protein synthesis." Can it be that at last the nerve impulse totters on its throne as the Alpha and the Omega of 'mind'?

32. *Hixon Symposium*, p. 65.

every informed person, whether scientist or not, appreciates that the integrity of the nervous system is a precondition of consciousness, remembering, and recollecting, but of the nature of the process we know no more than Aristotle knew. Further, whatever we may come to know of physiological processes and their physicochemical foundations, we shall still be removed from an understanding of how they issue in conscious states.

We seek to bridge the gap by mechanical fables, too easily confuse these with explanations, and lend them a fictitious reality in the hope of stilling our unsatisfied yearnings for real knowledge.

V. *Neurophysiological Concepts of Consciousness*

Nearly a century ago Hughlings Jackson wrote as follows about consciousness;

> We spoke of the substrata of consciousness as being the highest nervous arrangements. Yet to avoid misinterpretation we pointed out explicitly that we do not really suppose there to be one fixed seat of consciousness. . . . Consciousness is not an unvarying independent entity. Consciousness arises during activity of some of our highest nervous arrangements by which correspondence of the organism with its environment is being effected.
>
> Our present consciousness is our now mental state. It is such or such according to the correspondence now being effected. As this correspondence is continually changing, the nervous arrangements concerned are continually different. Psychologically speaking, our present consciousness is the present relation between the subject and the object.[33]

This lucid, and so often misquoted, opinion, corresponds closely with Lashley's view of cerebral organization in respect of the physiological substrata of consciousness and mental activities, though Jackson did not hold with him in wholly identifying mind with brain.

At the Laurentian Symposium[34] the term "consciousness" was a

33. *Selected Writings*, II, 242.
34. *Brain Mechanism and Consciousness*.

bone of contention, and its "localization" provided almost as many fables as we encountered in the *Hixon Symposium* in relation to memory. Here Bremer and Lashley rejected *in toto* the notion of a small circumscribed seat of consciousness in the brain, but there was a not inconsiderable measure of support for such an idea, and the "centre-cephalic integrating system," was a strong claimant for this role.

Yet an obvious fallacy inheres in the idea that because consciousness may ensue upon a focal destructive lesion in the reticular core of the brainstem, now become the reputed habitat of this integrating system, we must "localize" consciousness in this region. Lashley commented that we become unconscious when the heart beat stops, but that we do not locate consciousness in this organ.[35] Again if an electric circuit is interrupted, the light bulb in the circuit goes out, but we do not locate light in the wiring. The translation of a symptom into a function is too common in neurophysiological writing.

Lashley rejected this particular 'localization':

I have not been convinced by any of the evidence presented that the [reticular] system is more closely related to conscious processes than are other parts of the brain. It may serve as an activating system, but this is certainly all that can be claimed for it at present.[36]

In physiological language all that can be said is that for the cerebral cortex to maintain its normal level of excitability it requires afferent impulses from deeper regions of the brain, but even this needs qualification, for O'Leary *et al.* have shown that if the reticular core is destroyed less acutely than in Magoun's experiments the animal does not become unconscious,[37] but this significant finding has been ignored in later literature.

Bremer's stand at this symposium did not differ from Lashley's, and he expressed the view that "integration is a dynamic concept that is unlocalizable," while consciousness is the dynamic integration of all cerebral processes,[38] but that "at the present moment

35. *Ibid.*, p. 442.
36. *Ibid.*, p. 496.
37. J. O'Leary *et al., Journal of Neurosurgery,* XVII (1960), 1045.
38. *Brain Mechanism and Consciousness,* p. 497.

we are completely unable to explain accurately any state of consciousness in neurophysiological terms."[39]

During the course of this symposium, the variable meanings of the term "consciousness" were notable. As synonyms we find "arousal of awareness," "alertness" and "vigilance" all psychological terms implying a consciousness without content, an inconceivable entity.

The psychiatric contributions to the discussion revealed the immense difficulty of the topic. Kubie denied that consciousness exists, calling it an abstraction, but adding that "consciousness of something exists." Of these two terms the first is, as Kubie indicates, a universal, the second a particular. What he really asserts is that conscious states have contents and cannot be conceived of without contents, but his linking of a universal term with a particular confuses the issue.

All conceptual terms are abstractions, and when diluted to such ideas as "arousal of awareness" and "alertness" they become conceptually inadequate in the case of consciousness, as Jackson's dictum quoted earlier reveals. But Kubie's paper marked the essential difference between the neurophysiological and the psychological approach to the problem; the former is an etiolated idea that is unrelated to content, but the latter is realistic, even if its expression betrays a confusion between thought and things.[40]

Hebb's contribution showed the same confusion; thus, "The existence of something called consciousness is a venerable *hypothesis*; not a datum, not directly observable, but an inference from *other facts* [*sic*]."[41]

No concept is directly observable. In a later paper he writes

My proposition is that mind and consciousness, thought and perceptions, feelings and emotions, all consist of *nothing but* [italics added] the transmission of messages—nerve impulses—in and through the paths of the nervous system. . . . We must at the same time *keep in mind* [sic] the other side of the problem, all those aspects of mind such theory does not comprehend.[42]

39. *Ibid.*, p. 501.
40. *Ibid.*, p. 444.
41. *Ibid.*, p. 404.
42. "The Mind of Man" (Symposium) (Montreal: *McGill Medical Journal*, 1962) , 33.

Here Hebb seems to breach the law of contradiction in proposing that consciousness both is and is not "nothing but" nerve impulses, and leaves us with a mysterious bifurcation of mind which he does not explain in any way.[43]

The physiologist, R. W. Gerard has expressed the view that "One thing we know, ideas don't move muscles."[44] It is true that we do not know how ideas influence movements, but if it was not an idea that "motivated" him so to employ his relevant musculature to utter this opinion, what can it have been?

Whitehead has provided the adequate comment on this.

> In a criminal trial where evidence is circumstantial the demonstration of motive is a chief reliance of the prosecution. In such a case would the defence plead the doctrine that purpose could not direct the motions of the body, and that to indict the thief for stealing was analogous to indicting the sun for rising?[45]

What Gerard is asserting is that what we think does not influence what we do. If this were true, no doctrine of any kind could be acted upon, and no lost dog would ever be seen trying to find its way home. Indeed, human history would be a blank, with no scribe able to record and nothing to record.

It is necessary to make all these points for they reveal the absurdities in which a physicomathematical concept of psychology and physiology involves its expositors.

VI. *The Brain-Mind Relationship as Seen in a Mechanistic Neurophysiology*

Probably for many neurophysiologists this is a phantom problem to be solved by a process of linguistic analysis, the human person being a collocation of machines of no telic significance, arrived at mysteriously over countless ages by a process of random mutations since the first origins of life on the globe, and now

43. E. Straus points out that Thomas Hobbes (1588-1679) was the first writer, in his work *Leviathan,* to introduce the words "nothing but" that now so liberally adorn the writings of reductionist biologists.

44. See Polanyi's "The Two Cultures," *Encounter,* XIII, No. 3 (Sept., 1959), 62.

45. A. N. Whitehead, *Modes of Thought* (Cambridge: Cambridge University Press, 1938), p. 213.

greatly exercising the 'minds' of biologists in the endeavor to account for his astonishing endowments and achievements on the simple basis of a physicomathematical concept, which has at all costs to be saved from the grasp of the metaphysicians.

Thus, it can be with no sanguine expectations that we approach modern neurophysiological expositions on this greatest of all unsolved problems.

Lashley's views seem to have changed profoundly over the years that led to the famous confession of faith that has been cited here. A long quotation from his early paper "Basic Neural Mechanisms in Behavior" reveals his initial position:

> There seems to be most nearly a general agreement that the final explanation of behavior or of mental processes is to be sought in the physiological activity of the body and, in particular, in the properties of the nervous system. The tendency to seek all causal relations of behavior in brain processes is characteristic of the recent development of psychology in America. . . . It is rare that a discussion of any psychological problem avoids some reference to the neural substratum, and the development of elaborate neurological theories to 'explain' the phenomena in every field of psychology is becoming increasingly fashionable.
>
> In reading this literature I have been impressed chiefly by its futility. The chapter on the nervous system seems to provide an excuse for pictures in an otherwise dry and monotonous text.
>
> That it has any other function is not clear . . . but where the problems of psychology become complex and interesting, the nervous system is disposed with. . . . In more technical treatises the neurological explanations are made up mostly of assumptions concerning the properties of the nerve cell which have no counterpart in physiological experiment.[46]

It would be difficult to find a more cogent critique of some current neurophysiological discussions upon such problems as those of memory and consciousness. Yet in his final paper we find him writing as follows: "The problem [of consciousness] requires

46. *Journal of Psychology*, XXXVII (1930), 1.

an entirely different approach; a thorough analysis of the phenomena of consciousness, oriented with reference to the phenomena of neural activity."[47]

He then goes on to ask "how the brain knows that it knows"
and "how the brain thinks" and then concludes that

> The only conclusion that can be derived from experience is
> that thought exists. No psychologist has ever discovered the
> thinker. There are neither empirical nor logical grounds for
> assuming that the existence of consciousness implies a dis-
> tinct existence which is in the relation to it of a knower or a
> doer.

Here is a constellation of paradoxes! What can they mean? Only
the human person can think, communicate, possess knowledge,
and enjoy experiences. To make the brain the knower and the
doer, *in vacuo* as it were, is unintelligible if, in fact, neither of
these exists.

Of course, the perils of linguistic misunderstanding here are
immense, but at least we must assume that Lashley is invoking the
nervous system for his explanation of the psychological process of
thinking, a position he rejected earlier. All his later writings
reveal his complete adherence to a mechanistic and reductionist,
physicomathematical concept of life and mind. It is thus not
surprising to find him speaking of the concept of "free will" as
merely "a concession to certain ethical systems":[48] Yet few can
have displayed a free will more emphatically and fruitfully than
Karl Lashley, as long as he kept within the bounds of physiological problems and refrained from his reductionist philosophy,
which was not only unnecessary to them, but which also involved
him in inconsistencies.

Eccles has also endeavored to formulate the nature of the
brain-mind relationship. In brief his proposal is that neuronal
activity in the cerebral cortex may provide some special kind of
detector which "enters into liason with mind," but this is of such
a nature that our presently available apparatus cannot detect it.[49]

47. "Cerebral Organization," *ibid.*, pp. 1-18.
48. *Ibid.*, p. 8.
49. *The Neurophysiological Basis of Mind* (Oxford: Clarendon Press,
1953).

296   INTELLECT AND HOPE

In short, he is trying to account for the obscure by invoking the unknown, but this 'unknown' must be some mode of physical motion, and we are back where we began.

Reference is necessary to O'Leary's admirable review of modern electrophysiology of the nervous system, entitled "Cerebral Universe" in which, describing "traffic patterns" of nerve impulses in the cortex, he writes:

> These patterns provide the dance of life in all its intimate details. . . . No barrier reef separates mental from neural events, or the realm of the nerve impulse into two distinguishable worlds of brain and mind. . . . Together these encompass a tangible class of neural-mental events readily translatable into either sensation or into motor patterns. This stratum of functioning lies at the threshold through which *mind* examines the external world. [Italics added.][50]

He goes on to elaborate this hypothesis in one of the most closely argued mechanistic statements in the literature. He believes that mental events are no more than neural events, and yet he falls back on what he calls the "mind" as standing on the threshold *between* neural events and the external world which "it" examines. Why not say simply that neural events examine the external world, which is the true logic of his case? Yet, having rejected the mind, he finds as do all mechanists and reductionists that he is compelled to speak of it as though it had some kind of existence not synonymous with "neural events." Yet to put a hyphen between the words "neural" and "mental" and to beget the hybrid "neural-mental" is not to explain how the biophysical processes that are nerve impulses become perceptions and ideas in material bodies. Indeed, what could be less tangible than "neural-mental events" that can be translated equally into sensory or motor patterns? It is the "how" of this translation that is always omitted from these accounts which attempt to describe it.

This is clear from other passages in his review:

> The view adopted here is that consciousness is a product of brain and amenable to treatment as a function of that

50. *Journal of Nervous and Mental Diseases*, CLXI (1965), 1-15, 135-154, pp. 135-136.

entity. That is a matter of faith. . . . Our cleavage arbitrarily concedes what is called mind to philosophy and keeps only consciousness and its content as neural correlates.[51]

It cannot be seen that this "cleavage" does any more than to concede that philosophy as well as physiology has its own universe of discourse about the mind, yet 'consciousness and its content," being not only neural traffic but also "neural-mental events" can hardly be cleft from itself.

The cleavage is a judgment of Solomon that it is logically impossible to execute. Thus, seek to exercise it as he will, there remains a ghost—the mind—in O'Leary's machine, and with his permission. It cannot be got rid of by a reductionism that is ambivalent and can neither live with it nor live without it. It is part of nature and it cannot be expelled by a mechanist pitchfork.[52]

It would be to give an erroneous impression if I were to suggest that all neurophysiologists have addressed themselves to the problems of life and mind. Many have been content with the intensive study of this or that element in neural action and neural patterns of activity, not concerning themselves with the integration of its parts and its part functions into a comprehensive entity with relations to the other systems in the organism. In this way they have made many of the major advances in information about the nervous system of the past twenty-five years. Yet we must accept the consequences of this, namely, that attention has been focused on the parts, not as contributing to a comprehensive entity, but, as it were, for their own sakes, and the notion of a hierarchy of functional levels in the nervous system first clearly postulated by Jackson and recognized by Sherrington has suffered neglect. Dwelling amidst basic physicochemical processes, the lowest level in the hierarchy, they have come to assume that there are nothing else but physical and chemical processes involved. In this realm of inanimate nature there are no levels, and of its activity Whitehead has said:

This order of activity discloses no grounds for its own coherence. There is merely a formula for succession, but

51. *Ibid.*, pp. 148-149.
52. 'Naturam expellas furca, tamen usque recurret.' Horace, *Epist.* i.vi.i.

there is an absence of understandable causation, to give a reason for that formula for that succession,

But, he adds:

Of course it is always possible to work oneself into a state of complete contentment with an ultimate irrationality. The popular positivistic philosophy adopts this attitude.[53]

VII. *Brain Models*

Yet we still have to consider some reductionist "designs" and "models" of the brain. These have the advantage for the designers that they evade the awkward question of teleology, or seek to do so. The neurophysiologist, like everyone else, knows that purpose directs his actions, but *qua* biologist he may not say so. Ashby in his work *Design for a Brain* says of it that

No teleological explanation for behavior will be used. It will be assumed that a machine or an animal behaved in a certain way at a certain moment because its chemical or physical nature allowed it no other action. The biologist must view the brain, not as being the seat of "mind" or as something that "thinks," but, like every other organ in the body, as a specialized means to survival.[54]

Yet what sense does the word "survival" have when applied to physicochemical processes, and what can the expression "a means to survival" signify if not a belief in teleology? Ashby's atelic robot seems to embody that "contentment with an ultimate irrationality" of which Whitehead speaks.

A more elaborate "model" of the brain has been provided by J. Z. Young in which the language of physical science is stretched beyond its limits to sustain the mechanistic and reductionist idiom. Computers are "machines devised by brains to do the work of brains," and therefore "the words that brains use to talk about the machines can also be used of brains," though they are not the only relevant words. His thesis continues as follows: computers operate by systems of logical instructions or codes, and

53. A. N. Whitehead, *Modes of Thought* (Cambridge: Cambridge University Press, 1938) , p. 202.
54. W. R. Ashby, *Design for a Brain* (2d ed., rev., London: Chapman and Hall, 1960) , pp. 8-9.

"a code in this context is defined as any set of physical events that causes a system (specifically an automaton) to perform some organized task." The brain is "the central controller of a self-maintaining homeostat." It must be so planned as to be "able to take the right sorts of action," but physiology has not yet told us how this controller does produce appropriate patterns of action, but we may suppose that the "organism" makes decisions. Signals operate it by carrying "information" which is coded (encoded and then decoded). As machines assist "our" brains "we" shall learn from them a language much more useful than the present ones for speaking about "brains" and their "products," such as "mind."[55]

Throughout this painful struggle to find expression in an inadequate "basic English" restricted to the vocabulary of communication theory, we find the author repeatedly using the pronoun "we" as implying a knower and doer. Yet what kind of entity is here involved? The brain is already named as the controller engaged in coding and decoding signals as "specifically an automaton."

What is the role of "we" in this construct where, unnamed and unnameable except by this cryptic pronoun, lurks that human mind that he cannot do without if this enormous pretense is to carry conviction to himself as also to his readers? Yet can he tell us in ordinary language what are the nature and status of the "we" that learn to control the central controller of that self-maintained homeostat, the human person?

Or is it that we are only being given a tautology namely, that the brains control and speak about brains and are engaged in an as yet uncompleted process of giving the brain more scientific treatment? In plain terms, Professor Young's "we" resembles the non-existent Mrs. Harris whose name Charles Dickens' Sairey Gamp was so fond of invoking.

Perhaps the crowning irrelevance is to be found in his suggestion that

The supposition that the things of the spirit are necessarily dealt with in another language [than the author's] has

55. J. Z. Young, *Design for a Brain* (Oxford: Clarendon Press, 1964), pp. 1-16.

persisted only because we have not yet been able to extend *our* scientific treatment to the *brain*. Nor is there any reason to suppose that, as *we learn to control the brain better,* the results will be deleterious to human dignity. [Italics added.]

There will, of course, be many who are prepared to argue that all such usages are confusing and moreover degrading and derogatory to some central entity, the soul of man (perhaps also to God or some general principle of the universe) . . . . With the growth of information it will be found to fade away, leaving us better able to face these great problems about ourselves and the universe.[56]

Yet what room is there for a spirit or for "things of the spirit" or for "human dignity" in this mechanistic scheme, and what would be our fate if abandoning, as he anticipates, the "verbal traditions appropriate to an earlier state of knowledge," we were thrown back upon the stunted language he advocates? Thought, literature, even a philosophy of science would all be impossible.

Belief in God or in some "central entity" is irrelevant to our acceptance of what is a fantasy, for robust common sense of itself leads us to reject it. The truths of common sense are as valid as those of science even though they be less specifiable in their grounds.

The reader may well find the dissection of the various hypotheses that have been discussed somewhat wearisome, but it is imperative that the language of mechanism and reductionism should be sharply analyzed. Only thus can its incoherence and inadequacy be fully seen, and the impossible demands it makes upon our credibility be appreciated.

From all that has gone before we must still conclude that neurophysiology has not provided a feasible account of the brain-mind relationship, or adequate concepts of consciousness or memory in physiological terms, while the "models" proposed to us to illustrate brain functions are apter at confusing than enlightening. The unrecognized fallacy that an analogy is an identity creeps into the special pleading that accompanies the announcement of every new model. All are couched in terms of Whitehead's "nature lifeless."

In these circumstances it is difficult to understand the deter-

56. *Ibid.,* p. 6.

mined insistence upon reductionist ideas, which we are bidden to accept under pain of being thought unscientific.

Yet the explanations of consciousness and memory and the models so far offered to us *are not inferences from experiment,* but are what Lashley, the most determined of mechanists, called them, namely, *"assumptions from psychological events."*

There seems to be a feeling in the air that biology would be more respectable and more scientific if only it could find complete shelter under the umbrella of the physical sciences and mathematics; that is, if it were something that it is not and cannot be.

It is possible, however, to end on a more encouraging note, for Bremer, one of Sherrington's later pupils and a neurophysiologist whose work has always shown a remarkable generality of understanding, in discussing what neurophysiology has contributed to the problem of memory, goes on to comment as follows:

> It is necessary to say that impressive as these facts are, they provide no more than a glimmer of light in the night of our ignorance. They raise more problems than they solve.
>
> The striking differences which obtain between memories artificially evoked with their clarity and hallucinatory vividness, on the one hand, and ordinary recollections with their lack of detailed precision and their often deliberate distortions, are a symbol of the distance that still separates psychology from neurophysiology. The paths both may yet follow may be parallel, yet if in future they should unite and fuse, such a fusion will not, we may be sure, be the consecration of a mechanistic determinism tending to reduce the human person to the level of a robot or that of the social insects. [Translated][57]

From another source, this time a professor of logic and scientific method, we learn:

> . . . we construct electronic brains because we have no such brains ourselves. Thus we are not calculators. But we are constructors of calculators. . . . A calculator may be able, for example, to produce proofs of mathematical theorems. It may distinguish theorems from non-theorems, true state-

57. F. Bremer, *Aspects physiologiques de la memoire,* Conference held at University of Brussels (Brussels: Marcel Hayez, 1952), pp. 14-15.

ments from false statements. But it will not distinguish ingenious proofs and interesting theorems from dull and uninteresting ones. It will thus 'know' too much—far too much that is without any interest, the knowledge of a calculator, however systematic, is like a sea of truisms in which a few particles of gold may be suspended. It is only our human brain which may lend significance to the calculators' senseless power of producing truths.[58]

I have only one comment to make on this statement, namely, that the word "brain" might aptly have been replaced by the word "mind" in the final sentence. For the ability to select what is interesting and illuminating points to one of the characteristics that a machine does not share with the mind. When so many biologists equate the brain with a machine the distinction is critical.

Nevertheless, as Polanyi has pointed out;

The practice of science can be sound even when it is conducted in the name of false principles. For biologists to deny their use of teleological reasoning is quite harmless. . . . Think of recent explorations of the brain by electrodes of microscopic size which show the nervous system operating as a machine.

This splendid enquiry would be hampered by keeping in mind the fact that the assumption of the whole nervous system operating as an insentient automaton is nonsensical. They may be right therefore in ignoring the absurdity of the idea underlying their work.[59]

It would still be encouraging to be able to believe that all did in fact see this absurdity.

PART TWO.   PERSONAL KNOWLEDGE AND
NEUROBIOLOGY

Our comprehension of a living individual entails a subsidiary awareness of its parts which is not wholly specifiable in more detached terms. This understanding acknowledges a

58. Karl S. Popper, "Indeterminism in Quantum Mechanics; Part 2," *British Journal for the Philosophy of Science,* I (1950) , 194.
59. "On the Modern Mind," *Encounter,* XII (May, 1965) , 5.

particular comprehensive—i.e. 'molar'—achievement of the individual itself. Since our knowledge of this molar function is not specifiable in 'molecular' terms, the function itself is not reducible to molecular particulars; it must be acknowledged therefore as a higher form of being, not determined by these particulars. We can reach this conclusion directly by recalling that the understanding of a whole appreciates the coherence of its subject matter and thus acknowledges the existence of a value that is absent from the constituent particulars.[60]

This is the situation which every biologist has to face when contemplating and practising his science if he is not to become the profounder of a physics and chemistry of which chemists and physicists know nothing, namely, one which can fully account for the phenomena of life and of mind, and can now or later provide the language in which these can be described.

Do all biologists today understand that when dealing with living beings they must have *a logic of achievement* which is not a factor in the physical sciences of inanimate matter but which is at the very heart of biology? There are no 'acts' in chemical and physical processes, but in the living organism there are acts as well as chemical and physical processes, and the former are not specifiable solely in terms of the latter. Even in man-made machines there are working principles that cannot be subsumed in terms of physics and chemistry.

Chemical and physical *processes* cannot be described either as *performances* or as *achievements,* nor can we speak of the achievements of a machine, but only of its performances. These are specified by their human designer and are specifiable, as indeed they have to be before the machine can be patented. A computer, for example, is simply a device invented by man to extend his own natural powers of a certain order. The same may be said of automobiles, airplanes, or submarines which allow him to travel faster and in more dimensions of space than his natural powers permit. Yet these remain his creations and are neither his equals nor his models. Outside the realm of nature alive the term "achievement" has no place or meaning.[61]

60. *P.K.,* p. 327.
61. An achievement is something that might conceivably fail of success, but for physical and chemical processes there is neither failure nor success.

Man's capacity for achievements of various kinds exists and goes into action without man-made machines in many of the highest flights of his genius, and of these it may be said that they are neither wholly specifiable, nor predictable in kind or in order of genius.

Scientific thinking and the gift of scientific discovery involve much that is unspecifiable, and this even though their use does not conflict with the laws of physics and chemistry and needs the machine-like functions of the body for their display.

These three levels in a hierarchy from lowest to highest are inescapable for the biologist, and this is how it comes that a logic of achievement must be integral to his thinking. Yet this has no place in mechanistic and reductionist concepts of biology.[62]

Polanyi has defined biology as "life reflecting upon itself," but for the thoroughgoing reductionist it can logically be no more than "physics and chemistry reflecting upon physics and chemistry," with an incongruous "it" or a "we" inserted in the proposition to make this viewpoint less obviously incredible than it is.

It still remains true, of course, that the professed biologist despite his negative view of biology may by his discoveries of basic neural processes make advances of great value to neurobiology, the paradox of his ideas not impairing his technical ingenuity: this is the modern biologist's schizophrenia, arising from his exclusive preoccupation with parts and part-functions, and this in turn the consequence of the prevailing use of a single order of technique, both leading inevitably to reductionist and mechanist ideas.

Looking back over the history of the discipline we find that at its modern origins there was not great concern with the basic physicochemical processes in the structural material of living organisms, because there did not then exist the necessary collateral knowledge to deal effectively with this matter. Thus, the earliest observers devoted themselves to what Whitehead called

62. The terms "mechanistic" and "reductionist" are not wholly synonymous, but have overlapping references. The biologist who maintains that the living organism can be described as a machine or automaton has deprived the organism of its highest and most characteristic dimension, but the invoker of chemistry, physics, and mathematics as providing the ultimate level of description of the living organism is doubly a reductionist and has ceased to be even a mechanist, or even a biologist if this term has a meaning.

the "external understanding" of the nervous system:[63] namely, with the influence of the system upon the functions and structures of body which it innervated, and with the powers which this innervation and integration conferred upon the body in its commerce with the environment.

This was the order of Jackson's contribution, and later in the experimental field, Sherrington's achievement was largely of this kind. But this era of thought has gone and no one would now contemplate entitling a work on neurophysiology "The Integrative Action of the Nervous System." Interest has swung over to the intensive study of part functions by a particular order of technique, until the notion has insensibly grown that this reveals all that is significant and that it can be subsumed in terms of chemistry and physics, that is, in terms of inanimate nature.

Thus, in a sense, neurophysiology has become a discipline off-balance. Burns, himself a neurophysiologist, has summed up this situation with rare insight in the passage already cited (vide supra p. 283) and in terms that seem to justify the present criticism.

Thus, faced by the current belief of most neurobiologists, and indeed biologists in general, that they are accounting for the phenomena of life and mind in terms of physics, chemistry, and mathematics, Polanyi, in *Personal Knowledge* and in his other writings on this subject, has pointed out that they are doing nothing of the kind. What they are doing is *accounting for the dynamic properties of living organisms in terms of a mechanism founded upon the laws of physics and chemistry, but not explicable by these laws.*[64]

He has further pointed out that the concept of levels is not something we encounter for the first time when we pass from the study of inanimate nature to that of nature alive, for it inheres in all man-made machines. As an analogy he uses the wrist watch. This is kept going as a timepiece by its mainspring uncoiling under control of the hair spring and turning the hands that tell the time. These principles of operation define the watch's con-

63. *Modes of Thought,* p. 63.
64. M. Polanyi, "The Structure of Consciousness," *Brain* LXXXVIII (1965), 799.

struction and working, but they are not explicable in terms of inorganic aggregates. No component of the watch is formed by a natural equilibration of matter, but is artificially designed and connected to perform its function.

A complete physical and chemical topography of the watch would not reveal that it was a timepiece, but only that it was a composite object. Its operational principles transcend the chemical composition of its parts and are not explicable in terms of this.

If we turn from this analogy of levels within inanimate nature, to the living organism and take the example of a frog, it is clear that a complete chemical analysis of this would not tell us anything about it as a frog. It would not reveal the machine-like physiological processes, or the regulative principles by which these were co-ordinated and integrated. It would not reveal that we were dealing with a once living and resourceful creature. Here we encounter something qualitatively different from anything seen in man-made machines.

These instances raise *the general question of the validity of a reductionist concept when applied to a comprehensive entity*, and it is essential that this point should be explored and illustrated by examples comprehensible by educated persons who are not scientists. Therefore, I add another of Polanyi's analogies taken from the game of chess. *Rules* govern the movements of the different pieces, but obedience to the rules does not make an expert player, for there are *stratagems* in the game which while they are conducted within the rules are not explicable in terms of these, and transcend them.

The rules allow a wide freedom of play within what are called in physics the "boundary conditions" of the rules. Thus, we have here two levels of action, a higher and a lower, and the former is not specifiable in terms of the latter.

Of course, one might add another and physicochemical level, namely, the composition of the pieces, which may be made of wood or of ivory; but this level is wholly irrelevant both to the rules and to the stratagems, even though we could have no game without the pieces. The subtleties of chess cannot be reduced to a problem in chemistry and physics, or even to a problem of rules. Polanyi describes a machine as *a system in which the boundary conditions left open by chemistry and physics are controlled by certain structural and operational principles, and hence a machine cannot be described in terms of the laws of chemistry and physics.*[65]

It would surely be naïve to assume when we pass from the realm of inanimate nature to that of nature alive that we can escape the acceptance of a hierarchy of levels in such a comprehensive entity as a living organism, and that we can revert to a basic account of this in terms of chemistry, physics, and mathematics on a one-level plan.

Yet this is the hope and anticipation of many biologists, and an adherence to this view is required of us all, though the biologist, once he leaves his laboratory or his lecture room, does not believe it himself and does not act and think as though he did. Indeed, no one could live with such an over-all conception of himself. Yet convention requires that the manifestations of life and mind should be spoken of *as if* of their nature they were capable of full description in the language of the physical sciences. All ideas of purpose are excluded from this creed, and Polanyi quotes the saying that teleology is a lady of easy virtue whom the biologist rejects in public but lives with in private.

It is the liturgy of this faith that the biologist has formally to intone if he is not to risk being dubbed unscientific, if he is young, or demented, if he is not. No biblical fundamentalism could be more rigid and demanding, and for the human race it tacitly assumes that there is no valid universe of discourse outside the ring fence of the physical sciences. Of this attitude Polanyi has written:

. . . When the supernatural authority of laws, churches and sacred texts had waned or collapsed, man tried to avoid the emptiness of mere self-assertion by establishing over himself the authority of experience and reason. But it has now turned out that modern scientism fetters thought as cruelly

65. "The Modern Mind," *Encounter,* XII (May, 1965) , 3.

as ever the churches had done. It offers no scope for our
most vital beliefs and it forces us to disguise them in farci-
cally inadequate terms.[66]

Over and above the physicochemical processes and the machine-
like activities in the living organism there are principles that
cannot be formulated in terms of either of these levels. In the first
place we meet the *individual* for the first time, and we find in it
inventive and regulating functions which exploit and control the
boundary conditions of the lower levels.

A simple example is the maze-running of Lashley's mutilated
rats which still contrive to run the maze with such neuromuscular
synergies as are left to them after lesions of the nervous system,
retaining a memory and a purpose that evoked in each of them a
different set of operational principles to achieve a persisting aim.
This adaptive capacity reveals the presence of a central regulating force and also the principle of equipotentiality in the nervous
system, neither of these being an achievement within the scope of
any man-made machine, save within the narrow limits imposed
by their human designers.

Whitehead, writing of animal and human intelligence and of
man's unique place in nature, says:

> The final unity of animal intelligence is also the organ of
> reaction to novel situations, and is the organ introducing
> the requisite novelty of reaction. . . . Animal life can face
> conventional novelties with conventional devices, but the
> governing principle lacks large power for the sudden intro-
> duction of any major novelty. . . . When we come to man-
> kind, nature seems to have burst through another of its
> boundaries. The conceptual entertainment of unrealized
> possibility becomes a major factor in human mentality. . . .
> It is the entertainment of the alternative. In its highest
> development it becomes the entertainment of the Ideal. . . .
> The life of a human being receives its worth, its importance,
> from the way in which unrealized ideals shape its purposes
> and tinge its actions.[67]

I have given these two quotations from the writings of Whitehead and of Polanyi, because the one was a distinguished mathe-

66. *P.K.*, p. 265.
67. *Modes of Thought*, p. 36.

matician and the other a distinguished chemist before they became philosophers.

Thus both are immune from the scornful dismissal of philosophy and philosophers that characterized Lashley's final (1958) paper, where as a class philosophers were described as unreliable observers, incompetent psychologists, and weavers of fairy tales. This attitude is a belated hangover from the late nineteenth-century foible of natural scientists which arose during the debate about evolution and the doctrine of natural selection. Yet I have chosen these passages so that we may see what a deep, unbridged gulf lies between the views of these two scientists and philosophers and those offered to us by the mechanists and reductionists of today, which, I submit, fly in the face of human history and experience. The history of mankind is more than a narrative of animal behaviors.

The reiterated "nothing-buttery" of the reductionists rings hollow against the wisdom of these thinkers who have the insight to realize and the courage to state the inadequacy of the sciences of inanimate nature to give reasons for the manifestations of nature alive, that is, of life and mind.

So focally directed has been the attention of neurophysiologists to the basic physical and chemical substrata of neural functions, that that comprehensive entity, the nervous system as a whole, has been almost lost sight of amidst the minutiae of its activities.

This is characteristically exemplified by Jasper's criticism of Bremer's expressed view that "conscious integration is an integrative process of the whole brain," in the following words:

> The notion of the brain acting as a whole is, to my thinking and experimenting, rather sterile. It gives no possible conception of a real mechanism of integration. It leaves us completely without experimental approach to these problems (i.e. those of brain mechanisms and consciousness) .[68]

This comment reveals a complete confusion between *methods* and *ideas*. In the experimental study of a multifactorial physiological state it is necessary to break down the problem into its simplest components.

68. *Brain Mechanism and Consciousness*, p. 500.

As Whitehead had expressed it, "experiment is nothing else than a mode of cooking the facts to exemplify the law."[69] This involves a high degree of abstraction from the sum of phenomena presented. But because our methods call for fractionation, it is the more important that our thinking does not become disintegrated into isolated items, so that we lose sight of the rational aim of a physiological study, namely, the understanding of a comprehensive entity, and not merely the elucidation of a part-function which then becomes an end in itself. Bremer's well-known physiological studies have shown him to be an outstanding experimentalist whose interest has remained *focally directed towards a comprehensive understanding of the nervous system as a whole.*

Polanyi has also pointed out that in many behavioral studies it has been the practice to fractionate behavior into items which are separately considered and the "laws" of their occurrence sought. In this process of breaking down, the picture of the mind behind the behavior is quite lost, and the fragments themselves become meaningless.[70]

This brings me finally to his concept of *focal and subsidiary awareness,* which not only illuminates much dull writing on perception, but has implications for all studies of comprehensive entities. This idea has been developed in many of his recent writings.[71]

We may recognize a familiar face as a whole without being able to specify the many features that go to its composition. The situation is one in which *we know but cannot tell,* and is called "tacit knowledge" by Polanyi. While we are focally aware of the physiognomy we are subsidiarily aware of the details, which serve as clues *from which* we look to the whole, just as in a stereoscope we look *from* the two separate images to the stereoscopic image which is the focus of our perception and attention. The physiognomy and the stereoscope image have each a value and a quality which their components do not possess.

69. A. N. Whitehead, *Adventures of Ideas* (Cambridge: Cambridge University Press, 1933), p. 111.
70. "Structure of Consciousness," *Brain,* LXXXVIII (1965), 802.
71. *Ibid.,* pp. 799 ff. Cf. also *Review of Modern Physics,* XXXIV (1962), 601 ff.; *T. D.,* chap. I *et passim; Philosophy,* LXI (1966), 369-386.

In all these examples we find evidence of the stratification of nature, both inanimate and animate, of the principle of a hierarchy of levels, each with its boundary conditions which endow each ascending level with a greater range and flexibility of action, and render each level inexplicable in terms of lower levels. In brief, to quote Polanyi, "The higher principles which characterize a comprehensive entity cannot be defined in terms of the laws that apply to its parts in themselves."[72]

Let us take the example of the skills of the ballerina. At their foundation lie the physicochemical processes of muscular contraction and nerve impulses. Above this we have the basic level of simple motor co-ordination: reciprocal and double reciprocal innervation and co-contraction, still higher are the syntheses of local movements into ever-changing combinations, and finally the direction of all this into the humanly designed pattern of the ballet. All but the highest level in this hierarchy are without meaning *except as serving this determined pattern.*

Summing up such a situation Polanyi says:

> All meaning lies in higher levels of reality that are irreducible to the laws by which ultimate particulars of the universe are controlled. . . . What is most tangible has the least meaning and it is perverse to identify the tangible with the real. To regard a meaningless substrate as the ultimate reality of all things must lead one to the conclusion that all things are meaningless. We can avoid this conclusion only if we acknowledge that deepest reality is possessed by higher things that are least tangible.[73]

In conclusion, he regards the body and mind as two strata, in which the higher principles of mind rely for their operation on the lower principles of physiology, and postulates that no observations of physiology can make us apprehend the operations of mind, but that these operations do not run counter to the principles of physiology, nor even to the lower principles of physics and chemistry on which they rely. Yet since the operations of the mind rely on the services of lower bodily principles, the mind can be disturbed by adverse changes in the body, or be

72. *Brain,* LXXXVIII (1965) , 804.
73. *Encounter,* XII (1965) , 4.

offered new opportunities by favorable changes of its bodily basis.

While this concept leaves the final problem of the "how" of this association between these two levels unsolved, it points in the direction in which further understanding is to be sought and is the antithesis of the mechanistic and reductionist approach in which it is not possible to discern a future, for it has turned its back upon logic.

Eccles in his Eddington Lecture, while not attempting such a reasoned synthesis as Polanyi proposes, has had the courage to state explicitly that he is unable to believe that his conscious experiences are *nothing but* the operations of the physiological mechanisms of the brain. He adds that

> Contrary to this physicalist creed, I believe that the prime reality of my experiencing self cannot with propriety be *identified* with some aspects of its experiences and its imaginings—such as brains and neurons and nerve impulses and even complex spatio-temporal patterns of impulses. The evidence presented (in this lecture) shows that events in the material world are necessary but not sufficient causes for conscious experiences and for my consciously experiencing self. . . . I believe that there is a fundamental mystery in my existence, transcending any biological account of the development of my body (including my brain) with its genetic inheritance and its evolutionary origin. . . . I cannot believe that this wonderful gift of a conscious existence has no further future, no possibility of another existence. . . . At least I would maintain that this possibility of a future existence cannot be denied on scientific grounds.[74]

This confession of faith, the antithesis of those of Lashley and O'Leary, is in essence, from the point of view of science, no more than a rejection of the view that there is no other universe of discourse about man than that of science, and the statement of another view which is not put forward as a scientific statement.

Nevertheless, Eccles' view has been received with a derisory astonishment as one inappropriate to a scientist and as contrary

74. *The Brain and the Unity of Conscious Experience* (Cambridge: Cambridge University Press, 1965) , pp. 41-44.

to reason. Whether this response is an indirect claim to inerrancy by the critics, or merely a statement of the principle of philosophic doubt, in virtue of which you must doubt what the doubter doubts, but also believe what he is prepared to accept, is not clear, but whichever it is, it has no scientific legs to stand on.

Pirenne says that

> We are under no compulsion to believe that physiology gives us the whole truth about life and about ourselves. Physiology can be taken as referring only to certain aspects of reality. If we reserve our judgement as to the ultimate value of physiological findings, there is no difficulty in adopting the mechanistic standpoint as a methodological postulate, even in the field of sensory physiology. The Cartesian links between mind and body, which are not amenable to physiological investigation and whose introduction into physiological reasoning causes such confusions and obscurities, are thus avoided altogether.
>
> Such a method of approach does not deny the existence of the mind. It simply decides from the start not to deal with the mind, but only with the body. The fundamental problem of the body-mind relationship then remains, but as a metaphysical problem, not a scientific one.[75]

Here is the voice of Hughlings Jackson echoing across a century, perhaps as a reproach to those who now regard any acceptance of his views as no more than an expression of ancestor worship.

However, the human physiologist, at least, must be interested in the nature of the brain-mind relationship. What he does not have to do is to claim the problem as wholly within his own field of science, and to put himself forward, with his experimental techniques as the sole qualified expositor, competent to dispute more general views on the subject and to explain the problem in terms of scientific disciplines that are not really his own, namely, those of chemistry, physics, and mathematics. Physical scientists are, in general, not so bold.

In conclusion, the path that neurobiology now follows, dominated by mechanistic and reductionist ideas, must surely lead to

75. M. H. Pirenne, "Descartes and the Body-Mind Problem in Physiology," *British Journal for the Philosophy of Science* I (1950), 43.

its disintegration into the tale of the bloodless dance of action potentials and the shuttlings at synapses, divorced from the general body of biology, offering its explanations of life and mind in terms of atomic—and presumably in due time of sub-atomic-particles, and stating its generalizations in terms so remote from human experience as to have no explanatory value.

"A fortunate use of abstractions," writes Whitehead,

> is of the essence of upward evolution. But there is no necessity of such good use. Abstractions may function in experience so as to separate them from their relevance to the totality. In that case, the abstractive element is a flicker of interest which is destroying its own massive battle for survival.[76]

The submission of this paper is that we are not witnessing that fortunate use of abstractions in the generality of neurophysiological thought and writing. Whitehead, who had so much to say of value to biologists, having failed to reach their interest, it is strongly to be hoped that Michael Polanyi, whose message is of primary importance to them, will meet with more success in this regard, and that a younger generation of biologists, not yet so widely committed to mechanistic and reductionist ideas as many of their preceptors, may achieve through his writings a wider generality of understanding, a more liberal view of what their relevant literature should consist in, and the courage not to be intimidated by what can only be an ephemeral, but deadening, fashion in biology.

Life, the description and explanation of which is certainly within the proper scope of physiology, continues still to baffle us; but mind presents a problem to which so far it has provided no glimmer of an answer, save to evade it by mechanistic and reductionistic analogies and the invention of mechanical models. It is the writer's conviction that it must of its nature escape experimental physiology. Even its phenomenological description seems not within their general outlook, and only the psychologists in their own special language throw any light upon it, though not upon the nature of the brain-mind relationship.

76. A. N. Whitehead, *Modes of Thought* (New York: MacMillan, 1938), p. 169.

PERSONAL KNOWING AND MAKING

Harold G. McCurdy

For psychology, too, it is the best of times and the worst of times. At one moment it seems that psychology must inevitably harden into a technological ritual for promoting wars and insane asylums as it programs pigeons to guide bombs to the target and constructs tests to standardize people into "superior adult" or "psychopathic deviate." At another moment some gesture is made that hints at a truce or an act of love allowing the pigeons to fly free and all the people to rise up from their prisons and their graves, shouting, "I live, therefore I am!" But on the whole the present is very much like the past when a king with a large jaw and a queen with a plain face sat on the throne of England and a king with a large jaw and a queen with a fair face sat on the throne of France, and in both territories it was clearer than crystal that things in general were settled forever except for a few minor adjustments of the parameters.

What is so remarkable about Michael Polanyi is not that he takes up a third sovereign position, establishes a "third force" as some rebels in psychology like to call their little protest against the two major establishments, but that quietly, soberly, diligently he has developed a way of moving forward out of any established territory, whether affluent or barren, into new dimensions of reality.

Abraham Maslow, one of our more convincing rebels and by some miracle recently elected president of the American Psychological Association, has written in the preface of his latest book, which is concerned with "rehumanizing (and trans-humanizing) science," that he had planned to do a comprehensive treatise on the subject but was brought to a halt by "discovering Michael Polanyi's great book, *Personal Knowledge*, just as I had worked up a systematic outline and started writing." And he adds: "This profound work, which is certainly required reading for our generation, does much of what I had planned to do, and solves many of the problems which had concerned me."[1]

There in a few words we catch a glimpse of the state of American psychology and Polanyi's role in it. His work is just being discovered, and is meeting or about to meet a warm reception in certain quarters, along with a sense of recognition—"I was about to think this, too." It would be possible to define the situation more precisely, with some fullness of detail, and even to speak of crises of more than one sort; but I will confine myself to a comment on a title famous in its day. A few years ago Carl Rogers collided with B. F. Skinner in public debate under the banner question, "Persons or Science?"[2] That was in 1955. It is the "or" in the title to which I wish to draw attention. Perhaps, if Polanyi's influence could have been felt at that time, the "or" could have been tempered to "and" and the question mark removed. Science grows out of personal experience and is shaped by personal acts, even if it threatens destruction to persons. No matter how alien to ourselves it appears, it is something that we and our human comrades have devised.

In this narrow sense anyone willing to use a term like "person" at all might be expected to admit that science is personal. (Though I am not quite sure. There are those who say that culture makes persons, that science tells us who we are.) The sense is too narrow, however, to contain Polanyi's thought. He points to resources in us that not only produce science, but correct it, enlarge it, go beyond it, encompass it in a generous understanding capable of discovering truth. I think I can pay my homage to Polanyi best by trying to act in his spirit as I reflect on some matters that have engaged my attention as a psychologist. Other contributors to this volume are better qualified to examine his thought systematically.

1. Abraham H. Maslow, *The Psychology of Science: A Reconnaissance* (New York: Harper and Row, 1966), pp. xvi-xvii.
2. C. R. Rogers, "Persons or Science? A Philosophical Question," *American Psychologist*, X (1955), 267-278.

I

I will begin with a statement that may sound a bit antithetical to Polanyi. Often our explicit knowledge fails to get corrected because of a tacit conspiracy in favor of it. Though we may be covertly aware that a given method of inquiry has limits or indeed *compels* certain results, we may block off the realization of the fact by declining to test those limits. Our procedure may have general sanction within our specialty, and the results it leads to may reassure us by confirming our pet hypotheses. Under these circumstances, the wisdom which underlies our specific inquiry may be silenced to the point of repression.

It is the actions of which we have only subsidiary awareness that most imperil our search for truth. I will illustrate what I mean by a few examples.

We look to what we are focally aware of in our first endeavors to understand our world. Usually this means attending to what is out-there. When we have trouble fitting a key to a lock, we are prone to blame the lock rather than our choice of the key: the possibilities in our hand, the other keys, may be too obscurely present to consciousness to do us any good. This tendency, which may be innate in the human animal for all I know, is reinforced in professional psychology by the general ideal of scientific objectivity and the special influence of behaviorism. I will cite an amusing case. N. R. F. Maier developed an experimental technique for producing neurotic stereotyped behavior in rats. The animals were forced by a blast of air to leap across an open space toward two closed doors without any cue as to which of them was barred shut and which would open on contact; consequently they often bumped their noses against the barred door and fell sprawling helplessly into a net some distance below. Under these conditions it was usual for more than half of the rats to form the habit of jumping always toward the same door, regardless of whether it was barred shut or not, and to persist in doing so even when the other door was set open and the landing platform was visible through it. Some years ago two of Maier's research assistants, using rats from the same colony and working in adjacent rooms with similar equipment according to the standard procedures, got radically divergent results. One obtained the usual percentage of fixated position responses; the other, not a single one. The sole difference between the two which eventually emerged as they compared notes was that the unsuccessful experimenter *felt sorry for the rats* and may have petted them between trials a little more than other researchers using the same technique.[3] As Maier suggests, it would be well for experimenters to take into account and describe their own role in such experiments. From the little he tells us we can infer that experimenters who feel sorry for their rats are rare, and that a powerful determinant of "success" in these experiments is a certain hardness of heart in the experimenters.

Experimenter blindness to subjective factors is shown in another way in a famous experiment on decreased sensory input done by Bexton, Heron, and Scott at McGill.[4] Not until they had run eight of their twenty-two human subjects through the experimental procedures did it occur to them that it would be useful to question the subjects on the most important phenomenon that was generated by the conditions, i.e., the vivid hallucinations. It is true that some of the early subjects had made reference to "having a dream while awake," but these references are said to have been "rather puzzling." Light dawned when one of the experimenters himself underwent the experimental conditions. As they report: "Then one of us, while serving as a subject, observed the phenomenon and realized its peculiarity and extent."[5]

Fortunately I am able to report an experiment in which the role of the experimenter was by no means overlooked. It constituted a part of the work done by Miss Joan Woodworth for an honors paper on the subject of smiling.[6] She had become inter-

3. N. R. F. Maier, "Frustration Theory: Restatement and Extension," *Psychological Review*, LXIII (1956) , 370-388. The incident cited is mentioned on pp. 375-376.
4. W. H. Bexton, W. Heron, and T. H. Scott, "Effects of Decreased Variation in the Sensory Environment," *Canadian Journal of Psychology*, VIII (1954) , 70-76.
5. *Ibid.,* p. 73.
6. Joan Dee Woodworth, "The Significance of the Smile in Interpersonal Relations" (Psychology Honors Thesis, University of North Carolina, 1966) .

ested in a theory sometimes propounded on the campus that students at the University of North Carolina, especially the girls, are unfriendly, as proved by the infrequency of smiles. She proceeded to gather data. As she walked across the campus between classes she looked carefully at approaching strangers and tabulated their responses. The yield of smiles was low: 5 per cent for the boys, 18 per cent for the girls. One might say that the results supported the theory, though not in the predicted direction. Miss Woodworth, however, was aware that her observations could not be made without some sort of involvement of the observer in the phenomenon observed. The percentages just reported were obtained when she observed with an unsmiling face. On other days she smiled as she observed. The yield of smiles was higher: 32 per cent for the boys, 63 per cent for the girls. That is hardly surprising, when we reflect on it. Yet how many experiments have been performed, and how much data collected, without the experimenter's once reflecting on his own role? How many hypotheses or theories have been supported by data generated, in a sense, by the hypotheses or theories themselves? In the present case, it is easy to see how the data could be made to support a misanthropic view of one's fellow students. One would simply observe carefully, perhaps skeptically and suspiciously as a good cautious scientist should, while withholding one's own smile.

Once we have become aware of our own participation in the events we observe, we can make certain corrections. One line of correction strongly favored in science is to remove the observer farther and farther from the thing observed. One-way mirrors, intervening apparatus, professional formality, and outright deceit are some of the devices employed in psychology. To go into detail would be tedious, and it is unnecessary, because most of the deviousness is just a rather pathetic obeisance to scientific method—the method that tries to obtain data uncontaminated by the observer. As Polanyi has truly remarked, this ideal of scientific detachment exercises a destructive influence in the field of psychology, however it may function elsewhere.

Suppose, then, that we move in the other direction. We acknowledge our own motives and manner of observing, and from time to time reflect on them. I was a little shocked the other day to catch myself secretly assessing a student with suspicion and a trace of contempt. The moment I recognized my mood I realized how little basis there was for it in the person before me; and, having caught it, I was able to dismiss it, relax my foolish and cruel guard, and begin to appreciate the unique, intelligent, and sensitive visitor whom up to that moment I had been treating with superficial, inattentive cordiality. The moment of awareness enabled me to move out from under my own shadow.

Obviously, if we start off in this direction we are headed for total involvement. Any attempt to find an observation-base where we can claim the immunity of detachment is doomed to failure. Consider Freud. He put his patients on the couch, he kept himself out of view, he blanked himself out, so that their self-revelations would not be distorted by his presence. And then he discovered that they tended to forget about their memories and private ruminations and to concentrate their attention on him. Some of them revealed by unmistakable signs and some by outright declaration that they had fallen in love with him. He called it transference, i.e., he attributed as much of the passion as he could to the resuscitation of earlier passion for someone else and regarded himself as far as possible as a bare screen on which they projected their romances. Even so, it became apparent that the heat was on—on him. Furthermore, however belatedly and tentatively, he recognized a reciprocal process in himself. He called that counter-transference, and explained away the immediacy of it in the same terms he applied to his patients. Nevertheless!

Observation, it seems, is not a neutral stance. If one human being merely listens attentively to another, something begins to awaken in the relationship that resembles love; and, as Freud remarks, no matter how much sickness there may be in transference-love, it can be real enough and charming enough to endanger the starched professionalism of the doctor. The person observing and the person observed move toward a new condition, toward union or communion, where talk of scientific objectivity becomes ridiculous.

II

There are two perils in such a state of affairs, from the point of view of objective science: (a) the cool detachment of the observer, the data-gatherer, breaks down into a warm partiality; and (b) the data begin to undergo transformations. But what is our scientific purpose? To describe an artificial stillness, typified by a specimen fixed on a slide, or an unvarying absolute, as in geometry? Or is it to grasp reality in process? In the situations above described there is process, and it is bipolar. If we avoid bipolar process we may indeed manage to obtain a fixed picture of something—a test score, an anatomy for an elementary textbook. But the more successfully we do that, the more remote will reality-in-process appear in comparison with our results. We must either suffer a split between our everyday life of process and our scientific knowledge so-called, or, as determined objective scientists, we must attempt to bring our life of process as close to a halt as our model demands and heal the breach by killing off ourselves. There are some indications that the latter alternative is being put into practice here and there.

Suppose, however, that we continue to experience bipolar process and perhaps do our best to cultivate it, can we make explicit knowledge of it? Clearly, the language we use about it must be dynamic, because it is process, not fixity, that we have to describe. But, moreover, both poles must be recognized even when attention is concentrated on one. To put it succinctly in an example: "She is growing beautiful" must not be dissociated from "*I see* that she is growing beautiful," or even "*Because* I look at her as I do, she is growing beautiful." "She is growing beautiful" can be as factual as "The rocket is accelerating," but the experiment is different. To be sure, the acceleration of a rocket also depends on some human preconditions. But in the case of "She is growing beautiful" the bipolarity of observer and observed is peculiarly essential. To report the fact accurately we must include ourselves in the description and admit that if our manner of looking has changed her, her manner of change affects in turn our manner of looking. We must describe, that is, a whole relational universe. Retrospectively, of course. Any de-

scription must be retrospective. The moment described is a moment gone. However, description of the past, even when quite
abstract, may suggest the possibility of renewal; may encourage
those who have not entered that region of reality to make the
trial; may have pertinence for the future.

The great temptation for the scientific strategist who admits
the importance of bipolar process is to step out of it himself and
treat it as purely objective. To use terminology that I find
indispensable, the S-O (self-object) relationship is, in the name
of scientific objectivity, turned into an O-O (object-object) relationship. Thus it has happened in recent times that the intimacy
of sexual love has been submitted to the usual techniques of
physiological observation, the sexual partners being attached to
sophisticated laboratory apparatus and minutely monitored
while they went about the business of caressing, embracing,
copulating, and reaching orgasm.[7] It is in harmony with this
relentless technological trend (the medical authors of the above
study have perfected an electrically controlled artificial coition
machine) that many of the books designed to instruct the inex-
perienced in the art of love dwell on such matters as the mechanical stimulation of precisely located erogenous zones. Such observers and technicians of the mechanics of sex are more in the
tradition of classical science in their demure objectivity than
Freud was; but, then, they never enter the region of Freud's
concern at all.

Such tough-minded products of a scientific civilization as those
just mentioned are not likely, in fact, to give much thought to
the problem of the observer. More interesting are those who are
keenly aware of the problem but who dispose of it by consciously
stepping out of the S-role themselves and forbidding it to others.
For example, Floyd Allport, in an address before the American
Psychological Association on the occasion of receiving a Distinguished Scientific Contribution Award, said:

> It seems as though we ought to remove the observer alto-
> gether, but still have the record. This of course is impossi-
> ble. The observer must also be left there as a *part* of the

7. William H. Masters and Virginia E. Johnson, *Human Sexual Response*
(Boston: Little, Brown, 1966). See the review by Kenneth Keniston in
Contemporary Psychology, XII (1967) 113-115.

world under observation. The problem is to adopt some criterion to assure us that what he is doing in this capacity is, in kind, just like what everything else in nature is doing. His act of observing and recording should present no "special case." He should be a participant but not a disturbing participant.[8]

Allport wants to deal with bipolar process in which there is an observing S, but he declines to be that S himself. ("Suppose that I try, in general, to observe my own observing. This I cannot do."[9]) However, he imagines that another observer could observe him observing and could do so exactly as he would observe two billiard balls colliding: an observer observing something is, to another observer, just the same as one billiard ball hitting another billiard ball. By this methodological maneuver it is proposed to translate the S-O relationship which was under consideration into an O-O relationship and cause the S to vanish into another part of the field, where, in the person of the observer of the observer, the S is no longer under scrutiny.

III

If in spite of difficulties we have become convinced that standing inside the bipolar process as a conscious S is a right thing to do—whether in the interest of psychology or some entirely new endeavor—then we shall find ourselves thinking about phenomena that objective psychology typically pushes aside and, doubtless, about other phenomena still that have never reached the level of consciousness where they *could* be consciously rejected, much less that level where they could be seriously entertained.

One of the most neglected of the wise formulations in psychology is Alexander Shand's first law, namely, "Mental activity tends, at first unconsciously, afterwards consciously, to produce and to sustain system and organization."[10] The truth of the law is

8. Floyd H. Allport, "A Theory of Enestruence (Event-Structure Theory): Report of Progress," *American Psychologist* XXII (1967), 1-24, at p. 3.
9. *Ibid.*, p. 4.
10. Alexander F. Shand, *The Foundations of Character: Being a Study of the Tendencies of the Emotions and Sentiments* (London: Macmillan, 1926; first published 1914), p. 21.

obvious if we take it as referring to man's various constructive activities, such as clipping hedges, building houses, painting pictures, assembling radios, drawing up constitutions, producing systems of philosophy, etc. Perhaps the outstanding example of its working within the usual limits of psychology (the obvious facts of human constructiveness somehow escape our view) bears the pathological label of paranoia. The paranoid individual organizes the world around himself in terms of a pervasive hostility: he sees conspiracy everywhere—the automobiles in the street regulate their course and speed to defeat him as pedestrian or driver, people designedly turn away from him or whisper about him, influences from a distance play upon him through the agency of spirits or electronic devices, etc. Now, paranoia has a bad name. But should we therefore hide from Shand's law? Is it not more realistic to see in paranoia the working of a general human principle, and take note of its working in ourselves, than to emphasize the diseased character of paranoia and fear the organizing tendency because in paranoia it is corrupted by the hatred pervading the system?

I wish to examine a few outlying instances of phenomena which seem to arise, in part, from the organizing tendency of the mind—instances not at all obtrusive. For that a mother's thoughts and all sorts of daily happenings in her experience get organized around her child and that lovers see the whole world in terms of their beloved—

> Nor did I wonder at the lily's white,
> Nor praise the deep vermilion of the rose;
> They were but sweet, but figures of delight,
> Drawn after you, you pattern of all those[11]—

these are notorious, even if little regarded, facts; and I do not want to belabor the obvious. The matters to which I wish to refer are more recondite. They are sometimes classified as superstitious or occult or, of course, mad, and often as "unscientific." I wish to maintain, however, that in their special style they witness to our tendency to organize our experience, and do so in such

11. William Shakespeare, Sonnet 98.

fashion that we get a sense of the world rather going out of its way to be compliant.

Take this. One evening (March 30, 1964, to be exact) I read to my wife a letter by Robert Louis Stevenson addressed to F. W. H. Myers in which he describes some peculiar experiences of his, for example:

> During an illness at Nice I lay awake a whole night in extreme pain. From the beginning of the evening *one part of my mind* became possessed of a notion so grotesque and shapeless that it may best be described as a form of words. I thought the pain was, or was connected with, a wisp or coil of some sort; I knew not of what it consisted nor yet where it was, and cared not; only I thought, if the two ends were brought together, the pain would cease. Now all the time, with *another part of my mind,* which I ventured to think was *myself,* I was fully alive to the absurdity of this idea, knew it to be a mark of impaired sanity, and was engaged with *my other self* in a perpetual conflict. *Myself* had nothing more at heart than to keep from my wife, who was nursing me, any hint of this ridiculous hallucination; the *other* was bound that she should be told of it and ordered to effect the cure. I believe it must have been well on in the morning before the fever (or *the other fellow*) triumphed, and I called my wife to my bedside, seized her savagely by the wrist, and looking on her with a face of fury, cried: "Why do you not put the two ends together and put me out of my pain?"[12]

My wife found this and the rest of the letter as confusing as the experiences themselves were to Stevenson, and made some remark on his phrase about joining the ends together. I commented in response that Stevenson knew Jekyll and Hyde in himself. She then left the room, and I continued to reflect on the theme of the joining of the opposites. I came thus to think of Jung's *Mysterium Conjunctionis,* a book I had recently purchased and had not read, which happened to be lying on the floor. I picked it up and quite randomly opened it at page 181. There my eye was caught by these words: "the crass identity of

12. F. W. H. Myers, *Human Personality and Its Survival of Bodily Death* (2 vols.; New York: Longmans, Green, 1954; first published 1903), I, 301.

opposites which we meet with in Jekyll and Hyde." At that moment it seemed to me that Jung's book had chimed into the conversation very aptly, or, to put it strongly, that the trend of my thoughts and the structure of the world had an uncanny congeniality. This impression was further strengthened by discovering, on consulting the index, that this was the sole reference to Stevenson in the entire book.

Here the organizing tendency of the mind, *my* mind, was pleased and a little astonished at the fitness of the passage in Jung's book to the theme that was developing as I read and talked and thought. Of course, when I think about it, I realize that the world around me in its most brute materiality is ready to be shaped by my purposes; with a little effort, often with very little, I can move rocks, plant a garden, make a birdbox, and, with the assistance of others, set in motion much larger enterprises that require the world to adjust itself to my wishes and plans. This fact is a commonplace that I take for granted in most of what I do. But it is evident that I do not take it for granted that the world, compliant though it is, is so compliant that a mere wish or interest on my part will bring it into line without further ado. Yet in the case I have described something like this seemed to happen. "A coincidence," one can say. But since it was a coincidence that aptly fed my organizing mental activity it gave me a sense of unusual co-operativeness, as if the book were a person sensitive to my preoccupations.

All of us, I think, have more of such experiences than we commonly admit, and perhaps we reflect on them too little, perhaps avoid reflecting on them because they challenge the assumption that the world runs on fatally like a mindless machine out of phase with our interests unless we deliberately turn a control knob somewhere. There are much more impressive episodes than the one I have cited. Here is one which, brief and simple though it was, almost made the hair rise on my head. It was the night of December 4, 1959. My wife and I went to bed about 11:30. She settled herself against my side and was soon asleep. Some time afterwards I, who had not yet gone to sleep, disturbed her by starting to turn over. She muttered something very thickly. I rose up on my elbow to listen. And then she said, very loudly and clearly and as if reproaching me for being still awake, "It's twelve-thirty!" I knew she was asleep by the tone of her voice, which was different from that of the waking or just-waking state. Shall I say that it sounded clairvoyant? At any rate, after a minute or two my curiosity got the better of my need for rest, and I went into an adjoining room with the bedside clock clutched in my hand in order to check the time. When I turned on the light for an instant, I saw that the clock read not more than a couple of minutes past 12:30. To be doubly sure, I checked it again a moment later, and was satisfied that my wife's somnambulic utterance had been strictly accurate. Notice, now, that *I* was the observer of this coincidence between the clock and the statement, and that it was only because I thought that the statement, though made in sleep, was made to me and about time as we ordinarily mean time, that I went to the trouble to check it against the clock. I was not observing like that impartial observer of Allport's who can regard all events in the world as if they were modeled on the collision of two billiard balls. I was organizing my world into a meaningful pattern connecting a statement, which *might* have been no more than the superfluous noise of a dream, with myself and our bedside clock, and was experiencing in the process a slight awe at my sleep-talker's accuracy.

Quite recently, March 5, 1967, I jotted down the following note.

Two or three nights ago in the midst of a long dream I encountered a very strange object, a monstrous living thing (i.e., ugly and strange, not big), which I saw first as a snake-like mouth opened menacingly toward me, in a head bent back toward me on a neck protruding from a larger organic mass. In another view of it, the body appeared to be laid open so that I could see the snakelike part embedded in a complex sort of structure of living tissue, like an abdominal dissection, or, very inaccurately, open vulva (more a Freudian afterthought than exact description). This repulsive thing was called a "sympathizer"—which seemed odd even in the dream. In another view I had of it, it was a sort of flattish, round, soft, grayish blob, like some specimen of sea-life washed up on shore—more than a jellyfish, less than a skate or devilfish. I can invent numerous associations for it, of course; but, as an object, it seemed in my dream and afterwards utterly strange, a living monstrosity without parallel in my experience. Today, however, I was sharply reminded of it by a picture appearing at the bottom of Betty Hodges' column in the Book Review section of the Durham *Morning Herald*: a pen-and-ink drawing suggestive of a medieval woodcut, showing a griffin attacking a serpentine dragon, the whole design with its complex confusing forms corresponding to the abdominal view of my monster, with the dragon as the originally recognized "sympathizer."

I have no doubt that it was *I* who saw the resemblance between the drawing and the monster of my dream; I was again organizing my experience, as Shand's law says our mental activity tends to do. Nevertheless, I must record that I felt a shock of surprise at the moment of recognition. It was far from my mind that I should ever see anything so nearly duplicating the virtually indescribable, loathesomely living thing of my dream. Up to that point the most appropriate parallel in my memory was the hideous sea-beast washed ashore in *La Dolce Vita*, and that was suitable only in its general meaning, not in its size or shape. Less than a month after jotting down the above note I was to encounter a human situation for which nothing could be a more terribly accurate symbol than the dream-monster. I even take some consolation from the matching emblem of the griffin attacking the dragon, with its implication of wisdom overcoming evil. For at this point in time I read the dream, the griffin-dragon picture, and the human situation together as constituting one complex meaning, about which I must be deeply concerned. I dare now to regard the dream as prophetic and to brood soberly over its connection with certain concrete particulars having to do with the fundamental issues of life, though a month ago I was only a little surprised and amused at the resemblance I detected in the newspaper picture.

I find some remarks appropriate to my theme in an old essay by Frances Power Cobbe,[13] although the tendency of her thought is to deemphasize the parapsychological reach of the phenomena

13. Frances Power Cobbe, "Dreams as Illustrations of Unconscious Cerebration," *Macmillan's Magazine*, XXIII (1871), 512-523.

more than I am at present inclined to do. Here is one such passage:

> Next to the myth-creating faculty in dreams, perhaps the most remarkable circumstance about them is that which has given rise to the world-old notion that dreams are frequently predictions. At the outset of an examination of this matter, we are struck by the familiar fact that our most common dreams are continually recalled to us within a few hours by some insignificant circumstance bringing up again the name of the person or place about which we had dreamed. On such occasions, as the vulgar say, "My dream is out." Nothing was actually predicted, and nothing has occurred of the smallest consequence, or ever entailing any consequence, but yet, by some concatenation of events, we dreamed of the man from whom we received a letter in the morning; or we saw in our sleep a house on fire, and before the next night we pass a street where there is a crowd, and behold! a dwelling in flames. Nay, much more special and out-of-the-way dreams than these come "out" very often. If we dream of Nebuchadnezzar on Saturday night, it is to be expected that on Sunday (unless the new lectionary have dispensed with his history) that the lesson of the day will present us with the ill-fated monarch and his golden image. Dreams of some almost unheard-of spot, or beast, or dead-and-gone old worthy, which by wild vagary have entered our brain, are perpetually followed by a reference to the same spot, or beast, or personage, in the first book or newspaper we open afterwards. To account for such coincidences on any rational principle is, of course, difficult. But it is at least useful to attempt to do so. . . .[14]

The solution she offers is the power of "unconscious cerebration" (a phrase invented by the physiologist W. B. Carpenter about 1868), "a power which (under conditions imperfectly known to us) obtains access to the entire treasury of memory, to the stores of facts, words, and transient impressions accumulated during our whole lives, and to which in our ordinary consciousness we have no means of approach."[15] The concept to which she thus

14. *Ibid.*, p. 516.
15. *Ibid.*, p. 518.

appeals has some kinship with Shand's first law, but I think that in her concentration on the *sources* of our information she slights what we *do* with it, namely, organize it into meaningful patterns.

It is just because of the tendency of the mind "to produce and sustain system and organization" that we encounter the problem of those uncanny "coincidences" that give rise to parapsychology. If we can tolerate neither the hypothesis of mere chance nor the hypothesis of supernatural intervention, we find ourselves being led to the conclusion that the tendency of the mind to organize is met by a corresponding tendency of the world to *be* organized, and to a degree and under circumstances going beyond the customary fact, which we too blandly accept, that we so easily, every day, control and shape the material environment with our hands and feet and adjunctive tools, and affect at least the human environment with a smile or a frown. The oddity and general unpredictability of the so-called parapsychological phenomena may point more to our own disharmony than to anything else. I mean that it is conceivable that more expanded and more trusting and more loving consciousnesses than ours would go through life less blind and isolated than ours do, and would not be reminded so fitfully that the universe is our home, a place of meetings rather than a place of secrets and separations.

IV

In the bipolar process it is the S-pole, the I, that tends to be elusive. The history of psychology demonstrates that it is much easier, almost fatally easier, to be aware of the distal object of our psychic activity, even of our *embodied* psychic activity, than of the proximal end which *can* say "I" if it only will. Now and then a Thomas Reid, a Maine de Biran, a Franz Brentano, a James Ward, a Michael Polanyi calls psychologists back from overattention to the object for the sake of noticing the activity of the subject. Again and again objectivity has triumphed by sneering, "You're being subjective!" And indeed there is the danger of solipsism. It is a merit of Polanyi that he is no solipsist: the out-there is a full match for the in-here—and more, since it invites infinitely to participation by the deepest inwardness in us. Nevertheless, he does call us back to ourselves, as constructors of the science we wrongly praise for its impersonality, as co-workers with other selves whom we wrongly treat as inert or tedious or expendable *res extensae.*

When we look to ourselves, not as isolated substances but as beings intending a world, one of the discoveries we make is that we exercise a power of selective attention: can look, listen, reach, savor, sniff, this way or that, and thus bring into prominence (or, conversely, suppress) particular segments of external reality, i.e., that which stands at the other pole of the S-O relationship; and, furthermore, can by an intensification of attention bring into prominence details of the selected segment that at the beginning were quite unnoticed. To this extent, certainly, we participate in the making of external reality.

The history of psychology reveals a good deal of fluctuation here between emphasis on the self and emphasis on the object. A classical reference-point is the difference between Brentano and Wundt. According to Titchener, in an article of 1921, though psychology owes a debt to both, and in particular for their clashing volumes of 1874, every psychologist must make a choice between them: "There is no middle way between Brentano and Wundt."[16] Most psychologists today do not even know that there is a choice: in the textbooks Wundt is always mentioned as the founder of experimental psychology, and the textbooks exemplify his style; the name of Brentano is rarely seen, and the great issue between them still more rarely discussed. The old issue creeps in as a modern disturbance, if at all, under the head of phenomenology or existentialism, off in the Latin Quarter of the humanists or under the Victorian couch of a few non-scientific clinicians. Yet in 1921 in America, Titchener, who had been more devoted to Wundtianism than Wundt, and who, some say, by an alchemical transmogrification turned into John B. Watson—Titchener wrote it out plainly in the *American Journal of Psychology* that there was a choice, and seems to have been paralyzed by it, for he concluded the article with "Which of the

16. E. B. Titchener, "Brentano and Wundt: Empirical and Experimental Psychology," *American Journal of Psychology,* XXXII (1921), 108.

two authors is right?" and was never able to complete "the long-projected and long-delayed work upon Systematic Psychology" of which this dilemma-posing article was intended to be the Introduction. It may be relevant to a volume dedicated to Polanyi to quote Titchener's brief summary of Brentano's views:

> Brentano defines psychology as the science of psychical phenomena. The term may easily be misleading: for the phenomena in question are very far from being static appearances. Generically they are activities; in the individual case they are acts. Hence they can properly be named only by an active verb. They fall into three fundamental classes: those, namely, of Ideating (I see, I hear, I imagine), of Judging (I acknowledge, I reject, I perceive, I recall), and of Loving-Hating (I feel, I wish, I resolve, I intend, I desire). We may use substantives if we will, and may speak of sensation and idea, memory and imagination, opinion, doubt, judgment, joy and sorrow, desire and aversion, intention and resolution; but we must always bear in mind that the psychical phenomenon is active, is a sensing or a doubting or a recalling or a willing.
>
> It is true we never act without content. When we ideate, we sense or imagine something; when we judge, we perceive something, acknowledge the truth of something, recall something; when we love or hate, we take interest in something, desire or repudiate something. This, however, is precisely the difference between psychical and physical phenomena. The latter are blank and inert: the color or figure or landscape that I see, the chord that I hear, the warmth or cold or odor that I sense, the like objects that I imagine, all these things are described when their given appearance is described; their appearance sums them up and exhausts them; they have no reference, and do not carry us beyond themselves. Psychical phenomena, on the other hand, are precisely characterized by relation to a content, by reference to an object; they contain an object intentionally within them; and this character of immanent objectivity, in virtue of which they are active, marks them off uniquely from the physical phenomena upon which they are directed or toward which they point. Even in cases where the content of a psychical phenomenon is not physical, but is another psychi-

cal phenomenon, the distinction holds good. For the act which becomes content or object of another act is not thereby deprived of its essential character; it is still active in its own right; and it is therefore by no means confusable with bare physical appearance.[17]

It would be a fierce injustice to reduce all of Brentano to an emphasis on selective attention, as this short passage brings out, but there is certainly that in him, and, considering what the history of psychology has been, it is much to have said, "Attention is a psychic act and carries its own consequences with it."

At a further remove from the obvious (if indeed it *is* obvious that we selectively attend) is the effect of attitudes or evaluative assumptions, often scarcely more articulate than a preliminary mood, on the assessment of the things to which we attend and on what we do about them. I have mentioned how I caught myself obeying a suspicious mood in an interview with a student. Fortunately, in that case, the mood had not reached unredeemable overt expression. I can recall to my shame other instances where the barbed word had flown before I knew my mood was preparing to launch it. It is not only human beings that we alienate by these semiconscious, very evasive states of ours, but Nature at large. In general, we have been taught for several hundred years to regard Nature with a hostile, cold, exploitative, or simply analytical eye. Wordsworth was against that attitude when he wrote, "We murder to dissect." But Lord Bacon was for it when *he* wrote, "Put Nature to the rack." We have put Nature to the rack, and have used her confessions against her. Now we are beginning to discover that it can be very dangerous to ourselves and our descendants to proceed with such callous recklessness against our Mother. Lynn White, Jr., tracing the history of the problem in the pages of *Science*, remarks that: "With the population explosion, the carcinoma of planless urbanism, the now geological deposits of sewage and garbage, surely no creature other than man has ever managed to foul its nest in such short order."[18] He attributes these and suchlike ills to a mainly Occi-

17. *Ibid.*, pp. 113-114.
18. Lynn White, Jr., "The Historical Roots of Our Ecologic Crisis," *Science*, CLV (1967), 1204.

dental and orthodoxly Christian attitude which stresses man's
right to exploit Nature—an attitude making us "superior to
nature, contemptuous of it, willing to use it for our slightest
whim."[19] The remedy he proposes is a change of heart, in the
direction marked out by St. Francis of Assisi:

> Francis tried to depose man from his monarchy over crea-
> tion and set up a democracy of all God's creatures. With
> him the ant is no longer simply a homily for the lazy, flames
> a sign of the thrust of the soul toward union with God; now
> they are Brother Ant and Sister Fire, praising the Creator in
> their own ways as Brother Man does in his.[20]

I myself am entirely of a mind with White and St. Francis, but
my reason for bringing them in here is just to underline the
proposition that attitudes have consequences for our intellectual
constructions and technological maneuvers, within the "impersonal" sphere of science as well as in our ordinary daily relations
with people, and, further, that a given attitude is not an absolute
necessity but, at some level, a choice we have made.

We know and we make. Our knowing in its purest cognitive
form is a kind of making, and what is most definitely a making
furnishes us with something else to be known. The two strands of
knowing and making cannot be separated: to know is to make
known, to make is to know concretely and in particular.[21]

Somewhere between the extremes of the purest knowing and
the most definite making lies imagination. Freud argues that
dream imagination is a making: the fulfilment of a wish by an
unconscious patching together of odds and ends of memories, a
sort of collage. But a dream may function as a knowing, too.
Old-style dream interpretation, that of the Biblical Joseph or of
Artemidorus of Daldis, insists on treating certain classes of
dreams as prophetic. A modern dream interpreter like Medard

19. *Ibid.*, p. 1206.
20. *Ibid.*
21. I think we should not shy off from the sexual connotations here: "to
know" is King James Biblical for sexual congress, "to make" is American
secular slang for the same thing. A significant theorist of poetry (i.e., making)
has openly declared for this sexual meaning of the poetic process. Frederick C.
Prescott, aware of Freud but not a Freudian, in his *The Poetic Mind* (1922)
specifically compares poetic creation to sexual generation.

Boss also treats the dream in this way—a knowing at least of one's present life-situation and sometimes as a distinct precognition. I have already touched on this theme. I return to it now with my attention more sharply focused on the relationship between knowing and making.

Dreams do not usually achieve the full clarity of absolute knowledge, as in the analytic propositions of geometry, nor the firm enduring structure of a work of engineering or art, *monumentum aere perennius*. As knowledge they are obscure, cryptic, ambiguous; as making they are flimsy, evanescent, deficient in unity. But one does know through them at times, it seems, though often not knowing that one knows; and starting from them one may make a poem or story or chemical formula, as Coleridge and Stevenson and Kekule did.

Let us look once more at the dream as a kind of knowing. A colleague of mine dreamed one night that someone brought him the half of a dead cat. He examined the cat closely to see if it was one of his own, and decided that it was not. When he awoke from the dream he could remember that on the previous evening he had stopped by the house of a friend and been introduced for the first time to their puppy, which was referred to by the wife of his friend as "half cat." Up to this point we seem to be dealing only with a memory rendered literally in the dream. But there was a sequel that morning when the dreamer went to work: his friend informed him that during the night, at about the time of the dream, their little puppy had unexpectedly died. With this information before him, the dreamer could regard his dream as accurate knowledge, symbolically expressed. It must be admitted that he did not have this conviction during the dream (though a death was clearly indicated) and when he woke up and remembered it he did not at once say, "I know my friend's puppy is dead." No, the knowledge, such as it was, was obscure and uncertain—until the new piece of information specifically tacked it down. It was more a preparation for knowledge, a readiness for it, then it was actual knowledge; yet it was clearly not senseless, and it added to the significance of the news received. Such a dream set against such information helps one feel one's unity with the world and, in particular, with one's friend.

Now, as to making. Sometimes what happens in a dream is carried over directly into waking life and becomes embedded there, as a novel and concrete item in the world. I have known dreamers who were for a considerable time after waking convinced that the snake or piece of money encountered in the dream was still somewhere in the folds of the bedclothes and had to be searched for. I have heard a young woman say that, when she was four, she was quite convinced after a dream that the baby she had dreamed of was actually present in her room, though she was unable to find it. Music and poetry have been composed in sleep, or rather have appeared fully formed in a dream, and afterwards become a part of the general cultural heritage. Coleridge's "Kubla Khan" is only one of the more famous of these productions. I will mention a single other, a minor piece included by John Masefield in a collection of his poems under the title "The Woman Speaks." In a prefatory note he describes the details of the vivid dream, concerned with a tall fashionable lady contrasting her past life with the sunny peacefulness of Lincoln's Inn Fields on a Sunday morning; he sees her and the things she sees with great distinctness, while simultaneously intensely aware of the poem which speaks her thoughts. He concludes his note thus: "as she passed out of the dream, the whole of the poem appeared engraven in high relief on an oblong metal plate, from which I wrote it down."[22]

That processes so powerful and fruitful in their knowing and making should cease at the threshold between sleep and waking seems most unlikely. In fact they do not. We can imagine when awake. Here I must resist the temptation to stray off into such matters as the visions that sometimes flash before us, revealing in pictorial and dramatic form judgments and wishes that we could quite readily put into commonsense abstract language; or the transformations of the body-image such as that almost-visible, almost-tangible, shadowy arm that I once experienced as extending from my body to touch the silky head of a robin ten feet away on a lovely spring morning when my mood was gay and tender; or the speculations of H. H. Price concerning an Ether of Images generated by individual minds and thrown off into independent

22. John Masefield, *Poems* (New York: Macmillan, 1929) , Part II, p. 272.

existence.[23] It is quite enough for now to stay with the main sense of imagining, i.e., our power to produce more or less concrete conceptions by which we foresee or foreshape the future. Every sort of daily action is typically preceded by such imagining, brief or sustained; and all the great human monuments and buildings and machines (e.g., the flying-machine) emerge into their Dr.-Sam-Johnson-kick-that-rock unquestionable material reality out of a long, long history of dreaming them up.

Much of the environment to which we most attend is quite strictly of our own making, straight out of the human imagination. Behold what Man has wrought! It is a fantastic compound of conveniences and hindrances, of ugliness and beauty, of comforts and terrors. If every human wish were fulfilled on the instant as soon as imagined, we should either become extremely cautious or experience life as extremely perilous. It is perilous enough as it is, even with the restraints imposed by the enormous amount of work and co-operation required for producing some of our more elaborate products, such as bombing-planes, nuclear-powered submarines, intercontinental ballistic missiles, rockets, and satellites. We should notice, also, that once an individual or a community has invested much effort and treasure in an imaginative venture, and especially while it is still in progress, there is the greatest reluctance to surrender it, no matter how useless or absurd or dangerous it may ultimately be judged to be. There must have been workmen on the Tower of Babel who had their doubts. Certainly there are bystanders and workmen today who question the American space program—for example, the editor of *Science*. But though the costs mount and the purpose of the manned moon-shot is unclearer than that of the Vietnam war, the distinguished editor's protests make a very feeble sound: "The advocates of a large continuing space program have made their report. A committee of nonspace scientists would recommend differently. However, they are not likely to be asked to do so."[24] It is often hard to believe that a Rube Goldberg machine, if it is

23. H. H. Price, "Haunting and the 'Psychic Ether,'" *Tomorrow*, V (1957) 105-126. This is a condensation and revision of his Presidential Address to the Society for Psychical Research, London, 1939.

24. Philip H. Abelson, "The Future Space Program," *Science*, CLV (1967), 1367.

very big and expensive, could have come out of the imagination of Rube Goldberg; while it was still on the drawing-board, perhaps yes, but once in production and backed by billions of dollars it looks more like Manifest Destiny.[25] Yet there *was* some little man back there, with his Idea.

Wishes come true. By a long or short route, they do. The route is imagination. It is a matter of no little consequence what human beings imagine. What we imagine we are on the way to having; there may be some doubt about arriving, but we are on the way. What we cannot imagine is perhaps beyond our achievement; though indeed the unimagined can happen to us, with or against our will. One reason for being pessimistic about the future of the human race is that few people are able to imagine a universal society in which every individual is genuinely and realistically happy, and imagine it with conviction. Most Utopias are thin and depressing; Paradises, too. Wars and Hells come on a lot stronger. Still, it is worth noting what people actually do imagine when they try to imagine happiness. Suppose one is given three wishes. Here is the solution of a second-grade girl:

> Once there were two little snow boys. They played in the snow every day. One day the sun melted one of the snow boys. The other snow boy ran around yelling, "My brother has melted!" Only, a little fairy heard him.
>
> The fairy said, "I will give you three wishes."
>
> The little snow boy thought and thought. He wanted to have good wishes. His first wish was to have his brother again.
>
> The fairy told him to turn around five times.
>
> The snow boy did as she said. When he stopped, there was his brother again. His second wish was that he and his brother would never melt.
>
> The fairy said to hold on to her and close their eyes.
>
> The snow boys closed their eyes. They felt themselves being lifted, they were turned around in the air and then put on the ground. The snow boys opened their eyes.

25. I wrote the above sentence April 10, 1967, in a first draft, in the evening. The sheet of paper was still in the typewriter when I read the next morning in the Durham *Morning Herald* for April 11, 1967, p. 4B, the headline: "Apollo's Wiring Like 'Goldberg Invention,'" referring to Rep. Fulton's critical remarks on the spacecraft.

The fairy told them that they had one more wish.
The snow boys thought and thought. They both agreed
to have children to play with.
The fairy told them to keep their eyes closed until she
finished counting to ten.
When they opened their eyes, there was a little girl and
boy. And the snow boys were happy ever after.

The use of the wishes here is very different from their use in
the more familiar fairy-story where, granted three wishes, the
man wished for sausages, his wife wished they would stick to the
end of his nose, and the third wish had to be spent on getting
them off again. In the second-grader's story, the thoughtfulness of
the snow boy, his desire to have good wishes, and the wishes
themselves—for the return of the lost, for eternal life, and for the
companionship of others—are not mere whimsies but profound
expressions of the girl who wrote the story. I have asked college
students to try to imagine a happy world and write it out, on the
spur of the moment, in fifteen minutes. Out of 41 students (28
male, 13 female), 8 declined the task or declared that a happy
world was impossible, 3 or 4 imagined scenes of sensual pleasure,
most of the remainder conceived of universal felicity in terms of
open, loving relations between human beings in a state of peace.
Five days later I asked them to estimate the *attainability* of a
happy world such as the majority of them had imagined. Over-
whelmingly, they declared such a world to be unattainable. Fear
of others and selfishness were frequently mentioned as major
causes why such a world could not be. In the main they were
saying, "We could be happy, and all the world could be happy, if
we could love; but we cannot love, because we are selfish and
afraid." Out of the heart are the issues of life, and the streams are
bitter at the source.

V

I conclude, then, that the means by which we know and make
the world in which we live, the human world of culture both
material and intellectual—from the crudest arrowhead and heav-
iest tank to the most gossamer fabrics of art and mathematics—is

flawed at the source and yet is the only means we have, as independent knowers and makers. By relying on our tacit knowledge and our tacit powers of attention, of attitude, and of imagination, and by continuing to prove and invent in company with others working with similar faulty equipment, we blunder ahead into worlds unrealized. Vast prospects open up, mean little gadgets dog our steps, foxfires delude us, pebbles and playing-cards comfort us, zero and the negative numbers and the infinite estrange us from our hearths, we discover in the midst of our riches our poverty, in our progress our perversity, in our knowledge our ignorance. We begin to know ourselves. Some, in the arrogance of fear, venture to propose that we can make or remake ourselves—by DNA, by LSD, by conditioning, by psychoanalysis, by behavior therapy, by computers. A few mutter with Ezra Pound,

> Pull down the vanity, it is not man
> Made courage, or made order, or made grace;[26]

or reflect with the atomic scientist, as he puts the turtle back on the ground where he picked it up, "I've disturbed the balance of Nature enough"; or, in complete anonymity, feel their hearts swell within them and the tears come hot in mingled pity and terror, as they see themselves helpless among the milling young, and cry into the great Silence, "My God, my God, why hast Thou forsaken us?"

26. *The Cantos of Ezra Pound* (New York: New Directions, n.d.), Canto LXXXI.

MAX WEBER AND MICHAEL POLANYI*

Raymond Aron

The reader will be surprised by the conjunction of these two names. The first does not occur in the index of *Personal Knowledge* and there is nothing to suggest that Polanyi has studied the work of the German sociologist. The intellectual temper of the two men appears as different as possible. The first is a philosopher of contradiction dedicated to science, but in suffering, with the covert sorrow of being excluded by the progress of science from the paradise of faith. The second is a philosopher of reconciliation, convinced that it is only through a misunderstanding of its true nature that science disenchants the universe. Between the knowledge of the verifiable and the intuition of the inexpressible, the former establishes a radical break and the latter a continuous progression.

Nor indeed is there any question, in the following pages, of comparing the minds or works of the author of *Wirtschaft und Gesellschaft* and the recipient of this volume. I was tempted, to begin with, to apply the theory of *Personal Knowledge* to the social sciences in general and to sociology in particular. But since this project seemed to me, on reflection, to exceed the scope of a short essay, I thought that the analysis of an objectivist[1] concep-

---

*When I wrote this essay, I had not read Professor Polanyi's *The Study of Man*, in which some of the problems touched on in the following pages are explicitly treated. On reflection, I have let the text stand, except for some minor corrections on the last few pages. My intention was to take my inspiration from the ideas of *Personal Knowledge*, not to expound them. In relation to *The Study of Man*, the reader may judge to what extent my analysis agrees or disagrees with Polanyi's thought.

1. In the sense given to that term by Michael Polanyi.

tion of social science would constitute an introduction to a project of this kind.

It might be denied that Max Weber developed an objectivist theory of knowledge; that, on the contrary, he bound knowledge to the person of the knower, since the constitution of the object and the selection of the facts stem from an extrascientific choice which may fairly be called personal. I should not dream of denying that Max Weber, admitting an objectivist interpretation of the natural sciences, sought to mark out the specific traits of historical or cultural science, traits inseparable from the human character of the field to be explored. But social science seemed to him not to be scientific, precisely to the extent to which it was personal. Thus he forced himself to separate, within knowledge, the universally valid parts from the subjective and historical elements, in which, indeed, he did not deny the inevitable intervention of the knower, but which seemed to him contrary to the essence of scientific research.

In other words, the epistemology of Max Weber represents a supreme effort to take account of the social sciences, and to establish and limit their objectivity, within the framework of a critical philosophy. Starting from the difficulties to which this philosophy was driven, I shall ask what contribution the postcritical philosophy of Polanyi might make to the theory of sociological knowledge.

I

Max Weber, as we know, borrowed his conceptual instruments from the so-called South-West German school, and in particular from Rickert's famous book *Die Grenzen der naturwissenschaftlichen Begriffsbildung*. He retained its point of departure, the inexhaustible and unformed given, and the two possible orientations of conceptualization, that is, either the generalization of the natural sciences or the unique singularity (*einmalige Einzigartigkeit*) of history. In this latter direction a second division arose: the reference to values permits us to grasp the individual characters of the elements, to specify the subject matter as cultural, but the sociologist is no less justified in establishing general propositions relative to cultural unity. The fundamental distinction, therefore, is that of the sciences of culture, the former establishing their subject matter by the analysis of constancies or regularities, the latter in relation to values, and both of them including, though in very different proportions, both generalizations and propositions relative to unique facts.

The criticism of Rickert furnished Max Weber with a language and gave him, as it were, a clear conscience. History, sociology, political economy could be sciences and universally valid, without sacrificing their own distinctive appeal, the originality of their subject matter, and their desire to grasp what is original in that subject matter: that is, to know the human character. It is from this character, according to Max Weber, that the intelligibility of historical and social facts proceeds. The facts are comprehensible (*verstandlich*), we can interpret (*deuten*) them directly. On this point, Max Weber, it seems to me, is following Jaspers, or more precisely Jaspers' conception of psychopathology.[2] Human behavior remains comprehensible in its psychological texture up to the moment when it becomes pure reflex or complete alienation, so that the logic of neuroses and in part that of psychoses can be understood. Max Weber does not deduce the meaning of human behavior from its relation to values, but sees in that relation the self-evident specificity of such behavior (and, to a much lesser extent, of the behavior of animals).

Since it is the nature of social science to understand (it is *verstchende Wissenschaft*), the crucial problem turns out to be that of discriminating between various interpretations (*Deutungen*). Most interpretations are in fact intrinsically probable, since they establish relations between motives and acts, between drives and reactions, between environment and decision, consonant with our psychological knowledge or with intuitions which though prescientific are beyond the range of doubt (that the victim of humiliation desires revenge or that the general desires victory needs no demonstration). Hence the key problem of the sciences of man, which can always explain but find their explanations hard to verify: how can we distinguish between the prob-

2. Expounded in his earliest book, *Allgemeine Psychopathologie*.

able and the true, or between an intrinsically intelligible account
and what really took place?

To this question, Max Weber has given a series of partial
answers, which are convincing in themselves but fail to solve the
essential uncertainty.

These partial and several answers are scattered throughout the
expositions of the *Wissenschaftslehre*. They concern the precau-
tions that must be taken in order not to confuse the intelligible
account as such (the propositions relative to the equilibrium of
the market or the logic of a certain legal system) with the
immediately experienced reality to which, in approximation,
these propositions or this logic may apply. Real capitalism must
not be confused with the ideal type of capitalism which we are
able to construct; the ideal type of market economy is not realized in historical market economies; the law conceived by a
judge, a barrister, or a litigant differs from the law elaborated by
a theoretician according to what he believes to be the necessary
implications of the texts. And the sociologist aims at the experienced meanings, that is, at capitalism, market economics, and
legislations as they have been or as they are being experienced.
Only the subjective sense is meant, because only it is or has been
real.

Thus at one blow Weber's 'ideal types,' so christened because
they do not belong to the species and genera of botanical or
zoological classification, or to Aristotelian logic, become mere
instruments. Resorting to the principles of nominalism, Max
Weber admits, or rather he proclaims, the right of the sociologist
or the historian to remodel the object of his study by remodeling
the questions he puts to it, that is to say, the concepts he applies.
Each person, depending on the interest that inspires him, will
construct a different ideal type of capitalism, and each of these
ideal types will underline one of the aspects of real capitalism, an
aspect chosen by the question that the sociologist has asked. Thus
the subjectivity of the knower, itself historically determined,
expresses itself in the inquiry; but this relativity of inquiry does
not communicate itself to the science, since the latter consists of
non-subjective replies to subjective questions, of verified answers
to questions freely put.

This theory of knowledge would be satisfactory on either of two conditions: (1) if it were possible to distinguish in reality between question and answer, or (2) if the experienced meaning could be rigorously grasped. But neither of these two conditions is satisfied, or at least Max Weber has not demonstrated that they are effectively satisfied. The discrimination between the experienced (real) meaning and the meanings produced by the rationalizations of the interpreter, and the verification of the agreement between experienced meaning and interpretation, which should have been the center of a theory of understanding, appear only here and there in the course of his arguments. Moreover, Weber placed in the category of ideal type all or nearly all the concepts of the social sciences, whether the elaboration of an individual whole (Puritan capitalism) or an historical concept with several examples (Western city), or the rational relations of economic theory, and hence he was unable to recognize the diversity of the relations between ideal types and reality, the diversity of senses in which one can speak of experienced meaning and the diversity of ways in which interpretations may be verified or confirmed.

Weber himself oscillated between the objectivism of the experienced meaning and the historicism of free choices. It is not sufficient, he said, that the interpretation should be satisfying for the mind; it must be true. That is, it must have been realized in the event or it must be verified by the constancy of its regular occurrence. But on the other hand, humanity, in its unpredictable development, ceaselessly creates new values and interrogates its past in the light of the values which arise out of the present. To forbid the living to interrogate the dead with reference to the values experienced today would be to forbid the creation of new values, or to decree that the dead have no more to say to us. The dialogue of the present and the past confers on historical science a personal character (in Polanyi's sense). But this character is hard to assimilate to the critical conception of science.

Max Weber borrows from the Kantian tradition the radical opposition between facts and values, between the is and the ought. There is no common denominator between ascertaining what, in fact, happened once or is happening, and determining what should be the conduct of the statesman or the citizen. But

346 INTELLECT AND HOPE

Weber goes beyond that classic antithesis. In order to save freedom as he understands it, he asserts that each person's choice of
his values is arbitrary, essentially irrational, without any possible
differentiation between reasonable and unreasonable choice. He
invites each of his hearers to follow the voice of his genius—
whether 'god or devil.' Moreover, the choice is essentially polemi-
cal, for values are not only numerous but contradictory. A thing
may be beautiful just because it is not moral. Not to resist evil is
cowardice, unless it is holiness. The man who chooses holiness
renounces the defense of his country.

Free in his choice in consequence of the plurality and incoherence of values, man is free in his conduct also because historical
reality does not admit global determinism. Puritanism is not the
cause of capitalism as such; it has been, in fact, one of the
conditions for the emergence in the West of certain specific traits
of capitalism. Every causal relation, whether accidental or adequate, is partial and analytic; it results from cutting up reality
into fragments; it does not apply to the sequence of totalities. But
this process of dissection is inseparable from our way of asking
questions and hence from our concepts. Causal relations are not
arbitrary, but they are dependent on an arbitrary choice of values
or of questions.

At this point, we may well ask if Weber has not finally dis-
solved the universal truth of science which he so passionately
desired to secure. To begin with, scientific truth itself, in his
philosophy, was only one value among others, and its affirmation
was neither more scientific nor more rational than its negation.
Besides, when Weber demanded imperiously of his hearers or his
adversaries that they distinguish as he did between facts and
values, science and politics, he was inviting them to subscribe to
his philosophy and to renounce their own. Why should not the
revolutionary adorn his own convictions with the prestige of
science if there is no more merit in being reasonable than impassioned, if success is the supreme objective in politics?

Not only does science cease to be justifiable by reason as soon
as it becomes the object of an arbitrary choice, but the role of
universal truth in a science founded on many and contradictory
questions remains indeterminable and evanescent. True, the so-

cial scientist aims at the real, and the latter does not permit just any interpretation he likes. But neither history nor sociology is able to discover so many causal connections that one can safely abandon to subjectivity all that would not be a necessary succession, unique or regular. Besides, social science is interpretation of meaning; and all interpretation has its place within a particular conceptual system. Is the plurality of conceptual systems legitimate or fruitful? Or does it rather mark the defeat of a science claiming universal validity? If the plurality of interpretations is legitimate, must we not reconsider the alleged irrationality of the choice of values, the incoherence of the questions asked? Must we not find, at a higher level, an ordering of questions, such that their multiplicity would then cease to be random?

In short, we should have to question the two antitheses which dominate the philosophical form in which Max Weber cast his scientific experience: established or demonstrated facts as against values freely affirmed; the arbitrary character of questions put to reality as against the universal truth of the replies. The replies cannot be universally true if the questions are arbitrary; and besides, why seek with such passion for universal truth if it is worth no more than any other existential decision?

II

It is not possible here to attempt even a resumé of the principal theses of *Personal Knowledge*. I shall presuppose an acquaintance with the book and limit myself to extracting from it some propositions or maxims which seem to me to be suggested, either implicitly or explicitly, by Professor Polanyi and which might serve as introduction to a theory of historical or sociological knowledge.

(i) Only the method of inquiry, of research or of demonstration in fact practiced by the creative scientist can reveal the nature of scientific knowledge: its subsequent arrangement in hypothetico-deductive form, whatever its utility, disguises the intention of the knower and consequently the essence of his knowledge. The same proposition might be translated into the following terms: the theory of science must not ignore the psychology of the scientist. It goes without saying that this last statement must be taken in a special sense. The psychology of the scientist that interests epistemology is that of the scientist as such, not of the man X, Y, or Z, who lives in such and such a century, loves his wife and children, and is a good or a bad patriot, but of Poincaré or Einstein in search of scientific truth, of the intellectual passion which inspires them in that search, of the sense of beauty which makes them accept this or that vision of reality. In other words, the meaning of science cannot be grasped unless we start from the intention of the scientist. But this intention is not that of the historical men who have lived in different historical contexts but have had in common the will to truth and the same conception of what a true, rational, beautiful explanation of nature must be.

Elsewhere, Polanyi affirms, "psychology cannot distinguish by itself between true and false inferences, and hence is blind to logical principles; but it can throw light on the conditions under which the understanding and operation or correct logico-mathematical reasoning may develop, and it may supply an explanation for errors in reasoning."[3] But later he points to a closer kinship between the theory of science and psychology. The latter studies the process by which living beings learn; it provides a theory of learning. And the theory of scientific knowledge is the last stage of a theory of learning which is in the first instance psychological:

> . . . it may seem questionable whether, in the study of learning, the acknowledgement of rightness which accounts for the success of learning and accredits its achievements with universal intent, may be lumped together with the study of the conditions and shortcomings of learning. My answer is that the distinction in question is sharply pronounced only in the case of highly formalized logical operations. It becomes blurred and should be allowed to lapse altogether, when rightness is achieved according to vague maxims which are effective only when applied with exceptional skill and understanding. Such, I believe, is the case

3. *P.K.*, p. 334.

for inductive inferences. The analysis of such operational principles is so closely interwoven with a study of the conditions under which they can operate or fail to operate, that the two aspects of the subject must be treated jointly. Thus in spite of the logical and epistemological affirmations contained in the theory of learning, we shall accept it wholly as a branch of psychology and authorize this branch to study- —as all biology does—certain achievements ascribed to living beings.[4]

In the social sciences the desire of the theorist to separate the psychology of the knower and the logic of knowledge is so much the stronger since knower and historical person seem more indistinguishable from one another. The sociologist of today who analyzes the mechanisms of the market or the administration of planning, who compares the classes of capitalist societies and the 'groups' of soviet societies, himself belongs to one or the other social types; his preferences tend this way or that. If the intention of the historian is not separated from that of the citizen, is not the scientific intention, that of universality, at once condemned? Or must we say that in the matter of societies and of color, love and hate inspire our curiosity and become the springs of knowledge?

It was to resolve this difficulty that Max Weber was forced to effect a rigorous distinction between subjective questions and objective replies and so assumed that the knower, having expressed his historical subjectivity in the question, proceeded to efface himself before the object. It is true that the historical person becomes an historian, in the modern sense of the word, only on condition that he transcend, through the effort of knowledge, the temptation to justify, to condemn, and to distort. The error of the Weberian formulation is to transform into an objective duality a duality in fact internal to the consciousness of the knower. Thucydides, who had been an unfortunate general, admired Pericles, detested Cleon, respected Nicias; it is the man who paints these characters, not a transcendental consciousness or a pure spectator. But if the historical account is never depersonal-

4. *Ibid.*, p. 370.

ized, neither is it ever reduced to a simple elaboration of prejudices and passions, at least so long as it preserves a scientific
character in the eyes of competent men.

Historical or social science is not a sort of theology, *fides
quaerens intellectum*; it is a trial, a trial of spontaneous passions
in contact with facts, of prejudices confronted with the prejudices of others, a trial of the legendary past of the contemporary
scene through the effort of understanding what has happened or
why it has happened. The intention of history and sociology does
aim in a certain fashion at universality, but that universality is
defined by the enlargement of consciousness through the criticism
of itself and its institutions. The objectivist superstition, on the
other hand, leads in the social sciences either to minute inquiries,
purely empirical and of no ultimate significance, or to a pseudo-
system of the world and of history, like that of Auguste Comte or
of Marx. Either outcome is absurd.

(ii) In fact—and this maxim holds against the temptation to
seek absolute objectivity through empirical moderation—it is
unreasonable to sacrifice the interesting to the demonstrated. In
the last analysis, no body of scientific knowledge is ever wholly
and definitively demonstrated. To recognize the impossibility of
demonstrating an axiom system and the rules operative within
that system is not a defeat of the mind, but the recall of the mind
to itself. Formalization and axiomatization are necessary, legitimate, and fruitful. But they do not create a collection of truths
which would hold good all alone, on their own, without the
intervention of the knower's endorsement, the commitment of
the person. Still more in physics or in biology, there always exist,
in every age, laws or explanations which are admitted as true
without our being certain of their truth or able to demonstrate
them. In short, even in the natural sciences, there are degrees in
the certainty and rigor of demonstration and there are, invariably, risks of error.

In history or in sociology, if we were to be sure of escaping
subjectivity and error, we should have to be satisfied with brute
facts (supposing that that notion were susceptible of precise
definition) or of microscopic inquiries. No historian, however
positivist, no sociologist of those who have left a name, has gone

very far along this path. Auguste Comte, Durkheim, Pareto, Seignobos were no less subjective and philosophical, despite their pretensions to pure and objective science, then Scheler or Max Weber, who assigned a role to subjectivity.

Indeed, in history and in sociology, the interesting questions are also those which entail the greatest uncertainty, those which most frequently permit divergent and even contradictory interpretations. With the progress of statistics, we can succeed without too much trouble in ascertaining with precision the distribution of families in various income tax brackets. But if we ask whether there are exact divisions between these levels of taxation, or whether certain levels correspond to a particular way of living and to a 'real,' in the sense of a self-conscious, 'group,' our answers will be much less exact because the questions themselves utilize concepts that are not absolutely precise and are concerned with phenomena that are difficult to grasp. Nevertheless, it is not the distribution of taxes in different categories that lends interest to the problem of classes, but our interrogation about the collectivity itself: unity or plurality, homogeneity or heterogeneity, co-operation or class conflict. We must not hesitate to ask the interesting questions arising from the reality itself.

(iii) Any science becomes self-contradictory which because of the nature it attributes to its object renders its own existence inexplicable and unintelligible. Humanity, consciousness, science would not exist in the world envisaged by mechanists or objectivists. Rediscovering the idea of Comte and of Cournot, of a scale of 'levels of reality,' the lower level being the condition or the means of realization, but not the sufficient cause of the higher level, Polanyi shows that the biologist starts from complex, living realities, and that physicochemical explanation never accounts completely for the phenomena of life, the interpretation of which is impossible apart from reference to the finality of functions and, even before this, the distinctions between the normal and the pathological.

The equivalent, in the social sciences, of the materialist attempt to explain life and consciousness by combinations of atoms or of elementary particles is the attempt of Pareto or Marx to explain the realms of the spirit by reducing them to the circumstances in which they had developed and by denying the specific intention to which each such realm owes its being. Let me explain. The interpretation of history in terms of the class struggle is presented by Marx as true; he judges it to be so. Thus he admits implicitly, in himself, his claim to universal truth. And at the same time he cannot, without contradicting himself, deny this intention in others, deny it in historical reality. The social sciences are indeed the work of historical individuals; they reflect in every period the prejudices and passions of individuals and of classes. But they would not exist as sciences if they did not also express the effort of historical individuals to test their convictions, to enlarge their knowledge, to confront their particular existence with other existences.

The analysis of the fascination of Marxism constitutes one of the most interesting chapters of *Personal Knowledge*.[5] It is through moral passion that Marx came to deny the efficacy of morality. Because in his eyes men were untrue to the ideals that they invoked, he came, through indignation or despair, to assert that appetites and force were all that counted. He imagined a universe in which human reconciliation issued inexorably from pitiless conflict much as consciousness has been thought to issue from the collision of atoms in the universe. But the energy which animates materialists, cynics, or nihilists has still a moral origin, and this energy is increased by the sanction which pseudo-science gives to their enterprise. The latter becomes a prison for the mind as well as the body because it justifies itself at one and the same time by necessity (explicitly invoked) and by morality (unconsciously active). To escape from the prison, we must break with the first step, the denial of morality as an effective aim of humanity, and with the representation of a determinism which would assure victory in advance to one party, with whom, nevertheless, we are invited to co-operate.

Thus a sociological interpretation cannot without contradiction dissolve the scientific intention without which its own existence would be denied. It cannot without contradiction deny the moral will to which it owes its inspiration. We may generalize these remarks and assert that sociological interpretations made

5. *P.K.*, pp. 227-239.

from outside a given universe presuppose the sociologist's understanding of the intrinsic meaning of the universe in question. If we did not begin by understanding the painting of Tintoretto to be in some sense beautiful, an exhaustive knowledge of Venice would not suffice to reveal it to us. Without this primordial recognition of the intrinsic meanings of spiritual worlds, or if you like of culture, an avowedly mechanistic science of culture could not even begin. It must first recognize what it then pretends to reduce or to exclude.

(iv) All facts presuppose a framework of interpretation. The latter is never definitely demonstrated, either deductively (since the non-contradictoriness even of a mathematical system is not demonstrable) [6] or inductively, since we have never eliminated the possibility of another framework nor considered all the facts capable of refuting the framework we have provisionally accepted. In the last analysis we can say that interpretative frameworks are never either refuted or demonstrated or imposed by the facts. These propositions, classic in the epistemology of research or of scientific progress now, become integral parts of the theory of science itself. What bearing have they in the case of the social sciences?

Without trying to reproduce Polanyi's own argument on this point, I shall assert that it is just as impossible to follow through to its logical conclusion the subjectivism of Weber as it is to do the same for the alleged objectivism of Marx. The conceptual systems of the social sciences are neither the result of arbitrary choices, as Weber presents them in his theory of scientific practice, nor reflections of a structure inscribed in reality itself. Both formulae falsify what we may call the dialogue or dialectic which constitutes the authentic experience of social science and social scientists.

This thesis would need an extensive commentary. In this brief essay, I shall simply indicate the most general reasons which account for the knower's being bound by the human reality that he wishes to understand. Consider first the case of a reality where the will to express, to communicate is undeniable. The interpreter can and must first inquire, what knowledge or what wis-

6. It is demonstrable that this non-contradiction is not finally demonstrable.

dom the speaker wished to transmit to his contemporaries or his descendants. Philosophers, artists, scholars have wished to create, to explain; the interpreter wishes to understand their message and if he is not bound to take as final the meaning consciously given by the creator to his work, so much the less has he the right to substitute the meaning which the message would have in his own universe. If the universe of the interpreter had no kinship with the universe to be interpreted, the interpretation would be impossible. If they were confused with one another, there would be no history. Between these two extremes lies historical understanding, which entails a renewal of perspective, but implies that the historically existent subject (the knower) is aware of the otherness and uniqueness of his object, that is, of the men who are no more but whose work has been preserved.

Now all societies are, from a certain point of view, comparable to persons who have accomplished the creation of a work. A culture is a system of values and obligations which the members of a collective achieve without necessarily knowing them, as language, conceived by the linguist, is the unconscious system of spoken language.

Let us proceed to consider from this point of view a problem of social organization, for example, the problem of classes, which has been the obsession of European sociologists for so many years. The quarrels over facts and interpretations have been in large part the consequence either of the free choice of conceptual systems or of the search for a perfect objectivity. Either it was supposed that the facts examined without prejudice would say the last word on the reality of classes, or it was assumed that one had the right to decree that such and such criteria were to define a class. The second path is indeed preferable to the first. But the normal path seems to me to be intermediate between the two.

Modern societies proclaim the legal and moral equality of all men; so the difference in material conditions becomes less acceptable and raises a problem for the moralist and the statesman: To what extent are these differences legitimate? To what extent do they compromise the collective unity? In the past all societies have entailed hierarchies, 'classes' whose inequality was legally recognized. But because legal inequalities are officially eliminated and racial, national, and religious heterogeneities tend to disappear in certain nations, we ask ourselves about the inequalities still existing in the economic and social organization of modern societies. Hence the three questions issuing from reality itself: How do the different sorts of heterogeneity (income, occupation, standard of living, etc.) combine with one another? Are these groups more or less distinct according to social type? Are they pledged to co-operation or to struggle? Whatever the precision or imprecision of the possible answers, we cannot neglect these questions, because they are those which the societies of today in fact put to themselves.

We may invoke here Polanyi's distinction of logical levels:

Natural science is regarded as a knowledge of things, while knowledge *about* science is held to be quite distinct from science, and is called "meta-science." We have then three logical levels: a first floor for the objects of science, a second for science itself and a third for meta-science, which includes the logic and epistemology of science. . . .

A science dealing with living persons appears now logically different from a science dealing with inanimate things. In contrast to the two-storied logical structure of inanimate science, biological science, or at least some parts of biology, seem to possess a three-storied structure, similar to that of logic and epistemology. . . . Once we have before us the deliberate behaviour of an animal, by which it commits itself to a mode of action which can be right or wrong, and which thus implies assumptions about external things that can be true or false, the understanding of such a commitment is a theory of rightness and knowledge. It is clearly three-storied.[7]

The study of living beings, as distinct from the study of inanimate objects, has a three-storied structure, because the animal may succeed or fail, exhibit a true or false knowledge of reality, and so its behavior evokes a theory of knowledge over and above the theory of practice (that is, of the living being in its spontaneous conduct).

By analogy, we may say that men in modern societies 'live' a certain distinction of classes. They live it implicitly in the man-

7. *P.K.*, pp. 344-345.

ner in which they behave towards one another, and they live it consciously (and perhaps falsely in relation to their behavior and their feelings) in their ideology of it. The sociologist does not give preference either to the level of practice or to that of ideology, but he seeks to grasp at one and the same time the level of experience and the ideological level, to put them both into a relation to the actual and historical facts, and finally to measure the gap between what this society wants to be and what it is (somewhat as the biologist ascertains the conformity of an individual to the norm of its species).

The understanding of a society by the sociologist, therefore, aims at a rigor, an exactitude, a coherence to which the spontaneous awareness that one of the members of the society has of it can make no claim, and yet such an understanding is by its nature nothing but the elaboration, through empirical concepts, of that same social consciousness. No discipline displays so clearly the precariousness of the opposition between objective and subjective meaning. The languages reconstructed by linguists were never thought of in this form by those who spoke the languages in question, and yet every linguistic system was present, included, in living speech. The sciences of man are essentially the elaboration, empirical and conceptual at once, of what is given in the universe experienced by men. There is no one single conceptual system implied by the existence of a society or a civilization, nor are there an unlimited number; still less is there a total freedom of choice.

(v) The verification of a proposition in physics by the facts, the 'validation' of an intellectual system, are always imperfect, subject to doubt and revision. Nor does any of the realms of culture exist other than in and through the community of those who elaborate it and live in it. While critical or empiricist thought erected a difference of kind between positive, demonstrated knowledge and moral, aesthetic, or religious judgments, Michael Polanyi is concerned to re-establish the continuity between them by discovering once more the presence of the person, the fiduciary commitment even in the first steps in the acquisition of knowledge, in learning. Science, for him as for Bergson or Teilhard de Chardin, is a feature of the emergence of man and of mind in a cosmic and living process. At the same time, the critical task confronting man is to mark out the differences between the various realms of the spirit, once their fundamental kinship through reference to the person has been clarified. Thus the knowledge of the intellectual systems in which men have lived is itself elaborated into a system of knowledge. The history or the sociology of *Weltanschauungen* is personal knowledge, as are also the *Weltanschauungen* themselves, but the personal character is not the same in the two cases, and this is the difference which a theory of social knowledge must grasp and disentangle.

Max Weber had formulated this difference in a simple and categorical fashion. The knowledge which we gain of metaphysical systems is scientific because it points to a reality and because it takes account of facts and of observable and demonstrable relations. The systems of metaphysics themselves, on the other hand, lean towards a kind of knowledge which by its nature and scope exceeds the limits of what is accessible to science. Michael Polanyi cannot formulate the opposition in the same terms, because he has rediscovered transempirical beliefs within science itself, and because he perceives in the world a hierarchy of real orders and in the mind a plurality of realms of culture, none of these real orders being reducible to that which precedes it, and no authentic realm of culture being explicable by its external circumstances alone. Both the realm of conceptions of the world and the realm of knowledge of conceptions of the world are authentic. In what respect and why can the last lay claim to a validity which the first does not achieve?

In one sense, the answer is simple: the conception of the world bears on realities external to man, though with ambitions and in a manner which do not accord with the demands of positive science. The knowledge of these conceptions of the world, on the other hand, bears on the realms of human life, on the realms of belief and faith in which the men of the past have lived. But this knowledge of human worlds must start from the meaning given to them by the men who have made their homes in them ("indwelling") [8] and it cannot but accept, deny, or correct this mean-

8. See *P.K.*, pp. 59, 64, 173, 195-202, 212, 272, 279-280, 283, 321, 344-5, 378 [eds.].

ing. In other words, the awareness of other human worlds is an element in a dialogue comparable to that which scientists have with one another or scientists with artists or priests. The knowledge of the sciences of man would no longer be a dialogue if all communion between the historian and the historical object were canceled. The world of the historian is expressed in the knowledge that he acquires of the human worlds of the past, not only in the question he sets himself, but in the meaning he gives it. Even when the historian is seeking, as he must do, for the meaning which the dead had given to their world, he is interpreting, at least implicitly, this meaning in his own world. It is the historian of Auguste Comte, formed by the disciplines of positivism, Lucien Levy-Bruhl, who created the ideal type of the primitive mentality.

But this answer, we must admit, is but a preface. True, critical thought and the primitive are engaged in dialogue, as is the Marxist with the liberal, Einstein with Newton, Hegel with Kant, the positivist with the Christian. But there are as many dialogues as there are spiritual worlds, and in addition to the dialogues within each world there are the dialogues of one world with another. To return to the case which interests us, that of the social sciences, the dialogue of the Marxist and the liberal is neither that of the positivist and the believer, nor that of Newton and Einstein.

A theory of the social sciences would develop from questions like these: How is economic or economic-sociological theory constructed? What is the role of elaboration comparable to that of mathematics? What is the role of political options or normative implications? What is the role, not of verification, but of experimental confirmation?

As an example, let me recall the refutation of the Marxist formulation by Schumpeter. If, he wrote, the rate of surplus value was such as Marx suggests, anyone at all employing human labor would derive benefits from so doing. A considerable gap between the surplus values of one branch or enterprise and the profits of that branch or that enterprise, is nothing more, in the eyes of Schumpeter, than the proof of the initial error in the theory. If the redistribution of profits does not answer to the expectations of the theory of surplus value, the reason is that the theory is not true. The average rate of profit is the equivalent of the so-called method of epicycles: supplementary hypotheses are multiplied in order to maintain the theory and to bring it into agreement with experience instead of starting over on a new foundation.

This argument, which I have very roughly summarized, fails to convince the majority of Marxists, even those who are not constrained by the police to unreason and orthodoxy. Probably agreement is wanting on the question of what is expected of or meant by theory. Probably the purely scientific intention, that of truth and universal validity, is crossed by political or metaphysical intentions. And yet it would be wrong to conclude from this that there is no truth in economic or sociological matters, and to affirm either that every scientist is the prisoner of his environment or that social consciousness is always the expression of historically particularized realities. The very person who formulates this proposition of thoroughgoing relativism is excepting himself in the very act of formulating it. What is true is that the sociologist's intention of stating universally valid truth is seldom entirely purified of all influence from historical subjectivity, and that even if such a purification were achieved the intention of the sociologist would still be imbued with historicity, because the framework of interpretation into which he sets his object inevitably stems from his own environment. But to infer from this a pure relativism, we should have to abstract from the element of fact which makes hypotheses or theories probable, improbable, or absurd, as for instance, the facts make absurd every schema of capitalism which implies pauperization; and we should also have to abstract from the coherence appropriate to abstract theories like those of economics. Further, we should have to ignore the presence of the same facts expressed in a different language within different theories, and finally the possible ordering of the theories themselves at the hand of the social problems which the sociologist discovers even in his own society and in history.

If the sociologist were not radically distinguishable from the man in society, there would be no scientific dialogue, but only the contradictory justifications of the parties in the case. But if, on the other hand, the sociologist were in fact totally separate from the man in society, the scientific dialogue would not be charged with political or moral implications. The theorist has only to observe the actual development of the scientific dialogue to hear the two extreme interpretations. Social science is a factor in social man's awareness of his society (or societies). It arises with the intention of achieving universally valid and demonstrated truth, and proceeds to exceed the limits within which such an intention could be realized. The science of society not only gives to human collectives the consciousness they have of themselves and their destiny, but it clarifies each of them in relation to itself and to other such collectives. So long as the state does not stifle the aim of science by transforming scientists into mouthpieces of official truth, social science will trouble easy consciences by obliging every society to see what disfigures it and forbidding it to ignore what it is among other societies.

III

What, finally is the relation between the leading ideas of *Personal Knowledge* and the epistemology of Max Weber? Let us enumerate Weber's fundamental propositions and notice briefly for each of them the answer that, as it seems to me, Polanyi has given to them, whether implicitly or explicitly.

(i) The sciences of culture are directed towards a specific kind of understanding, different from explanation as practiced in physics and chemistry, since the meaning grasped by the interpreter is in a sense internal to reality. Polanyi admits that understanding is the proper aim of the sciences of culture, but he uses the same word, "understand," for the intelligibility achieved by the sciences of nature. Without denying the peculiar traits of historical understanding, he sees in the latter a species of a genus, the ultimate term of an ascending series, rather than a break with the developments of the earlier sciences.

(ii) In the human world unique events, singular facts are no less interesting, in fact they are often of more interest than are general propositions. Polanyi would subscribe to this statement. When the object is truly rare, as in the case of a great man, the understanding of that unique object can give the same satisfaction as a theory gives in physics when, in its simplicity and beauty, it accounts for many different phenomena.

(iii) The historian or the sociologist is more profoundly committed in his interpretation of the past and the present than is the physicist or the chemist in his explanation of motion or chemical composition. Polanyi agrees to this, but not without adding that transempirical, transrational commitment is present also even in the most basic procedures of positive science.

(iv) Despite this commitment, symbolized by the choice of questions or centers of interest, the historian or the sociologist wishes to achieve a rigorously objective truth, partial but universally valid. It is on this point that the fundamental opposition arises. Polanyi denies the antithesis between the arbitrary choice of values or interpretative systems and the scientific establishment of facts or relations. On the contrary, understanding is in its very nature the grasp of facts in a context; if the contexts are arbitrarily composed and only the facts universally valid, science will be arbitrary, like the contexts, and not universally valid like the facts.

(v) Finally, for Weber, facts and values would be rigorously heterogeneous and every hierarchy of values indemonstrable. Values would be contradictory and the battle of the gods would pledge humanity to tear itself apart. Here again, Polanyi answers that the understanding of works or persons involves appraisal. History or sociology does not cease to be scientific for including praise or blame. Understanding in biology is impossible without reference to the norms (trueness to type) of the living organism. Similarly, the sociologist's understanding of the statesman or the judge must refer to the morality of his act or the equity of his verdict.[9]

But this comparison of epistemological principles will remain superficial unless we recall, in conclusion, the philosophical attitudes of Weber and Polanyi which we mentioned at the beginning of this essay.

That there was no science of values to be created or of conduct

9. See M. Polanyi, "The Message of the Hungarian Revolution," *The American Scholar,* XXXV (Sept., 1966) , 661-676.

to be followed, Max Weber saw less as a check to reason than as a safeguard for the person. In marking off the limits of historical determinism, he was refuting the pretension of prophets to dictate our actions to us in the name of a future written in advance. In forbidding professors to introduce politics into their lecture rooms, he was preventing the confusion of demonstrations with preferences, and reserving the right to act according to conviction whatever the consequences. But in affirming an opposition of kind between procedures that are bound together in existence, between the discovery of the real and the choice of an action, he conferred an appearance of irrationality on decisions which indeed are not scientific, but which ought nevertheless to be reasonable. Having no intermediate category between science and choice, he finished by presenting, in terms of sheer choice, what tradition has more appropriately called wisdom.

And, as he denied all possibility of establishing rationally a hierarchy between the values of life and of the spirit, as the conflict of the gods of Olympus seemed to him symbolic of the incompatible values offered to or created by humanity, the choice of the man of action reflected, on a lower level, the higher choice of man, choice by each one of his destiny in the irreducible solitude of consciousness. But for such an unjustifiable choice, there is nothing to prevent its being the choice of the devil.

The commitment in which Max Weber's philosophy issues is a substitute for religious belief, the ultimate defense against a science which would violate our consciences by revealing their secrets or dictating their duties. But this last word of Weber is to be explained only by the hypothesis from which he had started. He accepted the objectivist vision of the world, ostensibly inspired by mechanistic science, before revolting against it. It is impossible to live in a world devoid of sense; if science eliminates religion and disenchants the world, then political and metaphysical commitment becomes, in its very irrationality, the expression of the condition set to man by the knowledge which explains the facts but strips the totality of meaning. But in such commitment, man escapes necessity, only to be lost in arbitrariness.

Michael Polanyi ignores or transcends these painful contradictions. The commitment of faith, he believes, is present from the first stage of knowledge and the hierarchy of spiritual worlds is ordered towards an ultimate goal. The existentialism of Polanyi issues in reconciliation because it moves towards religion. Thus the confrontation between Max Weber and Michael Polanyi over and above the epistemological problem, illustrates the dialogue of two persons: the man of tragedy and the man of reconciliation. The science of Polanyi leads without a break to faith; the science of Weber keeps a space for the faith which condemns it and which it denies.

"MORAL INVERSION"—OR MORAL REVALUATION?

Zdzislaw Najder

I

If we, for a moment, disregard the pertinent social factors and try to analyze the contemporary moral predicament in purely intellectual terms, we shall certainly notice a strange twist in the ethical role of science. For some three hundred years science has been undermining all traditional moral authorities; and finally, in our time, has wound up decisively explaining that there is no direct, logically tenable connection between facts and values, between scientific statements and ethical prescriptions.

At the same time, however, by ousting former spiritual mentors, science has taken their position in the minds of a great number of people. And because until quite recently scientists themselves, speaking *ex officio*, were rather outspoken on moral issues, the two factors: the force of traditional expectations, and the dethronement of the old authorities by science, mutually support each other in creating a situation in which more and more people expect ethical guidance from science. It is a paradoxical situation precisely because by demonstrating that moral precepts do not, cannot, follow from scientific statements, science has provoked expectations of becoming a supplier of such precepts.

I do not know whether Professor Polanyi would approve of the way I am trying to describe, very one-sidedly, the "scientific aspect" of our moral predicament—but I have found in his work an exceptionally acute awareness of its existence. In *The Tacit Dimension*, his latest book, he characterizes this predicament from another point of view,[1] but all his work is permeated by the consciousness of the specific moral responsibility of scientists and men of learning in general. This rare sensitivity is what attracts me in his work, in spite of all my objections. And I thought I should begin by this personal confession, in view of all critical remarks which are to follow.

I am going to attempt an analysis of one particular aspect of Polanyi's immense program of rebuilding the philosophical framework of knowledge. Such "sectional" approach presents, I am aware, a danger of misinterpretation. However, not being equipped to undertake a fuller review of Polanyi's theory, I have no choice but to test it on a particular group of problems. Luckily, I can find a justification for doing so in Polanyi's own work—namely, in his description of how the academic community co-operates in vindicating or refuting theories which cannot be tackled by any single discipline.[2] And, after all, it is only sensible to assume that the applicability of any new conceptual structure, however broad and general, has to be tested on particular cases.

II

Polanyi's concept of "moral inversion," with which I am concerned, involves, in fact, both a conceptual proposal and a certain historical, social, and political theory. Consequently, for the sake of clarity and at the risk of appearing excessively pedantic, I shall discuss it separately under those two headings.

As a conceptual proposal, the notion of "moral inversion" is evidently supposed to provide a tool to analyze certain problems of morality and moral behavior, of ethical change and of mass psychology.

We encounter the concept, used explicitly, for the first time in *The Logic of Liberty*, where it is introduced as follows:

> In such men, the traditional form for holding moral
> ideals had been shattered and their moral passions diverted
> into the only channels which a strictly mechanistic concep-

1. *T.D.*, p. 4.
2. *P.K.*, pp. 216-218.

tion of man and society left open to them. We may describe this as a process of *moral inversion*. The morally inverted person has not merely performed a philosophic substitution of moral aims by material purposes, but is acting with the whole force of his homeless moral passions within a purely materialistic framework of purposes.[3]

In the earlier *Science, Faith and Society* we have a similar phenomenon described, without the term in question being used.[4] The concept appears fully developed in *Personal Knowledge*; "moral inversion" is conceived there to be an outcome of two modern developments: the growth of moral self-doubt and the simultaneous growth of moral radicalism. Both these processes combined result in a substitution of non-moral principles in the place of moral ones, and in an exploitation of moral passions for "immoral" purposes.[5] The only examples given here, or anywhere else, are those of Marxism and Nazism.

In *Beyond Nihilism* Polanyi characterizes moral inversion twice in brief, definition-like statements:

> . . . there is a progression from Robespierre to his successors *which transforms Messianic violence from a means to an end into an aim in itself.* Such is the final position reached by moral passions in their modern embodiments, whether in personal nihilism or in totalitarian violence. I shall call this transformation a process of *moral inversion.*[6]

A few pages farther on he describes moral inversion as "a condition in which high moral purpose operates only as the hidden force of an openly declared inhumanity."[7]

Although the tenor of these explanations is generally consistent, they are by no means fully equivalent nor unambiguous (e.g., is moral inversion a process or a state?). The first problem consists in deciding what precisely is their frame of reference. Are the specific characteristics of moral inversion to be found basically in psychological processes, in sociohistorical tendencies, or in axio-

3. *L.L.*, p. 106.
4. *S.F.S.*, pp. 77-78.
5. *P.K.*, pp. 231-235.
6. *Beyond Nihilism* (Cambridge: Cambridge University Press, 1960), p. 20.
7. *Ibid.*, pp. 25-26.

logical structures (i.e., in the way ethical systems are organized)? In other words, is moral inversion a psychological (as the terminology suggests), or a sociohistorical trend (to which the examples point), or an axiological scheme (which is implied by the general sweep of the concept)? Considering Polanyi's integrating intentions, we should probably understand the concept's function as linking all the three spheres together. Thus, to explore its full meaning and to test its integrating applications, we have to approach the concept, in turn, from three directions: psychological, sociological, and axiological.

III

From the psychological point of view the first striking thing about Polanyi's concept, seen in the comprehensive context of his views on morality, is that he regards "moral forces as primary motives of man."[8] This is asserted without any arguments although, as Polanyi himself is well aware, it would be challenged by many anthropologists and sociologists.

More important, however, is that Polanyi assumes also that moral *passions* are inherent in all men—while moral *ideals* are not: this separability of the sphere of passions from the sphere of ideals forms, in fact, the core of "moral inversion." According to Polanyi, men can preserve and exercise their moral passions while shedding moral ideals for the sake of "immorality." Seen in this light, the meaning of the predicate "moral" seems to be rather difficult to ascertain: what precisely differentiates moral passions from other kinds of passions?

Looking for some elucidation, we notice that Polanyi believes in a "coherence of all men's consciences in the ground of the same universal tradition."[9] Such coherence must, presumably, consist in some convergence of their moral passions. But if so, then their passions must have some concrete moral aims—and must be, in a word, indistinguishable from certain very general ideals.

However, the concept of conscience itself is never clarified by

8. *P.K.*, p. 234.
9. *S.F.S.*, p. 82.

Polanyi. His usage of this term suggests that he understands it entirely ahistorically. But if we conceive of conscience as a general psychological faculty, not as a reflection of man's moral evolutions, revealing to him his changing obligations and guilts—then the notion turns out to be useless in our quest for solving the passions-ideals riddle.

Another perplexing assumption, fundamental for the concept analyzed, is that we are witnessing an unprecedented tendency to moral perfectionism. Polanyi reiterates this point many times,[10] stressing the disastrous consequences of excessive moral demands, imposed on man by the modern temper. But he never explains that this recent moral perfectionism or radicalism is neither theoretical nor psychological, but primarily *social*. I do not think that the last two thousand years have produced any more exacting ethical doctrines than those found in Christianity and the great religions of the East. What has been on the increase for the last two hundred years, and what we are now watching rapidly expand, is the awareness that the implementation of many basic moral rules has been, socially and geographically, very limited. Contemporary "perfectionists" simply wish that, e.g., the principle of man's dignity be observed not only with regard to the upper parts of societies or in the richer countries of the world. Even if it can be argued that this process of a "sociogeographical expansion" of moral consistency is concurrent with a sharpening of moral consciousness—still the two developments should be differentiated. And both of them have, in fact, little to do with any sharpening of moral demands under which an average individual puts himself: in this respect we are indubitably more self-tolerant than our ancestors.[11]

IV

The concept of "moral inversion" refers ostensibly to a process, or a situation, which is not individual but social in kind. It is, therefore, a little disturbing to find in the exposition of this

10. *L.L.*, pp. 109-110; *P.K.*, pp. 235-236; *Beyond Nihilism*, p. 1; *T.D.*, pp. 57-59.

11. Polanyi seems to be disregarding these distinctions when he protests (in *Beyond Nihilism*, pp. 1-2) against accusing our age of "moral weakness."

concept no cues which would explain the social mechanism of the phenomenon in question. How does it happen that societies, or their parts, substitute "purely materialistic" purposes for moral rules? By what communal routes do they proceed from Messianism to "totalitarian violence"? What are, in a word, the social determinants of the whole process?

We shall not find any clear answers to these questions in Polanyi's work. When he describes, very vividly and persuasively, the disintegration of traditional moral values and the resulting consciousness of "living in a spiritual desert"[12]—he does it in purely individualistic terms. That this is not simply an omission, made for the sake of brevity, is indicated by the fact that Polanyi does not ever mention social or group interests giving rise to genuine moral standards or even moral dilemmas. All moral rules, of which he approves, are individual-oriented. No matter what the social and economic conditions of men, Polanyi seems to suggest, moral rules remain the same. But it is almost a commonplace that ethics and morals are a product of communal life. It seems strange that Polanyi, who pays so much attention to the role of man's environment and upbringing in shaping his beliefs, disregards the social determinants of morality.

The theoretical source of this disregard seems to be Polanyi's antirelativism. Any discussion of the problems of morality in sociological terms almost inevitably shows moral norms as not absolute, but functionally relative. But Polanyi does not even consent to a purely descriptive use of the term "moral"—"moral" is, for him, always "morally commendable." It is difficult to imagine an analysis of the social roots of "moral inversion" undertaken without such a neutral concept of "the moral."[13]

Polanyi's use, very frequent, of the words "liberty," "freedom," and "free" is another illustration of his neglect of sociological ramifications. He uses these words always in a general, unspecified sense, as if their meanings were absolutely unambiguous; he

12. *P.K.*, p. 236.
13. Without indulging in a prolonged discussion of the necessity to have both descriptive and evaluative usages of certain terms, I shall only add that cultural anthropologists would find their task impossible without "moral" being used in a descriptive sense. Cf. Talcott Parsons, *The Social System* (New York: MacMillan, 1951), p. 50.

makes no conceptual allowances for the possibility that freedom may not be a static condition, independent from historical, social, and economic circumstances. Thus "free" becomes for him a sort of magic incantation, as it was for the eighteenth-century liberals. Opposing the existentialists, he still uses their concept of freedom as an absolute, ontological condition. Stressing the role of social intercourse in making man a human being,[14] he still treats man's freedom as a purely personal and ahistorical fact. But, as we all remember, freedom is always situational, always a freedom *from* or freedom *to*.[15]

Seen from the axiological angle, Polanyi's concept of moral inversion reveals certain paradoxical traits. He concedes, for example, that—in view of the fact that "universal statements commonly held by men" cannot be verified[16]—important human beliefs can be upheld only by an "explicit profession of faith" rooted in tradition.[17] This would certainly find support among most contemporary philosophers and sociologists of morals. However, Polanyi calls these important beliefs "eternal truths," which changes his framework from empirical to idealistic. Furthermore, although he openly admits that his moral values are derived from nineteenth-century English and American liberalism,[18] owing to his general theoretical standpoint he claims universal validity for them. Thus, his position can be described as one of "ethnocentric absolutism."[19]

As I have observed above, Polanyi uses the term "moral" only in an evaluative sense: the rules, with which he does not agree, are not "moral." The very concept of moral inversion rests on the assumption that people can have a code of behavior, applied to situations calling for moral decisions, which would not be a

14. *P.K.*, pp. 133, 205-207.
15. Cf. Isaiah Berlin, *Two Concepts of Liberty* (Oxford: Oxford University Press, 1958) , *passim*, esp. pp. 10-11, 33.
16. *S.F.S.*, p. 82.
17. *Ibid.*, p. 83.
18. *S.F.S.*, p. 80; *L.L.*, p. 96; *P.K.*, pp. 222-223, 245; *Beyond Nihilism*, pp. 16-18; and elsewhere.
19. Cf. *S.F.S.*, p. 83, where Polanyi says that we are "finally committed from the start" by "accepting uncritically a large number of traditional premisses of a particular kind." For the concept of "ethnocentrism," see Clyde Kluckhohn, "Universal Categories of Culture," in *Anthropology Today*, ed. A. Kroeber (Chicago: University of Chicago Press, 1953) , pp. 507-523.

"moral" code. However, if the basis of the claim to the universal validity of a man's moral standards lies in his personal commitment,[20] then on what grounds are we going to decide which commitments result in "moral" and which in "immoral" precepts in Polanyi's sense of the term? Polanyi's suggestion is that the commitments fostered by a truly "free" society are moral, but those fostered by "totalitarian" societies are not. Leaving aside the question whether this classification would be universally helpful (Was Athens a free society? Was republican Rome? Cromwellian England? If so, then not in the same sense) —two objections can be raised here. First is that the definition of a "free society" seems to be based precisely on its "morality,"[21] which would involve us in a vicious circle. Secondly, even if the danger of circularity could somehow be removed, still we are faced with the task of evaluating, not a system of rules of behavior, but a society giving rise to this system. I am not concerned here with the spurious problem of an infinite regress in valuation, but only wish to point out that the criteria for judging societies obviously have to be historical and economical. Therefore Polanyi's claim to universal validity of moral standards has to be upheld on some other grounds.

And, in fact, the grounds are there—in Polanyi's own work, although they are tacitly assumed rather than openly accepted. How frequently we read about "spiritual reality,"[22] "transcendent obligation" to truth, justice, and charity,[23] about "truth" and "justice" in an absolute, openly idealistic sense.[24] That this is not only a matter of style is plainly shown by the example of "beauty," which Polanyi also treats as absolute.[25] All these concepts have to rest on certain specific ontological assumptions, and Polanyi's remarks on God and religion reveal these metaphysical foundations.[26] Of course, if we accept the existence of God and supernat-

20. *S.F.S.*, pp. 82-83; *P.K.*, p. 377.
21. The description of the functioning of "free society" in *P.K.* (esp. pp. 222, 213-214) suggests this very strongly.
22. *S.F.S.*, pp. 65, 78-79.
23. *Ibid.*, p. 83.
24. *L.L.*, p. 102.
25. *S.M.*, pp. 74, 80. That we talk about the "beauty of a physical theory" is evidently only a metaphor.
26. *T.D.*, p. 62; *S.F.S.*, pp. 83-84.

ural forces, we shall be provided with adequate grounds for claiming that the values to which we are committing ourselves are indeed absolute.

The trouble is, however, that Polanyi tucks away these fundamental ontological premises and opens his whole axiological structure to accusations of inconsistency and arbitrariness. Worse still, his mentions of God and religion are confoundingly vague: we do not know what concept of God and what kind of religion he has in mind. His sweeping remark that "no society can live up to Christian precepts"[27] does not help us much. If Polanyi had ever explained what he thinks about, e.g., Maritain's "Christian humanism," his own position would have become infinitely clearer.

I believe that the whole conceptual knot discussed here can be disentangled by introducing a distinction between the language of a given moral system and the metalanguage of moral philosophy.[28]

Let us define "a value" as any principle ultimately justifying our judgments, choices, and preferences.[29] Accordingly, the language of a given moral system (or any other system) is a language in which the evaluative predicates (like "good," "honest," "evil," "free," etc.) derive their force from certain value-principles peculiar to this system and tacitly or openly accepted. If somebody wants to use "moral" as an evaluative predicate, he can do it within such a system, given the appropriate rules of usage. While within the scope of such a language, we can claim the universality of our values, providing that our system in fact covers all imaginable situations of moral choice.

A metalanguage of moral philosophy is a language in which we analyze the structures of particular moral systems. The rules of such language have logically nothing to do with the value-principles under scrutiny, and are determined by the exigencies of logic and currently accepted standards of scientific inquiry.

27. *Beyond Nihilism*, p. 4.
28. The following remarks are based on my work-in-progress, "Values, Ethics and Aesthetics."
29. More precisely: "S is a value" means "The name or description of S appears in a proposition which is used as a final justification or reason of an action or a judgement."

Such a metalanguage enables us to study and compare the origins, functions, and results of the workings of particular value systems.

As the knowledge of the comparative grammar of Indo-European languages does not preclude my writing in Polish or English, so the use of metalanguage for analytical purposes does not bar us from working, for practical purposes within the scope of the language of a chosen moral system. However, keeping these two apart enables us, I believe, to cope with the problems with which the concept of "moral inversion" deals.

"Moral inversion" becomes "moral revaluation"—a shift from one system to another. We do not then require any additional premises about moral forces[30] and passions being separable from moral ideals; we escape the dangers of ethnocentrism, and also the risks of axiological circularity. We are, to be sure, liable to lose a large part of the direct emotional appeal of our discussion, which will be no longer studded with praises and condemnations. But in academic discussion the emotional appeal should stem from facts, not from concepts: if our moral ideals are workable, if they result in an increase of human well-being and happiness, these results will speak for themselves.

V

To wind up my discussion of "moral inversion" as a conceptual proposal, I wish to add a few words on one characteristic of Polanyi's mode of thinking: his inclination to employ absolute terms and polar oppositions. This is a habit no reader of his books can overlook, and it is most apparent in chapters concerned with moral, political, and historical problems. Perhaps enough has been said above about "absolutism," although instances could easily be multiplied.[31] One of its results is that Polanyi sometimes accuses a moral system of self-contradiction—failing to notice that the system is self-contradictory only if regarded from the point of view of Polanyi's own "absolutistic ethnocentrism."[32] Polar opposition is the most frequent form of

30. *P.K.*, p. 215.
31. "Morality" as an absolute term, *P.K.*, p. 226.
32. *Ibid.*, p. 228.

presenting a problem: freedom and absolute government,[33] free society and totalitarianism,[34] rational and pathological behavior,[35] rational and causal explanation,[36] etc.

This method of forcing a choice between two extremes does not, of course, allow for any closer examination of intermediate cases; it also results in sharper condemnations and more uncritical approvals. This tendency to polarize, to divide everything into two opposed categories, is a feature which Polanyi shares with the political ideologies he most fervently attacks. However, what is understandable and even justifiable in a doctrine aiming at practical success is not so excusable in academic writings, and betrays a strong political passion in the author.

VI

This political passion, discernible in the very method of reasoning, is fully revealed by the other aspect of the concept of "moral inversion," as a historical, social, and political theory. I have to say that I am approaching the task of discussing this other aspect with great reluctance. Frankly, I find Professor Polanyi's political and social views often hard to comprehend. I am also fully aware that the differences of opinion involved are partly due to the differences of our backgrounds. I had the doubtful pleasure of experiencing personally the workings of both political systems with which Polanyi is particularly concerned: Nazism and Stalinism. However, I do not wish to give the impression that I consider these biographical incidents to play a decisive role in my argument: these experiences do not give me any special authority, only some knowledge of facts.

The problems involved are so numerous and complex that any detailed discussion would carry us far outside the limits of an essay. I am, therefore, going to touch upon only the more relevant points; I shall also refrain from explaining at length the more obvious factual confusions concerning the history of Marxism and international Communism.

"Moral inversion" is for Polanyi not only a concept, but a

33. *S.F.S.*, p. 63.
34. *P.K.*, pp. 213-214.
35. *S.M.*, p. 90.
36. *Ibid.*, p. 91.

concrete historical and political fact. According to him, modern totalitarianism, in the shape of Marxism and Nazism, perfidiously exploits philosophical scepticism and the increase of moral sensitiveness, substituting for "genuinely moral ideals" "materialistic" and "inhuman" purposes.

Marxism and Nazism are coupled together as belonging to the same category; differences between them are barely mentioned. Not once does Polanyi refer to the fact that whatever transgressions Stalin committed, they were indeed "transgressions" in the light of Marx's teachings and Stalin's own doctrines. Nobody can quote Marx or Lenin as advocating the establishment or justifying the existence of labor camps. However, it is certainly possible to deduce concentration camps and the extermination of Jews from *Mein Kampf* and Rosenberg's *Mythus*. Nazism was a rare case of an openly antihumanitarian, racist, and terrorist ideology; Stalinism was a case, in this respect like many others, of a blatant discrepancy between word and deed. The implications of this difference are obvious, and have been becoming even more evident for the last fourteen years.

It is rather difficult to discuss Polanyi's interpretation of Nazism and Marxism, since it is most unclear on what sources he relies. He does not give a single reference to Hitler's or Rosenberg's writings, or to any history of Nazism, and the only book quoted about the subject is Crankshaw's rather journalistic volume on the Gestapo. Consequently his picture of Nazi ideology is vaguely impressionistic. There is no word on the social and economic background of the movement, the absence of which gives it an air of freakishness.

More obscure still are the sources of Polanyi's statements about Marxism, which plays in his books the role of the arch-villain of recent history. At one point Polanyi says that "Throughout this chapter the term 'Marxism' is used rather for describing a current ideology, than the hypothetical beliefs of Marx himself,"[37] but this is an understatement. In fact, he makes no distinction whatsoever between Marxism and the Stalinist political and ideological practice.[38] Moreover, he accomplishes this identification in a most carefree manner, without even once quoting Stalin or, for

37. *P.K.*, p. 228 n. 2.
38. E.g., *Beyond Nihilism*, p. 24.

that matter, Marx himself. Instead, several times he quotes a remark made by Bukharin in a private conversation in 1935,[39] without inquiring how that remark stands against the background of Marxist tradition and contemporary pronouncements.

It is therefore not difficult for him to blame Marxism even for the rise of Nazism[40]—a thesis so grotesque that it is better passed over in silence. Much more serious are the charges that Marxism wilfully discredits all moral ideals to establish in their place its own system of rules.

Marxist ethics is, in fact, subject to contradictory interpretations.[41] It is, however, a different thing to point out, that there is a logical discrepancy between the scientific and the moral claims of any theory[42]—and to suggest that Marxism fosters "the love of state power,"[43] "denies the reality of moral motives in public life,"[44] or "openly declares inhumanity."[45] Whatever the ambiguities and internal contradictions of Marxist ethics may be, it is certain that Marx himself never "said that violence alone must be the aim of a scientific socialism"[46] and that none of his adherents has ever subscribed to such a slogan. Polanyi seems here to be mistaking for Marxists, Dostoevski's caricatures of Russian revolutionaries.

This blatant arbitrariness obscures certain genuinely important issues raised by Polanyi: the danger of means becoming substituted for original ends, which leads to the elimination of ethical considerations for the sake of political ones,[47] and the danger of logical confusions leading to a moral confusion.[48]

39. *S.F.S.*, p. 8; *P.K.*, p. 238; *T.D.*, pp. 3, 60.
40. *L.L.*, pp. 101, 106.
41. Cf. Eugene Kamenka, "Marxian Humanism and the Crisis in Socialist Ethics," in *Socialist Humanism: An International Symposium*, ed. Erich Fromm (Garden City, N.Y.; Doubleday, 1965), pp. 118-130; also other essays in that volume.
42. *P.K.*, p. 230.
43. *S.F.S.*, p. 79.
44. *T.D.*, p. 59.
45. *Beyond Nihilism*, p. 26.
46. *Ibid.*, p. 25.
47. This is, however, only a particular case of the age-old problem of political expediency and of means being glibly justified by ends. Marxism, because of its sweeping claims, is simply in a particularly vulnerable position. Still, considering Polanyi's individualistic conceptual framework, better instances could be found in part I of Burckhardt's *Civilization* or in a biography of Talleyrand.
48. Cf. *P.K.*, p. 233.

Anyway, whether or not the criticism of internal discrepancy between the allegedly scientific statements and moral precepts can be leveled against Marx himself,[49] it can surely be leveled against any "scientific" system of ethics. Herbert Spencer and Julian Huxley have also claimed that evolution provides scientific grounds for moral rules.[50] And the accusations of "scientific disguise," in which Marxism cloaks its political doctrine, sound hollow in the context of abstractly psychological interpretation, in which there is no word on Marx's social and economic theories. Karl Mannheim, who was no Marxist but understood the social functions of this doctrine well, saw much more clearly the role of reason in Marxism: "The proletarian mode of life is essentially rational because its position in the world compels it to plan revolution on a calculatory basis even more than the bourgeoisie had done."[51]

VII

The issue of Marxism, although it blurs the intellectual horizons of Polanyi's work most obtrusively, is only an offspring of a larger problem or revolution and the historical process in general.

In *The Study of Man* Polanyi presents his model of hierarchically arranged levels of understanding in knowledge: from physics to "dramatic history" of prominent historical personages.[52] When we analyze this hierarchy we are struck with the total absence of any sociological discipline or social problematics.[53] I do not think it is a case of a simple omission of a link which can be supplemented without any change in the whole structure. Sociology and cultural anthropology cannot simply be "inserted"

49. Eugene Kamenka in *The Ethical Foundations of Marxism* (London: Routledge & Kegan Paul, 1962) defends Marx against such a charge.
50. Cf. Herbert Spencer, *The Principles of Ethics* (London: Williams & Hargate, 1892) and Julian Huxley, *Evolutionary Ethics* (London: Oxford University Press, 1943).
51. Karl Mannheim, *Essays on Sociology and Social Psychology* (London: Routledge & Kegan Paul, 1953), p. 91.
52. *S.M.*, pp. 73-97.
53. To be sure, Polanyi talks about "material and social rootedness" affecting "the mental life of man" (*ibid.*, p. 87), but then, significantly, changes his terminology into "local rootedness" and does not elaborate on any social factor.

at a level of complexity lower than individual history, since social and ethnic groups consist of and are influenced by individuals. Conversely, we cannot put sociology on a higher level, since individuals are to a large extent products and parts of their environment; it is simply impossible to describe, or even define, an individual without setting him apart from others. Furthermore, social studies, which in certain ways are more complex than studies of individuals, seem to be at the same time closer to natural sciences in their methods. But the opposite can also be maintained: from neurophysiology to psychology there is but a step; sociology does not border comfortably close to any natural discipline.

I am not dwelling on this subject for the sake of sheer pleasure in picking holes in Polanyi's neat fabric. I am doing it to demonstrate that Polanyi's neglect of social, economic, and sociohistorical factors is deeply embedded in his theory of knowledge, in spite of all appearances to the contrary.

All his mentions of the "oppressed" notwithstanding, Polanyi's concept of society is basically solidaristic: fundamentally, he regards it as a homogenous whole[54] and never discusses social conflicts and cultural cleavages. A fragment in *Personal Knowledge* (p. 213) is for me particularly revealing. There he equates the statements "society accepted its own structure as permanently established" and "a hierarchical social structure was for the most part regarded as essential to the very existence of the body politic," and concludes that "for the first 2300 years of European history" there arose "no fundamental tension . . . between power and thought in society." This means to play down not only the early impact of Christianity, but also Thomas Münzer, the Levellers, and innumerable, although unsuccessful, social revolts.

Polanyi goes on to say:

> Only after the American and French revolutions did the conviction gradually spread over the world that society could be improved indefinitely by the exercise of political will of the people, and that the people should therefore be sovereign, both in theory and fact.

54. *P.K.*, p. 203.

This movement gave rise to modern dynamic societies. . . .[55]

The upshot is that social change is a result of "convictions," i.e., intellectual trends. Consequently, Polanyi never pays attention to social and economic causes of revolutions and upheavals, but tends to brush them aside.[56] According to him, intellectuals are drawn to Marxism solely for muddled psychological and philosophical reasons[57]—not because they see an urgent necessity of political change.

In this atmosphere of History as Symposium, it is not surprising that all revolutions seem to be vile and absurd.[58] That revolutions are sometimes outbursts of counterviolence, that the oppressed cannot possibly see the "truth" of their own condition before they are liberated, etc.[59]—simply does not come into the picture. The only reason why the English, American, and French revolutions are approved of seems to be that they have been successful; but the violence and bloodshed of these three is never mentioned.

VIII

Essentially, Polanyi is a reformist, and a reformist of a very definite kind. His best words of praise are reserved for the European liberalism of the nineteenth century, and he simply idolizes the Anglo-Saxon democracies. Undoubtedly, there is a lot to be said for these sentiments—providing they are not carried to the extreme.

The idyllic picture of Europe at the end of the nineteenth century presented in *The Logic of Liberty* looks too good to be true—and it is not true. In fact, from Poland alone more than "a few hundred people were forced into political exile":[60] thousands were serving long prison sentences. The statement about

55. *Ibid.*, p. 213.
56. Cf. *S.F.S.*, p. 78.
57. Cf. *P.K.*, pp. 236-237.
58. Cf. *Beyond Nihilism*, p. 23.
59. Cf. Herbert Marcuse, "Ethics and Revolution," in *Ethics and Society*, ed. R. T. De George (Garden City, N.Y.: Doubleday, 1966), pp. 133-147.
60. *L.L.*, p. 96.

the nonexistence of censorship is also inaccurate: there was political censorship in Prussia, Austro-Hungary, Spain, Italy, Greece, and other countries. Millions of people were living in a state of national oppression. It was indeed possible to travel without a passport everywhere outside Russia and Turkey, but very few could afford it: freedom of movement was most extensively exploited by starved emigrants to America. There was no country with universal suffrage.

When we read about "the peak of freedom and idealism achieved [in Europe] thirty years ago" (i.e., in 1914),[61] we have to ask: For whom was it "the peak"? Surely not for the Irish, Southern Slavs, Poles, Rumanians? In fact, it was the period immediately following the war of 1914-1918 which brought the most radical expansion of political liberties in Europe.[62] It seems to be no accident that the same period marked a sudden decline of the liberal parties: it was the liberals who found themselves unable to explain why the whole glossy structure of "peaceful, free and idealistic" Europe collapsed in 1914. In Polanyi's terms this collapse also seems to be unaccountable.

The glorious examples of political progress held forth by Polanyi are England and America. The development of civil liberties in these countries is shown as an outcome of "an intellectual process, moved by its own passions and guided by its own standards."[63] These processes were usually "evoked in the first place by persuasive individuals devoted to the advocacy of one particular reform."[64] That most of these changes came about as a result of strong social and/or economic pressure, that the English lawmakers were frequently yielding to threats of open revolts,[65] that in the United States a bloody war was fought ostensibly over a major social and racial problem (which still remains unsolved) —about all this we do not read a single word. The fact

61. *S.F.S.*, p. 80.
62. Cf. H. F. Gosnell, *Democracy: The Threshold of Freedom* (New York: Ronald Press, 1948), pp. 12-77.
63. *P.K.*, p. 223. On the same page again: ". . . broader changes of civic culture, which form the dominant matrix of legislative reform, are determined by a process of thought guided by its own standards and prompted by its own passions." Cf. also *L.L.*, p. 98.
64. *P.K.*, p. 223.
65. Asa Briggs, *The Making of Modern England: 1783–1867* (New York: Harper, 1960), pp. 294, 416, 429-435, 504, *et passim*.

that nineteenth-century England and America were the world's richest countries in economic resources, that England had her colonies and America her frontier and Negroes to cushion the bumpy ride of social progress—is again passed over in silence. The idealistic principles of sensible Englishmen prevented them neither from oppressing the Irish[66] nor from establishing the first concentration camps in history.[67]

Polanyi quotes, with understandable horror, the case of Nechaev—the Russian nihilist who had a fellow-conspirator murdered apparently for fear of betrayal.[68] Nechaev's story is rather obscure; he was, quite probably, a raving megalomaniac.[69] But questions of his sanity apart, we have to remember that Russian revolutionaries of that time did not conspire against a state observing the rules of fair play: they were risking their lives, they were engaged in a ruthless war. Have we not heard about intelligence agents being killed as "risks," or abandoned for certain death,[70] because such were the exigencies of the situation? Assuming that Nechaev acted in good faith—his behavior seems almost excusable if compared, for instance, with the execution of Roger Casement—completely harmless in prison, caught at the moment when he intended to call off an uprising in Ireland.[71]

In *The Logic of Liberty* Polanyi identifies the "fall of liberty" in Europe with the fall of liberalism.[72] This may be simply a matter of definition; but when elsewhere he maintains that Polish and Hungarian events of 1956 were a revival of the old-style liberalism,[73] he is dangerously mistaken. The "truth" looked for then and there was not the traditional, individualistic truth of

66. When they finally yielded, it was to open revolt, not to ideals. See A. J. P. Taylor, *English History: 1914-45* (Oxford: Oxford University Press, 1965), pp. 153-161.
67. G. H. L. Le May, *British Supremacy in South Africa: 1899-1907* (Oxford: Oxford University Press, 1965), pp. 94-110.
68. *Beyond Nihilism*, p. 23.
69. Cf. René Cannac, *Netchaiev* (Paris: Payot, 1961). Dostoevski, who modeled on Nechaev his Peter Verkhovensky in *The Possessed*, was later himself not sure whether the portrait had any semblance to the original (Cannac, p. 175).
70. John Hospers, *Human Conduct: An Introduction to the Problems of Ethics* (New York: Harcourt, Brace, World, 1961), p. 223. The reference is to the British Intelligence during World War II.
71. Taylor, *English History*, pp. 56-57.
72. *L.L.*, p. 103.
73. *P.K.*, p. 244.

the liberals.[74] One of the songs most frequently and with a renewal of conviction sung by Polish workers during the events of 1956 was "The Red Banner"—a symbol of the 1905 revolution, the traditions of which were revived both spontaneously and consciously.

IX

In this rather one-sidedly presented political and historical context, "moral inversion" emerges as the true villain of modern history. Judging by Polanyi's examples, the only restrictions on freedom have been in our century imposed by "moral inversionists." There is no mention of contemporary Spain, Portugal, or Turkey; no word on the prewar regimes in Hungary, Poland, or Greece. Needless to say, problems of freedom outside Europe are not touched upon. Against this background Polanyi's pleas for political and moral restraint and moderation[75] sound distinctly conservative. What he describes as the "suspended logic" of English and American liberalism, which avoided the pitfalls of sudden and disturbing upheavals,[76] was not a result of a moderate program accepted from the outset—but an outcome of bargaining and of the mellowing of much more radical demands.

Therefore, the call to action which Polanyi issues at the end of *Beyond Nihilism* rings to me a little false. A call to an action, which has as its avowed aim an extension of liberties, should not insist so much on telling the well-fed and free that they are doing fine. The basic moral and political problem of today is still the problem of implementation: how to expend economic safety and the order of democratically guaranteed liberties beyond the "happy few" of the nations. And the main danger is not that of "moral inversion"—but of cant and indifference.

X

Many crucial passages in Polanyi's work, dealing with the formation of consciousness, seem to agree in principal and to

74. *Beyond Nihilism,* p. 31.
75. *P.K.,* pp. 244-45.
76. *S.F.S.,* p. 77; *Beyond Nihilism,* pp. 16-18.

provide new arguments for the ideas commonly associated with Mannheim's "sociology of knowledge." This refers particularly to his argument, which I wholeheartedly support, that all our actions are charged with valuations, and, at the same time, are changing slightly the existing systems of operating values.[77] However, it seems to be no accident that Mannheim (or, for that matter, any other prominent sociologist) is never referred to by Polanyi. In spite of all appearances and all talk about "social lore," "conviviality," "fellowship," and "environment"—Polanyi's conceptual framework remains thoroughly individualistic or rather, to be more precise, rests on a sort of an individualistic-intellectualistic syndrome.

All his remarks on "sociology" are abstract and elusive. "Free society" is described in very general, inconcrete terms, with no mention of its components, institutions, historical or economic determinants.[78] Although the problem of sociocultural unity of a given group is most important for his theory of environmental origin of consciousness, he gives it only passing and inconclusive attention.[79]

In contrast, pronouncements on the role of thought and prominent individuals abound in Polanyi's work. Some of them I have quoted above, but many more can be easily added.[80] All in all, the problems of individual consciousness versus social ramifications, thought versus socioeconomic conditions, personal versus environmental factors in man's spiritual life—are never fully faced. Polanyi's mankind consists of individuals, inhabiting a world of semi-abstract ideas.[81]

XI

To supplant the strongly evaluative "moral inversion" with the descriptive concept of "moral revaluation" seems to have

77. See esp. *P.K.*, pp. 207-209.
78. Cf. *S.F.S.*, pp. 72-73.
79. Cf. *P.K.*, p. 221, where the issue of "philistinism" emerges for a moment but is not discussed.
80. *Beyond Nihilism*, p. 15; *T.D.*, pp. 50-51, 57-58.
81. This bears a striking resemblance to the intellectualistic-middle class outlook, as characterized by Mannheim, *Ideology and Utopia* (New York: Harcourt, Brace, 1936), pp. 221-222.

some advantages also from the sociological and historical point of view. It diminishes the risks of oversimplification, hasty judgment, and tendentious interpretation of history; at the same time it does not prevent us from investigating, and ultimately condemning, the perfidious manipulating of moral drives, as in the case of the Nazi appeals to the New Order.

To talk about "moral revaluation" means, in academic discussion, to aim at a separation of factual statements from evaluative judgments. I agree with Polanyi that such separation is ultimately impossible.[82] However, I am strongly convinced that it should remain a postulate, and that much can be done towards its realization. Both theoretical considerations[83] and my private experience corroborate the validity of the rule that the best, in fact the only reliable, weapon against political sorcery is a patient sifting of facts from dogmas, descriptions from commendations.

I think this can be done by tracing and isolating value-principles, which underlie our thoughts and assessments. When isolated, these values can be discussed as to their consequence, theoretical and practical, their historical sources, social concomitants, economic prerequisites, etc. Herbert Feigl and others have demonstrated convincingly that the dictum "de principiis non disputandum est" is by no means unshakable.[84]

I do not think that we should meekly settle down upon the diagnosis that we have to "accept uncritically a large number of traditional premises of a particular kind." Were this true, no great moral and social reformers, who started by anything but by being uncritical, would have been possible. Understanding our commitments, we should watch out for the danger of turning them into condonations: this is why we are obliged to be most searchingly critical of what is dearest to us; this is why I have attacked so strongly some of Polanyi's pronouncements about

82. Although I am accepting this on slightly different grounds; namely, I do not subscribe to Polanyi's "accreditive" concept of truth, which I am unable to discuss here.
83. Cf. C. H. Whiteley, a review of *Personal Knowledge, Mind,* LXVIII (October, 1959), 558.
84. H. Feigl, "De Principiis Non Disputandum . . . ?" in *Philosophical Analysis,* ed. Max Black (Ithaca, N.Y.: Appleton Century, 1950), pp. 119-156; cf. also I. Berlin, "Rationality of Value Judgments," in *Rational Decisions,* ed. C. J. Friedrich (New York: Atherton, 1964), pp. 221-223.

liberalism. To be faithful to the best traditions of European liberal thought cannot mean to advocate the return to the "suspended logic" of nineteenth-century England and America.[85] It means to commit ourselves to the future, not to the past; even the Roman Catholic church, as the last encyclical *Populorum Progressio* shows, points that way.

At this juncture the role of professional intellectuals seems to be paradoxically twofold. They should, I believe, busy themselves with the task of studying values and their workings; at the same time, however, they should do their utmost to persuade people that nobody is going to liberate them from the burden of moral decisions. Not that there are no candidates for the role of the Grand Inquisitor; they, however, would only exchange the duty to choose for the duty to obey. It is a myth, persistent but pernicious, that science can help us out of our moral predicament: it only can and should be used to make our choices more conscious and better documented.

Professor Polanyi's work goes a long way in showing us that we cannot escape our commitments and that we should be more aware of them, undertake them both more passionately and more responsibly. His position of an "engaged intellectual" must be dear to any East European heart, disagree as we may about particular issues. His sincere insistence on commitment evokes respect; but in academic discussion respect commands the strictest standards of judgment. Hence the severity of my criticism.

85. *Beyond Nihilism*, p. 36.

IN PURSUIT OF DISCOVERY*

Donald L. Weismann

Physiologists long ago established that the way we see an object is determined by our awareness of certain efforts inside our body, efforts which we cannot feel in themselves. We are aware of these things going on inside our body in terms of the position, size, shape, and motion of an object, to which we are attending. In other words we are attending from these internal processes to the qualities of things outside. These qualities are what those internal processes mean to us. The transposition of bodily experiences into the perception of things outside may now appear, therefore, as an instance of the transposition of meaning away from us, which we have found to be present to some extent in all tacit knowing.

We start the pursuit of discovery by pouring ourselves into the subsidiary elements of a problem and we continue to spill ourselves into further clues as we advance further, so that we arrive at discovery fully committed to it as an aspect of reality. These choices create in us a new existence, which challenges others to transform themselves in its image. To this extent, then, 'existence precedes essence,' that is, it comes before the truth that we establish and make our own.[1]

About ten o'clock one Sunday morning in January, I formally placed myself in a kind of laboratory. The laboratory was princi-

* A variant form of this essay will appear as part of *Language and Visual Form: The Personal Record of a Dual Creative Process,* to be published by the University of Texas Press.
    1. *T.D.*, pp. 13-14, 80.

pally of my own making, and consisted, insofar as its physical attributes were concerned, of two chairs, one at a table at which I would write, the other at a large slant-top desk at which I would paint. Near the writing table I had built a set of wall shelves and on these I had put about thirty books—books which I had long liked and which I had guessed I would be going to during periods of virtual inability to move forward in the series of events which I hoped was soon to begin. My bed was off in a corner. It was rigged with a light for night reading just as the table and desk were rigged with lights for night work. The room in which these things found their places was about fifteen by twenty feet with a dark red tile floor and walls of a light gray-blue plaster. It had windows on three sides and on the fourth side a door opening on to a long deck that shot out over the first floor of the house. Out of the south window, the one directly behind the writing table, I could look over the stubble of cornfields, up a long undulating slope covered with adobe houses to the blue-green shape of Mount Ajusco standing against the sky. Out the north window, the one directly above my painting desk, I could look over the winding road that runs from Huipulco to Xochimilco and on across cornfields toward the other side of the Valley of Mexico. The west window gave to the country between—hilly, crossed with stone fences and maguey, covered with eucalyptus and pepper trees, and accented with the dark trains of lava that once flowed molten from Ajusco.

This part of the laboratory, this workroom, was about thirty kilometers from Mexico City. The bus fare, then, was fifteen centavos—about two cents—and the trip took only forty-five minutes; but as the months from January to September passed, my interest in the work of the laboratory deepened and intensified and I found that I might just as well have been hundreds of miles from the city. It may be true that never before had I been so fortunate in finding both time and space in such ample compatible disposition—in finding so congenial a situation for a task that lay ahead. There was this place in which to work, tailored to the best of my hunches as to the color, shape, and texture that the undertaking would assume. Things were at hand. The singleness of my obligation to time gave me a feeling of its purposeful continuity. I could count on weeks and months of effort uncompromised by anything but the exigencies of the main task itself. Time and space were ready to go hand in hand in an unfettered way—in a way ample and flexible enough to allow for the natural development of a *modus operandi* organically suited to the dual creative effort to which end all things had been set in readiness.

Certain things were clear to me at the outset of work on that Sunday morning. It was clear, for instance, that I would start writing a book and that this book would try to tell a story of self-discovery. For my protagonist I had chosen the name of Richard Westermann, and if his story were to parallel or analogize that of anyone I knew, it would most likely be myself. It was clear to me that I would attempt also to paint parts of this history—to present in the visual terms of shape, line, color, and texture another kind of insight into the story I wished to tell. I felt strongly that the pictures I would make would not illustrate the words I would write, but rather that both the pictures and the words might conspire to illuminate the experience common to both. I accepted the possibility that in some cases pictures might precede words, and that in others words might precede pictures. And since I had painted for many years prior to that Sunday, and had often attempted to write, though never out of the kind of impulsion that I now felt driving me, it was clear at the outset that the thing I hoped to accomplish could not spring fully mature like Minerva from the head of Jove, but would evolve by fits and starts, through periods of rapid growth and periods of slow, long-drawn-out maturing, through periods of that excited activity that rides with every new clue to coherency, and through periods of laborious piecing and fitting together of the best that would be revealed in those flashes of optimum awareness.

I had already discovered that I could not make an outline of what I was about to try to objectify in language and visual form. I go about accomplishing a thing, rather, by beginning on the thing itself: beginning where I must or where I can—in the middle, at the end, sometimes at what later develops as the artistic beginning—and from that evolving a feeling for the still undisclosed whole. This means that I have become accustomed, especially in painting, to obliterating, doing over, saving the bit that matches the unspecified feeling of "rightness" in me, and gradually evolving a pattern that in its entirety "looks right" in the same way as does the good bit. Although I know that a creation is best when form, feeling, and idea fuse to one end, I do not favor the feeling of contrivance in a finished work. This does not necessarily mean that I rely on some mystic intercession of forces or even accidents to reveal the nature of my work to me. It may mean, instead, that I give generous place to the possibility of an idea or feeling having within itself clues for its own development, and that only by dwelling in those ideas and feelings and by responding to the askings of their particular qualities will they point me toward a larger thing such as a concept or a work of art.

I had sensed that my undertaking would not follow a rigid plot, since such a plot, if it existed at all, had not evidenced itself to me. I knew, simply, that a very large body of material—a wealth of experience, contemplation of which interested and moved me deeply—was asking for some kind of formulation and expression. The meanings in this body of experience had not evolved, and I felt that they could not become at all clear except in the process of working with it in the media of language and paint. I had thought a great deal about this material. I had ranged over it and worked it in imagination. It, as well as I, had suffered and gained through metaphorical thinking and analogical extension, but with the exception of forty or fifty short written sketches and a few dozen drawings and paintings, this material lay largely unformed within me—certainly without so sophisticated an organization as a plot. Yet this plotless body of remembered and imagined experience had assumed a color, if not a clearly defined shape. The contemplation of it; the attempts I had made in the past to objectify some of it in language and paint must have worked some kind of unifying persuasion over it, and I had perceived this as a particular color or tone—felt it as a wind blowing continually from the same quarter. I had come to live with this mass of experience in a spirit of searching. I came to identify it as quest, even going so far as to write, a few months before I began to work, that I presumed the book and the pictures would be the history of a personal quest—one that continued without its protagonist knowing its name or its object.

These things I seemed to know from the beginning. There were others, such as a fairly good estimate of my energies and of the difficulty of the work before me; but they seemed neither so specific nor so significant as the kind I have mentioned. What I had not at all adequately realized beforehand was that my moving into this physical laboratory—this workshop prepared in the shadow of an extinct volcano in a foreign country—would prove the step that was to bring me to a door which subsequently opened into the laboratory that was my self. And once having taken the step across the threshold, I was in the presence of my whole life. It was something like the afternoon many years before, when, while I was swimming in the upper Milwaukee River, a side drift eased me toward a powerful eddy. Before I knew what was happening I was drawn toward the center of a tightening circle. Then, rapidly revolving, I was pressed down the stem of a funnel. Yellow-green turned to blue-green, and it was colder. I was drowning. And before consciousness ebbed away, I had this feeling of being all at once in every part of the life I had lived up to that moment.

In both these cases I had the feeling of the presence of my entire life, replete, in some way, with the cities I had known, the intimate details of rooms in the houses where I had lived, the colors and textures of the streets I had walked, the seasons I had felt against my skin—their blending from hot to cold and from rain to snow; the people—all of them—their gaits, their clothes, the way they held their heads and hands, the sounds of their voices and the implications of their conversations; the thousands of skies, millions of sounds and sights, textures and smells, and the billions of transmutations of these in the events and feelings that were my life. In the river incident I had passed out, was somehow freed from the pull of the whirlpool, and drifted into calm water from which I was taken and revived by a companion. In Mexico I willingly passed into the laboratory of my self, understanding that if meaning were to be evolved out of the mass of experience that was my life I must find its substance in grappling with it. For ten months following that first Sunday morning I grappled with that mass of experience and in so doing added to it another mass which emerged as a piece of writing in excess of a hundred thousand words and a series of twelve gouache and casein paintings. This body of work, as it stands in fourth revision today, hardly makes the coherent statement it seeks. It stands as a kind of record of the first major stage in evolving meaning out of a bulk of past experience. But however that may be, I do not propose to speak of either the writing or the painting as accomplished tasks. By far the most fruitful part of this dual creative experience was not these partial achievements managed at the end of those months, but rather the mode of existence that came with the experiencing of the process itself during all the time my efforts were seeking those achievements.

If from my life I have learned one thing for certain, it is that nothing is simple, nothing static, and that everything impinges in some way on everything else. I can remember as a small child standing on a footstool before an open window in a house in downtown Milwaukee, taking a deep breath, blowing it out east toward Lake Michigan and feeling entirely convinced that all the air above the earth would move differently because I had blown so, and that everything in Michigan and New York and in Spain and Holland would in some way respond. And then I would blow into the west, toward Iowa, convinced that even though it might take a long time and the effect would be slight, something would happen on the other side of the world where east met west. For a period, when I was a young child, thoughts like this prompted a good deal of mysterious conduct aimed at modifying conditions on the other side of town, in my family's life, among the people and animals of Africa, the ships at sea, and the fires burning at the center of the earth. It was a kind of conduct that a group of us children shared for a while in a mixture of intense excitement, pleasure, and terror. We even had feelings for our responsibilities in pushing the universe around the way we were. But a little time and some refinement brought us to other living and freed us forever from concern about how, if we were not very careful which way we breathed in Milwaukee, we might blow a ship aground off the coast of Cuba. Still, something of this

profound respect for the continuity and interrelatedness of everything remained and was strengthened. Life kept demonstrating
its functional truth. The infinitely effective possibilities of every
living being became a notion to ponder seriously, and its entertainment precluded any chance of believing in a simple, static
world. This conviction enriched and complicated the business of
living. It became increasingly difficult to give a straight *yes* or *no*
answer to all but the most banal, point-blank kinds of questions.
It made clarity of statement difficult of achievement for all the
parenthetic qualifications an evolutionary concept of life demanded. But this notion of the infinite possibilities for affecting
life—for discovering other dimensions of its order—had strong,
personally appealing charm, and helped to effect in me an enthu-
siasm not only for discovery, but for expression, no matter how
difficult. This desire for expression did not take the form of
soap-box oratory or the leadership of pressure groups eager to
cast a whole new world. It took the form of simply making new
things and then setting them about in the world for other people
to see and possibly be influenced by. The writing and painting
that I accomplished in Mexico is of the lineage of that enthusiastic desire to sense and embody the ever-dawning aspects of reality.
This may help to explain how it comes that the telling of even
the early stages of the process through which the writing and
painting came into being is not simple, even in this first part
where I am dealing with it only in general terms.

   Before going any further I should like to say that I do not feel
at all out of my role as creator in attempting to do this. If what I
worked at in Mexico is not a fully achieved thing, but rather part
of a continuing process that emanates from some creative desire,
it may well be true that no one is in a more favorable position to
reveal the intimate nature of that process than he who is part of
it. A New Zealander telling of his homeland may make a very
inaccurate picture of it to a group of Boston professors. No one is
infallible or wholly trustworthy. Yet the native New Zealander
may still be able to reveal more about New Zealand than any of
the Boston professors can, if only because his person persists in
being part of what he speaks. Only recently has the artist come to
talk about his art, or the public been interested in listening.

Historically, the artist has been lionized in the reception hall, and then stood like an umbrella in the umbrella rack while certain, usually unblessed, spokesmen for his art took over in the drawing room. With him out of the way, conversation blew full, was capitalized, italicized, and attempted to overhistoricize, journalize, and devitalize his art. We have grown accustomed to this. There is a danger of mistaking the art spokesman for the artist, of considering the artist as only a pretext for something else. It is my hope that the relationship that exists between the artist, the work of art, and the experience that goes to make both will be helped into proper focus by functioning naturally in this essay.

I cannot remember when it was that I first felt a strong urge to create something substantial out of my experience. I presume all of us are always trying in some way to make sense out of our lives, but I am thinking a little beyond that level of activity to another level on which overtures in the direction of philosophy or art are made. It seems that I have always been interested in making things. I have painted with serious intent since I was twelve years old. I was an exhibiting member of the professional society of painters of the state of Wisconsin when I was fifteen. I have been trying to write a story ever since I entered college that same year, but not until after the Second World War did I begin to think of writing as something like my painting. It was only with some naïve conviction concerning the dynamic power of experience itself to seek its own form through language that I made some simple beginnings in writing. Before other responsibilities intervened, I had written twenty pieces, all about two thousand words in length, and had observed that all of them were nibbling away at some larger, more inclusive story or personal history. And strangely enough, the principal character about whom I thought I was writing emerged as only a foil for the larger intention. Later, two of these short pieces, and then four others, were published, and this strengthened the desire to accomplish something in writing. Before I wrote any more, I had made a series of rather unsuccessful illustrations for this group of sketches and had collaborated in the writing and illustrating of several children's books. It was not until an autumn several years later that I again had the opportunity to devote almost full time to painting and writing.

Something about the physical separateness of my studio that autumn worked to make it assume a mood sympathetic to creative effort. This opportunity to withdraw for periods seems to be one of the conditions for any kind of whole-hearted participation in the modes of discovery and creation. For, although such withdrawal has provided caricaturists with the phoney stereotype of the eccentric, anti-social, half-starved artist, it does reflect some underlying truth. The artist, as artist, finds that he must periodically suspend the purely normal course of his existence and separate himself from something in order to get closer to something else.

Without wishing to solemnize this fact too roundly, I should like to mention that this separation from something in order to get closer to something else functions also in the doctrinal belief in the purifying power of individual prayer and communion. Saint Augustine speaks precisely of this in the tenth chapter of the seventh book of his *Confessions*: *"Divine things are the more clearly manifested to him who withdraws into the recesses of his heart.* And being thence warned to return to myself, I entered into my inward self, Thou leading me on. . . . And I entered . . . and Thou didst beat back the infirmity of my sight, pouring forth upon me most strongly Thy beams of light. . . . And I heard . . . as things are heard in the heart, nor was there room for doubt. . . ." It may not be pure coincidence, indeed, that certain of these same elements of humbleness and submission have proved to be components of what I have discovered the most fruitful attitude in which to approach a creative task.

The necessity for periods of withdrawal and for an attitude of humble submission before the creative task was a discovery I had made long before going to Mexico, but it was in pursuing the painting-writing task that it crystallized into something like the beginning of a *modus operandi*. What actually happened, it seems, was that certain ways in which I attended from what was going on inside of me to conditions external to myself were brought to a level approaching conscious procedure.

Then, on that Sunday morning in January to which I have

already referred, I had breakfast at about eight o'clock, and by ten I was seated at my writing table and wondering how one begins to paint and write a story. The sun was shining on the fields outside and I wondered why I had worked so hard to get this opportunity to do something I seemed to know nothing about. As I said earlier, my entire life came about me that Sunday morning. From out of every corner of my mind there came countless images of places I had been, things I had seen and persons who had touched my life. I could feel the texture of the broom handle I held when I was four; I could smell the chocolate factory three blocks from the house where I lived when I was eight; I could taste the coal dust blowing across the viaduct when I was six; I could feel myself hold my breath as I watched my youngest brother being born in the room off the dining-room when I was seven; and I could hear the swooshing of rockets as they tore over my head on the beach at Leyte in 1944.

The sun kept shining on the fields of stubble outside my window, and a patch grew across the red tiles of the floor. For a while I rested in it, feeling that I had made a great mistake—that I should be out in the sun, back in the Middle West, painting some landscape I knew, instead of sitting alone here in this room, hearing the distant, garbled Spanish of some Indian trying to get his burros over a crumbling stone wall.

I remember going over to a window and watching until the burros were safely on the other side. And then I stood there watching them become smaller as they went up the slope toward Mount Ajusco. Something in the limpid clarity of the air— something that reminded me of a day twenty-two years before when Eddie Nolan and I had left high school at noon and had gone swimming in Murphy Lake on the edge of town—moved me to want to paint the landscape I was looking at. I went over to my painting table and began. In half an hour the beginning had crumbled into a shapeless, colorless configuration on the board, and I abandoned it to write a letter to Eddie Nolan. I wrote my address at the top of a clean sheet of typing paper. I wondered how Eddie would pronounce Xochimilco. He had never finished high school and the course he had followed while he was a student had carefully avoided geography, history, and foreign languages. I wrote the date below that. And then, instead of writing the letter, I wrote:

> Long ago, when the smoke looked so pretty coming from the chimney of the bungalow across the street, the mailman brought a small red package to Richard's house on Island Avenue. He had seen the mailman coming because he was standing on the chair at the bay window watching the smoke through an opening in the frost that he had made by pressing his hands, first one and then the other, to the ice-covered glass. Summer had gone away. Where was it now? Maybe it was in Holland where the windmills are; maybe in Spain where Miss Stanley said the colored sailing ships are; maybe it went away into many warm corners like down in the basement of Sandy's Bakery where little green plants were growing near the ovens. Then summer must be broken up into pieces—a million million pieces down in warm corners and all over the world. But how does summer put itself back together again, and how can so many little pieces be made back into summer? Little drops of rain make rivers, and if you stop the rivers, then lakes come. Summer must be an island in a lake, and it comes from the rivers full of warm pieces where little green plants grow. Rivers must carry the million million little pieces and make them back into the island of summer.

I had, in fact, written the first paragraph of my story. I cannot tell at all exactly out of what this paragraph came. I cannot really tell why I wrote down that particular paragraph. It might be argued that it came from an attempt to analogize the then very present state of my feelings in that room—to represent those feelings, if possible. It might be submitted that thoughts of Eddie Nolan called forth the "long ago" at the beginning of the paragraph; that looking out the window recalled the frosty window of thirty years before, and that I went ahead in the supposition that the general ambiguity of my feelings could be expressed by writing such a line as "How does summer put itself back together again, and how can so many little pieces be made back into summer?"

But strangely logical as this may seem I am not sympathetic to it. There is something about this kind of interpretation which makes me feel that it short-circuits the actual pattern of energy. Granting that a heightened state of mind and body existed prior to writing this first paragraph, I cannot believe that what I did was merely an attempt to *analogize* or *represent* that state. To do that, I feel, would be to confuse the body-mind state as a kind of *end in itself* rather than recognizing it for its value as a symptom or a *clue to something else*. In the limited and active sense, this *something else* was the individual *qualities* of things present and recalled in that room in Mexico. In the largest sense, this *something else* was the constellation of those qualities—or, to put it another way, the pattern of *meaning* in my life. It was toward that constellation that I wished to move. For that was the ambivalent allure, the all-present but undisclosed coherency I sought to meet and know.

It pays to know that the way one moves toward coherency and meaning is not simple. It is often indirect; intentions double back on themselves. Clear clues are often misread, and even the most sophisticated of us finds himself in the ancient game of trial and error. I cannot take at face value, for instance, Edgar Allan Poe's statement concerning how he wrote "The Raven."[2] He says that "no one point in its composition is referable either to accident or intuition; that the work proceeded, step by step, to its completion with the precision and rigid consequences of a mathematical problem." I am inclined to regard his earnestness in such disclosures as being of the same sort as his earnestness in developing his tales based fictively in science. I am inclined, going a little further, to credit more completely the *means* by which Poe develops his thesis of direct, rigidly consequential creation than I am the *ends* toward which he directs those means. His means are those of an explorer, an artist, not those of a journeyman mathematician, and his "Philosophy of Composition" is developed and climaxed with all the artistic genius evident in "The Raven" itself. Rather than a cold exposition of the arithmetical and other such matters concerning the creation of this poem, his essay succeeds mainly in creating an *analogy* of it. Poe's very use of metaphorical language in the essay; i.e., "elaborate and vacillat-

2. "The Philosophy of Composition," in *The Works of Edgar Allan Poe* (Cambridge, Mass.: Stone and Kimball, 1905), VI, 33.

ing crudities of thought . . . true purposes seized only at the last moment . . . innumerable glimpses of ideas that arrived not at the maturity of full view . . . fully matured fancies discarded in despair as unmanageable . . . painful erasures and interpolations . . . the wheels and pinions, the tackle for scene shifting, the stepladders and demon traps, the cock's feathers, the red paint and the black patches, which in ninety-nine cases out of the hundred constitutes the properties of the literary *histrio*" cancels out in some important way the decisive validity of such bald statements as "Nothing is more clear than that every plot, worth the name, must be elaborated to its denouement before anything is attempted with the pen."

In my attempts to understand what specifically sets in motion a creative process, I have, by virtue of my own experience, come to be sympathetic to such accounts as Walter Van Tilburg Clark's concerning the inception of his short story, "The Portable Phonograph:"[3]

> I didn't, naturally, start with a notion of saying something about the finality of war and out of that melancholy fog evolve a set of rules, and out of them a story. The process was not that orderly. First, I just began to write. I can't remember exactly what set me off. Probably it was some intensifying item of the day's news, stirring me when I had time to sit and brood on it until I had to get rid of the emotion it built up, and the first, suggestive images began to appear. Almost always, whatever may have been working up to it in my mind, recognized, it is some image suddenly coming alive and suggesting more to follow, or to precede, that makes me reach for a pencil.

What we are talking about here is, of course, the creative impulse or "inspiration"—the energy that raises the sluice gates and initiates the creative flow. Clark quite frankly says he cannot remember what set him off and that "First, I just began to write." But he neatly qualifies that with the suspicion that it might have been some "intensifying item of the day's news, stirring me when I had time to sit and brood on it until I had to get rid of the emo-

3. "The Ghost of an Apprehension," *The Pacific Spectator*, II (Summer, 1949) , 256, 257.

tion it built up." Something particular may have been troubling him, he says, but he implies that nothing came of it until he "had time to sit and brood."

This was very much like the situation in which I had found myself immediately before writing that first paragraph. I had months of time ahead in which to brood on the very generalized problem of meaning in my life. I had been brooding on it, and I felt I had to do something about the tensions it had built up. For me it meant doing more than producing something which merely described or presented those tensions. It meant doing something more subtle than just "getting rid of the emotion" as Clark put it. For me it meant that I must recognize and value these tensions as positive aids to perception. All the preparations made before beginning actual work were in some manner part of my attempt to perceive what it was that these building tensions were transmitting as clues to what lay beyond them. Planning the trip to Mexico, finding the house in which the work was to be done, setting chairs and tables and lights in place, arranging paints and brushes and writing materials and sharpening pencils were all part of it. And the necessary attitude of humility took hold when I felt the magnitude of the task in comparison to the uncertainty of my talents. The period of humble and submissive brooding spent in helplessly staring at my sunlit room, in feeling past and present in the landscape at the window, in feeling some mysterious incongruity that I was once a boy lying awake at night in a cold bedroom in the Italian district of Milwaukee, and now stood in this room far south of the Tropic of Cancer wondering how to make this thing I wanted so badly to make, heightened the intensely moving character of my own predicament and sent me to my painting table to *do something* about it—anything, perhaps, that might induce a condition of congruity, a condition for which I suspected my perception may now have been especially sharpened. The painting didn't work. I abandoned it. I started a letter to Eddie Nolan, and it turned into the first page of a book that over a long period of time was to move me closer to the coherency and meaning I must have been seeking.

This deep-going and powerful feeling of need to bring one's self into a better relationship with the world—this feeling of

terror and lostness and beauty and melancholy, shot through
with an intense yearning for resolution in gracious, satisfying
objective form, is the million-threaded radix that searches out in
every way for its death in consummation. Anything come upon
might prove the beginning of this process of consummation. For
me it might have been the patch of sun lying on the tile floor, the
sounds of Spanish coming across the fields, the odor of drying
clay in the road below—any remembered or imagined scene,
person, word, or event. Anything, absolutely anything, might
have proved the touchstone for the long drawn out pleasure-pain
process that would consummate this feeling with its death in
objective form.

I think it is true that, in my case, it was essential that frustration should arise and cause me to abandon the kind of highly
directed effort I had been making up to the time I started the
letter to Eddie Nolan. The willingness to abandon the "great
project" in favor of writing that old friend may be an instance of
what Polanyi describes as "pouring ourselves into the subsidiary
elements of a problem." Somehow, then, the letter turned me
back in the direction of the "great project," and I just began to
write. This series of events made me feel further affinity with
such concepts, for instance, of Bosanquet's that "In creative art
the production is as it were a form of perception; it is subordinate to the full imagining, the complete looking or hearing."[4]

At the end of that first Sunday of writing—it was close to ten in
the evening when I quit my table—I had salvaged a little over
eight hundred words from the three or four thousand that I had
put down in longhand. These eight hundred I had typed out on
sheets and pinned in sequence to a two-by-ten foot board in front
of the table so that I could easily refer to any of them. Before I
closed shop entirely, I read them over. That might not have been
necessary since I already knew them by heart, but I read the eight
hundred words over, slowly and out loud. I can remember that in
some way, for myself, they pleased me; but later, as I walked in
the night street, I wondered what they meant—what they could
portend for the whole story of which I felt they were a part. I

4. Bernard Bosanquet, *Three Lectures on Aesthetics* (London: Macmillan,
1923), p. 34.

wondered if, by chance, I had actually started so easily at the beginning of my story, or whether the beginning was still to be evolved in subsequent efforts. I thought it might easily be possible that I should have to discard this first day's work as I had the two or three thousand words that helped form the eight hundred I had salvaged.

The thought of having to discard everything I had done that day and start all over the next frightened me a little, not because of losing the eight hundred words, but because I could imagine this going on forever: writing a day, destroying a day; then painting another day and destroying that, *ad infinitum*. I had a picture of leaving Mexico a year from then with nothing at all to show for the time and struggle between. I found myself walking faster, faster down the Calle del Diez-y-seis de Septiembre, and back to the house. I hurried up the stairs to my room, turned on the light over my table, and read again the first eight hundred words. They sounded empty and foolish. I wanted to tear the sheets from the board and start all over, right then. But I didn't. Instead, I went downstairs, had a cup of tea, looked at *La Prensa*, came back upstairs, read the eight hundred words another time and felt some comfort in believing that at least I had begun— that whatever the eight hundred words were moving toward lay in a circle all around them, and that I would find my way of extending them. And in the long meantime that extends from that long-ago room in Mexico to this very place and moment I can rejoice in the good existence that this search keeps making possible for me.

SENSE-GIVING AND SENSE-READING

Michael Polanyi

I propose to inquire here into the way we endow our speech with meaning and into the way by which we make sense of speech that we hear spoken. I shall show that, notwithstanding their informal character, these acts possess a characteristic pattern, a pattern that I shall call the *structure of tacit knowing*; I shall show that to form such a structure is to *create meaning*. Both the way we endow our own utterances with meaning and our attribution of meaning to the utterances of others are acts of tacit knowing. They represent *sense-giving* and *sense-reading* within the structure of tacit knowing. My inquiry will outline the total structure of language, comprising both its formal patterns successfully established by modern linguistics and its informal semantic structure, studied so far mainly by philosophy.

I. *The Triad of Tacit Knowledge*

Tacit knowing joins together three coefficients. This triad is akin to the triad of Stoic logic: "A means B to C." But I shall prefer to write instead: A person A may make the word B mean the object C. Or else: The person A can integrate the word B into a bearing on C.

But to integrate a thing B into bearing on some C amounts to endowing B with a *meaning* that points at C. An obvious way to do this is to choose as B a finger pointing at C. Suppose a lecturer points his finger at an object and tells the audience: "Look at this!" The audience will *follow the pointing finger* and *look at the object*.

There is a fundamental difference between the way we attend to the pointing finger and its object. We attend to the finger by *following its direction* in order to look at the object. The object *is then at the focus of our attention*, whereas the finger *is not seen* focally, *but as a pointer* to the object. This directive, or vectorial way of attending to the pointing finger, I shall call our *subsidiary awareness of the finger*.

It is our subsidiary awareness of a thing that endows it with meaning: with a meaning that bears on an object of which we are focally aware. A meaningful relation of a subsidiary to a focal is formed by the action of a person who integrates one to the other, and the relation persists by the fact that the person keeps up this integration.

We may say, in slightly more general terms, that the triad of tacit knowing consists in subsidiary things (B) bearing on a focus (C) by virtue of an integration performed by a person (A) ; and may say also that in tacit knowing we attend *from* one or more subsidiaries *to* a focus on which the subsidiaries are brought to bear.

II. *Various Types of Tacit Knowing*

Consider now the range of different instances in which we meet this structure of meaning in tacit knowing.

(*a*) We have an instance of this in the practice of a skill. In a skill we have a set of elementary motions, integrated in fulfilment of a joint performance. These elements are the subsidiaries of this focal act. They possess a joint meaning in being co-ordinated to this common purpose. We are attending *from* them *to* their integrated result.

(*b*) The same applies to the reading of a physiognomy. The several features which express the mood of a person are clues, or subsidiaries, bearing on the moody impression which they jointly compose. We attend *from* these features *to* the mood by integrating them to the appearance of the mood; and this physiognomy and the mood expressed by it are the meaning of these features.

The faculty of identifying a physiognomy is used in medicine for diagnosing the appearance of certain diseases and even more widely for the identification of specimens in zoology, botany, and geology.

(c) Our next example is the way we find our way blindfold by the use of a stick. The impact made by the near end of the stick on our hand holding the stick is used for sensing the position of an object touched by the far end of the stick. Indeed, we feel the impacts made on our palm and fingers as if they occurred where the stick hits an object. In other words, the impact made on our hand *means* the position of the object where it hits an object. A similar integration takes place when we use a tool. We come to feel the impact on our hand holding a hammer at the point where the hammer hits a nail.

(d) We may take finally the case of a speculative skill. A chess player conducting a game sees the way the chessmen jointly bear on his chances of winning the game. This is the joint meaning of the chessmen to the player, as he decides from their position the choice of his next move.

III. *Knowing Our Body: A Paradigm of Tacit Knowing*

In all our transactions with the world around us, we use our body as our instrument. Such uses are skilful. To fix our eyes on a moving object and to see rightly what it presents to us is to perform a watchful, intelligent operation. It jointly interprets dozens of clues in our eyes, in our memories, in muscles of every kind, and in the labyrinth inside our skull.

And this applies to all the examples of tacit knowing that I have listed. The expert recognition of specimens, the use of probes and tools, the major skills of our body and mind are all based on a meaningful integration of our body and of the sensations felt by our body.

Throughout these exercises we are subsidiarily aware of the elements that we integrate inside our body and where our body touches things outside it. This is how we are usually aware of our body. Our internal parts are focally felt only when we are in pain; and the external appearance of our body is rarely observed by us; people having no large looking glasses know very little of their bodies externally. It is the subsidiary sensing of our body that makes us feel that it is *our* body. This is *the meaning our body normally has for us.*

Things like our clothes, spectacles, probes and tools, when in use, function like our body, and resemble our body closely by the fact that we rarely know them focally. Indeed, whenever we experience an object outside us subsidiarily, we feel it in a way similar to that in which we feel our body. And hence we can say that in this sense all subsidiary elements are *interior to the body* in which we live. To this extent we dwell in all subsidiarily experienced things.

The way we see a pair of stereo-pictures illustrates strikingly the parallelism between integrating things in our body and similar things outside. We are normally aware of a pair of retinal images only subsidiarily as they contribute to stereoscopic vision and we can use a pair of stereo-pictures likewise only by seeing each with one eye through a stereo-viewer.

To sum up, meaning arises either by integrating clues in our own body or by integrating clues outside, and all meaning known outside is due to our subsidiary treatment of external things as we treat our body. We may be said to *interiorize these things or to pour ourselves into them.* It is by dwelling in them that we make them mean something on which we focus our attention.

This view presents us with two important features of *sense-giving.* Our body and the organs in our body are given to us as our own by birth, and there can be no question of embodying them in order to endow them with meaning. To enrich the meaning of our body, we have only to co-ordinate our motions and to integrate the sensory clues due to the impact of external events. The matter is different when we endow *external* things with meaning. The process of integration assimilates them to our body and to this extent *deprives them of their character as external objects.* We have, for example, two external stereo-images to start with, which we can look at as separate objects; when we interiorize them, these objects vanish into a single image of depth in space. There is also a change in the appearance of spoken or written words when their meaning is established and we attend *from* the words *to* that which they mean. A word focally observed—that is as a sequence of sounds or of marks on paper—appears to us as a meaningless external object; while its assimilation, which makes it a subsidiary thing, deprives it of the opaque externality of an object. The meaningful use of a word which causes it to lose its bodily character makes us *look through the word at its meaning.*

Yet another strange fact emerges from this context. When we co-ordinate parts of our body to achieve some external performance or make sense of impacts on our sentient organs, we include in our operations many hidden internal parts, commonly unknown to us. It is characteristic of our body that it submits to operations the particulars of which are virtually unknown to us and that these largely unspecifiable operations cannot be replaced effectively by any focally controlled operations. This offers us evidence of our capacity *to integrate and endow with meaning things of which we possess only a subsidiary awareness.*

This faculty is present also in sense-giving outside our body. In viewing a pair of stereo-pictures we integrate tiny differences of the two pictures, which we could hardly ever see in themselves, so that they form the spatial appearance of their joint image. The sense of a physiognomy and the characteristic appearance of a sickness or of a zoological or botanical specimen are all largely based on features that are hardly identifiable in themselves. And we may add that scientific discovery is notoriously guided by many unidentifiable clues, and so is to an important extent our ultimate decision of accepting the claims of a scientific discovery as valid.

These facts are essential to the study of language. There could be no phonology if we could not control and use meaningfully a complex pattern of vocal actions without any explicit knowledge of what we are doing when relying on these sounds for our utterance of words. Nor is the pattern of grammar on which we rely for composing meaningful sentences commonly better known to us. We can know them well only from linguistic studies. We usually conduct these delicate and meaningful integrations without our being able to give more than the crudest account of such subsidiary performances.

These unspecifiable powers of the mind will yet be clarified.

But in conclusion to the present section, I shall add that *sense-giving* has its counterpart in the reverse process of *sense-deprivation*. I have described the changes in the appearance of external things when we endow them with meaning. They lose their bodily character and become as it were transparent. This is achieved by turning the focus of our attention away from the external object and attending *from* it *to* something else which has become its meaning. The reverse process works by switching the focus of our attention back on the object, which is thereby rendered once more external to us. And as it acquires the status of externality, the object loses its meaning. It is well known how a word we speak can be reduced to a meaningless utterance of sounds by repeating it a number of times, attending closely to our lips and tongue and the sounds they make. The fact that exteriorization kills meaning confirms the sense-giving powers of indwelling.

IV. *Communication: A Triad of Triads*

It may seem puzzling that so often the C on which we are focusing our attention is even more meaningful than the B *from* which we are attending to C. While the features of a face have their meaning in a mood, the mood itself is even fuller of meaning than the features are. And again, while the meaning of a string of words lies in the sentence they form, the sentence is even more meaningful than the words which form it.

Such consecutive levels of meaning are widespread, but it yet seems reasonable to identify the several triads composing them. Take the example of speech. Suppose we have a series of spoken sounds that mean a word and a series of spoken words that form a meaningful grammatical sentence, while a sequence of such sentences forms a meaningful piece of prose. A person A writing a piece of prose performs a whole series of consecutive integrations simultaneously. The sequence of triads that he controls can be described as a hierarchy of levels in which each lower level functions as subsidiary to the next higher level.

There is in fact another sequence of triads which throws a closer light on the main problem of sense-giving and sense-reading. Suppose we travel in a country we have not visited before. By the end of a morning we will be full of new experiences and may report them by letter to a friend so that he may read our message and try to understand our experiences. This is a sequence of three integrations. The *first* is an intelligent understanding of sights and events, the *second* the composing of a verbal account of this experience and the *third* the interpretation of this verbal account with a view to reproducing the experience which it reported. The first two integrations are the work of one person, while the third is done by another person, the friend addressed by the first. We may note also some variation in the character of the three consecutive integrations. The first triad is mainly cognitive; it has the structure we met in the process of perception and, more strikingly perhaps, in the identification of a specimen by an expert. The second triad, which puts the result of the first into words, resembles more the performance of a practical skill, while the third returns once more to the cognitive type which integrates clues to a meaningful experience. The *first* triad is more a sense-*reading*, the *second* more a sense-*giving* and the *third*, once more, a sense-*reading*.

These two directions of using meaning can be illustrated by a small episode from my own experience.[1] My correspondence arrives at my breakfast table in various languages, but my son understands only English. Having just finished reading a letter, I may wish to pass it on to him, but must check myself and look again to see in what language it was written. I am vividly aware of the meaning conveyed by the letter, yet know nothing of its words. If I look then and find that the letter is in a foreign language, I tell my son its content in English. These two phases clearly show that we can possess the meaning of a text without knowing the text itself, and can put this inarticulate meaning into words. It illustrates also the kind of inarticulate knowledge first acquired by the traveler by an act of sense-reading: this is the original meaning of his experience. It is the kind of understanding that we share with intelligent animals.

The fact that we can possess knowledge that is unspoken is of

1. Described in *P.K.*, p. 57. The ideas on language developed in the present paper were largely anticipated in this book, particularly in chapter iv on Skills, pp. 49-63, and in chapter v on Articulation, pp. 69-124.

course a commonplace, and so is the fact that we must know something yet unspoken before we can express it in words. It has been taken for granted in the philosophic analysis of language in earlier centuries, but modern positivism has tried to ignore it, on the grounds that tacit knowledge was not accessible to objective observation. The present theory of meaning assigns a firm place to the inarticulate meaning of experience and shows that it is the foundation of all explicit meaning. To this I shall yet return.

V. Sense-Reading

We shall see more fully what is involved in tacit semantic acts, and particularly in sense-reading, if we introduce a measure of difficulty that needs to be overcome by an effort. Take first two typical cases of sense-reading. First, noticing at night a strange outline in our garden, we strain our eyes to make out what it is; second, from an inkling of a meaning suggested by a text, we strive for a fuller understanding of it. And third, as a case of sense-giving, we may feel what we want to say, yet must grope desperately for words to say it.

These tacit efforts can perhaps be appreciated better if we note that each of them has a major form in which it manifests its powers more fully. Students of biology have for years past noticed the presence of certain cells of microscopic shapes which they called Golgi bodies. Most histologists accepted the claim that these shapes represented biological organs, but there were some who were sceptical, until the electron microscope proved that the Golgi bodies were real organs.[2] Take another similar case. Early in the nineteenth century the apparently integer value of atomic weights based on hydrogen induced William Prout to suggest that all elements were built of hydrogen. But sceptics rejected this claim on the grounds that the approximation to integer values was but crude. Their objections prevailed for nearly a century, until atomic physicists proved them wrong: matter was shown to be built of particles like hydrogen atoms.

We see here how heavily the course of scientific inquiry may

2. See J. R. Baker, *Journ. Roy. Microscopic Society*, LXXXII (1963), 145-157.

rest on deciding whether certain regularities should be taken to be significant or be set aside as accidental. This is true also for juries drawing conclusions on the grounds of circumstantial evidence. They must decide whether certain suspicious circumstances do establish beyond reasonable doubt the guilt of the accused, or are to be set aside as pure coincidences.

Such decisions are open to argument, but yet remain substantially dependent on an informal judgment, which in the case of science may require exceptional powers of insight. It is to these powers that we owe our capacity for recognizing in our experience a meaning that can then be stated in words.

These instances of inarticulate sense-reading apply to the first of the consecutive integrations which make up the transmission of an experience to another person. Leaving aside for the moment the process of verbalization, which is a sense-giving, I pass on to the third integration—that is the reception of the message—which is another act of sense-giving. When a message reaches the person to whom it is addressed, he will try to make sense jointly of its text and of the experience described by the text. For the understanding of a verbal communication of a meaningful experience, we can usually rely on our previous understanding of familiar experiences. But we often have to understand language for which this does not hold. Our education is largely based on absorbing communications about experiences that are novel to us and are recorded in a language we do not understand.

Some time ago I described the arduous process by which a medical student learns to interpret radiograms of pulmonary diseases.[3] He begins by watching in a darkened room the shadowy traces on a fluorescent screen placed against a patient's chest, and hears the radiologist commenting to his assistants, in technical language, on the significant features of these shadows. The student is completely puzzled, for he can see in the X-ray picture of a chest only the shadows of the heart and the ribs, with a few spidery blotches between them. The experts seem to be romancing; he can see nothing that they are talking about. But as he goes on listening for a few weeks, looking carefully at the pictures

3. *P.K.*, p. 101.

of different cases, gradually a rich panorama of significant details will be revealed to him: of physiological variations and pathological changes, of scars, of chronic infections and signs of acute disease. He has entered a new world. He still sees only a fraction of what the experts can see, but the pictures are definitely making sense now, and so do most of the comments made on them. Thus, at the very moment when he has learned the language of pulmonary radiology, the student will also have learned to understand pulmonary radiograms.

An unintelligible text referring to an unintelligible matter presents us with a dual problem. Both halves of such a problem guide our minds jointly towards solving them and will in fact be solved jointly by the understanding of the objects referred to and the words referring to it. The meaning of the things and of the terms designating them is discovered at the same time. I have said that this dual act of sense-reading is the paradigm of the educational expansion of our mind; it also bears on the process by which a child learns to understand speech, which is a basic problem of linguistic theory. I shall lead up to this as I go on.

VI. *Experience and Report*

Let me return then to the scene when I received a letter, took in its content, and remembered it, though I had forgotten in what language the letter was written. The knowledge I thus retained was the meaning of the letter as I understood it. Suppose the letter described a scene its writer was witnessing at the time he wrote to me. He had an understanding of the scene and this was its meaning to him; we may ask then how the meaning of the scene that I gained from this letter compares with the meaning it had for him who wrote it.

We may say that the observed meaning of an experience differs structurally from one conveyed by a letter. They are the focus of two very different triads. The first triad is formed by the integration of perceived objects impinging on our senses, while the second triad integrates the meaning of written words. In the first case we experience sensory qualities that cannot be gained by reading a letter. We may say that the first meaning is *immedi-*

ately experienced, while the second is *only present in thought.*

We find similar differences between various semantic triads. When I point my finger at an object I mean that object, and so this object is the meaning of my pointing finger. This relation can be expressed also verbally by naming the object at which I am pointing. But the appearance of the object is never quite the endpoint of our attention, for even when we look at a real, clearly circumscribed object, we know that it could be observed also in many other ways. In other cases the range of our attention can be altogether intangible. A stereoscopic picture is intangible and so is—to take another example—the strategy pursued by a chessplayer. In such cases our attention is not focused on an object before us, but is fixed instead on distant matters towards which our proximal experience is pointing. The less tangible is the focus, the more purely mental is its object; from a meaning that consists in an object we pass to a meaning consisting in a conception.

Thus the conflict between the view that denotative language bears on objects and the classical view, which holds that language bears on conceptions, is resolved here by admitting both possibilities and establishing a continuous transition between the two.

But to speak of conceptions evokes an ancient logical problem. The traveler who admires a landscape sees a particular image of trees, fields, rivers, and peaks, and nearer to his position he hears church bells ringing and sees villagers walking to attend service. His experience is composed of particular instances of the classes denoted by the terms "tree," "river," "peak," "church bell," "villagers," "walking," "religious service," etc., but when he *reports* the scene he is admiring, his experience will be represented in these general terms, which will not transmit the particular instances that his senses are witnessing. While these experiences will remain his private recollections, his report will convey to its reader merely a conception of the writer's experience. The question is how such a conception can apply to a multitude of disparate instances of it, so that the mention of the conception can tell that an instance of it has been observed. The ancient problem of how one general word can cover a multitude of disparate things comes back here as a problem of verbal communication.

We meet this problem in the reverse direction in the way a writer selects words for reporting on his experience. Let us now study this action. I have described the tacit process of understanding experience and that of understanding a report on an experience as two acts of *sense-reading*. In the process by which a writer picks his words for describing his experience, we meet an act of *sense-giving*. And in view of the use he makes of universal terms, we may say that this sense-giving is an act of *conceptual subsumption*, while we may call the intelligent reading of a description an act of *conceptual exemplification*.

To understand verbal communication requires therefore that we resolve the problem of universals: we must explain how a single word can apply to an aggregate of objects that differ in every particular. An attempt made by F. Waismann in 1945 to answer this question has gained wide attention. He pointed out that general terms have an "open texture," which admits differences in the instances to which it applies. But this merely shifts the question. For to ascribe "open texture" to a word is merely to imply that among an indefinitely extending series of different objects the word properly applies to some objects and not to the rest. The question how this is done remains open, exactly as before.

Kant wrote of the process of subsuming particular instances under a general term that it was "a skill so deeply hidden in the human soul that we shall hardly guess the secret that Nature here employs." The secret was indeed inaccessible so long as one looked for an *explicit procedure* to account for the subsumption of particulars under a general term, but the secret can be found in a tacit operation of the mind. Take as our paradigm the viewing of stereoscopic pictures. There is a slight but decisive difference between each pair of corresponding particulars in the two pictures, and when the two are viewed jointly, these disparities are fused to a single image possessing a novel quality. No explicit procedure can produce this integration. This is our key to the problem of general terms. Our conception of man, for example, is formed in a similar way. It arises by the tacit integration of countless experiences with different human beings: with men and women, with black, white, and yellow people; with people of all ages; people long dead and with countless others who too have reached us only by reports of them. All these encounters are included in forming the conception of man; they are all used subsidiarily with a bearing on the conception of man, which is what we denote by the word "man."

When groping for words to describe an experience, we are using this very path. We use the particulars we have seen and heard as clues to conceptions covering them and we then designate these particulars by the names of these conceptions.

Conversely, a general term can be readily used as a guide to its instances. When reading about meadows, church bells, and village folk we can readily think of possible examples of them. In a description composed of a number of general terms these will mutually restrict the range of their possible instances, and this is what a description conveys to the reader.

VII. *Nature of Meaning*

We have now explained an important example of sense-giving and a corresponding sense-reading by the powers of tacit integration. But we must yet deal with the more elementary fact that a word can mean anything at all, for example a single object. The brilliant advances of modern linguistics in phonology and generative grammar have cast no new light on the strange fact that language means something. This failure is due to the same reason which rendered the function of universals inexplicable. The relation of a word to that which it denotes is established by a tacit integration in which we rely on a subsidiary awareness of the word for directing our attention on its meaning.

We have seen how this integration deprives the word of its existence as an observed body and makes it in a way transparent. And we have also seen that the interiorization of the word and the meaning acquired through its interiorization can be wiped out by switching the focus of our attention back on the word and turning it thus once more into an opaque, meaningless object.

This is in fact what happens if we try to interpret meaning by an explicit procedure. Listen to the following formulation of this attempt by Charles Morris: "The sign vehicle itself is simply one object, and its denotation of other objects resides solely in the fact that there are rules of usage which correlate the two sets of objects."[4] This is to convert words into mere sounds and then to subject them to the operation of rules corresponding to the meaning they possessed before. But this does not work. Any rules that will operate on meaningless sounds endowing them with such powers as they would possess if they had a meaning, will be found to include actions—like pointing at something—which introduce the very kind of meaningful integration which the operation was to eliminate.

The explanation of meaning by a habitual association of sounds and objects, which has recently been renewed by W. V. O. Quine,[5] fails likewise to account for the actually observed function of words to mean something, for to observe the frequent coincidence of certain sounds with a particular sight keeps the sound and the sight equally in the focus of our attention and this necessarily keeps the sound opaque and meaningless.

The kind of meaning that the sound of a word actually conveys is destructible by switching our attention from the thing meant to that which means it; to explain such meaning we must explain its destructibility, as I have done. A positivistic analysis of meaning would evade the necessity of explaining the actual meaningfulness by offering an explicit substitute for this meaning. But this is pointless; it would be pointless even if such substitutes were feasible, which they are not.

Some writers have noticed the inequality in the status between language and the things meant by language and ascribed to this inequality the functions of meaning. Erwin Straus writes:

> That which is to function as a sign must not only be lowered in rank and value, it must be closer and more accessible to me than the designate. . . . The sign and the designated, therefore, cannot exchange their roles within a single semiotic relationship. The semiotic role belongs to a three-cornered relation if one may put it so. Only because in this world one thing is to us less important, closer, and more accessible than another, can it function for us as a sign of

4. *Foundations of the Theory of Signs* (Chicago: University of Chicago Press, 1938) , p. 24.
5. *Word and Object* (Cambridge: M.I.T. Press, 1960) .

the other. Its only purpose is to point beyond itself towards something else, to be in its own nullity a sign of *the other*. This opens up in detail a wide range of subjective interpretation. The semiotic reference is inseparable from our egocentricity, from the bodily subjection of our existence.[6]

Earlier still, Susanne K. Langer had observed the relative worthlessness of signs: ". . . little noises [she writes] are ideal conveyors of concepts, for they give us nothing but their meaning. This is the source of 'transparency' of language on which several scholars have remarked."[7]

However, words would not lose their meaning, even if cast in gold while referring to mere flies, and the content of a priceless medieval bible is the same as that of the shabbiest copy of the *same* text. Our capacity to endow language with meaning must be recognized as a particular instance of our sense-giving powers. We must realize that to use language is a performance of the same kind as our integration of visual clues for perceiving an object, or as the viewing of a stereo-picture, or our integration of muscular contractions in walking or in driving a motor car, or as the conducting of a game of chess—all of which are performed by relying on our subsidiary awareness of some things for the purpose of attending focally to a matter on which they bear. These are exercises of an integrative power which can comprehend a triad in which the person A sees a B as bearing on a C, or else uses a B for the purpose C; and these integrations can be seen to be essentially and irreducibly tacit.

VIII. *Inference—Tacit and Explicit*

Let me insert here a *caveat*. I have spoken of the two kinds of awareness comprised by tacit knowing as a lower and a higher level. But it would be a mistake to identify subsidiary awareness with subconscious or preconscious awareness or with the fringe of consciousness described by William James. When writing a letter

6. Erwin Straus, *The Primary World of Senses* (Glencoe, Ill.: Free Press, 1963; London: Collier Macmillan, 1963), Pt. II, chap. B, sect. 3, p. 149. This chapter was first published in German in 1956.
7. S. K. Langer, *Philosophy in a New Key* (New York: Mentor Books, 1941), p. 61.

I am fully aware of the pen and paper I am using. The fact that I am not focusing my attention on these particulars, but attending *from* them *to* that which they mean, reduces them to a subsidiary status, but does not render my knowledge of them subconscious or preconscious, or such as one has of an indefinable Jamesian fringe. The clues of tacit knowing and the elements of tacit performing are usually difficult to identify, and sometimes they are quite unspecifiable. Again, tacit integration may often take place effortlessly unnoticed by ourselves. But all this does not make a subsidiary state an unconscious one.

Conversely, when an integration meets with difficulties, and this evokes a deliberate effort in us, this does not make the integration any less tacit. The sailor straining his eyes to make out what he sees on the horizon, or the athlete concentrating every fiber of his body while approaching the barrier for a high jump, do not proceed by calculations. And even in the highest mathematical sciences, the pursuit of discovery is essentially a tacit operation.

It is the *function* of a subsidiary item that counts in classing it as subsidiary. We may call it its *logical function*. When I see visual clues as a coherent object, the relation between my awareness of the clues to the knowledge derived from them is similar to that between premises and conclusions derived from them: it is a logical relationship. The clues enter here into a procedure of *tacit inference*, with integration replacing deduction. The performance of a skill can also be regarded as a logical operation by regarding a skilful co-ordination of several moves as a process of construction, like the construction of a triangle from three elements. Here integration takes the place of operations by ruler and compass.

But if these claims of tacit knowing are accepted, what is left of explicit knowledge arrived at by explicit inference? If the meaning of language is the work of tacit integration, surely the same holds of mathematical formulae, and thus tacit knowledge seems to swallow up all discursive thought.

The answer is not far to seek. In my paradigm of the traveler, we have met a purely tacit knowledge of an experience; both its subsidiary and its focal awareness were tacit. At the next stage, this focal awareness of an experience was introduced subsidiarily into a communication which was a piece of explicit knowledge, the meaning of which was tacit. *All knowledge falls into one of these two classes: it is either tacit or rooted in tacit knowledge.*

The ideal of a strictly explicit knowledge is indeed self-contradictory; deprived of their tacit coefficients, all spoken words, all formulae, all maps and graphs, are strictly meaningless. An exact mathematical theory means nothing unless we recognize an inexact non-mathematical knowledge on which it bears and a person whose judgment upholds this bearing.[8]

The false ideal of a strictly explicit knowledge was pursued with greatest zeal in the twentieth century by modern positivism. The attempt of Charles Morris to identify the meaning of language in operational terms, as well as Skinner's behaviorist representation of language leading up to Quine's associationist definition of meaning, all flow from a compelling desire to eliminate any reference to a tacit structure of meaning, which is necessarily mental. The most important achievements of modern linguistics were due to turning attention to the sound of language, as best suited to an exact, objective investigation and going beyond this only in the study of formal relations underlying the grammatical structure of language. The fact that language is nothing unless it has conscious meaning was set aside as a temporary difficulty for modern strictly empirical linguistics.

However, a distinct tendency to break with strict empiricism and to revive the classical conception of language, which recognizes the mental character of meaning, has been expressed recently by Noam Chomsky,[9] and my present study supports this by showing that speech has the fundamental structure of all meaningful uses of consciousness in animals and men.

IX. *The Dynamics of Tacit Knowing*

I shall now turn to two problems of linguistics defined by Chomsky, who regards them as crucial.

8. *T.D.*, p. 21.
9. Of his own "generative grammar" Chomsky writes that "its roots are firmly in traditional linguistics." Noam Chomsky, *Current Issues in Linguistic Theory* (The Hague: Mouton, 1964), p. 20.

1) "It seems plain (writes Chomsky) that language acquisition is based on the child's discovery of what from a formal point of view is a deep and abstract theory—a generative grammar of his language—many of the concepts and principles of which are only remotely related to experience by long and intricate chains of unconscious quasi-inferential steps."[10] The question is how the child can possibly discover the highly sophisticated generative grammar of his language.

2) Another great problem is "the fundamental fact about the normal use of language, namely the speaker's ability to produce and understand instantly new sentences that are not similar to those previously heard in any physically defined sense . . . nor obtainable from them by any sort of 'generalisation' known to psychology or philosophy."[11]

Of the grounds on which language is learnt, Chomsky writes: "The language-acquisition device is only one component of the total system of intellectual structures that can be applied to problem solving and concept formation; in other words, the *faculté de langage* is only one of the faculties of the mind."[12] But he goes no further in defining these faculties. My view is that the use of language is a tacit performance; the meaning of language arises, as many other kinds of meaning do, in tacitly integrating hitherto meaningless acts into a bearing on a focus that thereby becomes their meaning. I would try to trace back the roots of this faculty to primordial achievements of living things. All animals are capable of tacitly integrating their bodily actions; indeed, meaningful integration can be found in the very process of coherent growth. But I shall refer here only to the intelligent forms of this power, as exercised by the higher animals.

Lashley has demonstrated in a famous experiment the powers of 'latent' learning in animals. When a rat, trained to run a maze, was severely mutilated, including blinding its eyes, the animal still succeeded in finding its way—however clumsily—through the maze. Mutilated rats performing this feat invoked unhesitat-

10. Noam Chomsky, *Aspects of the Theory of Syntax* (Cambridge, Mass.: M.I.T. Press, 1965) , p. 57.
11. *Ibid.*
12. *Ibid.*, p. 56.

ingly muscles and senses not used before in learning to run the
maze and thus improvised a totally unprecedented integration of
their bodies. Such instantaneous practical integrations are
matched in the conceptual powers of animals by which they
recognize disparate individuals of a species. They instantly identify very different specimens of a class, e.g., different human
beings.

We can see here in the behavior of animals the sources of man's
power promptly to utter or understand unprecedented sentences.
This relationship was observed a number of years ago by G. H.
Humphrey, who even then aligned the capacity to express knowledge on an unlimited variety of spoken terms with the capacity of
a rat to manifest its knowledge of a maze in an unlimited number
of different actions.[13]

But the mere kinship of man's linguistic performances with a
rat's varied expressions of its understanding of a maze cannot
satisfy us here. We must acknowledge the fact that speech is the
application of complex rules of phonetics and grammar and must
show how the theory of tacit knowing accounts for the acquisition and practice of such rules.

Our knowledge of linguistic rules and our application of them
in speech is commonly called an unconscious knowledge applied
unconsciously. I shall call it a subsidiary knowledge and call its
application a tacit integration. The difference is essential. To say
that we are subsidiarily aware of a thing or action is to attribute
to it a particular function, namely, a bearing on its meaning,
which is at the focus of our attention. The level of consciousness
at which we are aware of a subsidiary particular may vary over
the whole range of possible levels. Some subsidiary things,
like the processes in our inner ear, of which we are aware in feeling the position of our head, are profoundly unconscious, strictly
subliminal. But we are not unconscious of a pointing finger the
direction of which we are following, nor of the features of a face
that we are seeking to recognize, nor of the paper and pen used
with a bearing on the content of a written message we are
composing. A pianist who, having improved his touch on the keys

13. G. H. Humphrey, *Thinking* (London: Methuen, 1951), p. 262.

by a spell of finger practice, integrates this skill to his musical performances, has rendered his awareness of it subsidiary, but still feels the working of his fingers. He has not lost consciousness of it.

I have said that to switch our attention to a subsidiary particular deprives it of its meaning. Such action admittedly does make us more fully conscious of such a particular, but its loss of meaning is due not to this but to the accompanying loss of its subsidiary functions. This is how generative grammar appears to us when set out in formal, explicit terms. To look at these formulae does not make them work as they do when we rely on their guidance for putting something into words. Our task is now to discover how such rules are developed within our subsidiary awareness and how they perform their functions from this subsidiary condition in controlling the behavior on which they bear.

I shall take as my first example a skill by which a person does no more than carry out a purpose of utmost simplicity, and yet cannot do so, except by the use of a skill implemented by subsidiary operations.[14] If you put on spectacles which make you see things upside down—or inverted between right and left—you feel completely lost. You are unable to use your hands or to walk about the room. Yet you seem to have a perfect solution to your problem. It is obvious that what you see above you through upside-down spectacles is really below you—while what you see below you is in fact above you; and with horizontally inverting spectacles, what you see on your right is at your left and vice versa. But this prescription, which appears to be all you have to know, is useless: it does not prevent you from responding to what you falsely see.

By contrast, a persistent effort to find one's way while wearing inverting spectacles will correct the inversion. Stratton first discovered this fact in 1896 and after eight days overcame the upside-down glasses he was wearing. Other observers have confirmed this result; but for half a century and more it was almost universally misinterpreted as the reversal of the visual image.

14. A similar, somewhat briefer, account of the following illustration was given in my "The Creative Imagination," *Chemical and Engineering News,* XLIV (1966), 85-93.

Even today it is little known that the observations of Snyder and Pronko (1952) [15] and of Kottenhoff (1961) [16] have proved that the position of the visual image remains inverted when the subject has learned to move around with inverting spectacles. Kottenhoff has shown that the subject gets to find his way around because he has acquired *a new way of seeing things*, which appropriately co-ordinates his inverted vision with his muscular feelings, his sense of balance, and his hearing.[17] This reintegration of sense impressions produces a novel sensory quality to which the usual terms of "upside down or right way up" or "right or left" do not apply. A subject wearing right-left inverting glasses will say that "depending on whether I attend more to my hand or to the rest of the visual field, I would ascribe to it the quality of rightness or leftness."[18] Kottenhoff writes that at this stage "the question whether something is to the right or to the left was felt to be rather annoying."[19] Snyder and Pronko[20] observed the same tendency to confusion as follows. The subject, wearing upside-down inverting spectacles, "was observing the scene from a tall building. Suddenly someone asked, 'Well, how do things look to you? Are they upside down?' The subject replied, 'I wish you hadn't asked me. Now, when I recall how they *did* look *before* I put on these lenses, I must answer that they look upside down *now*. But until the moment that you asked me I was absolutely unaware of it and hadn't given a thought to the question whether things were right-side-up or upside-down.' "

Thus, not only was the obvious explicit interpretation of the

---

15. F. W. Snyder and N. H. Pronko, *Vision with Spatial Inversion* (Wichita, Kansas: University of Wichita Press, 1952).

16. Heinrich Kottenhoff, *Was ist Richtiges Sehen mit Umkehrbrillen und in welchem Sinne stellt sich das Sehen um?* (English translation: "What Is Right Seeing with Inverting Spectacles and in What Sense Is Seeing Re-inverted?"), *Psychologia Universalis*, V (1961) (Vlg. Anton Hain, Meisenheim am Glan). Kottenhoff's enquiry was carried out as a doctoral dissertation in the Institute of Experimental Psychology of the University of Innsbruck under Professor Th. Erisman. It was completed in 1956.

17. G. M. Stratton, *Psychological Rev.*, IV (1897), 341-360, 463-481, does *not* claim that the right way of seeing with inverting spectacles (achieved after eight days) consists in the turning back of the visual image. He identifies the result with "upright vision," for, he says, "the real meaning of upright vision" is a "harmony between touch and sight."

18. Kottenhoff, *op. cit.*, p. 78.

19. *Ibid.*, p. 80, also p. 64 *et passim*.

20. Snyder and Pronko *op. cit.*, p. 113.

inverted images useless, but it was disturbing to remember it. The reason being, as Kottenhoff observes, that these corrections use the words "right," "left," "up," and "down," which refer to the normal integration of sensory data and thus confirmed this integration just when it had to be discarded and replaced by a novel integration.

Explicit directions for correcting the vision presented by inverting spectacles are ineffectual then for two reasons. First, they do not tell us that we have to reintegrate our senses; on the contrary they confirm their normal integration and hinder their reintegration; second, even if some rule did tell us what we have to do, this would be useless, since we cannot directly control the integration of our senses.

What is it then that brings about the solution? What causes a process of reintegration to take place, of which we have no focal knowledge, and which we could not carry out in response to such knowledge even if we had it? The process does not take place spontaneously: it is the result of a protracted, sometimes strenuous, effort. We try to see rightly, and it is established by all observers that only sustained practical efforts to find one's way about will lead to success. Kottenhoff analyzes this effort in two parts. (1) The attempt to revise the meaning of the inverted image in the sense of our tacit experiences. (2) The attempt to extend this reinterpretation to the surroundings of the field of vision. For we must comprehensively revise *our visual ideas* in the sense of our reintegrated vision, if the revision is to be stable.[21]

We must conclude then that it is the effort of our imagination, seeking to reinterpret our vision in a way that will control the scene before us, which produces the right way of seeing inverted images. This is *the dynamics of tacit knowing*: the *questing imagination vaguely anticipating experiences not yet grounded in subsidiary particulars evokes these subsidiaries and thus implements the experience the imagination has sought to achieve.*

This principle has already been touched upon above when I spoke of the way we integrate the muscles moving our limbs,

21. Kottenhoff *op. cit.,* p. 111.

without any focal knowledge of this muscular performance. This was first described by William James as the structure of all voluntary motion, and he also observed that it was set in motion by the imagination striving to anticipate the result of the action. It would seem that we can move our body only indirectly by thrusting forward our imagination, which then evokes subsidiarily the means of its own implementation.

Another simple example of tacit dynamics will illustrate its principles further. Think of the way we keep our balance when riding a bicycle. The cyclist counteracts at every moment his accidental imbalance by turning the bicycle into a curve having a radius proportional to the square of his velocity divided by the angle of his imbalance. This rule, explicitly stated, is useless in learning to ride a bicycle. Most people would not understand it, and even if they did, there would be no way of focally sensing the particulars to which it refers, and no way of directly controlling them. The practice of this rule can be acquired and kept operating only subsidiarily; the cyclist can have only a theoretical knowledge of it and no focal experience of practicing it.

We can see here clearly the work of the imagination by which a practical knowledge of focally ineffectual rules is acquired. The learner's imagination is fixed on the aim of keeping his balance, and this effort of the imagination implements its aim by subsidiarily evoking an observance of the rules that secure the cyclist's equilibrium.

This broadly answers the first problem of linguistics I quoted from Chomsky. To the question of how a child can learn to perform a vast set of complex rules, intelligible only to a handful of experts, we can reply that the striving imagination has the power to implement its aim by the subsidiary practice of ingenious rules of which the subject remains focally ignorant.

This kind of rule can be acquired tacitly and *only* tacitly and it can also be practiced *only* tacitly. The elaborate systems of grammar discovered by linguists in the speech of "the idealized native speaker" belong to this class of rules.

The second fundamental question of linguistics, how we can instantly understand and produce totally novel sentences, can also be readily answered now. For in riding a bicycle we do something quite similar. We keep our balance at each moment by applying the equilibrium equation to ever new sets of values taken on by its variables. The cyclist's striving imagination, which has discovered within a few weeks a whole tacit system of balancing, may well be credited with the performance of instantly reapplying this system to new conditions. The *faculté de langage*, which can discover a whole system of tacit grammar, might be credited likewise with evaluating it instantly for meeting any new case for its application.

X. *Heuristics and Language Acquisition*

My scheme of tacit dynamics is obviously incomplete; the self implementation of the imagination of which I have spoken must have limits. My white hair will not turn black however assiduously I strain my imagination to accomplish this. There must be some principle which excludes mere fancies and selects feasible, or at least possibly feasible, tasks for the imagination to strive for.

We meet this principle of reasonable endeavor in the scientist's choice of a problem. But I shall approach this matter indirectly by looking first at the way a bright idea emerges to solve a scientific problem. Discovery takes place in two more or less separate stages, an arduous straining of the imagination is followed by a virtually spontaneous appearance of the solution. In his classic study of heuristics, Poincaré has described cases in which these two phases were sharply separated: the effort of the imagination had ceased for several hours when the bright idea turned up. Poincaré thinks that first a strenuous search loosens possible bits of a solution and that discovery is then achieved by an effortless integration of these bits. He calls this integration an illumination; I shall name it intuition.

Intuition, as I understand it, ranges widely. It stands for integrative acts taking place at any stage of a scientific inquiry, from start to finish. The scientist's intuitive powers consist first in the faculty for surmising with a fair degree of probability the presence of a hidden coherence in nature. It is this faculty that espies a problem, the pursuit of which the scientist may accept as his task. The inquiry goes ahead then, guided by a series of surmises, which also have a reasonable chance of being right. Thus a discovery is reached—or may be reached—which solves the problem.

Poincaré emphasizes that illumination does not come without the previous work of the imagination. This applies also to what I call intuition. A problem fit for inquiry comes to the scientist in response to his roaming vision of yet undiscovered possibilities. Having chosen a problem, he thrusts his imagination forward in search of clues and the material he thus digs up—whether by speculation or experiment—is integrated by intuition into new surmises; and so the inquiry goes on to the end.

But the kind of intuition which starts off a successful inquiry, and then serves to guide it, differs somewhat from the final integration of the solution which Poincaré has called illumination. To start on an inquiry that may take years of effort and consume all his current resources—and to repeat such enterprises throughout his professional life—the scientist must be sure that a problem on which he enters has a fair chance of being well founded. A good problem must not only tell him the probable presence of something hidden in a certain direction in nature, but also assess the chances of reaching this hidden truth and anticipate with a reasonable degree of reliability whether the result will be worth the time, effort, and money that will be needed for finding it. This requirement is conspicuous in the pursuit of technical inventions, for practical advantage is central here, but it is important also for the pursuit of the natural science.

One might try to recognize the kind of clues that will lead to a hidden coherence in nature. Many successful scientific inquiries have started from an unexplained regularity in nature, but others, on the contrary, from an unexplained deviation from regularity or from any strange unexplained phenomenon. Others again have started from an apparent conflict between two established principles, and some, on the contrary, from the apparent chance of deriving one principle from another. In any case, such clues can merely offer a possible occasion for discovery: they do not tell us how to make a discovery. For this one must either discover a problem that no one has yet sighted, or hit upon new ways for solving a known problem. The scientist who achieves this is usually not better placed than others, but he is more gifted. He possesses to an exceptional degree the faculty for integrating signs of potentialities, a faculty that we may call the power of *anticipatory intuition*.

Compare this with the *final intuition* that Poincaré called illumination. A final intuition is a claim to discovery and is thus at the point of being proved true or mistaken, while a problem—a feat of anticipatory intuition—can usually be justified only after a long and uncertain pursuit. Both a problem and a suggested solution are in the nature of surmises, but they differ in their degrees of explicitness. A suggested solution can usually be clearly communicated and its convincing power be transmitted to others, for its grounds are largely tangible. By contrast, a problem—or any other surmise arising in the course of an inquiry—is difficult to explain to others, let alone to make convincing to them, for its grounds are mainly unspecifiable.

From the inception of an inquiry to its successful conclusion intuitive judgments become progressively more concrete, more fully grounded in focally observed evidence, but this should not obscure the essential kinship of heuristics and verification. For if this be lost sight of, we can understand neither the logic of scientific inquiry nor the grounds on which a discovery is accepted.

We have arrived now at the mechanism by which the imagination implements its aims, as purified and guided by intuition. Intuition thus fills the gap I left open in my previous section on the dynamics of tacit knowing. After this it is easy to fill the part of intuition also in such sensorimotor feats as the mastering of inverted vision, or learning to ride a bicycle; we need not pursue this here.

But let me introduce a further feature of tacit dynamics that comes out most clearly in sensorimotor achievements. To learn a skill or to invent one, whether a skill of the senses or of the muscles, is an essentially coherent task. It sets out to solve a coherent problem, and any progress towards its mastery will but fill in the body of this anticipatory outline. Random trial and

INTELLECT AND HOPE

error unguided by such a perspective will never add up to a skilful performance.

This applies also to the progress of a scientific or technical inquiry. A steady unity of purpose, sustained from start to finish, is perhaps more marked in practical research, the aim of which is set from the start and is rarely modified in the course of its pursuit. But any initial clues of a purely scientific inquiry—of which I have listed examples in my list of possible problems— usually determines the framework of the enterprise from beginning to end. We shall find a similar persistence of basic ideas prevailing in the course of language achievement.

Let me start by applying this mechanism of imagination-cum-intuition to the production of a single sentence. In his contribution to the *Hixon Symposium* of 1948, entitled "The Problem of Serial Behavior," K. S. Lashley shows that associative chain theories fail to explain the production of a spoken sentence. He describes what actually happens.[22] Prior to the internal or overt enunciation of the sentence, an aggregate of word units is partially activated or readied. This shows in the fact that words, destined for a sentence, may be found scrambled in a hasty utterance of it. I regard this as the period described by Poincaré in which the imagination loosens potential elements for solving a problem. Given sufficient time for intuitive reorganization, this would lead to a solution in the form of a correct sentence, but in a premature utterance the words will come out in disorder.

This mechanism explains in general the formation of a time sequence, each item of which is related to all the others by their joint meaning. This was in fact the general problem raised and left open by Lashley in his contribution to the *Hixon Symposium*.

We can now approach at last the question, how language is acquired by the child. Rejecting current attempts to explain language acquisition by the assumption of behavioral psychology, Noam Chomsky writes:

> The real problem is that of developing a hypothesis about initial structure that is sufficiently rich to account for acqui-

22. At p. 119.

sition of language, yet not so rich as to be inconsistent with the known diversity of language.[23]

The dynamics of tacit knowing has made this problem more manageable. We are no longer faced with the question of how people who learn to speak a language can identify, remember, and apply a set of complex rules known only to linguists. They do not identify these rules, let alone memorize and explicitly apply them, and do not need to do so. According to the dynamics of tacit knowing, the rules are acquired subsidiarily, without focal knowledge of them.

But this dynamics must be kept moving by the combination of intuition and imagination. We have met this combination of imagination-cum-intuition at work in the utterance of a single sentence, and we may add now that such utterances, as well as the intelligent listening to a spoken sentence, can make a contribution to the development of language.

A sentence spoken during childhood and adolescence will not infrequently include a word never used before and thus expand the speaker's vocabulary. The same happens when taking in the meaning of a sentence—be it heard or read—if it contains words not met before. Moreover, with this growth of the vocabulary, the clarity of understanding and the precision in using speech will continue to improve. The moment more than a minimum of words is used, some rules of grammar emerge and increase in range and complexity as the speaker's vocabulary expands further, while the observance of grammatical rules will become ever more precise.[24]

This type of language acquisition can of course only proceed from one stage of language to the next. But even so, its range is immense. It extends from the first babbled morpheme used as a word-sentence and from the child's response to similar sounds used by adults, to the eventual mastery of literary language and culture. From its very start, it takes up the problem which will guide its quest throughout—the task of improving communica-

23. Chomsky, *Aspects of the Theory of Syntax,* p. 58.
24. This is true in general for the discovery or learning of skills. New principles make their appearance first in mere tendencies which are then sharpened and eventually consolidated.

tion. The growth of the vocabulary and the acquisition of ever more complex and subtle grammatical rules are both actuated by the imaginative search for further enrichment and greater precision of communication. Symbolic sense-giving and sense-reading are striven for ever further, as the twin powers of intuition and imagination work towards this from start to finish.

The manifest parallelism of this conception to the heuristics of science and technology is clear. To apply it more closely, we may note that pure science discovering meaning in nature is a pursuit of *sense-reading*, while technical invention which makes things into instruments for a set purpose is a *sense-giving*. Thus a language achievement that develops a rudimentary beginning of language to its fullness bears analogies to the pursuit of scientific discovery combined with technical inventions.

But I would liken language achievement rather *to a sequence of advances* in a basic problem of science or technology. Think of the consecutive discoveries of classical mechanics extending over more than two centuries from Galileo to Hamilton; or of the successive inventions which improved the airplane from the first model of the Wright brothers to the giant supersonic machine about to be constructed today—these consistent creative developments of a single idea may offer a paradigm of the way a mature language is formed from its rudimentary beginnings by successive stages of a growing intelligence.

But we must yet take a look at the previous development of the infant which leads from empty babbling to rudimentary speech. The child's discovery of symbolic sense-giving and sense-reading arises within a multitude of parallel achievements. His imagination is at work from the start exploring the nature of the things he is encountering. The conception of enduring objects is formed, along with the knowledge of persons. New skills of crawling, standing, and walking and the use of objects for various purposes are mastered. Within such ceaseless action of sense-reading and sense-giving, the child may well come to feel puzzled by the talking of adults and also sense the possibility of making himself better understood by imitating them. This should set his heuristic powers at work.

This rough sketch of the way language may arise in the midst of the earliest growth of human intelligence must suffice here. But there is an ancient question to which I must yet respond. If language is rooted in primitive faculties which we share with the higher animals, why can animals neither invent language nor learn to speak? An ape can learn to ride a bicycle, tacitly discovering ingenious operations that might well rival in complexity those used by small children when they speak. Why can the ape be so clever at one thing and not at another?

Note first that the tacit acquisition of an ingenious operation is no mark of high intelligence; the proper standard is the degree of abstraction presented by a problem. The cycling ape has his problem of keeping his balance right in front of him and he has the clues to solve the problem too within his immediate experience. Not so the child. His problem, both to discover what adults mean by talking and to learn to address them in similar terms, is a highly speculative enterprise that transcends by far the child's immediate experience. Animals cannot master such abstract problems, and this explains why animals have not invented language as man has, nor can even learn to speak, as children do.

When language is understood as tacit knowing, and the acquisition of language is accordingly explained by the dynamics of tacit knowing, man's linguistic powers appear to be due simply to his higher general intelligence.

A BIBLIOGRAPHY OF MICHAEL POLANYI'S SOCIAL AND PHILOSOPHICAL WRITINGS[1]

compiled by
Richard L. Gelwick

Books and Brochures

Beyond Nihilism. London: Cambridge University Press, 1960. The Eddington Lecture, Cambridge University, 1960.

The Contempt of Freedom. London: Watts and Company, 1940.

The Foundations of Academic Freedom. Society for Freedom in Science, Occasional Pamphlet No. 6, 1947.

Full Employment and Free Trade. Cambridge: Cambridge University Press, 1945.

Handbook to the Film Unemployment and Money, 1938.

   Supplement to a film by Michael Polanyi prepared with the assistance of Miss Mary Field, Mr. R. Jeffryes, and Professor J. Jewkes.

The Logic of Liberty. Chicago: University of Chicago Press, 1951; London: Routledge and Kegan Paul, 1951.

Personal Knowledge. Chicago: University of Chicago Press, 1958; London: Routledge and Kegan Paul, 1958; New York: Harper Torchbooks, 1964.

   Contains, with additions and revisions, the Gifford Lectures, 1951–52.

The Planning of Science. Society for Freedom in Science, Occasional Pamphlet No. 4, 1946.

---

1. A bibliography of scientific papers compiled by John Polanyi may be found in *The Logic of Personal Knowledge* (Glencoe, Illinois: The Free Press, 1961), pp. 239-247.

Pure and Applied Science and Their Appropriate Forms of Organization. Society for Freedom in Science, Occasional Pamphlet No. 14, 1953.

Rights and Duties of Science. Society for Freedom in Science, Occasional Pamphlet No. 2, 1945.

Science, Faith and Society. Chicago: University of Chicago Press, 1946; London: Oxford University Press, 1946; Chicago: Phoenix Books, 1964.

The Riddell Memorial Lectures, University of Durham, 1945.

The Study of Man. Chicago: University of Chicago Press, 1959; London: Routledge and Kegan Paul, 1959; Chicago: Phoenix Books, 1964.

The Lindsay Memorial Lectures, University College of North Staffordshire, 1958.

The Tacit Dimension. Garden City, New York: Doubleday and Company, 1966.

The Terry Lectures, Yale University, 1962.

USSR Economics. Manchester: Manchester University Press, 1935.

Articles Appearing in Books

"Beyond Nihilism," *History and Hope,* ed. K. A. Jelenski. New York: A. Praeger, 1962. Pp. 17-35; and *Crisis and Continuity in World Politics,* ed. George A. Lanyi and Wilson C. McWilliams. Random House, 1966. Pp. 214-227.

"Clues to an Understanding of Mind and Body," *The Scientist Speculates,* ed. I. J. Good. London: Heinemann, 1962. Pp. 71-78.

Commentary on "The Genesis of the Special Theory of Relativity," by Adolph Grünbaum, *Current Issues in the Philosophy of Science,* ed. Herbert Feigl and Grover Maxwell. New York: Holt, Rinehart and Winston, 1961. Pp. 53-55.

Commentary on "The Uses of Dogmatism in Science," by Thomas Kuhn, *The Structure of Scientific Change,* ed. A. C. Crombie. London: Heinemann, 1962. Pp. 375-380.

"The Foundations of Freedom in Science," *Physical Science and*

Human Values, ed. E. P. Wigner. Princeton: Princeton University Press, 1947. Pp. 124-132; "Discussion," pp. 132-143.

"John Dalton's Theory," *L. Farkas Memorial Volume,* ed. Adalert Farkas and E. P. Wigner. Jerusalem: Research Council of Israel, 1952. Pp. 13-15.

"My Time with X-Rays and Crystals," *Fifty Years of X-Ray Diffraction,* ed. P. P. Ewald. Utrecht: N. V. A. Oosthoek's Uitgeversmaatschaapij, 1962. Pp. 629-636.

"A Postscript," *History and Hope,* ed. K. A. Jelenski. New York: A. Praeger, 1962. Pp. 185-196.

"Preface," *Science and Freedom*: Proceedings of a Conference Convened by the Congress for Cultural Freedom, Hamburg, 1953. London: Martin Secker and Warburg, 1955. Pp. 9-11.

"Profits and Private Enterprise," *Economic Problems in a Free Society.* London: Central Joint Advisory Committee on Tutorial Classes, 1948. Pp. 50-62.

"Pure and Applied Science and Their Appropriate Forms of Organization," *Science and Freedom*: Proceedings of a Conference Convened by the Congress for Cultural Freedom, Hamburg, 1953. London: Martin Secker and Warburg, 1955. Pp. 36-46.

"Science and Man's Place in the Universe," *Science as a Cultural Force,* ed. Harry Woolf. Baltimore: Johns Hopkins Press, 1964. Pp. 54-76.

Articles and Papers[1]

1935

"U.S.S.R. Economics—Fundamental Data, System and Spirit," *The Manchester School,* VI (November 2, 1935), 67-89.

1936

"The Struggle between Truth and Propaganda," *The Manchester School of Economic and Social Studies,* VII (1936), 105-118.

1. Most of the published articles and all of the unpublished papers listed here are available on microfilm in the *Collected Articles and Papers of Michael Polanyi,* compiled by Richard L. Gelwick (Berkeley: Pacific School of Religion, 1963).

"The Value of the Inexact," *Philosophy of Science*, III (April, 1936), 233-234.
  Letter to the editor.

1937

"Congrès du Palais de la Découverte," *Nature*, CXL (October 23, 1937), 710.

1938

"The 'Settling Down' of Capital and the Trade Cycle," *The Manchester School*, IX (November, 1938), 153-169.

1939

"Rights and Duties of Science," *The Manchester School of Economic and Social Studies*, X (October, 1939), 175-193. Published also 1945.

1940

"Economics on the Screen," *Documentary News Letter*, August, 1940.
"Economics by Motion Symbols," *The Review of Economic Studies*, VIII (October, 1940), 1-19.
"Science in U.S.S.R.," *The New Statesman and Nation*, XIX (February 10, 1940), 174.

1941

"Cultural Significance of Science," *Nature*, CXLVII (January 25, 1941), 119.
"Extract From a Letter of 27th June, 1941, "First Statement in 1941 on the principle of deficit spending—a reply to a memorandum circulated by the cabinet officers. (Jewekes–Robbins).
"The Growth of Thought in Society," *Economica*, VIII (November, 1941), 428-456.

1942

"The Revaluation of Science," *The Manchester Guardian*, November 7, 1942. Letter to the Editor.

1943

"The Autonomy of Science," *Memoirs and Proceedings of the Manchester Literary and Philosophical Society,* LXXXV (February, 1943). Published also 1945.

"The English and the Continent," *The Political Quarterly,* XIV (October–December, 1943), 372-381. Published also 1944.

"The Hungarian Opposition," *The New Statesman and Nation,* XXVI (September 25, 1943), 216-217.

"Jewish Problems," *The Political Quarterly,* XIV (January–March, 1943), 33-45.

"The Obligations of our Heritage," *The Christian News-Letter,* December 15, 1943.

"Research and Planning," *Nature,* CLII (August 21, 1943), 217-218.

1944

"England and the Continent," *Fortune,* XXIX (May, 1944), 155-157, 178, 182, 185. Published also 1943.

"Patent Reform," *The Review of Economic Studies,* XI (Summer, 1944), 61-76.

"Reflections on John Dalton," *The Manchester Guardian,* July 22, 1944, pp. 13-15.

"Science and the Decline of Freedom," *The Listener,* June 1, 1944, p. 599.

"Science—Its Reality and Freedom," *The Nineteenth Century,* CXXXV (February, 1944), 78-83.

1945

"The Autonomy of Science," *The Scientific Monthly,* LX (February, 1945), 141-150. Published also 1943.

"The Planning of Science," *The Political Quarterly,* XVI (October–December, 1945), 316-326.

"Reform of the Patent Law in Britain," *Nature,* CLVI (July 14, 1945), 54.

"Science and the Modern Crisis," *Science, The Universities and the Modern Crisis,* from Vol. LXXXVI of "Memoirs and Proceedings of the Manchester Literary and Philosophical

Society," Sessions 1943-45, Published: Manchester, June, 1945. Pp. 7-16.

1946

"Can Science Bring Peace," *The Listener,* April 25, 1946.

"Civitas: A Proposed New Quarterly," Journal to be published by The Manchester Literary and Philosophical Society, circulated privately as a memorandum, 1946.

"Free Trade Through Full Employment," *University Liberal,* III (December, 1946), 1-2.

"Policy of Atomic Science," *Time and Tide,* August 10, 1946, p. 749.

"Re-Dedication of Science in Germany," *Nature,* CLVIII (July 13, 1946), 66.

"Science: Academic and Industrial," *Universities Quarterly,* 1946.

"Social Capitalism," *Time and Tide,* April 13, 1946, pp. 341-342.

"Social Message of Pure Science," *The Advancement of Science,* No. 12 (April, 1946).

"Soviets and Capitalism: What is the Difference?" *Time and Tide,* April 6, 1946, p. 317.

"Why Profits," *The Plain View,* No. 8 (July, 1946), pp. 197-208.

1947

"The Foundations of Freedom in Science," *The Nineteenth Century,* CXLI (April, 1947), 163-167.

"Old Tasks and New Hopes," *Time and Tide,* January 4, 1947, pp. 5-6.

"Organization of Universities I," *Time and Tide,* July 19, 1947, p. 777.

"Organization of Universities II," *Time and Tide,* July 26, 1947, pp. 802-803.

"Science: Observation and Belief," *Humanitas,* I (February, 1947), 10-15.

"What Kind of Crisis?" *Time and Tide,* October 4, 1947, pp. 1056-1058.

"What to Believe," *Credere Aude,* I (December, 1947), 9-10.

1948

"Ought Science to Be Planned?, The Case for Individualism," *The Listener,* September 16, 1948.

"The Place of Universities in the Community," *The Advancement of Science,* V (April, 1948) , 13-15.

"Planning and Spontaneous Order," *The Manchester School,* XVI (September, 1948) , 237-268.

"The Universities Today," *The Adelphi,* XXIV (January–March, 1948) , 98-101.

1949

"The Authority of the Free Society," *The Nineteenth Century,* CXLVI (December, 1949) , 347-360.

"The Nature of Scientific Convictions," *The Nineteenth Century,* CXLVI (July, 1949) , 14-28.

1950

"Economic and Intellectual Liberties," *Zeitschrift Für Die Gesamte Staatswissenschaft,* CVI (3 Heft, 1950) , 411-447.

"Scientific Beliefs," *Ethics,* LXI (October, 1950) , 27-37.

"Der Glaube an die Wissenschaft," *Physikalische Blätter,* Jahrgang VI (Heft 8, 1950) , 337-349.

"The Logic of Liberty: Perils of Inconsistency," *Measure,* I (Fall, 1950) , 348-362.

1951

"Autorität und Freiheit in der Wissenschaft," *Physikalische Blätter,* Jahrgang VII (Heft 3, 1951) , 97-102.

"Die Freiheit der Wissenschaft," *Physikalische Blätter,* Jahrgang VII (Heft 2, 1951) , 49-55.

"The Hypothesis of Cybernetics," *The British Journal for the Philosophy of Science,* II (February, 1951) , 312-315.

"Totalitarianism," review of Hannah Arendt, *Origins of Totalitarianism, Time and Tide,* August 25, 1951, pp. 801-802.

1952

"Skills and Connoisseurship," *Atti Del Congresse di Metodologia,* Torino (December 17-20, 1952) .

"The Stability of Beliefs," *The British Journal for the Philosophy of Science,* III (November, 1952) , 217-232.

"Science and Faith," *Question,* V (Winter, 1952) , 16-36, 37-45. Published also as "Science and Conscience," 1953.

1953

"Protests and Problems," *Bulletin of the Atomic Scientists,* IX (November, 1953) , 322, 340.

"Science and Conscience," *Religion in Life,* XXIII (Winter, 1953-1954) , 47-58. Published also as "Science and Faith," 1952.

"A Theory of Poetry," from a letter dated May 19, 1953.

1954

"On the Introduction of Science into Moral Subjects," *The Cambridge Journal,* VII (January, 1954) , 195-207.

1955

"From Copernicus to Einstein," *Encounter,* V (September, 1955) , 1-10.

"On the Limits of Economic Planning" (Intervention at the Milan Conference, September, 1955). (Mimeographed.) 2 pp.

"On Liberalism and Liberty," *Encounter,* IV (March, 1955) , 29-34.

"Strategy of Freedom," The Future of Freedom: An International Conference Sponsored by the Congress for Cultural Freedom, Milan, 1955. (Typewritten.)

"Words, Conceptions and Science," *The Twentieth Century,* CLVIII (September, 1955) , 256-267.

1956

"Ethics and the Scientist," *The Bulletin of the Institute of Physics,* (July, 1956) , pp. 1-21.

"The Magic of Marxism," *Bulletin of the Atomic Scientists,* XII (June, 1956) , 211-215, 232. Published also in *Encounter,* VII (December, 1956) , 5-17.

"Passion and Controversy in Science," *The Lancet,* CCLXX (June 16, 1956), 921-924. Published also 1957.

"Pure and Applied Science and Their Appropriate Forms of Organization," *Dialectica,* X (September, 1956), 231-241.

"This Age of Discovery," *The Twentieth Century,* CLIX (March, 1956), 227-234.

1957

"Beauty, Elegance and Reality in Science," *Symposium on Observation and Interpretation,* Bristol, April 1, 1957, pp. 102-106.

"The Foolishness of History: November, 1917—November 1957," *Encounter,* IX (November, 1957), 33-37.

"Passion and Controversy in Science," *Bulletin of the Atomic Scientists,* XIII (April, 1957), 114-119. Published also 1956.

"Problem Solving," *The British Journal for the Philosophy of Science,* VIII (August, 1957), 89-103.

"Scientific Outlook: Its Sickness and Its Cure," *Science,* CXXV (March, 1957), 480-504.

1958

"Apartheid and the World's Universities," *Science and Freedom,* No. 10, June 10, 1958.

"The Impact of Science," unpublished, University of Manchester, June 27.

"Die Magie des Marxismus," *Der Monat,* XI Jahrgang, Heft 123 (December, 1958) pp. 3-15. Published also 1956.

"On Biased Coins and Related Problems," *Zeitschrift für Physikalische Chemie,* Neue Folge, Frankfurter Ausgabe, XV (April, 1958), 290-296.

"The Outlook of Science: Its Sickness and Cure," lecture at Austin, Texas, November, 1958. (Typewritten.)

"Tyranny and Freedom, Ancient and Modern," *Quest,* Calcutta, 1958.

1959

"The Organization of Science and the Claim to Academic Freedom," *Science and Freedom,* No. 13 (November, 1959), pp. 1-9.

Review of *Darwin and the Darwinian Revolution,* by G. Himmelfarb, *The New Leader,* August 31, 1959, p. 24.
"The Two Cultures," *Encounter,* XIII (September, 1959), 1-4.

1960

"Beyond Nihilism," *Encounter,* XIV (March, 1960), 34-43.
Congress for Cultural Freedom, closing address, Berlin, June
22, 1960.
Congress Lyceum, speech delivered at a dinner given by the
Congress, *Quest,* Bombay, December, 1960.
"Le Comte du Noüy Foundation Award to Michael Polanyi,"
acceptance speech, *The Christian Scholar,* XLIII (March,
1960), 57-58.
"Freedom and Responsibility," *Science and Freedom,* No. 11,
April 12, 1960.
"Morals—A Product of Evolution," review of C. H. Wadding-
ton's *The Ethical Animal* (George Allen and Unwin), *The
New Scientist,* December 22, 1960, pp. 1666-1667.
"On the Use of International Seminars," Cairo, December, 1960.
(Mimeographed.)
Review of *The Phenomenon of Man,* by Pierre Teilhard de
Chardin, *Saturday Review,* XLIII (January 30, 1960), 21.
"Towards a Theory of Conspicuous Production," *Soviet Survey,*
XXXIV (October–December, 1960), 90-99.

1961

"Faith and Reason," *Journal of Religion,* XLI (October, 1961),
237-247. Published also as "Scientific Revolution," 1961.
"Guiding Principles of the Milan Conference," personal letters
to: M. P. Sinha, Indian Committee for Cultural Freedom;
V. B. Karnik, Indian Committee For Cultural Freedom
(January, 1961).
"History and Hope: An Analysis of Our Age," lectures delivered
at the Thomas Jefferson Center for Studies in Political Economy, University of Virginia, 1961. Mimeographed for private
circulation only. Published also 1962, in part.
"Knowing and Being," *Mind,* LXX (October, 1961), 458-470.

"Science: Academic and Industrial," *Journal of the Institute of Metals,* LXXXIX (1961), 401-406.

"Scientific Revolution," *The Student World,* LIV (No. 3, 1961), 287-302. Published also as "Faith and Reason," 1961.

"The Study of Man," *Quest,* Calcutta, April–June, 1961, pp. 26–35.

"Syllabus of Class on Unspecifiable Elements of Knowledge," Oxford, 1961. (Mimeographed.)

1962

"Conspicuous Production," Broadcast on RIAS, Berlin, December 12, 1962. (Mimeographed.)

"History and Hope: An Analysis of Our Age," *The Virginia Quarterly Review,* XXXVIII (Spring, 1962), 177-195. Published also 1961.

"The Republic of Science, Its Political and Economic Theory," *Minerva,* I (October, 1962), 54-73.

"Tacit Knowing: Its Bearing on Some Problems of Philosophy," *Reviews of Modern Physics,* XXXIV (October, 1962), 601-616. Published also in *Philosophy Today,* VI (Winter, 1962), 239-262.

"The Unaccountable Element in Science," *Philosophy,* XXXVII (January, 1962), 1-14. Published also in *Philosophy Today,* VI (Fall, 1962), 171-182.

1963

"Notes About Mind and Body," February, 1963. (Mimeographed.)

"Points from a Conversation with Paul Tillich on February 21, 1963." (Typewritten.)

"The Potential Theory of Absorption: Authority in Science Has Its Uses and Dangers," *Science,* CXLI (September, 1963), 1010-1013.

"Science and Religion: Separate Dimensions or Common Ground?" *Philosophy Today,* VII (Spring, 1963), 4-14.

1964

"Conspicuous Production," *Quest* (Bombay), (April–June, 1964). Published also 1962.

"The Feelings of Machines," *Encounter,* XXII (January, 1964),
85-86.

1965

"On the Modern Mind," *Encounter,* XXIV (May, 1965), 12-20.
"The Structure of Consciousness," *Brain,* LXXXVIII (Part 4,
1965), 799-810.

1966

"The Creative Imagination," *Chemical and Engineering News,*
XLIV (April, 1966), 85-93. Published also 1967.
"The Logic of Tacit Inference," *Philosophy,* XLI (October,
1966), 369-386.
"The Message of the Hungarian Revolution," *Christianity and
Crisis,* XXVI (October, 1966), 240-243; *The American
Scholar,* XXXV (Autumn, 1966), 661-676.

1967

"The Creative Imagination," *Tri-Quarterly* (Winter, 1967),
11-124.
"The Growth of Science in Society," *Minerva,* V, No. 4 (Sum-
mer, 1967), 533-545.
"Life Transcending Physics and Chemistry," *Chemical and Engi-
neering News,* XLV (August, 1967), 54-66.
"Science and Reality," *British Journal for the Philosophy of
Science,* XVIII (1967), 177-196.
"Sense-Giving and Sense-Reading," *Philosophy,* XLII (October,
1967), 301-325.

1968

"Logic and Psychology," *The American Psychologist,* XII (January, 1968), 27-43.

REVIEWS AND CRITICISM OF MICHAEL
POLANYI'S WRITINGS

Adams, E. M. "The Theoretical and the Practical," *The Review
of Metaphysics,* XLIII (June, 1960), 642-662.
Bennett, John W. "A Review of *The Study of Man,*" *American
Anthropologist,* LXII (October, 1960), 885-887.

Bright, Laurence. "A Review of *Personal Knowledge,*" *Black-friars,* XL (May, 1959) , 236-237.

Brodbeck, May. "A Review of *Personal Knowledge,*" *American Sociological Review,* XXV (August, 1960) , 582-583.

Buchanan, James M. "Politics and Science, Reflections of Knights' Critique of Polanyi," *Ethics,* LXXVII (July, 1967) , 303-310.

Buehler, Walter J. "A Review of *The Logic of Liberty,*" *The New Scholasticism,* XXVII (January, 1953) , 120-121.

Caldin, E. F. "Interpretation and Deduction," a review of *Personal Knowledge, The Tablet,* CCLXXXIX (February, 1959) , 178-180.

"Comprehending Experience," a review of *The Study of Man, The Times Literary Supplement,* April 3, 1959, p. 197.

Coulson, C. A. "A Review of *Personal Knowledge,*" *The Hibbert Journal,* LVII (April, 1959) , 310-311.

Cranston, Maurice. "A Review of *The Logic of Liberty,*" *The Spectator,* CLXXXVIII (August, 1951) , 219-220.

Crosson, F. "A Review of *Personal Knowledge,*" *New Scholasticism,* XXXV (April, 1961) , 258.

"February Authors," a portrait of Polanyi, *The Scientific Monthly,* LX (March, 1945) , 202.

"For Significant Contributions," *The Commonweal,* December, 1959, p. 278.

"Freedom to Choose," a review of *The Logic of Liberty, The Times Literary Supplement,* June 8, 1951, p. 359.

Friedrich, Carl J. "A Review of *Personal Knowledge,*" *Natural Law Forum,* VII (1962) , 132-148.

Gelwick, Richard L. "*Michael Polanyi: Credere Aude,* His Theory of Knowledge and Its Implications for Christian Theology," Th.D. Dissertation, Pacific School of Religion, Berkeley, 1965.

———. "Michael Polanyi—Modern Reformer," *Religion in Life,* XXXIV (Spring, 1965) , 224-234.

Hamilton, Bernice. "Morality and Social Progress," *Blackfriars,* XLI (December, 1960) , 468-478.

Harrod, R. F. "A Review of Full Employment and Free Trade," *The Manchester Guardian,* (November 9, 1945) , p. 3.

Hartt, Julian. "The Realities of the Human Situation," *The Christian Scholar*, XLIII (Fall, 1960), 231-236.

Ignotus, Paul, *et al*. *The Logic of Personal Knowledge: Essays Presented to Michael Polanyi on His Seventieth Birthday*. Glencoe, Illinois: The Free Press, 1961; London: Routledge and Kegan Paul, 1961.

Kelly, Michael. "A Review of *Personal Knowledge*," *Archives for Internal Medicine*, (January, 1963), pp. 785-788.

Knight, Frank H. "Virtue and Knowledge: The View of Professor Polanyi," a review of *Science, Faith and Society* and *The Foundations of Academic Freedom*, *Ethics*, LIX (July, 1949), 271-284.

Kolaja, Jiri. "A Review of *Personal Knowledge*," *The Personalist*, XL (October, 1959), 397-398.

Langford, Thomas A. "Michael Polanyi and the Task of Theology," *Journal of Religion*, XLVI (January, 1966), 45-55.

"The LeComte du Noüy Foundation Award to Professor Michael Polanyi," *The Christian Scholar*, XLIII (March, 1960), 54-58.

MacKinnon, Edward. "A Review of *Personal Knowledge*," *Modern Schoolman*, XXXVI (May, 1959), 294-296.

Moore, Edward C. "A Review of *Personal Knowledge*," *Philosophy of Science*, XXVI (July, 1959), 270-272.

Mukherjee, Nirmal. "Belief and Knowledge," *The Radical Humanist*, Calcutta, April, 1963, pp. 181-182, 184.

"Nothing Succeeds," a review of *Beyond Nihilism*, *The Times Literary Supplement*, April 8, 1960, p. 225.

"Polanyi's Logic," *Encounter*, XXVII (September, 1966), 92.

Orwin, C. S. "A Review of *The Contempt of Freedom*," *Economica*, VIII (May, 1941), 211-215.

Oakeshott, Michael. "The Human Co-efficient," *Encounter*, XI (September, 1958), 77-80.

Robin, Richard. "A Review of *Personal Knowledge*," *Philosophy and Phenomenological Research*, XX (March, 1960), 429.

Ross, Ralph. "A Review of *Personal Knowledge*," *The Annals of the American Academy of Political and Social Science*, CCCXXIII (March, 1959), 201.

Sawyier, Fay. "A Review of *The Study of Man*," *Ethics*, LXXI (October, 1960), 62-63.

Scott, William T. "A Course in Science and Religion Following the Ideas of Michael Polanyi," *The Christian Scholar*, XLVII (Spring, 1964), 36-46.

Scott, William T. "Polanyi's Theory of Personal Knowledge: A Gestalt Philosophy," *The Massachusetts Review*, III (Winter, 1962), 349-368.

Thompson, Manley. "A Review of *Personal Knowledge*," *The Philosophical Review*, LXIX (January, 1960), 111-115.

Van Lennep, D. J. "A Review of *Personal Knowledge*," *The British Journal for the Philosophy of Science*, XI (February, 1961), 344-345.

Whiteley, C. H. "A Review of *Personal Knowledge*," *Mind*, LXVIII (October, 1959), 556-559.

Williams, J. H. "Economics by a Diagrammatic Film," *Adult Education*, June, 1941.

Ziman, John. "The Two Towers," *The Cambridge Review*, October 21, 1961, pp. 33-37.

APPENDIX, INDEXES, AND
NOTES ON AUTHORS

*Appendix**

Some of Polanyi's critics have been generous enough to concede the operation of tacit and unspecifiable elements in the achievement of all knowledge, even the importance of these elements to an adequate account of knowing. Many of these same critics, however, balk at what they regard as the "laziness" or "looseness" of Polanyi's theory since, presumably, it invites the kind of latitudinarianism (as they would regard it) which has evoked a deep phobia in the West, at least since Cartesian doubt and the demand for explicitness have governed our intellectual style. They tend to hold, therefore, that even granting that there are unspecifiable particulars upon which we rely in feats of achieving knowledge, these elements, unspecifiable *in fact*, are nevertheless *specifiable in principle*. Since we have a responsibility to the ideal of intellectual rigor and since the ideal is a meaningful one, we must not be seduced into dalliance with a more flaccid standard by an interest in the merely *de facto* unspecifiable elements of knowledge.

To establish the unspecifiability *in principle* of the particulars of our feats of knowing against those who deny this possibility is difficult indeed. They demand that one meet the test of a criterion which it is the comprehensive effect of Polanyi's thought to render imprecise. The import of his general view is, among many things, to revise—though not explicitly so—the force of the phrase "specifiable in principle." The root innovation of Polanyi's thought lies just here.

The modern philosophical tradition originated in Descartes, whether empiricistic or intellectualistic, has generally prized the *explicit* component in knowledge—though its representatives

---

* Polanyi has commented in greater amplitude upon the consequences of the many indeterminacies of knowing in "Logic and Psychology," *The American Psychologist,* XIII (January, 1968) , 27-43.

have of course differed widely in their account as to how it is
achieved; and it has generally overlooked, relegated to the domain of "mere psychology" or denominated as "conditions of
knowledge," whatever components are not explicit—though various exponents of the tradition have differed widely among themselves in their analysis of these.

In Hume's analysis of knowledge, which may be taken as an example of the empiricistic element of the tradition, the antecedent
and inert "psychological" conditions of reflection, that is, conditions of knowledge properly speaking, are the "principles of
association."[1] In Kant's analysis, where we may see the intellectualistic emphasis exemplified, the antecedent and "transcen-
dentally" psychological conditions of *Wissenschaft* are the forms
of sensibility and the categories of the understanding. There are
certainly broad analogies between Hume's principles of association and Kant's forms and categories, on the one hand; and much
of what falls within the antecedents of explicit knowledge for
Polanyi, namely, the tacit domain, on the other. By the same
token, the "antecedents" of explicit knowledge, as viewed by the
philosophical tradition, have a relation to the explicit which is
analogous to that between the tacit and explicit dimensions in
Polanyi.

However, the antecedents of the explicit, as viewed by the
tradition, are not usually seen themselves as forms of proto-knowl-
edge, but are mere "passive" conditions of it and, *a fortiori,* are
not comprised of actions or of proto-actions of any sort.

Contrary to the philosophical tradition which in general begins its formulation of a theory of knowing by taking the accomplished fact of *explicit* knowledge as its paradigm, Polanyi, taking seriously the continuity of unique human powers of knowing
with more primitive forms of animal intelligence, thinks of a
knower primarily as a living, sentient, active being, exercising
its subtle sensory, motor and conceptual powers in a world in
order to realize an achievement. He is thereby led to see that

1. It is difficult to know what motion to use here. It is not at all clear
that Hume would regard the "principles of association" as laws describing
psychological facts. Equally, it is unsatisfying to say that they are tokens in a
"transcendental" psychology which led Kant to deduce the categories of the
understanding.

the antecedents of the explicit knowledge which is paradigmatic of *human* intellection, are tacit *actions* whose formal structures are already pregnant with the coherency which comes to be called "logical" when it is rendered explicit.

The philosophical tradition then, in assimilating the concept "know" to the concept "explicitly know," has the tendency to pre-empt "logic" for the realm of the explicit alone and, on the whole, to relegate all else to the realm of psychology—variously construed.

The consequence of the construal has been the identification in the tradition of the phrase "in principle" with "logically necessary," both sharply contrasted with "in fact" and "contingent." Hence the difficulty one has in claiming that the particulars of a feat of knowing are not merely "as a matter of fact," that is, "contingently" unspecifiable; but, rather, are "in principle," that is, "necessarily" so. The objection that Polanyi has not demonstrated his thesis to be *logically* necessary is derived from a persistance in the sharp polarization between "the contingent" and "the necessary."

What, in fact, are those demanding who insist that only a defense of tacit knowledge by an argument to its unspecifiability in principle is responsibly rigorous and compelling?

In so far as they have assimilated "knowledge" to "explicable" —that is, "specifiable knowledge," they may be taken to hold that "in principle" anything subsidiarily known can be focally known, anything informally known can be formally known, anything we attend *from* can be attended *to*. Polanyi's rejoinder would be that while, in a trivial sense, such a view is *conceivable,* it does not bear upon the crucial problem; and that in any case, it seriously misleads us as an epistemological ideal.

While much of what he says suggests otherwise, Polanyi could argue that it is not the psychological impossibility, say, of *focusing* at once both on the center and on the periphery of a perceptual field which is the principal embarrassment to the case of his critics. Where this is concerned, more devastating is the fact that what is known peripherally is not *the same thing* as what may come to be known focally. That which is first known informally undergoes a change by being formalized. It is therefore impossible to have a formalized knowledge of *the same thing* one has antecedently 'known' in an informal mode. To come to know *explicitly* what one has hitherto known only *tacitly* produces not only an existential transformation in ourselves as knowers, but a coordinate transformation in the character of the objects known. From being more or less indeterminate, they become determinate.

Even so much, however, is of only tertiary importance. Taking seriously Polanyi's insistence upon the *from-to* structure of tacit knowledge, it becomes clear that, if we rely on unidentified clues *from* which we attend *to* the comprehensive entities in our knowledge which these clues jointly mean, then the entities *explicitly* known and the clues which are *tacitly* known, are not on the same level. The forces of the concept, "know," in the two cases, are not logically/psychologically[2] on the same footing. Tacit clues, being those particulars upon which depends our discernment of the order in comprehensive entities, they are "radical" and "necessary" *grounds* of that discernment. They are the *conditiones sine quibus non* of the "derivative" explicit knowledge which is achieved and sustained by our reliance upon them. And it simply makes no sense, amidst these conceptual innovations, to wonder whether this "necessity" is logical or psychological.

Conversely, in any feat of specifying, so far as is possible, the particulars upon which we have logically/psychologically relied in achieving our *explicit* knowledge, the same asymmetry holds. It is the comprehensive entity itself *from* which we attend, upon knowledge of which we tacitly rely as we seek to discover, from an infinity of possible particulars, those very particulars *to* which we will attend as we specify *some of them* as the (hitherto tacitly but now) *explicitly* known clues of our present *tacit* knowledge of the (hitherto explicitly but now *tacitly* known) comprehensive entity which they did (and do) jointly mean. Here, too, we find that the relation of the entity *from* which we attend *to* the particulars upon which we have relied is a "radical" and "necessary" one: our reliance on our now tacit knowledge of the com-

2. I use this awkward device to indicate that at this point the sharp dichotomy, logical-psychological is no longer licit.

prehensive entity is the *conditio sine qua non* for the identification of the constituent particulars *of* that entity in our knowledge. And here equally it makes no sense whatever to ask whether this "necessity" is logical or psychological.

Those who hold to the possibility of a specification "in principle" of all the particulars upon which we rely in feats of knowing are then demanding a dissolution of this logical/psychological hierarchy which *necessarily* obtains in all actual feats of incarnate, human intellection by covertly appealing to the model of a discarnate, god-like knower for whom all the terms of knowledge are simultaneously on the same logical/psychological footing. Only a discarnate knower could know everything *explicitly* and *simultaneously*. To such a knower there are no heterogeneous logical/psychological foci. Knowledge, according to this model, does not have a *from-to* structure. Unlike our own incarnate selves, such a god not only need not, but cannot, *learn* anything. On the contrary, personal knowledge is essentially knowledge that has been achieved *in time*.

This model is the epistemological form of the Laplacean ideal of explicitness, which Polanyi has successfully demolished in its original formulation.[3]

Another way to enlarge upon the differences between Polanyi's analysis of knowledge and the theories of those in the tradition who have, by and large, restricted the use of "knowledge" to cases of explicit knowledge and who have taken the accomplished fact of explicit knowledge as the paradigmatic point of departure, is to call attention to his genetic analysis of the facts of human knowing. It is this which enables Polanyi to consult the data of experimental psychology without the embarrassment felt by the tradition,[4] a readiness in him which alone is often enough to discredit him among some philosophers and to render him suspect among some psychologists.

Since Polanyi is willing to explore the analogies between the *structure* of cognitive acts and that of motor acts (despite the more manifest disanalogies upon which the tradition has been

3. See especially *P.K.*, pp. 139 ff.
4. In this, as in many respects, he has affinities with the phenomenologist, Maurice Merleau-Ponty.

content to rely) new relations are made noticeable to him. Hitherto, speaking loosely, the investigation of the structure of a cognitive act was regarded as being the explicit analysis and deployment of the *logical* relations obtaining among its several component particulars—considering, for example, the conditions (in, mainly, the sense of 'logically necessary conditions') of the knowledge of any object whatsoever. At the same time, the investigation of the structure of motor acts was carried out in physiological or psychological *causal* categories. And these enterprises were taken to be theoretically distinct.

In Polanyi, by reason of his sweeping conceptual innovation, this dichotomization is blurred. The anology upon which he trades is this: in the structure of both cognitive and motor *acts*,[5] we can remark the propriety of the particular components of each to the totalities which these components jointly mean in each. This is possible because Polanyi has chosen to view both cognition and motility under the category of action. To remark this structural analogy between cognition and motility is to show what rationality *is* in these two cases. In this unfamiliar permissiveness—that is, thinking of cognitive acts (of what the tradition would call the human mind) and motor acts (of what the tradition would call the human body) as analogously embodying rationality—Polanyi shows yet another way in which he innovates.

Now, consider the bearing of these observations upon the altered force of the conceptions "matter of fact," "in principle," "contingent," "necessary," "psychological" and "logical." The import of Polanyi's general view is to regard acts of human cognition as the "contigent" achievement of human powers of knowing—whether viewed phylogenetically or ontogenetically; even as human acts of motility are viewed as the "contingent" achievement of a coordination of the several motor particulars to a comprehensive feat of movement.

This obviously has the effect—though it is not made explicit nor even recognized by Polanyi—of altering the force of "con-

---

5. I am fully aware that the logical force of the concept "act" is importantly altered according to whether it is modified by "motor," "cognitive," "moral," etc.

tingent" and hence of "necessary": the effect is not, however, such as to render the use of these concepts otiose. Instead, for Polanyi to say of a relationship, a form of order, that it is 'necessary,' is for him to say that it is radical or primitive in relation to any form of order or relationship which is judged to *depend* upon it; or conversely, to say of any relationship or form of order at a *remove* from this 'necessity' that it is dependent, is for Polanyi to say that it is 'contingent.'[6] Furthermore, the force given by the philosophical tradition to "*psychological* necessity" as opposed to "*logical* necessity" will be changed. Polanyi's conceptual innovation suggests that, however incontrovertibly the proper range of "logical" may diverge from that of "psychological" at many levels (and may usefully be claimed to diverge), their range will converge at the most radical level: the discernment of order and coherence and its accreditation by the human mind can with equal radicalness be remarked in terms of the *discerned order* which is a *terminus ad quem* of a process (a 'logical' account) or, contrariwise, in terms of the *process of discernment* itself which has its inception at a *terminus a quo* (a 'psychological' account).

It would not be exact to say that Polanyi is interested in logic as something that is actively embodied in feats of intellection and views the logical rules as the explicitly derived principles which have informed this act, whereas the philosophical tradition is rather inclined towards an exclusive interest in those principles in abstraction. It would not be exact to say this, but it would be suggestive to do so.

W. H. P.

6. The terms "depend," "dependent" and "remove" as used here are puzzling, but are, I believe, best left vague.

7. Polanyi's treatment of a child's *tacit* reliance upon a "generative grammar," later made *explicit* by linguists sheds further light upon this relation between the 'logical' and the 'psychological' in his discussion of language acquisition at p. 429 *supra.*

Index

Abbott, Charles D., 223n
Abelson, Philip H., 337
Adams, E. M., 443
Adrian, Lord (Edgar Douglas), 279
Aeschylus, 223
Alain (Emile Chartier), 33
Alaka, M. A., 251n
Alexander, Samuel, 120n
Allport, Floyd, 322, 323, 327
Andrews, D. A., 255n, 269n
Anscombe, G. E. M., 137n, 153n, 168n
Arendt, Hannah, 225n
Aristophanes, 45
Aristotle, 65, 99, 100, 112, 115, 118, 122, 124, 125, 287, 288, 289, 290
Artemidorus of Daldis, 334
Ashby, W. R., 298
Aubrey, John, 289
Auden, W. H., 211, 213n, 223
Austin, J. L., 169-197 *passim,* 212n
Ayer, Alfred J., 163, 205, 206, 207

Bachelard, Gaston, 167
Bacon, Francis, 333
Baker, J. R., 409n
Barker, Ernest, 93n-94n
Barnes, Hazel, 20n
Barrett, Cyril, 164n
Battan, Louis A., 244n, 269n
Bennett, John W., 443
Bergeron, Tor, 251
Bergson, Henri, 20, 66, 111, 123, 356
Berkeley, George, 162, 190n
Berlin, Isaiah, 370n, 384n
Bernard, Claude, 282
Bexton, W. H., 318
Black, Max., 192, 384n
Blanshard, D. C., 273n
Bosanquet, Bernard, 400
Boss, Medard, 334
Braithwaite, R. B., 215, 216, 217
Bremer, F., 291, 301, 309, 310
Brentano, Franz, 330, 331, 332, 333
Bridgeman, Percy, 282n
Briggs, Asa, 380n

Bright, Laurence, 444
Brodbeck, May, 5n, 444
Brooks, Cleanth, 211
Buchanan, James M., 444
Buehler, Walter J., 444
Bukharin, N., 376
Burke, Edmund, 109
Burkhardt, Jacob, 376n
Burns, D. B., 283, 305
Buytendijk, F. J. J., 46n
Byers, H. R., 266n

Caldin, E. F., 444
Campbell, C. A., 167
Camus, Albert, 164
Cannac, Rene, 381n
Cardozo, Benjamin N., 103n, 104n
Carpenter, W. B., 277, 329
Casement, Roger, 381
Cassirer, Ernst, 254n
Cezanne, Paul, 200, 205, **209**
Chomsky, Noam, 418, 419, 424, **428**
Clark, Walter Van Tilburg, 398, 399
Cleon, 349
Cobbe, Frances Power, 328
Coleridge, Samuel Taylor, 335, 336
Collingwood, R. G., 157n
Comte, Auguste, 350, 351, 358
Copernicus, Nicholas, 161
Coulson, Charles A., 444
Cournot, Antoine Augustin, 351
Crankshaw, E., 375
Cranston, Maurice, 444
Crombie, A. C., 433
Crosson, F., 444

Daly, C. B., 141n
Danzig, Allison, 211
Davis, M. H., 272
De George, R. T., 379n
Delafresnaye, J. F., 287n
Desan, Wilfred, 20n
Descartes, Rene, 6, 17, 19, 22, 39, 54, 58, 59, 65, 82, 121, 122, 125, 126, 204, 233, 234, 276

Dilthey, W., 112, 127, 128, 129, 130, 131, 132, 133, 158n
Diotima, 45
Dostoevski, Fyodor, 376, 381n
Duguit, L., 93
Duns Scotus, 233
Durkheim, Emile, 351

Eaton, M. A., 255n, 269n
Eccles, J. C., 287, 295, 312
Eichmann, R., 106n
Einstein, Albert, 43, 161, 348, 358
Eliot, T. S., 231n
Erikson, Erik, 204n
Ericksson, B., 256n
Erisman, Th., 422n
Euripides, 185, 223
Evans, D. D., 189n
Ewald, P. P., 434

Farber, Marvin, 116n
Feigl, Herbert, 384, 433
Ferrier, Sir David, 278
Fessard, A., 287
Feuerbach, Ludwig, 20
Fichte, J. G., 20
Field, Mary, 432
Fletcher, N. H., 266n
Flew, Anthony, 149n
Flitner, Andreas, 130n
Freud, Sigmund, 164, 209, 320, 322, 334
Freyd, Bernard, 94n
Friedrich, Carl J., 93n, 97n, 98n, 101n, 102n, 105n, 107n, 109n, 384n, 444
Fritsch, Gustav, 278
Fromm, Erich, 376n

Gadamer, H.-G., 133
Galileo, Galilei, 276, 430
Gaius, 104n
Geach, Peter, 156n
Gelwick, Richard L., 57n, 432, 444
Genet, 56
Gény, F., 93
Gerard, R. W., 293
Gierke, Otto Von, 93n-94n
Gilman, D. L., 269n
Gilson, E., 123n
Goldberg, Rube, 337, 338
Gomulicki, Bronislaw R., 285
Good, I. J., 433
Gosnell, H. F., 380n
Goudsmit, S. A., 266n
Gould, Wesley L., 105n
Grene, David, 223n

Grene, Marjorie, 69n, 77, 86n, 276
Grünbaum, Adolph, 282, 433
Grünbaum-Leyton, Albert S. F., 282

Haines, Charles Grove, 93
Haldane, Eliz. S., 82n
Hamilton, Bernice, 444
Hamilton, W. R., 430
Hampshire, Stuart, 168n, 207n
Harari, Manya, 204n
Hare, R. M., 191
Harris, E. E., 167
Harrod, R. F., 444
Hart, H. L. A., 95n
Hartt, Julian, 445
Harvey, William, 289
Hastings, Warren, 109
Hauriou, M., 93
Head, Henry, 286
Hebb, O., 292, 293
Hegel, G. W. F., 112, 131, 358
Heidegger, Martin, 27n, 28, 30, 44n, 112, 128, 133, 158n, 167
Heron, W., 318
Hibbs, J. R., 269n
Himmelfarb, Gertrude, 441
Hitler, Adolph, 104, 105, 375
Hitzig, Eduard, 278
Hobbes, Thomas, 95, 96n, 293n
Hocking, L. M., 272
Hodges, H. A., 128n
Holmes, G. M., 286
Horace, 297n
Hospers, John, 381n
Hume, David, 23, 58, 59, 60, 61, 62n, 63, 81, 82, 163, 195, 276, 450
Humphrey, G. H., 420
Husserl, Edmund, 20, 35, 39, 42, 112, 116, 121, 158n, 167
Huxley, Julian, 377

Ignotus, Paul, 445

Jackson, Hughlings, 277, 278, 279, 280, 281, 282, 284, 286, 290, 292, 297, 305, 313
Jaeger, Werner, 130n
James, William, 416, 424
Jaspers, K., 167, 309, 343
Jeffress, J. L., 288n
Jeffryes, R., 432
Jelenski, K. A., 433, 434
Jewkes, J., 432
Johnson, Virginia E., 322n
Jordon, L. L., 251n
Jung, Carl, 325, 326

Kamenka, Eugene, 376n, 377n
Kant, Immanuel, 6, 19, 20, 59, 60, 61, 62, 63, 65, 74, 75, 108, 123, 126, 128, 134n, 240, 358, 413, 449
Karnik, V. B., 441
Kekule, F. A., 335
Kelly, Michael, 445
Keniston, Kenneth, 322n
Kenny, Anthony, 168n
Kepler, J., 237
Key, V. O., 107n
Kierkegaard, Søren, 20, 22, 164, 210, 230n
Kluckhohn, Clyde, 97, 370n
Knight, Frank H., 445
Koenig, L. Randall, 250
Kohler, Wolfgang, 7, 289
Kolaja, Jiri, 445
Kottenhoff, Heinrich, 422, 423
Krabbe, H., 93
Kroeber, A., 370n
Kubie, L. S., 292
Kuhn, H., 116n, 124n, 134n
Kuhn, Thomas S., 161, 162, 163, 433
Kurtz, H., 131n

Landau, L. D., 257n
Landgrebe, L., 128n
Langer, S. K., 416
Langford, Thomas H., 192, 193, 445
Lanyi, George A., 433
Laplace, P. S. de, 112, 207, 254
Lashley, K. S., 281, 284, 286, 287, 288, 289n, 290, 294, 295, 301, 308, 309, 312, 419, 428
Laskin, P. L., 269n
Lasswell, Harold D., 99n
Leibniz, G. W., 116
Le May, G. H. L., 381n
Lenin, N., 375
Lerner, Daniel, 99n
Levine, Joseph, 257n
Lévi-Strauss, Claude, 167
Levy-Bruhl, Lucien, 358
Lewis, H. D., 149n
Leyton, (See Grünbaum-Leyton)
Liddell, H. S., 280, 282
Lifschitz, E. M., 257n
Lilly, Douglas K., 256n
Lipps, T., 158n
Litt, Theo., 130n
Llewellyn, Karl, 101, 102, 104n
Locke, John, 60, 276
Lorenz, K. Z., 279

Ludlam, Frank H., 256, 273
Lullus, Raimundus (Lully, Raymond), 116

MacCready, Paul B., Jr., 258n
McCulloch, W. S., 289
Mace, C. A., 168
McKeon, Richard, 97n
MacKinnon, Edward, 445
Macmurray, John, 167
McWilliams, Wilson C., 433
Magoun, H. W., 291
Maier, N. R. F., 317, 318
Maine de Biran, F.-P.-G., 330
Mairet, P., 46n
Malcolm, Norman, 137, 140n, 164n, 166n
Mannheim, Karl, 8, 377, 383
Marcel, Gabriel, 31, 42n, 167, 204n
Marcuse, Herbert, 379n
Margenau, Henry, 254n
Maritain, Jacques, 372
Marx, Karl, 108, 164, 350, 351, 352, 353, 358, 375, 376, 377
Masefield, John, 336
Maslow, Abraham, 315
Mason, B. J., 266n
Masters, William H., 322n
Mathieu, Georges, 209
Maxwell, Grover, 433
Mayo, Bernard, 168n
Meiner, F., 131n
Meldon, A. I., 168n
Merleau-Ponty, Maurice, 31, 42n, 55, 149, 202n, 453n
Michaelangelo, 43
Michelson-Morley, 168
Mill, J. S., 20
Montaigne, Michel de, 122n
Moore, Edward C., 445
Morgan, Lloyd C., 120n
Morris, Charles, 414, 418
Mottern, R. E., 269n
Mukherjee, Nirmal, 445
Munzer, Thomas, 378
Murdoch, Iris, 21
Myers, F. W., 325

Nechaev, Sergey, 381
Newton, Sir Isaac, 254, 358
Nicias, 349
Nietzsche, F., 130, 164
Nohl, H., 130n

Oakeshott, Michael, 5, 6, 445
Occam, William of, 202n

Ogura, Y., 256n.
O'Leary, J., 279, 284, 285n, 291, 296, 297, 312
Orwin, C. S., 445

Pareto, V., 351
Parsons, Talcott, 369n
Pascal, Blaise, 19
Passmore, John, 163
Péguy, Charles, 164
Penfield, Wilder, 277n
Perelman, Chaim, 233n, 240n
Pericles, 349
Phillips, John P., 280, 282
Piaget, J., 7, 33, 239
Pirenne, M. H., 313
Plato, 30, 46, 58, 59, 61, 65, 66, 67, 75, 82, 87, 112, 121n, 122, 123n, 124, 125, 135n
Poe, Edgar Allen, 397
Poincaré, Henri, 348, 425, 426, 427, 428
Polanyi, John, 432
Popper, K. R., 239, 259n, 263, 302n
Poteat, W. H., 190n
Pound, Ezra, 340
Prescott, Frederick C., 334n
Price, H. H., 149, 336
Prini, Pietro, 167n
Pronko, N. H., 422
Prout, William, 409

Quine, W. V. O., 415, 418

Ramsey, I. T., 194n
Rawls, John, 96n
Reid, Thomas, 330
Renard, R. J., 251n
Rickert, H., 342, 343
Riehl, H., 251
Robespierre, M., 366
Robin, Richard, 445
Rogat, Yosal, 106n
Rogers, Carl, 316
Rosenberg, Alfred, 375
Ross, G. Ralph T., 82n, 445
Rossby, C.-G., 251
Rousseau, Jean-Jacques, 13, 17, 233, 234, 285
Ruestow, Alexander, 108n
Russell, Bertrand, 20, 142, 169
Ryle, Gilbert, 156, 158, 163n, 206

St. Augustine, 13, 16, 17, 18, 122n-123n, 125, 224, 233, 394
St. Francis of Assisi, 334

Sartor, J. D., 272
Sartre, Jean-Paul, 20-25, 27-39, 42, 44, 46, 47, 49-55, 112, 133, 164
Sawyer, Fay, 446
Scheler, Max, 8, 351
Schumpeter, Joseph, 358
Scott, T. H., 318
Scott, William T., 244n, 446
Seignobos, Charles, 351
Shakespeare, William, 324n
Shand, Alexander F., 323, 324, 328, 330,
Sherrington, C. S., 279, 280, 281, 282, 297, 301, 305
Silber, John, 202n
Simpson, J., 255n, 257n, 269
Simpson, R. H., 255n, 269n
Sinha, M. P., 441
Skinner, B. F., 316, 418
Smith, Colin, 202n
Snow, C. P., 5, 6
Snyder, F. W., 422
Socrates, 122, 124
Sophocles, 223
Spencer, Herbert, 377
Spinoza, Baruch de, 46, 50, 74
Spranger, E., 130n
Squires, P., 257n, 268, 273
Stalin, Joseph, 375
Stammler, R., 109n
Stenius, Erik, 153n
Stevenson, C. L., 141n
Stevenson, Robert Louis, 325, 335
Stratton, G. M., 421, 422n
Straus, E., 286, 287n, 293n, 415
Strawson, P. F., 177, 178, 192, 207n

Talleyrand, 376n
Taylor, A. J. P., 381n
Teilhard de Chardin, Pierre, 356, 441
Thomas Aquinas, 125
Thompson, Manley, 446
Thucydides, 349
Tillich, Paul, 129n
Tintoretto (Jacopo Robusti), 353
Titchner, E. B., 331, 332
Todd, Clement J., 258n, 268
Tolman, E. C., 7
Troeltsch, Ernst, 93n
Turner, J. S., 257n
Twomey, S., 268

Ulpian, 104n
Urmson, J. O., 169n, 190n, 212n

Van Lennep, D. J., 446
Von Frey, Max, 282
Vonnegut, B., 269n

Waddington, C. H., 441
Waismann, F., 136, 149, 413
Walshe, F. M. R., 282n, 283n
Ward, James, 330
Warnock, G. J., 162, 169n, 190n
Watson, John B., 331
Weber, Max, 341-363 *passim*
Weismann, Donald L., 13n, 57n
Whewell, William, 234
White, A. R., 168n
White, Lynn, Jr., 333, 334
Whitehead, A. N., 59, 79, 80, 87, 88,
  89, 276, 293, 297, 298, 300, 304, 308,
  310, 314
Whiteley, C. H., 384n, 446
Whyte, L. L., 279

Wigner, E. P., 434
Wild, John, 124n
Williams, J. H., 446
Wisdom, John, 166, 168, 206, 208n
Wittgenstein, Ludwig, 30, 136-168
  passim, 181n, 207, 208, 212n
Wolf, Erik, 93n-94n, 108n
Woodcock, A. H., 273n
Woodworth, Joan, 318, 319
Woolf, Harry, 434
Wordsworth, William, 333
Wright Brothers, Orville and Wilbur,
  430
Wundt, Wilhelm M., 331

Young, J., Z., 298, 299

Ziman, John, 446
Zuurdeeg, W., 190

Notes on Authors

RAYMOND ARON, occupant of the Chair of Sociology at the Sorbonne, came to this ultimate academic post from, amongst others, Toulouse, and l'Institut d'études and l'Ecole nationale d'administration. He is widely known as a political commentator, editorialist for *Combat* and *Figaro,* as well as editor-in-chief of *France Libre.* He is a member of the American Academy of Arts and Sciences, the author of *Introduction to the Philosophy of History, The Opium of the Intellectuals, Contemporary German Sociology, The Century of Total War,* and others.

THE REVEREND CAHAL B. DALY is Reader in Scholastic Philosophy in Queen's University, Belfast, Northern Ireland. He has contributed to *Prospect for Metaphysics,* London, 1961, and has written articles on Wittgenstein and on contemporary British ethics in *Philosophical Studies* (Maynooth, Ireland).

CARL J. FRIEDRICH is Eaton Professor of the Science of Government at Harvard, where he has taught since 1926. His books include *The Philosophy of Law in Historical Perspective* (1958) and *Man and His Government* (1963), and hundreds of scholarly articles.

RICHARD L. GELWICK is Chairman of the Department of Philosophy and Religion, Stephens College. He studied with Polanyi during the latter's tenure at the Center for Advanced Studies in the Behavioral Sciences, Stanford, California. He compiled on microfilm the *Collected Articles and Papers of Michael Polanyi,* wrote his doctoral dissertation on Polanyi's epistemology and its implications for Christian theology, and has published several articles on Polanyi's work.

MARJORIE GRENE, Professor and Chairman of the Department of Philosophy at the University of California, Davis, was a lecturer in philosophy at Queen's University, Belfast, Northern Ireland, from 1960 to 1965. Dr. Grene is also the author of *A Portrait of Aristotle, Dreadful Freedom* (issued in paperback as *Introduction to Existentialism*) and other books on subjects in the history of philosophy. She has written extensively in scholarly journals on metaphysics and epistemology and has been increasingly concerned with the philosophy of biology. Her most recent book is *The Knower and the Known.*

HELMUT KUHN is Professor of Philosophy in the University of Munich, Rector of the Academy for Political Sciences, Munich, late President of the *Allgemeine Gesellschaft für Philosophie in Deutschland,* author of *Das Sein und das Gute,* Munich, 1962, *Freedoms Forgotten and Remembered, Encounter with Nothingness, et al.*

THOMAS A. LANGFORD is Professor and Chairman of the Department of Religion, Duke University. A recipient of a Danforth Distinguished Teacher Award, he was in residence at Cambridge University in 1965-1966 doing research in twentieth-century English theology. He is coauthor of *Philosophy of Religion* and has contributed to *The Christian Scholar, Journal of Religion, Religious Studies, Interpretation,* and other journals.

HAROLD G. MCCURDY is Kenan Professor of Psychology at the University of North Carolina, Chapel Hill, where he has taught since 1948. He previously taught at Meredith College (1941-1948) and Milligan College (1938-1941). He has published *A Straw Flute, The Personality of Shakespeare, The Personal World, Personality and Science,* and *Barbara: The Unconscious Autobiography of a Child Genius,* and sundry articles in psychological journals on experimental and theoretical topics, as well as a sprinkling of poems here and there.

ZDZISLAW NAJDER, literary critic and scholar, lives in Warsaw, where he was born in 1930. He has studied philosophy and literature in Warsaw and in Oxford. He has taught aesthetics and literature at Yale, Columbia, and the University of California, Berkeley. He has published many essays and articles on literary and philosophical subjects, and has edited several volumes of Polish, English and American authors. One of his two books on Joseph Conrad, *Conrad's Polish Background,* was published in 1964 by Oxford University Press.

CHAIM PERELMAN is former Dean and Professor of Logic, Ethics, and Metaphysics at the Free University of Brussels, past President of the Belgian Philosophical Society and of the Belgian Society of Logic and Philosophy of Science, member of the International Institute of Philosophy, General Secretary of the International Federation of Philosophical Societies, Visiting Professor at Pennsylvania State University and McGill University (Montreal), recipient of the Franqui Prize (1962), de la Justice (1945), Rhetorique et Philosophie (1952), author of *Traité de l'Argumentation* (1958), *The Idea of Justice and the Problem of Argument* (1963), *Justice et Raison* (1963), *An Historical Introduction to Philosophical Thinking* (1965), and over a hundred papers published in scientific journals.

EDWARD POLS is Professor of Philosophy at Bowdoin College. His philosophical outlook is most completely expressed in *The Recognition of Reason.* A book on Whitehead is in press. He is currently writing on the person and the mind-body problem.

WILLIAM H. POTEAT is Professor of Christianity and Culture at Duke University. He has written chapters and articles for *View Points,* ed. Pittenger and Coburn; *Philosophical Interrogations,* ed. B. and S. Rome; *Religion and Rationality,* ed. D. Z. Phillips; *Philosophy and Phenomenological Research; Philosophical Quarterly; Hibbert Journal; Mind; University of Maine Law Review; Journal of Religion; Theology Today,* etc.

IAN RAMSEY, late Nolloth Professor of the Philosophy of the Christian Religion and Fellow of Oriel College in Oxford University, is now Lord Bishop of Durham. In all his books, of which the latest is *Christian Discourse: Some Logical Explorations,* he is concerned to meet constructively the challenge of contemporary empiricism to religious belief.

WILLIAM T. SCOTT is Professor of Physics at the University of Nevada. His principal preoccupations are theoretical cloud physics, multiple scattering, and quantum theory. He was formerly at Smith College and spends summers at Brookhaven National Laboratory, the National Bureau of Standards, etc. A sabbatical (1959-1960) was spent at Yale University in the Physics Department and Divinity School. He is author of *The Physics of Electricity and Magnetism, Erwin Schrödinger: An Introduction to His Writings,* and numerous research articles.

SIR FRANCIS WALSHE, now in semi-retirement, is the dean of neurophysiologists in the English-speaking world, as is attested by the issue of *Brain,* LXXXVIII, Pt. IV (1965), which paid him tribute on his eightieth birthday. Though a practicing and consulting neurologist (to University College Hospital, the National Hospital for Nervous Diseases, and others), he has published reports on his own researches as well as articles dealing with some of the philosophical implications of his science. His academic affiliation has been with The Institute of Neurology, University of London.

DONALD L. WEISMANN, Professor of Art History, University Professor in the Arts and Director, Institute of Arts and Letters, the University of Texas, member of the National Council on the Arts, Washington, D.C., has paintings and collages exhibited in principal galleries of the U.S. and circulated nationally by the American Federation of Arts. Author of "Jelly Was the Word," Pemberton Press, 1965, he has in press *Language and Visual Form: The Personal Record of a Dual Creative Process,* soon to be published by the University of Texas Press.